D1564335

THE AMERICAN AS ANARCHIST

The American as Anarchist

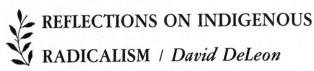 REFLECTIONS ON INDIGENOUS

RADICALISM / *David DeLeon*

THE JOHNS HOPKINS UNIVERSITY PRESS

Baltimore and London

This book has been brought to publication with the generous assistance of the Andrew W. Mellon Foundation.

The Johns Hopkins University Press, Baltimore, Maryland 21218
The Johns Hopkins Press Ltd., London

Photographic assistance: Roy Sparks

Library of Congress Cataloging in Publication Data

DeLeon, David.
　The American as anarchist.

　Bibliography: pp. 196–235
　Includes index.
　1. Anarchism and anarchists—United States—History.
　2. Radicalism—United States—History.　I. Title.

HX843.D44　　335'.83'0973　　78–58290
ISBN 0–8018–2126–6

To My Parents and Other Teachers

I do not wish to remove from my present prison to a prison a little larger. I wish to break all prisons.—Ralph Waldo Emerson

What do you suppose will satisfy the soul, except to walk free and own no superior?—Walt Whitman, *Leaves of Grass*

CONTENTS

FOREWORD

BY ROBERT N. BELLAH

In this book David DeLeon pursues with single-minded determination (Weber would have called it "one-sided accentuation") that central strand in the American tradition that might be called radical anti-institutionalism. He documents both the suspicion or indifference to institutions that is so extreme that it pushes in the direction of anarchism, and the implicit paradox that a culture with so powerful a strand of anarchism can coexist with a society with great centralized structures of power—governmental, military, and economic. Today, these institutions threaten to deprive the individual of any meaningful control over his or her own life. Since the anarchist culture preceded the centralized structures we must even ask whether there is not some deep inner connection between these two apparently contradictory tendencies.

DeLeon has rooted American anarchism in three features of American life: religion, an environment of great physical space, and capitalism. It would be difficult to detect in religion, particularly in the Protestantism that DeLeon emphasizes, any source for our increasing tendency toward centralization. In spite of the emergence of national bureaucracies in most Protestant denominations in recent years, the basic unit remains, as DeLeon notes, the local congregation. Tendencies toward centralization in the denominations seem to be more a response to, than a cause of, the centralization of other social structures. The last decade has shown how precarious many of the denominational bureaucracies have been, and how drastically they can be reduced when congregational support fails.

An environment of great physical space, or rather, our decision to remain one people politically while expanding into that space, seems a more likely candidate to help explain the rise of centralization. One great republic rather than many small republics has created problems of scale that seem manageable only through centralized administration. The centralizing tendencies of the great republic were at first muted by the simplicity of our economy and the degree to which our ocean moats kept foreign dangers at bay. Today we are, whether we like it or not, a superpower, and in a world of competing superpowers and intercontinental ballistic missiles, an extraordinary degree of centralization would seem necessary for survival. Thus the great physical space of our nation has created not only the frontiersman and the frontiersman mentality that has outlived him but also the potentiality and perhaps even the necessity for the garrison state.

But it is surely capitalism, in spite of its continuing idolatry of the individual entrepreneur, that has provided the most dynamic impetus toward centralization. Great concentrations of economic power, made possible by extraordinary technical and organizational inventions, became first national and then multinational corporations. The growth of federal government in the United States seems to be a direct response to the disruption of the fabric of American life caused by the rise of corporate capitalism. Welfare capitalism, with its growing federal bureaucracy, was a necessary development that kept under control for a while the tendencies of expansive capitalism to destroy the social conditions for its own continuing growth. Thus, however much capitalism has contributed to the mythology of radical egoism ("making your own way"), its actual history has strengthened those tendencies most inimical to a practical anarchism.

And yet the paradox remains. The rise of statism has not seen the rise of a statist ideology in America. Corporate capitalism still masquerades in the ideology of "free enterprise," whose hero is the autonomous, inventive, individual entrepreneur. Anyone who would understand America would do well to take this book as an instructive text. It helps us perceive how certain powerful tendencies toward centralization remain ideologically illegitimate, and thus generate severe tensions in our public life. It helps us understand how authoritarian radicals and romantic conservatives, so allergic to radical anti-institutionalism as scarcely to see it, much less understand its significance, have been so mistaken in their analyses of American life and so peripheral in their political influence.

The question remains whether it is possible to make a genuinely American critique of such fear of institutionalized authority, a critique that may be the necessary premise for any adequate solution to our present and growing problems. It is not DeLeon's purpose to answer that question. In the fascinating last chapter, "The Future of the Radical Past," he catalogues both the weaknesses and the potentialities of the several "ideal types" of libertarianism. His final model of a "mass democratic movement" that would emphasize decentralization and local control is an attractive one. But one might wonder whether the various forms of anarchism could ever supply sufficient content for a movement that could genuinely challenge, not merely expressively protest, the present structures of power. Would not the shared ideology of which DeLeon sometimes speaks have to contain common beliefs beyond the mere assertion of individual and small group liberties? And from where would such common beliefs come? Perhaps from our religious traditions that never wholly accepted untrammelled individualism, or from the admittedly meager element of republicanism in our political tradition that has always existed uneasily alongside our liberalism. But how could these alternative elements in the American tradition be reappropriated in convincing form today? Again these are questions that DeLeon's book implies but that he does not set himself to answer. He confines himself to the extraordinarily useful task of making us take a full, undiluted look at our central traditions of radical libertarianism. In our time, and in coming days, these traditions will be our hope and our despair.

PART I

THE GENESIS OF REVELATION

OVERVIEW

American radicalism can be divided into two general camps: indigenous and imitative. The imitators of foreign radicalism, and those who interpret American movements by foreign terms, are the most widely recognized in this culture, but they are in fact the least culturally significant. In terms of the usual categories of mass parties, class consciousness, and popular use of the stereotyped vocabulary of the Left, American dissidents have been a resounding failure; but such concepts are usually irrelevent to American conditions. This study could be entitled "The American Radical" in the same sense that Emerson wrote "The American Scholar" in 1837, calling for the decolonization of our literature and the construction of an authentically American culture built from national experience. My work has the similiar purpose of identifying some varieties of radicalism as intellectual imports while showing that others represent enduring traditions.[1] Borrowed, imitative art still has its equivalent in borrowed, imitative radicalism.

Perhaps it is time to recognize, after two hundred years of political independence, that our native radicalism is fundamentally different from that of Europe, Russia, China, or the Third World. By native, I do not mean baptized by the Indians. I imply that it draws upon basic beliefs of the general culture for its meaning. This indigenous radicalism is rooted in centuries of our history and assumes that however much this society may be changed or transformed, it is unlikely to become something *wholly* dissimilar to what it has been. It is radical, then, in the sense that it is a complete realization of the democratic potential it perceives within our past. My book, following Emerson's advice, is an intellectual declaration of independence from alien modes of interpretation, finding the spirit of our radicalism not in Lenin but in Debs, not in the USSR, but in the IWW, not in Chinese peasants, but in the Populists. It assumes, as Emerson did, the existence of "new lands, new men, new thoughts." De Crèvecoeur realized earlier that the American is *new*, a difference in *kind*, not simply in variety.

What, then, is American about this American radicalism? Unlike Scandanavian social democracy, Fabian bureaucracy, and Soviet communism, our traditional critiques of the existing order have been pervaded by suspicion, if not hostility, toward any centralized discipline. The essence of this heritage—which has been expressed in both individualist and communal forms—could be named "antistatism," "libertarianism," or more provocatively, "anarchism." Like Proudhon, who defined this last term positively in 1840, we have frequently assumed that there is an order inherent in nature, that society is self-sufficient, and that government is likely to interrupt the vital functions of individuals and voluntary associations. Homegrown critics from both the individualist right and the communal left have often counterposed society against the state, or even the individual against the structures of society. Some rebels have always gone beyond implicit resistance to institutional authority to explicit rejections of such authority. Our radicals have concentrated on emancipation, on breaking the prisons of authority, rather than on planning any reconstruction. They are abolitionists, not institution-builders; advocates of women's liberation, gay liberation, liberation theology, black liberation; prophets, not priests; anarchists, not administrators. They generally presume that the freed spirit will require little or no guidance.

This implicit ideology of American radicalism has been expressed in several varieties of criticism: liberalism, right libertarianism, and left libertarianism. Each contains an element of anarchism that distinguishes it from statist (and often foreign) radicalisms. None of these libertarian currents, however, would necessarily eliminate all authority. We must erase the cartoon image of the anarchist as a shaggy-headed Frankenstein's monster, with a crazed glint in its eyes, loaded down with an armful of bombs. Anarchists have usually advocated new forms of order, not chaos. While the statist would rely primarily upon institutions, libertarians prefer other means of social control. Mores can regulate far more powerfully than administrators (Emerson's "government without governors"). Tocqueville noted in the 1830's that a seemingly atomized population, by expecting allegience to its basic values, could be extremely cohesive and authoritarian.

Similarly, it is quite possible to envision a highly authoritarian culture that is also stateless. *Ánarchos* (being leaderless) is not incompatible with *ñomos* (law, custom, usage). A society without a state could be repressive in other ways, as even "primitive" societies might instruct us. This realistic possibility will become clearer when the types of anarchist organizations are outlined.[2]

Each form of libertarian radicalism covers a spectrum that evolves toward the most explicit, from laissez-faire liberalism to Anarcho-Capitalism (organizing society entirely on the basis of the market), or from community control advocates to Anarcho-Communists and syndicalists. Such tendencies have been historically repeated, but often without an understanding of their precedents. As one labor historian has remarked: "The only bona fide American radical tradition is anarchy, and that, in spite of Thoreau, has been *much less a doctrine than a fact.*"[3]

This study will attempt, for the first time, to discuss this "fact," classifying different libertarian perspectives within a general theory of American radicalism, as others have done for American liberalism or conservatism. It will bring to consciousness, or focus, the historical repetition of certain themes. Such continuities or recurrences will be presented as "pure types," used to capture the characteristic features of forms of criticism—as useful typifications or sketches of generalities, rather than as actual beings. Thoreau gave voice to the actual complexity of our pragmatic anarchism: "I quietly declare war with the State, after my own fashion, though I will still make what use and get what advantage of her as I can, as is usual in such cases."[4] Consistency is not an anarchist virtue.

The first section of my book will survey the social and cultural enviroment that generated this anarcholibertarian sensibility. The interaction of three factors will be stressed: the Protestantism of most of the colonial founders, the expansive opportunities they encountered, and their business relations. These cultural, geographic, and economic influences were crucially different from other areas of even the New World, such as the Latin, Catholic, and Mediterranean elements that struggled with large-scale Indian civilizations in much of South America. Here, each factor tended to disintegrate traditional definitions of community that favored ideals of organic solidarity, hierarchy, status by birth, and deference to precedent, often rooted in a fundamentally agrarian society following the slow natural rhythms of the seasons. Instead, these influences have promoted relationships based upon changing associations to satisfy particular functions; egalitarianism; status by activity; and constant innovations for the technological control and utilization of nature. Although we live in a community with a common language and unifying symbols, traditional society, as an ideal type, is a "lost world." One of our most stable beliefs is the inevitability of change. Our relationships are generally formed by the shifting needs of the marketplace in an atomistic society where people are often treated like interchangeable parts.[5]

Religion commands the premier rank in this transition because of the universal truth expressed by Mircea Eliade: "the beginnings of culture are rooted in religious experience and beliefs." Radical values, like others in our culture, "cannot be correctly understood if one does not know their original religious matrix, which they tacitly criticized, modified, or rejected in becoming what they are now: secular cultural values."[6] If this had been a Buddhist culture, obviously our common perceptions of linear progress, active humanity, and personal responsibility might have been dramatically altered.

It was not only Christianity, but one specific tendency of it that was crucial in our history. By the 1770s, one historian has claimed that approximately 85 to 90 percent of the population bore "the stamp of Geneva," of the radical Reformation that had weakened or destroyed Catholic definitions of community.[7] Although such groups labored to build their own purified institutions, ultra-Protestant ego has sometimes justified the conservative's fear of it as "the dissidence of dissent."[8] At the very least, this has promoted a sense of self-reliance. In 1820, when de Maistre first used the term "individualism," he christened it political Protestantism. The traditional role of religion in providing holistic or transcendent values became a rationale for every pilgrim's separate progress. In the 1970s, more than 80 percent in one poll agreed that "willpower" was the key determinant in success, and that "whenever I fail, I have no one to blame but myself." Self-sufficiency was admired. In another study, up to 90 percent of blue-collar workers refused to attribute their failures to outside conditions. Despite the power of modern institutions, individual effort and individual solutions have been emphasized.[9] Protestantism has helped to replace community with privacy—an English concept, absent from other languages, which have terms only for separation or isolation, not for privacy. For radicalism, this has sometimes raised a counterforce to the state's claim to ultimate power by emphasizing a law higher than that of institutions, the law of personal conscience.

Second, American capitalism has also tended to replace community with individualist anarchism, the "I" spirit instead of the "we." Whereas capitalism in other societies has been modified by precapitalist or anti-capitalist institutions and mores (resulting, for example, in the paternalism of Japanese corporations), in the United States capitalism exists in perhaps the purest form in the world. It is one of the assumptions most Americans take for granted in a society that has 5 to 6 percent of the world's population but uses more than half its resources, has a gross national product surpassing a trillion dollars, and has a higher standard of individual consumption than any of the communist countries.

In our culture, community is often identified with the market—a bargaining society, a society of contract. Earlier moral injunctions against the love of mammon have generally been replaced with a narrow self-seeking. Tocqueville, in the 1830s, perceived an almost antisocial society where individuals were concerned with "the petty pleasures of private life," although he also warned that when personal comfort was threatened, people might repudiate social liberty to defend their personal security. History, of course, has confirmed *both* of Tocqueville's themes—anarchy and authority. The common vision of freedom and the general experience of conformity have been a dialectic throughout our culture, although most commentators have understood only one or the other. But the dialectic continues, since our libertarian ideals are neither fully achieved nor annihilated. The hardy persistence of this heritage is the core of my book.

Third, atomism has been encouraged by an environment of great physical space and social opportunity, where optimistic Americans have been unlikely to maintain the sense of sin and limitation that might be so useful to conservatism. Rather, sunny views of human nature and civil or natural society have prevailed. Government, in this pleasant world, may be regarded as useful, but not as a vital barrier to human cruelty or a major umpire that can ration scarcity.[10]

Many of the core values nurtured by this history—which forms the basis of much of our past—are radical, liberatory, utopian. The United States has, comparatively, one of the most egalitarian societies in the world, in which there are few philosophical conservatives who praise class orders, suspicion of the common people, veneration of the old, organicism, or the necessity for a strong leader. In Emerson's terms, Americans usually identify with the party of the future, not of the past; of the movement, not the establishment. The mental landscape of Americans is filled not so much with solid institutions of the past and present as with visions of human will, progress, and change. Our literature is "more relentlessly self-critical than any other,"[11] the intelligentsia frequently serve as an idealistic conscience against imperfection; our ideas are particularistic and pragmatic (or, as one person labeled the thought of William James: "philosophic Protestantism"); our language is simple and direct; and our social manners are relatively democratic, free of formal titles and officiousness.[12] Of course, this antiorthodoxy and anti-elitism has its own assumptions, often held with dogmatic certainty. In the candid words of Paul Goodman: "I have a democratic faith—it's a religion with me—that everyone is really able to take care of himself, to get on with people, and to make a good society. If it's not so, I don't want to hear about it."[13] This is a common faith among Americans.

The most moderate expression of this radical belief in democracy is liberalism. Perhaps because this is the oldest liberal democracy in the world we forget how utopian are the commonplaces lauded even in McGuffey's readers, honoring a "free community" in which there are no "privileged orders" and opportunity is open to ability alone.[14] Although Tocqueville argued that America had been "born free," it would be more accurate to portray a slow and often painful revolution, over several centuries, to liberate blacks, women, and many others to be equal competitors in the capitalist marketplace. This dream, and the constant tension between the ideal and the actual, has been a vital source of radical thought and action in our society.

Throughout our history, it has encouraged the kind of spontaneous antimonopolism often found in the Anti-Federalists, the Jacksonians, the Knights of Labor, and the Populists, with fears that "the people" were losing their liberties and economic chances. The alternative to concentrations of wealth and power have been sometimes individualist, sometimes cooperative, but they have almost invariably been critical of undemocratic power.[15]

Themes of liberation have also been applied to groups of people. For blacks, it has been reflected in Garrison's newspaper the *Liberator*; in Frederick Douglass's broad definition of slavery as the lack of control over one's own life (by which he often included women and wage laborers); in John Brown's scorn of "talk—what is needed is action—ACTION" (what the anarchists would call propaganda of the deed); in the phrase from the "Battle Hymn of the Republic," "as He died to make men holy, let us die to make men free"; and in modern criticisms that "we have made a mockery of being our brother's keeper by being his jail keeper."[16]

Liberation from confining sexual roles was expressed by the first women's rights convention in the world, held at Seneca Falls, New York, in 1848. These daring Americans called for equal rights in the professions, schools, politics, and religion, equal status in marriage, equal wages and equal property rights. "Know your place" has been changed, slowly but steadily, to "woman's place is everywhere." Increasingly, there have been real personal choices in sexual freedom, careers, marriage as a relation of equals ("democracy begins at home"), communal living ("explode the nuclear family"), and abortion ("our right to choose"), as aspects of a critique of social/sexual definitions that limited both men and women, straight and gay (e.g., James Baldwin's reference to "the male prison").[17] By the 1970s, the American women's movement was the largest independent feminist force in the world, far more systematically radical than perhaps any other (the Communists, for example, casually scorn sexual pleasure as "petty bourgeois indulgence" and consider nonconformists "deviants" to be "rehabilitated," or worse).

The ideal of liberation has also been applied to "ageism" (treating children and the elderly as representatives of a category, rather than as individuals); to schools (John Holt has called them "children's prisons"); to civil rights in the military, including free speech, press, and assembly; to abolishing laws against "crimes without victims" (as in drug use, sexual behavior, pornography, and gambling); or to prison criticism (most radically enunciated by Eugene Debs: "while there is a soul in prison I am not free").[18]

While liberalism has generally sought to achieve such radical freedom by moderate means, it also includes a history of direct action, like the sit-downs of the 1930s, pray-ins at segregated churches, sit-ins at segregated lunch counters, wade-ins at segregated beaches, boycotts, and demonstrations. But the impossibility of realizing such utopian ideals by limited means—the unfulfilled promises of liberalism to achieve liberation—has fostered more explicit forms of radicalism. A moderate liberal might fantasize that problems had been solved—like a complacent individual of the 1920s or the 1950s—only to be shocked to reality by the Great Depression or the social upheavals of the 1960s. In the late 1970s, the basis for another period of struggle may be evident in such statistics as the Urban League's claim of 25 percent unemployment for blacks (and up to 50 percent for black youth), one-third of blacks below poverty level and a growing gap between the average white income and average black income, or in the disproportionately large number of women in jobs with the lowest status and pay. Clearly, we continue to live with the legacy of centuries of racism and sexual discrimination, whatever our progress.

Liberalism, beyond these charges of inadequacy, has been burdened with the contradiction that it has often used institutional means to guarantee equality while popular sentiment has been deeply skeptical about "bureaucracy" (even when it has called it into existence to achieve its hopes). Notice Whitman's hatred of "the swarms of cringers, suckers, doughfaces, lice of politics, planners of sly involutions for their own preferment to city officers or state legislators or the judiciary or congress or the presidency."[19] Though all forms of indigenous radicalism have deep roots in the liberal center and its idealism, they are more dramatically libertarian.

The first, which I will define as right libertarianism, trusts in a society organized on the basis of voluntary agencies. Its most moderate expression can be found in various laissez-faire liberals, and its most extreme, in Anarcho-Capitalists who repudiate the state. Since modern intellectuals easily equate radicalism with communitarianism (and hierarchical authority), this tradition is frequently overlooked. Nonetheless, it is a genuine expression of utopian individualism, as represented by Emerson, in "The American Scholar," yearning for an individual "like a sovereign state." While anarchism, in the form of *movements*, has been most pronounced in Europe, expressed as Anarcho-Communism, syndicalism, and other types of communitarianism, American anarchism—even when explicit—has been distinctively separate. A 1907 comparison between European and American anarchism remains valid: "European anarchists are less introspective than us. They concern themselves more with the mass movement than we do; they fight the capitalist; we fight Comstock. Instead of participating in the trade unions, organizing the unemployed, or indulging in soap-box oratory, we rent comfortable halls and charge ten cents admission. Added to that are, in many cases, ten cents carfare, and Anarchism has become a luxury. Instead of inspiring the workers with revolutionary ideas we teach them speculative theories of liberty."[20] Especially in America, anarchist theories have had many ties to middle-class egoism.

However, another variety of antibureaucratic radicalism will also be identified—left libertarianism, which ranges from decentralists who seek to limit state power to syndicalists who want to abolish it. While individualist anarchism is one possible form of capitalism taken to an extreme, left libertarianism represents an alternative tradition. While resistance to institutional authority, praise for local decision-making, and mass participation (if not consensus) are also hallmarks of this criticism, it is directed toward creating a society of communal sharing rather than individual assertion.

The conclusion of part 2 will contrast these forms of indigenous radicalism with the strange gods of what I have termed "statist radicalism." All expressions of this tendency have usually cast off our libertarian history for the neatly ordered usable past of some other society's legends, symbols, shrines, "holy days," patriotic songs, and heroes. As one Communist asserted in the 1930s, the main task of the CPUSA was to "bolshevize" the party rather than to Americanize it.[21] More recently, a Marxist historian belittled any plea for a "red, white, and blue left" with the condescending claim that "our revolutionary 'heroes' must be understood to be expansionists and the oppressors of workers, slaves, women, and national minorities. . . . We must avoid identification with the bourgeois revolutionary tradition of imperial expansion built into the U.S. from its inception."[22]

Radicals in other countries have sometimes noticed this remarkable abandonment of all national symbols, so unlike the USSR looking back to popular champions from its pre-1917 history, the People's Republic of China preserving the memory of peasant insurrections, Cuba speaking of its present revolution as continuing the long struggle for independence, Vietnam invoking a thousand years of conflict to become a separate entity, or other states calling themselves defenders of radical nationalism (Peru, Syria, Egypt). Radicals in most other societies have been passionately engaged in building their programs upon local traditions, demonstrating how they continue or fulfill many of the central aspirations of their cultures.

Americans meeting with representatives of the National Liberation Front were once chastized, however, because "you American friends have not yet found your own identity: you do not identify with your own people or your country and its traditions." On another occasion, a United States delegation was greeted by the Vietnamese revolutionaries as "the finest sons and daughters of Washington and Jefferson." American radicals are likely to be startled and appalled by such comments. Such reactions are shared by both libertarians and statists, who may be reflecting the moralistic, ahistorical, atheoretical, and eclectic character of this society in their confusion about their own history, rejection of whatever does not immediately "work," contempt for their imperfect predecessors, and affirmations of universal ideals; but the statist radicals have suffered most because their solution to these quandaries has been to retreat to alien models.[23]

Each foreign system has its outpost in America, loyally staffed: Soviet Marxism (the Communist Party, USA), Maoism (the U.S. Communist Party, Marxist-Leninist), and "true" Trotskyism (the Workers' League, the Socialist Workers Party, and the Spartacist League). In 1977, for example, the U.S. Communist Party, Marxist-Leninist, was given the sole American franchise to distribute Maoism. A member of the Chinese politboro, at a Peking banquet honoring the obscure leader ("Chairman Klonsky") of the USCP (M-L), grandiloquently announced that "the founding of the Communist Party (M-L) of the United States has reflected the aspirations of the proletariat and other working people of the United States and is a new victory for the Marxist-Leninist movement in the United States."[24] Such delusions should require little comment.

To emulate theories developed in preindustrial socities, often struggling for national independence, is to obscure the American present (where any revolution would not be against a czar, a Chiang Kai-shek, or a Batista) and the potentialities of a fully libertarian industrial America. The Old Left has been culturally arid and politically withered because, in an innovative, libertarian culture, it has been seeking to turn back the historical clock. As some left liberatarians rebuked the statists: "We fight on the most advanced terrain in history—a terrain that opens the prospect for a post-scarcity society, a libertarian society, not a substitution of one system of hierarchy by another."[25] By dismissing several hundred years of American libertarian radicalism as petty bourgeois and ideologically obsolete (when it may be avant-garde), statist radicalism has been reduced to esoteric cults, like American Buddhism (or, in this case, Maoism), that appeal essentially to radical snobs and alienated intellectuals. A major movement capable of having a deep and lasting impression on this society is unlikely to develop without building upon some existing foundations. The conclusion of part 2, then, is a call for a self-conscious, postcolonial radicalism that is authentically American.

Part 3 centers on the contemporary revival of these native traditions and speculates on their prospects. Certainly the failures of conventional socialism reinforce my thesis. The austerity measures often adopted by labor governments, the absence of popular control in nationalized industries, and the obvious hypocrisies of revolutionary states have done much to validate Proudhon's fear of "the socialism of the barracks" and Bakunin's warning of "workhouse socialism" where the new elite would merely constitute a red bourgeoisie.

Nationalization, for example, has not been synonymous with democratization. Rather, power is often more remote. Workers still have little voice in what happens at their workplace. They are still subject to appointed managers, their unions are usually powerless, and they often cannot strike against "their" state. One British coal miner complained that it was "like working for a ghost" instead of a definite group of capitalists. Michael Polanyi was probably correct when he observed that a worker in a nationalized mine no more felt that he "owned" the mine than he felt that he owned the royal navy.

Nationalization, then, has not solved inequalities of power; it has only substituted officials for owners. Under the direction of this new elite, an enormous and highly centralized bureaucracy reduces the local unit to insignificance. Top-down management, a cretinizing division of labor, production quotas that resemble speedups, praise of stoical efficiency above personal happiness, and limits on popular control are at least as stringent as those in capitalist society.[26] This has been bureaucracy, not democracy, and Fabians have been as guilty of it as Leninists, Trotskyists as much as Stalinists. This is the socialism of five-year plans, growth rates, and dams and factories, but it is not everyday democracy.

In fact, socialism has generally meant the restriction, rather than the expansion, of freedoms found in liberal society: discussion, reading, publishing, art, travel, organization of public employees, voting, religious beliefs, conscientious objection to military service, privacy, the right to strike, emigration, assembly, and the rights of nonconformity (for example, the freedom in American schools—legally guaranteed—not to salute the flag).

By contrast, none of the Marxist-Leninist states permits the formation of any open opposition, or the printing of opposition literature, or the holding of opposition meetings. Most Americans are aware of the military suppression of the working class in Hungary, East Germany, Poland, and Czechoslovakia. Even in China, the stuggle for power after the death of Mao Tse-tung was not openly debated but was the result of cliques, monster rallies, and bombastic denunciations of "the Gang of Four" as wreckers, spies, "agents of the Kuomintang," ultrarightists, and even "capitalist roaders"!

By the end of the 1970s, it was more difficult for American radicals to avoid historical dilemmas by turning to foreign models. Abroad, the Labour Party lacked the enthusiastic support of most British workers, the socialist party of Sweden was voted out of office after decades in power, the German socialists nearly met a similar fate, and much of the idealistic aura of the

Soviet and Chinese revolutions had been diminished by the realities of power politics, such as Chinese support for dictators like Suharto and Marcos, recognition of the Chilean junta, and approval of the Nixon visits. We were living in a time of decaying idols, ''after the fall.''

At home, Americans were less convinced that mammoth systems would necessarily satisfy their personal needs. Was the modern city more comfortable than neighborhood communities? Was a factory more pleasant than a workshop? Was corporate capitalism ecologically, humanistically, and financially desirable? These were issues of the most fundamental radicalness, for which the seemingly exhausted imagination of the welfare state and the Old Left had few answers that were attractive to the public. The ''successes'' of Social Democracy and Communism may yet force a reevaluation of the ''failed'' truths of anarchism.[27]

Let us turn, then, to the origins of this vision of decentralism, which may now form one of the few historical sources of hope.

Courtesy of Community Press Features

CHAPTER ONE

CONSCIENCE AND COMMUNITY

The only obligation which I have a right to assume is to do at any time what I think right.

Any man more right than his neighbors constitutes a majority of one already.

I was not born to be forced. I will breathe after my own fashion.

—Henry David Thoreau, American Protestant saint, "On Civil Disobedience"

I cannot give unconditional loyalties to any institution, man, state, movement or nation. My loyalties are conditioned upon my own convictions and my own values.
—C. Wright Mills, in *Listen, Yankee*

In the American beginning, there was Protestantism. Unlike France and Spain, which officially permitted only orthodox Catholics to emigrate to the New World, the American lands of England were dominated by representatives of the militant Reformation. Although fervent believers in Puritanism, Anabaptism, and Quakerism were a minority, they laid many of the basic foundations for a new society.

Most of them began by rejecting Catholic definitions of community. Catholicism maintained the mythology of apostolic succession, embracing all of society and the centuries within institutions. Although the Church of England had preserved this claim, most Protestant communities tended to be narrower, excluding rather than including. They generally built upon the basis of individual soul, individual minister, and individual congregation. With varying degrees of thoroughness, the Protestants abolished most of the institutional mediators between God and the believer. The unseating of the pope, the demotion of the saints, the disruption of much ritual and tradition and the destruction of the awesome order of the cathedral weakened all authority, since the church and the state were so profoundly interrelated. The weight of eternity fell upon the individual, unaided by a hierarchy of priests, unrelieved by confession, unassisted by the saints, and forbidden to claim that earthly works might contribute to salvation. The individual, though instructed by ministers and the concerns of a congregation, had to experience conversion individually. The believer was less restrained by obvious barriers against what the Puritan fearfully called "enthusiasms," at the same time that reading the Bible and reflecting upon it contained unavoidably subjective elements.[1] Although "con-scientia" originally meant knowledge of anything shared with another person (in other words, social knowledge), a personal conscience did not always agree with the consensus of the church membership. Then, community could rupture. It became more arduous to balance the historic tensions within Christianity between the gospel and the law, grace and works, internal authority and external authority, spirit and structure, conscience and church. Most Protestants were acutely aware of emotional and doctrinal dangers and labored to forge new forms of discipline that would renew the ancient social ideal of an organic community, bound together by a common faith.[2]

The earliest settlers consciously sought to build new communities with the Mayflower Compact of 1620, Winthrop's speech on Christian charity before stepping onto American soil in 1630, the founding of Harvard in 1636 for an educated leadership, and the numerous laws regulating social status and economic life. As Winthrop believed, guidance was necessary so that the colonists would not "shipwracke" by following solely their own "pleasures and profits." Drawing upon traditional models and a rational understanding of their needs, Winthrop urged repeatedly in his address that the colonists "be knitt together" as one.

The Plymouth settlers had already illustrated the contradictions that lay like silent fault lines within Protestantism, making it vulnerable to collapse. These colonists simultaneously broke the institutional continuity of the Church of England, claimed to preserve the simple heritage of the early church, and established their own new order. Conservatism and radicalism mingled, if not at times merged, within their organizations. When the Mayflower Compact was approved in 1620, they once again conserved the principle that government was God's law while demonstrating that it might be a conscious creation. Against their pious intentions, they built a working model of what Rousseau would abstractly term "a social contract," or our age would call "an intentional community." Because they deliberately acted to "combine our selves together into a civil body politick, for our better ordering and preservation," their institutional life carried the insidious implication that they were a people "subject to no law but that which they consented to impose on themselves."[3]

Winthrop's model was also provocatively flawed. The Puritan vision of a city on a hill that would be a moral beacon to a sinful world was capable of stimulating outbursts of perfectionism. The very founding of Massachusetts implied that civil government was indeed a voluntary agreement based upon free will, and that government might be an agency for the creation of such a

New Jerusalem. This possible *communitas* was in painful contrast, however, to the reality of a society divided into the elected brother and the separated other (just as only 35 of the 102 passengers on the *Mayflower* were full Pilgrims). The chasm between the real and the ideal was obvious to these purifiers and contributed to what some scholars have called a frustrated utopianism in American life.

These ambiguities were an especially heavy cross for the Puritans. Whereas the Pilgrims had broken free from the established religion and publicly identified themselves as separatists, the Puritans suffered painful doubts about their continued ties to the Church of England. The question of authority was agonizingly complex for them. These stern sectarians had technically remained within the state church, while castigating it for Catholic liturgical remnants, Anglican approval of bishops, and moral and theological "corruption." The violent friction between their urgent pleas for reform and the inertia of institutions flared into fanaticism among themselves and others. Although they were not separatists, some of them left their comfortable homes, traveled several thousand dangerous miles, and gave their lives and fortunes to construct the first major settlements in the Massachusetts Bay area during 1630-40. While pleading loyalty to the church, they added fuel to the English Civil War in the 1640s. Their efforts to recreate religious order, in both England and America, were radically disintegrated by some of their own principles. Thus, Puritan denunciations of existing imperfections, even when based upon "conservative" pleas for the purity of Christ's original church, fostered more extreme purifiers, such as the Quakers. The Puritans were cruelly destined to confront unruly spirits who mocked them with some of their own implications of an irrepressible radicalism.

By 1636 Roger Williams had demonstrated that a saint could also be a subversive. He was cast out of Massachusetts for pleading that church and state be separated. He had become convinced that forced belief was "soul-rape." If Protestanism encouraged even "the simplest man or woman to search the Scriptures," it must now allow them to find their own truths, free from coercion. A state church, then, was a Romish perversion of conscience that sullied faith upon "the Dung heape of this earth." Consider, he argued, the history of the English church since 1529—Catholic, Calvinist, Anglican. People's beliefs had been (in his words) "tost up and down (even like Tenis-bals)." No, each person must have the liberty to "try all things"—knowing that while he or she would suffer no political persecution, the ultimate sanction would be eternal salvation or damnation![4]

Moderate Puritans strained to protect an official faith, doubtful that civil and religious harmony could be maintained by such radical conscience. While they admired much of Williams's zeal and agreed that fallible human beings, organized as a government, might enforce false doctrines, they denied that a state church was necessarily "a stench in God's nostrils." "Williams' position, from [their] point of view, looked like anarchy."[5] The New Jerusalem of the Puritans had to be defended from splintering into a Protestant Babel. Indeed, the later separation of church and state in Rhode Island pulled down a conservative pillar that had persisted since the last days of the Roman Empire. Such government lost the powerful emotional support of a state religion.

Of course, this did not convict Williams of explicit anarchism. He remained convinced that the state was divinely mandated to preserve civil peace, and that churches could be God's instruments (although he joined none, taking the title of "seeker"). In either domain, opinions that might disrupt the public order were prohibited. Yet, just as Williams had bedeviled the leaders of Massachusetts with his jeremiads against the bondage of the church by the Babylon-state, he was in turn set upon by even more ferocious critics of organized power, such as Samuel Gorton and William Harris. Any Catholic might have predicted the growing crowd of protesters claiming the authority of their own consciences. By 1657, the exasperated Williams had condemned some of his adversaries as "common opposers of all authority" and placed a treason indictment against one radical religionist

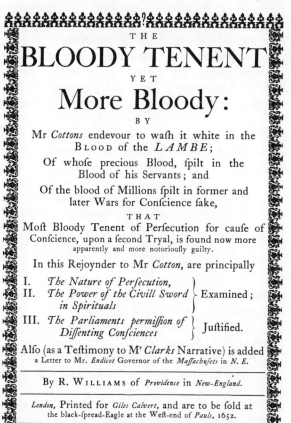

THE

BLOODY TENENT

YET

More Bloody:

BY

Mr *Cottons* endevour to wash it white in the BLOOD of the *LAMBE*;

Of whose precious Blood, spilt in the Blood of his Servants; and

Of the blood of Millions spilt in former and later Wars for Conscience sake,

THAT

Most Bloody Tenent of Persecution for cause of Conscience, upon a second Tryal, is found now more apparently and more notoriously guilty.

In this Rejoynder to Mr *Cotton*, are principally

I. *The Nature of Persecution,*
II. *The Power of the Civill Sword in Spirituals* } Examined;

III. *The Parliaments permission of Dissenting Consciences* } Justified.

Also (as a Testimony to M[r] *Clarks* Narrative) is added a Letter to Mr. *Endicot* Governor of the *Massachusets* in *N. E.*

By R. WILLIAMS of *Providence* in *New-England.*

London, Printed for *Giles Calvert,* and are to be sold at the black-spread-Eagle at the West-end of *Pauls,* 1652.

Roger Williams on "The Bloody Tenent" of coerced belief

"for saying that it was against his conscience to yield to any human order amongst men."[6]

Meanwhile, the saints of Massachusetts had perservered in their battle to enforce religious, social, political, and economic authority. But the result was not the "narrow and cold prison" that V. L. Parrington once portrayed—or, if it was, its inmates were a turbulent lot, and even the guards sometimes questioned the justice of their own power. Puritan belief that humanity was sinful and that its rulers could not be trusted with arbitrary power, which was reinforced by their opposition to Stuart absolutism, became a deep cultural inhibition against absolute power. Constitutional social compacts were encouraged as bulwarks against abusive authority.

However, even these forms of governance contained the seeds of their own self-criticism, if not self-destruction, by the admission that God could speak directly to, and through, the individual. Anne Hutchinson demonstrated the destructive possibilities of this during the mid- and late 1630s. A Puritan morality play began quietly when Hutchinson opened her Boston home for meetings to summarize recent sermons. She had no initial thought of challenging the ministerial function of guiding the believers. but only of restating the content of sermons for those who had missed them and for others of the pious. Her gossipy descriptions, however, rapidly became analyses, an easy error for a literate and introspective laity. She then trespassed into territory that was jealously guarded by ministers and, even worse, carried along subversive beliefs. Hutchinson began to insinuate that the clergy and magistrates were usually representatives of the Old Testament who were severely limited to a knowledge of external appearances, such as visible obedience to rules. But the new dispensation of Christ had released believers from these chains. The godly were no longer sanctified by obligations to law or by their works (a delusion of the Jews and papists) but were purified by the covenant of grace, "the indwelling of the spirit." These elect were subject not to corrupt, external laws and imperfect institutions, but to an inner law known only to themselves. When Hutchinson was asked how she knew that it was God who spoke to her, she boldly answered: "by an immediate revelation." The deputy governor was astonished: "How! An immediate revelation?" Hutchinson: "By the voice of his own Spirit to my soul."[7]

This appeal to direct revelation was an ominous threat to all authority, religious and civil. Although Hutchinson was no revolutionary who yearned to put a torch to all existing order, she had unwittingly conjured up the specter of anarchist subjectivism. If someone could act upon the direct command of God, what was the status of churches, ministers, governments, rulers, and even the educated elite? They might all be relegated to some inferior rank before such a direct power. Captain Johnson recalled one of the heretics making such a reasonable conclusion: "I had rather hear such a one that speaks from the meere motion of the spirit, without any study at all, than any of your learned Scollers, although they may be fuller of Scripture."[8] Leaders of the colony, such as the Reverend John Wilson, became increasingly resentful and alarmed that Hutchinson and her disciples were reducing God's faithful servants to "Nobodies."

In 1637, she was accused of eighty-two doctrinal errors, many of them covered by the term antinomianism: being "against the law." Although she fervently declared that intuitive knowledge would not counsel license, since it meant direct access to divine law, her opponents ridiculed her as a Jezebel who appealed to emotions. Her beliefs were scorned as libertine, seditious, and "anarchical." Like Williams, she was banished, and—also like Williams—her followers split into factions. Governor John Winthrop was properly horrified at the implications of her ideas: "She walked by such a rule as cannot stand with the peace of any State; for such bottomless revelations . . . if they be allowed in one thing, must be admitted a rule in all things; for they being above reason and Scripture, they are not subject to controll."[9] Winthrop upheld the powers of the magistrates and the ministers with his severe judgment on the disruptive potential of her principles. But the Puritans were never able to purge themselves of their contradictions by expelling Hutchinson, Williams, and many others. They were frustrated by a basic riddle of Protestantism: Who or what is authority? Although the Puritans had not desired to become ancestors of anarchism, this rebel progeny was among their bastard descendants.

Another form of militant Protestantism, the Society of Friends ("Quakers"), also illustrated the possibilities for radical disintegration of authority. This was dramatically evident in Quaker faith, where each believer followed the vision of his or her own inner light, partially directed by the voluntary discipline of the meeting. This spontaneity flowed naturally from the Protestant emphasis on conscience and "the priesthood of all believers." The inward covenant of grace had full primacy over the old covenant of works. Even the authority of Scripture was subordinate to the direct insight of the spirit, which revealed the "new law written within, on the tables of the heart."[10] Quaker disdain for the frailties of man-made law, emphasis on revelation, refusal to take political oaths, rejection of war taxes, tithes, and military duty, and repudiation of various social conventions (such as removing their hats before magistrates and other rulers) earned them a reputation as subverters of all order. This was an understandable fear. If anarchism could be achieved in spirit, civil authority was likely to be attacked by some of the believers. Religious antinomianism might become secular antinomianism, where self-reliance threatened social institutions.

However, few Quakers uniformly applied their spiritual philosophy and practice to physical society. In 1682 William Penn solemnly prayed that the government of his colony be respected as "a part of religion itself, a thing sacred in its institution and end."[11] Most people should not meddle in politics but should live quiet lives of work and devotion. Yet, even as Penn upheld the power of the magistrates in nonreligious matters, he character-ized most earthly laws as "superficial" compared with the immutable and "fundamental laws" that were sensed by conscience. This religious freedom—combined with other circumstances—shattered Penn's admoni-tions for conventional politics. Even when it was not ignored or flouted, the regime was held in little awe. During most of 1681–96, no taxes were im-posed. When one of Penn's governors arrived in 1688, no one greeted him. He later "found the council room deserted and covered with dust and scat-tered papers. The wheels of government had nearly stopped turning."[12] While authority was always reasserted and Quakerism became embodied in powerful social and political institutions, its foundations were never entirely secure, and it relied more on appeals to norms than on direct coercion.

The revivalist movements that erupted in the 1720s and 1730s, although their social perspectives were often conservative, paradoxically added to this anarchist heritage by their appeals to emotion rather than reason and by their creating, through camp meetings, a sense of community without a church. The "prepared heart" of Puritan theology (with its implied mysticism) finally burst all its structural bonds to become spontaneous belief. Guardians of tradition like the Harvard faculty were dismayed by revival ministers who distracted people from their normal business, under-mined the basis of rational theology, and, *"which is worse*, and *it is a Natural effect of these Things*, [caused the people] to despise their own Ministers."[13] Those in power often feared the revivalists as disrupters of the established order.

These suspicions were overstated but not illusory. Religious ferment was a yeast capable of unexpected results. Sometimes it revivified old churches, sometimes it unsettled or burst them. A crusading spirit might find its form in repressive laws or, on other occasions, utopian colonies. But in all the manifestations of revivalism, it was the individual who achieved "new light." If God could reveal Himself directly to any person, the power of in-stitutions was diminished. Most evangelicals heartily agreed with Peter Cart-wright, a famous circuit rider, that "Christ had no literary college or univer-sity, nor theological school or Biblical Institute, nor did he require his first ministers to memorize his sayings or sermons [or] to take a theological course."[14]

By the early 1800s, religious contributions to the character of American radicalism were clearly defined: the Protestant emphasis on conscience, moral purity, and natural law could challenge worldly authority. The belief that individual conscience might perceive a higher law than that of civil gov-ernment, and that disobedience to "unjust law" is a moral duty, has been repeated from the days of the Puritans and the Quakers. Thomas Paine announced that his own mind was his church, and the revolution against England was justified as an affirmation of God-given inalienable rights that were self-evident to everyone. This revolution was another reformation.

Conscience—for some of the critics—could also become the judge of all. Emerson later rejected the "corpse-cold rationality" of the Unitarian church for spontaneous nature, insight, transcendental ego, and "illimitable freedom": "Judge for yourself . . . reverence yourself. It is the inevitable effect of that doctrine . . . to make each man a state" (or, we might say in the case of Margaret Fuller, each woman).[15] It was comfortably assumed—by Hutchinson, Williams, Penn, Emerson, and others—that conscience was direct understanding of natural law, or immediate communication with God.

In 1850, when the president supported a fugitive slave bill, the Congress approved it, and the Supreme Court upheld it, Emerson was not impressed: "I will not obey it, by God!" Thoreau agreed, saying that institutions were usually wrong. They had been created by past revelations, matured and decayed like people, and became decrepit, senile, and contemptible. Institutions were natural reactionaries, crucifying Christ, excommunicating Copernicus and Luther, and rejecting Jefferson and Washington. But the rebel's sense of universal justice had an immediate validity that would triumph over "the party of the past." Ideally, this spirit of protest would result in a permanent revolution against the dead letter of all organizations, including those of Protestantism. Emerson concurred that "the Office of America is to liberate."[16]

Similar voices of defiance against structures of control have continued. Twain describes such a conflict in *Huckleberry Finn* (1885), when Huck must decide whether he should betray his friend, Nigger Jim, by returning him to slavery. This would uphold the conventions of property and the then-teachings of Southern churches but deny his own sense of justice. The God of society is watching him, but Huck turns away from organized religion, saying "All right, then, I'll *go* to hell." Many of the pacifists of World War I, the members of sit-ins for civil rights, and the antiwar demonstrators of the 1960s were also asserting a perfect moral freedom. Some did so moderately, as when Norman Thomas pleaded that the flag should not be burned, but cleaned, while his opponents followed a more extreme conscience and reenacted the drama of William Lloyd Garrison, who set fire to a copy of the constitution because it was a covenant with hell that sheltered slavery.[17]

Such freedom has rendered it difficult, if not impossible, to organize these radicals. Just as their critical spirit has been antitheoretical and antiinstitutional, so has their work. William Ellery Channing was a true American critic when he expressed "a peculiar dread and abhorrence of the passion for power." When such Americans have been unable to avoid organizing, they have been attracted to voluntary associations, like the autonomous congregations of most American religions.[18] Once formed, these groups have been more active in moralizing than in politics; they have sought generally to transform individuals through moral appeals ("a change of heart") rather than to attain political power. Discipline, whether as an organizational principle or a goal, has often been defeated by such eloquent rebels as Bronson Alcott, who valued the sanctity of his own soul above loyalty to an organization: "Church and State are responsible to *me*; not I to them. They cease to deserve our veneration from the moment they violate our consciences. . . . Why should I employ a church to write my creed or a state to govern me? Why should I not write my own creed? Why not govern myself?"[19] Channing lauded this self-governed individual as the glory of our culture, and he predicted a social evolution toward individualism that might eventually eliminate any necessity for government, where "soul" would finally defeat "force." This was an American version of the withering away of the state.

Such visions of a perfect moral freedom to achieve a perfect moral order have been both repressive and liberating. Explicit radicals and average Americans have a strong predisposition to believe in simple definitions of good and evil and to condemn their opponents as the latter. Conventional politics is hindered by this standard, which implies that all politics is corrupt because power cannot avoid sordid compromises of principle. Ask the typical American what comes to mind first when the word politician is spoken. He or she will probably have few, if any, kind thoughts, since politics in America (in general contrast, let us say, to England or West Germany) is not an honored profession. Even a president can indulge in such stereotypes. Can one imagine a prime minister or a chancellor casually announcing that while being executive was "a fascinating experience," he had "no great liking . . . for the word 'politics' "?[20]

This pervasive idealism is also expressed in unprecedented aspirations (such as achieving a classless society or abolishing poverty) and frequent harsh criticism of the gap between utopian ideals and the existence of racism, inequality, sex discrimination, and "hypocrites in high places." Thus, many Europeans were somewhat startled by the furor over Watergate, since a less idealistic society might have been more complacent about the realities of power. In many ways, the City of Man continues to be measured by the City of God. Our most revered critics, like Norman Thomas or Martin Luther King, Jr., have spoken from deep moral convictions, preaching to Americans as a congregation. Radical movements that have been relatively popular are equally moralistic, reflected in C. Wright Mills's characterization of the New Left as an ethical upsurge, and by Staughton Lynd and Paul Goodman calling upon young people to "come out of Babylon" and make a "New Reformation."[21] Less successful have been those who have offended this need for ethical absolutes, whether typical Marxists, northern civil rights students who disregarded Southern religious feelings, or many Black Panther leaders with their early atheism. These people have generally isolated themselves from the masses.

CAPITALISM AND COMMUNITY

Conservation of the old modes of production in unaltered form was . . . the first condition of all earlier industrial classes. Constant revolutionizing of production,
uninterrupted disturbance of all social conditions, everlasting uncertainty and agitation distinguishes the bourgeois epoch from all earlier ones.—Marx and Engels, *The
Communist Manifesto* (1848)

There is, let us admit it, no revolutionary movement on earth today which is reshap-
ing human society and the face of nature as vastly, as precipitously as the American
business community. Metternich, speaking for conservatism old style, proclaimed
himself "the rock from which the waves recoil." But our jet-set managers, administrators, and systems analysts are a storm beating upon every coast.—Theodore
Roszak, introduction to *Sources* (1972)

Anarcho-libertarian impulses have also been generated by capitalism,
which has broken down many of the traditional frameworks of authority
in this culture, generally replacing them with self-interest. Capitalist
rhetoric about "the free enterprise system" as a voluntarist society of free
choice, not compulsion—however removed from hard realities—contributes
to our common definition of "the pursuit of happiness" as consumerism
and of liberation as personal gratification. The radicalism that grows out of
this is most often individualist, but, when communal, it also has been
remarkably preoccupied with issues of decentralization and fears of the
tyranny of organization.

We cannot understand American radicalism unless we understand
American capitalism, which forms most of the core of our history and vitally
influences all life in this most capitalistic of nations. Even the one-third of
our working class that is unionized is neither socialist not Communist,
unlike that of any other major industrial country, but officially speaks for
private property. Virtually every radio station, every large newspaper, every
billboard, and every mass publication should be interpreted as capitalist
propaganda. Since its values are everywhere, we seldom realize how distinctive they are. Many of our everyday assumptions are not shared by most peo-

ple in the world, who do not stress individual achievement or evaluate people as commodities. Our common forms of speech—the very way most of us think—are formed by these commercial concepts: "I'll buy that!" "You'd have to sell me on that." "You pays your money and you takes your choice." "How have you been spending your time?" "I wouldn't take a million dollars for her." "I'd put my money on that." "I don't have a personal investment in it." "Put your money where your mouth is." "We can certainly capitalize on that." "We're in business." "I've no use for him." "He's a loser." "Winner take all!" It would be profitable to examine this going concern.

Capitalism is being used here not as a synonym for business, profit, or greed, but as the proper name for a general system based upon the private ownership of the means of production (such as land and raw materials) by small numbers of people. The great majority own one commodity, their labor. Unlike slaves and serfs, however, they can move, change jobs, and attempt to bargain for the best sale of themselves.

The motive force of this system is profit, or surplus value, which is the difference between wages and the cost of production, on one hand, and the selling price of the manufactured goods or services on the other. Hence, if a worker produces five hundred dollars worth of goods in a week and receives three hundred dollars in wages, the remainder, minus production costs, enriches the owner. Conflicts arise because the capitalist desires the highest profit while the worker seeks the highest wage. These conflicts are usually resolved in favor of the capitalist because the system assumes economic production for private profit. If a capitalist cannot achieve what is considered a satisfactory profit from, let us say, selling food, then food is not produced (or the supply may be artificially restricted or efforts made to stimulate demand, most recently through advertising). But the motor of the system remains profit.

We have all been born into such a profit culture, in which the buying and selling of labor and land are considered normal. This seems to us the only "natural" way to live. Yet, for most of human history, and throughout much of the world today, capitalism is an aberration.[1] The novelty of this system, so destructive of most definitions of community, can be highlighted by comparing it with the system of medieval Europe, which it gradually defeated.

The socioeconomic ideal of that period was an organic community in which everything and everyone had its proper place, as defined by tradition. This goal of stability—attractive because these were often violent, rather than placid times— was perhaps exemplified by the cathedral, which rose from a broad base (like society),

From *Common Sense*
(June 1974), p. 4.

with its narrowed spires (like the temporal and spiritual elites) reaching toward heaven. In our day banks, supermarkets, and department stores might embody the symbolically central.

In medieval society, it was universally assumed that economic processes were moral questions that were answered by objective standards established by God and revealed in the Scriptures and the teachings of the church. For us, profit and personal advancement are dominant.

Earlier, land and labor were not in a free market. Land, for example, was the key to power and status. A lord would no more sell land than the governor of Maryland would sell a county. And the labor force (whether serfs, peasants, or the few townspeople) was seldom legally free to move about or to change occupations.

Business was often feared as a corrupting activity that focused too much attention on wordly things, an attitude that was reflected in such occasionally strident mottoes as "no Christian ought to be a merchant" and "business can scarcely be conducted without sin," along with the less extreme maxim (in canon law) that "to fornicate [that is, to commit adultery] is always forbidden to anyone, but to trade is sometimes allowed and sometimes not."

Other common practices of capitalist society were equally foreign to this world, such as the "sinful" practice of taking interest on loans, which could be interpreted as selling God's time or having money "unnaturally" breed more money. Prices and wages should be set not by demand but by standards of intrinsic worth. If a person needed some item but was under no compulsion to buy it, the "just price" was that fixed by convention. A merchant was not morally correct in raising his prices simply because demand had increased or to offset losses suffered in other areas, which were the judgments of God or the result of personal folly. Disregarding the just price could turn laudable industry into hellish avarice. Thus a seller was morally obligated to point out defects in a product, while the buyer was expected never to profit from the seller's mistakes. Augustine gave the illustration of the seller of a precious manuscript who was ignorant of its real worth. The buyer—who is evidently Augustine—pays the just price, which is substantially higher than the one demanded by the stupid seller. (Augustine would not have been a successful used-car salesman.) It was crucial to avoid the slithering snake of greed lurking in the transient wealth of this world. The ideal life avoided such problems by monastic retreat.

Practice, of course, often deviated from these standards, but they were central economic concepts of the official ideology of that day. There were individual capitalists who were aggressive traders, bankers, voyagers, greedy moneylenders, avaricious tax collectors, and the like, but these people were not participants in a systematic and rational way of life. They operated within a context that often specified maximum limits on profits and wages and usually denied them clear legal status on interest for loans. They might be able to overcome these barriers, but the fear of social and divine retribution was strong. Treasure in heaven was more to be sought than treasure on earth.

Capitalism, as a system, was a transformation that began within this medieval framework. The old order had functioned in rather primitive agrarian societies. Much of medieval Europe was essentially a nonmoney economy of self-sufficient local agriculture. Prices and wages in this kind of society were not likely to fluctuate too wildly. The traditional price was commonly assumed to be the "just price." Prices seldom changed rapidly, except when there were crop failures. But, by the eleventh and twelfth centuries there was already a money economy in some Italian cities, and financial expansion came with the crusades and later explorations. A commercial civilization (which was slowly emerging) required a new ideology. Signs of this change included technological innovation, increasing urbanization, accumulation of capital, the interconnection and expanding trade of Europe, population growth, and the opening of an era of overseas expansion. A new system began to form, based on the systematic, rational acquisition of goods, long-term capital investments, and standardization of finance and production.[2]

This transitional period was also marked by the disintegration of the hegemony of the Catholic church, which had generally preserved the older ideals of community. The relationship between the rise of capitalism and the destruction of the universal church is an extremely complicated one, but it can be said that those who rejected the halfway measures of Luther and the English state were to have some radical influences on business practices, as did John Calvin and the citizens of Geneva, beginning in the 1530s. Whereas most leaders of the Reformation remained essentially medieval in their social, economic, and political thought, Calvin, the "godfather" of the Puritans, virtually repudiated the entire Hebraic and Aristotelian heritage on the subject. While he agreed that excessive interest (undefined) was a sin against charity, he concluded that brotherhood and justice did not forbid the common practice in Geneva of charging 5 percent on loans. While Luther continued to denounce usury, and a later Catholic bishop, Bossuet, remarked that "usury is the brat of heresy" (which was not necessarily true), the Calvinists had changed.

In the New World this influence was most vitally expressed by the Puritans, who were the dominant elements of the Great Migration of 1630–40. During this time, the population of New England grew to about twenty thousand. Although there had been earlier settlements, such as Jamestown in 1607, they were shaped by other sorts of people and circumstances. Most of the South afforded rich land that eventually yielded much with relatively little effort (compared with stony New England); it was also characterized by extensive slave labor, a geography that thwarted the creation of a network of closely associated towns, more upper-class leadership, and a major role for Catholicism and Anglicanism. In the course of history, the South became a regional curiosity, whereas the Puritan-influenced New Englander became the model "Yankee."[3]

Overall, Puritan thought encouraged the growth of a capitalist culture, although, like any ideological response to a period of change, it did not merely reflect the new order but contained considerable, and not always compatible, elements of the old. The earlier ideals were represented by such men as John Winthrop, who believed in a Christian commonwealth that would be upheld by both religious and political authority. Such leaders of New England hoped to create a New Canaan by inculcating and legislating extensive social controls. These controls ranged from status laws—defining who was qualified to identify himself as Master or Goodman, or what women could wear silk hoods (their husbands had to be worth at least 299 pounds), to upholding the ancient principles of just prices and wages. Thus, from 1633 to 1641, the Court of Assistants in Boston set maximum wages, with more for skilled laborors such as carpenters and thatchers, and less for common labor. The colonial governments also frequently examined the quality of exported goods such as leather and pipe staves to insure the good reputation of local products.

No one consciously defended unrestrained business egoism. Regulations were variously described as "the sinews of society" and the mortar that held a brick building together. As one minister intoned: "For if each man may do what is good in his owne eyes, proceed according to his own pleasure, so that none may crosse him or controll him by any power; there must of necessity follow the distraction and *desolation* of the whole, when man hath liberty to follow his owne imagination and humerous devices and seek his particulars, but oppose one another, and all prejudice the publike good."[4]

God-fearing merchants were expected to work within the bounds of this moral principle of social responsibility, with its specific applications of reasonable rates in labor and goods, to observe the rankings of social and political hierarchy, and to avoid "immodest and costly apparel" and all else that diverged from "the simplicitie of the gospel and...God's word."[5] Businessmen were also expected to be charitable and to labor in the service of the church and the state. For forty years the merchant Robert Keayne put aside one penny of every shilling for the poor. When Governor Endicott died in 1665, he had met his duties so well that he had "died poor, as most of our rulers do"—and John Hull, the author of this comment, made extensive loans to the government, many of which were never repaid.[6] Such men were often as concerned with the public interests as with their own, if not more. They were fulfilling John Winthrop's aspiration of constructing "a model of Christian charity" to the whole world—a New Jerusalem.

If Protestant saints like these had been common and without ambiguities in their own lives, the holy commonwealth would have killed the egoistic "spirit of capitalism." But Puritan practice was a valiant failure. The "inner-directed" Puritan was at first controlled by a social conscience, but, as Perry Miller perceived, "at every point, economic life set up conflicts with ideology."[7] Or perhaps the older ideals in the Puritan ideology conflicted with the newer modernizing, capitalist aspects. The Puritan community contained its own gravediggers. As Cotton Mather was to remark in *Magnalia Christi Americana* (1702); "Religion begat prosperity and the daughter devoured the mother." Many businessmen soon gravitated toward their own immediate interests, fragmenting the order of the community, because of elements within Puritanism.

This occurred first, and most superficially, in the eliminating or modifying of many of the roadblocks to business (like the usury laws).

Second, it had the traditional notion of vocation, but in a more militant form. Everyone had a "calling" in life, even if only to be a lowly shepherd. Diligent labor in one's calling was a kind of worship. They combined it with the earlier Christian notion of humanity as the temporary "steward" of God's wealth to form a virtual sacrament of labor. As Luther commented, to be a good cook was like cooking for God, and to be a good housekeeper was like keeping house for God. Even when traditional images of work might be used, the content had been transformed. To the medieval church—represented, let us say, by Aquinas—work was a punishment for sin. There was no work ethic that glorified labor. Aquinas urged that rich people abandon the pursuit of further wealth for the study of religion. The Puritans rejected this as a monkish retreat from the struggles of everyday life and placed an unprecedented emphasis on work as a positive good rather than primarily as a divine retribution for Adam's iniquity.[8] All were expected to labor: the idle poor and the idle rich were both condemned.

This emphasis on individual work was reinforced in America by direct material encouragements. A small artisan could indeed become a merchant; a poor servant might come to own land. They could live better than people of similar classes in Europe. Edward Johnson praised the Massachusetts Bay Colony twenty years after its founding: "There are not many towns in the country, but the poorest person in them hath a house and land of his own, and bread of his own growing, if not some cattle."[9]

Third, Puritans suffered anxiety about their salvation and often sought proof of santification. "Success" might be taken as a visible sign of inward grace, although few dared to make this argument, since the wealthy could quite easily be wicked.[10]

Fourth, the asceticism of Puritan life also stimulated a prosperity that tended to dissolve the stern commandments that had helped produce it. If Puritans were successful, they were urged not to spend their profits on themselves, but to reinvest them. Reinvestment was good stewardship of God's wealth, made a greater contribution to the community, and protected one from the temptations of vanity that lurked in consumption.

While these were values of the Puritan community, they ultimately threatened social cohesion. Hard work, denial of luxuries, and reinvestment of profits were godly acts, but prosperity could bring increased temptations toward personal vanity. Thus, while the Puritans passed laws on just wages, prices, and other aspects of business and social life, "at every point economic life set up conflicts with ideology."

In 1639 the future of Puritan economic laws was captured in a prophetic social drama. Robert Keayne, a model and perhaps almost saintly Puritan merchant, was vehemently accused by both court and church of "oppression"—that is, profiteering. He was originally accused of exceeding the just price on a bag of nails; then other members of the community, placing the blame for high prices solely on greedy merchants, further denounced him for overcharging on some large gold buttons, a bridle, and a skein of thread. Today this may not sound like a heinous crime, but the charge of exploiting other members of the community was damnable and illegal in a Puritan society pledged to be "knite togeather as a body in a most stricte and sacred bond and covenante of the Lord. . . . Straitly tied to all care of each others good, and of the whole by every one and so mutually." Keayne, in his business practices, was charged with subverting the community and offending God.

He was eventually censured "in the Name of the Church for selling his wares at excessive Rates, to the Dishonor of Gods name, the Offense of the General Cort, and the Publique scandall of the Cuntry." For this he was fined an extraordinary sum (later reduced), and he abjectly and tearfully confessed his covetous heart in church. With the payment of the fine and his "penitential acknowledgement" the case was officially closed. The governor, John Winthrop, sighed that humanity was naturally corrupt and that Keayne was a godly man who had not consciously sinned but had fallen into error and should be admonished rather than excommunicated.[11]

It was significant that the more merchant-oriented magistrates objected to the decision of the General Court. They argued that there was no explicit law against Keayne's variety of extortion, that everyone charged high rates, and that "it is the common practice in all countries, for men to make use of advantages for raising the prices of their commodities." Though this view did not prevail, and Keayne was formally defeated, his case still presaged the time when the countinghouse would control the meetinghouse or—as often—ignore it. As the pious William Bradford lamented by 1653, the goals of the Plymouth Colony had also been subverted by "that subtill serpente" who "hath slylie wound in himself under faire pretences of necessitie and the like."[12] Just as radical Protestantism could devolve into individual egos, so the early social controls of the colonists would be challenged by economic egoism.

Other settlers were less apologetic about their self-aggrandizement. When Cotton Mather told one group near Boston that religion was the main motive for colonization, a prominent member replied: "Sir, you are mistaken, you think you are preaching to the people at the Bay; *our* main end was to catch fish." Much later, when the founder of the College of William and Mary informed a Southerner that education would save souls, he was bluntly repelled: "Damn your souls! Make tobacco!"[13] The cloven hoof of the wayward merchant was on the path not to the City of God, but to the City of the World. This was to be the future.

The liberation of business would mean the weakening of community. Capitalism was a vital, progressive force when it cracked the structures of feudalism, allowing the emergence of a society of choice, a society of constant change. People were no longer locked into a social mosaic of customs, rank, and community but were forced to be free. In the famous words of Marx and Engels: "Conservation of the old modes of production in unaltered form was. . . the first condition of all earlier industrial classes. Constant revolutionizing of production, uninterrupted disturbance of all social conditions, everlasting uncertainty and agitation distinguishes the bourgeois epoch from all earlier ones." This is the permanent revolution of capitalism.[14]

Such a radical, innovative system demanded a degree of social mobility that destroyed controls on men like Robert Keayne. In the new society, the individual was supposedly free to choose his own occupation, work contract, religion, and marriage partner—and to try to get the "best bargain" in each choice. All individuals were to follow their own particular self-interests, living within the freedom and constant uncertainty of the marketplace, where ideas, institutions, and people were all commodities. Even the most eminent theoretician of Anarcho-Communism interpreted this activity by capitalism as liberating: "millions of transactions are made without the slightest interference of government, and those who enter into agreements have not the slightest intention of breaking bargains."[15] But if this was the positive dimension of capitalism for Kropotkin, its immoral or amoral ego was its darker side. He was no admirer of an ethnic of "grabbing" for oneself, of "possessive individualism." Whereas such qualities have been partially restrained elsewhere by vestiges of an organic community (such as the "paternalism" and permanent employment of Japanese firms) or by powerful nationalistic sentiments that may limit capitalist self-interest (such as the selling of English or German firms to foreigners), American capitalists have been remarkably free from these restrictions. Profit is their first principle. As Jefferson observed: "Merchants have no country. The mere spot they stand on does not constitute so strong an attachment as that from which they draw their gains." Certainly for American capitalists, self-interest is supreme.

At a minimum, this system has encouraged self-reliance, just as radical Protestantism had sometimes liberated the individual beyond its own expectations. The owners and workers, reinforced by religion, were under less external compulsion, being impelled by both self-interest and self-discipline. Secular society would later develop the themes of individual "Wealth" through "Self-Reliance" (two of Emerson's prominent essays) for its more-or-less official ideology. It was assumed that individual effort would be rewarded and that such striving in the marketplace would "work out best" for all of society. Even in 1976 the president of the United States could reveal that Horatio Alger had been his favorite childhood author.[16]

If the individual failed, business and religion both proposed a government that was deaf (or nearly so) to cries for assistance. Failure likely was a deserved punishment for a dronish disposition or a welcome suffering that would purify the soul. The first almshouse was not established in Boston until 1660. The image of the "welfare chisler" as lazy, sexually irresponsible, and dirty is still prevalent today. Welfare, to many, is parasitism. In 1972 the official ideology was crisply enunciated by President Richard Nixon in his Labor Day address. He sternly lectured the nation that the presidential election of that year was a titanic struggle between the staunch old "work ethic" and the evil allure of the "welfare ethic." Speaking to workers, he confidently declared: "The work ethic builds character and self-reliance, the welfare ethic destroys character and leads to a vicious cycle of dependency. The work ethic builds strong people. The welfare ethic breeds weak people. . . . This year, you are not only to choose the kind of leadership you want, you are going to decide what kind of people Americans will be."[17]

Few people thought it strange that the head of one of the largest bureaucracies in the world was praising individualism. His pronouncements merely restated old verities like "stand on your own two feet!" and "pay your own way." Whether this folklore bears any relation to reality is a question few public figures will ask.

Any interpretation of American radicalism must understand the pervasive powers—economic, social, and psychological—of American capitalism. Above all, it has been generally perceived as incredibly successful. Collectively, Americans are in the wealthy First World whose necessities are often considered luxuries in the Third World. A history of resilient business and abundant production, distributed far more equitably than in most of the world, may not have produced what Lord Bryce once called a land of happy monotony, but Americans have become generally accustomed to a fatalistic optimism about progress. This explains much of our innocence of the general reality of the world—poverty, famine, disease, "overpopulation," revolution, and limited hope—and our general difficulty in understanding or feeling sympathy for noncapitalist societies. Just as F. Scott Fitzgerald once said that "the very rich are different from you and me," Americans are different from most other peoples. There has been no major depression since the 1930s, and the country remains the strongest of the capitalist nations. Whereas Japan, the third largest economic system, imported 80 percent of its energy resources and more than 50 percent of its food in 1976, the United States has the potential for self-sufficiency. In both food production and advanced technology, it also remains vastly superior to the Soviet Union.[18]

Although claims that this is a classless society are not convincing to me, it is nevertheless significant that these can be made and believed by many— which would be unlikely in Great Britain, France, Italy, or elsewhere. Marx said that the workers had nothing to lose but their chains; yet what chains do most Americans think they have to lose? The Industrial Workers of the World asserted that the working class and the employing class had nothing in common, but few agreed. The material success of capitalism has created bonds of belief, fostering the hegemony of capitalist values in this society, giving us the unreasoned assumptions through which we "see" the world. The boundaries of capitalism form the limits of the average imagination, of what seems "natural." Work is not simply imposed by the system but becomes a vital source of self-meaning, even when it has little hope of financial achievement or high status. Those who "don't make anything of their lives," whether "lazy hippies" or irresponsible welfare recipients, are commonly scorned as an insult to the self-esteem of the working class.[19]

But, despite these often shared values and aspirations, most of society is atomized. We live in a community, but it is a community of competition. We are divided from nature; people are perceived not as a part of a continuum with nature, but as the aggressive, exploitative dominators of it. We are separated from others by competition or because of the increasing specialization of labor. The interests of city and country, work and play, reason and emotion are also separated. Absolutes of all kinds, whether of religion, systematic philosophy, or tradition, are disintegrated by the demands of utilitarian self-interest. T. S. Eliot described such a world of uncertainty, where everything had to be "named" again, and the poet must be a beginner, not a continuer:

> Trying to learn to use words, and every attempt
> Is a wholly new start, and a different kind of failure...
> ...And so each venture
> Is a new beginning, a raid on the inarticulate.[20]

While older societies were often based upon historically evolved social statuses, this organic union has been replaced by mechanical solidarity, by contractual relations for specific purposes. An impersonal society means living together but not knowing your neighbors. Instead, the individual is evaluated primarily as the proprietor of self and the appropriator of others, in a society that ideally is composed of free and equal atoms like the millionaire in Saul Bellow's *Henderson the Rain King*, crying out "I want, I want, I want." Already in the 1840s Emerson observed that industrial capitalism had destroyed the independence and satisfactions of craft labor, turning the workers into commodities to be brought, sold and used—into a collection of walking monsters, here "a good finger, a neck, a stomach, an elbow," but never a whole person.[21] More recently, if you worked in the auto factory in Lordstown, Ohio, in 1976, the cars went by you at the rate of 101 an hour. Every 33 seconds you had to mechanically repeat certain motions. If you were a telephone operator, a keypuncher, or a steel worker you might have the same response to such a division of labor:

You're there just to handle the equipment. You're treated like a piece of equipment.

You do it automatically, like a monkey or a dog would do something by conditioning. You feel stagnant; everything is over and over and over. . . . This makes the average individual feel sort of like a vegetable.

That's mechanical; that's not human. . . . We sweat, we have upset stomachs and we're not about to be placed in the category of a machine.[22]

The images are all nonhuman: a vegetable, a monkey, a dog, a machine.

This resentment can be neutralized, however, by other forms of individualism. Many people, if they are unhappy or unemployed, believe the official ideology that it is somehow their fault. Others are gratified because their pay buys them a sense of freedom as a consumer. Consumerism then becomes a kind of spectacle that controls people by convincing them they have meaning through products: "Come alive, you're in the Pepsi generation," "Suzuki [motorcycle] conquers boredom," and "Take a puff and it's springtime." Even those who become disillusioned are often caught in "the golden chains" of installment buying; they now have something to lose if they rebel. Trotsky inadvertently touched upon this question when he described his family's 1917 living quarters in New York City: "We rented an apartment in a workers' district, and furnished it on the installment plan [!] That apartment, at $18 a month, was equipped with all sorts of conveniences that we Europeans were quite unused to: electric lights, gas cooking-range, bath, telephone, automatic service-elevator, and even a chute for the garbage. These things completely won the boys over to New York."[23]

Business has often been willing to further encourage this individualism with such techniques as profitsharing, company pensions, teams of workers, and more flexible working hours. These are all excellent forms of social control: "quit and you lose your pension!" "We're speeding up the line to increase your profitsharing." Or, "buy a share in YOUR company!" While most of these changes are cosmetic, merely giving the appearance of humanistic management, most radicals have been insensitive to the power of such devices to meet minimal human needs. Elinor Langer, who took a job at a telephone company so she could write about it, soon realized that the "busy little world" of small rewards and loyalties could assuage the impersonality of most existing work situations. For business, "the pattern of co-optation...rests on details: hundreds of trivial, but human details."[24] Capitalists have generally understood this better than leftists, who are still quoting Marx from 1848, or the IWW from 1905.

A contemporary exemplar of capitalist radicalism might be John D. Rockefeller III, a banker, Republican, and author of *The Second American Revolution* (1973). Although he opens his book with the delightful understatement that "the name Rockefeller does not connote a revolutionary," his goal is an American utopia: an open society where each person can develop his or her potential free from limitations of race, sex, or class. Though all people should be guaranteed adequate food, clothing, and shelter, further status must depend upon ability alone. For Rockefeller, this is not only a practical question of utilizing resources but the moral responsibility of America's "transcendental mission." The latter is rather ill defined, but Rockefeller leaves no doubt that it can be most fully achieved by a "humanistic capitalism."[25]

He immediately laments the incomplete realization of this vision by American society. He invokes an eminently respectable group to preface his own complaints, the 1971 White House Conference on Youth, appointed by Richard Nixon. They had affirmed "the high ideals upon which this country was ostensibly founded" and challenged the government to act upon them: "We are not motivated by hatred, but by disappointment over and love for the unfulfilled potential of this Nation." Rockefeller, like some Puritan moralist, then launches into his own jeremiad against the corruption of America. A crisis of faith has been provoked by such realities as "the exploitation and destruction of nature's beauty," too much money for the "haves," hunger, greater emphasis on efficiency than on humanity, "the military-industrial complex," racism, sex discrimination, "the dehumanization of work," unresponsive bureaucracy, and a society where "competition predominates over compassion." What sounds like a litany of the New Left is delivered by a capitalist with impeccable credentials.

How will these problems be overcome and his American ideal of full human liberation be attained? Centralist "elitism" is considered and rejected as stifling local creativity and initiative. Instead, he lauds a "participatory democracy" that will keep the large institutions of politics, business, and labor open to the opinions of average people. As models of such physical and intellectual liberation, he eclectically praises Ralph Nader's consumerism, co-ops for housing, marketing, and agriculture, tax reforms, black capitalism, and feminism. These activities, he says, are "in the best

American tradition of individual initiative.'' Government should encourage this by revenue sharing, ''privatizing'' many of its functions (emulating the postal service), and decentralizing many of its bureaus. He optimistically concludes that this second American revolution has already begun and will culminate not in ''selfish individuality'' or nineteenth-century laissez-faire, but in a renewal of the voluntary societies that were described and cherished by Tocqueville.[26]

Some will dismiss Rockefeller's book as the ravings of a crazy capitalist, as sham and hypocrisy, or as chuckleheaded nonsense, but I believe it is a sincere interpretation of many basic assumptions in our capitalist culture. Its liberalism represents the continuing American revolution of business, which prefers to organize society by the market rather than by the state. More aggressively antistatist versions of this will be investigated in the chapter on right libertarianism.

CHAPTER THREE

SPACE AND COMMUNITY

Before putting these representatives of libertarianism on the stage, however, we must complete the essential background by adding a further element. Besides Protestantism and capitalism, a third factor that has diffused traditional authority in America is physical and social space. Behind the immigrants were three thousand miles of ocean, separating them from the crown. Before them was the vastness of America:

> East were the
> Dead kings and remembered sepulchres:
> West was the grass.[1]

For some, arriving here was like the moment of creation; it suggested the promise of a second Eden. Old limits no longer seemed as reasonable. In England land was precious; here it was abundant. This was a place in which visions could be realized. Opportunities were everywhere.

When problems arose, the colonists were often required to solve them locally. Whereas France and Spain encouraged centralization, the English government practiced benign neglect, allowing the colonists immense freedoms that were further magnified by the absence of regular passenger service between London and America until 1755. Self-reliance, already rooted in religious dissent and incipient capitalism, was further stimulated.

Even when institutions of authority were constructed, critics could always secede by moving to other lands, whether Rhode Island or the forest. In such an environment, highly stratified societies were not a stable possibility.

This menace to community horrified some of the earliest leaders, who sensed the danger of political, religious, and social dissolution. One of the founding documents of our culture is the Mayflower Compact (1620), written before the settlers had touched American soil. It was a product of the conflict between organization and anarchy. Whisperings of insubordination had been heard from both the non-Pilgrim majority and the ranks of the believers. The rebels implied that "when they came a shore they will use their owne liberties; for none had the power to command them." The compact was intended to restore order, calling upon the colonists to unite in "a civil Body Politick." In fact, while "some discontents and murmurings" continued, this task was probably accomplished more by nature: the struggle for collective survival during the winter, an inhospitable site, and the death of half the group bound them together by necessity, not words.[2] Although following years brought the economic and sectarian isolation of Plymouth, the controversy at its founding was symbolically significant.

It became a general pattern that attempts to maintain traditional order—such as the Puritan economic laws—were doomed. Small farmers with their own land and small artisans with their own tools were often independent-minded people, a fact generally lamented by those in power. In 1705 the royal governor of Massachusetts was riding in his carriage along a snow-banked road when he was obstructed by some lowly wood-gatherers. He imperiously commanded them to move aside, whereupon they instructed the astonished governor that they were as good as he, and that *he* would have to move. Governor Dudley also bemoaned the arrogance of common folk who refused to pull off their hats in his presence.[3]

This "insolence" was prompted by many reasons, but partly by the isolation of most from the pomp of European government, urban officials, or even—for many—the power of local government and taxes. Crèvecoeur, in the late 1700s, was amazed that in some areas people seemed beyond the reach of government. He sketched the American prototype of the perfect anarchist—a self-reliant person free from the regulations, taxes, and traditions of huge states, armies, and official churches. The American's individualism was directed toward the goal of creating each person as a universal being, guided not by simple egoism but by rational self-interest. American individualists lived within self-regulating communities that Europeans praised for their citizens' equality in dress, speech, and social relations. While Crèvecoeur objected to this apparent lawlessness as "a perfect state of war," he conceded that such freedom from authority liberated Americans to enter new areas of activity and to dream new visions.[4] As the country grew, adding regions like California and Texas that were as large as or larger than entire countries like Germany and France, early problems of transportation and communication within these regions and with the central government, along with local pride, encouraged self-reliance. When people had a need they did not automatically turn to the central government but frequently relied upon ad hoc structures that unconsciously realized Kropotkin's theories of mutual aid: local organizing of defense, some sharing of building and farming tasks, voluntary churches, and social gatherings. Although military aid against the Indians or money for local projects might be enthusiastically urged, control by the state was certainly not a popular ideal. This contributed to a fragmented society bound together not by "a single republic" but (as *The Federalist* believed) by "a compound republic."

This type of society was possible not only because of space, but because of nature's unique generosity to Americans. While other societies evolved elaborate bureaucracies or rituals to distribute limited resources and wealth, American opportunity could allow for anarchy. Physical hunger and hunger for land have been more easily gratified than in European nations like France or in most of the rest of the world. During 1750–76, the colonial population almost doubled, and political barriers to expansion were challenged. Our experiences were evidence to Thomas Paine that "man, were he not corrupted by governments, is naturally the friend of man, ...human nature is not of itself vicious."[5] Indeed, nature appeared to be governed by universal and benevolent laws. Tocqueville later observed that American self-satisfaction over a flexible society and constant improvements favored "the idea of the perfectibility of man."

Space and opportunity, along with some values, militated against elites and organizations, whether in politics, religion, education, or society. Institutionalized orders were often criticized because they "artificially" denied the potentiality for action and abundance. Thoreau characteristically belittled a cathedral by comparing it to the sacred grandeur of a forest; American government, by European standards, was often pathetically impotent; formal schools for lawyers and doctors were resisted as antidemocratic plots; and Bayard Rush Hall even discovered that his institutional education made him "hated and villified as the supposed instrument of aristocracy."[6]

This attitude, at its most extreme, could virtually condemn formal organizations as unnatural. Thoreau, though a Harvard graduate, extolled the wilderness as "absolute freedom," an oasis in the desert of our urbanizing civilization.[7] His eyes, like those of most other Americans, were focused on Oregon, not on Harvard or Washington, D.C., and certainly not on Europe. His social criticisms, his moral witness, his hut near Walden Pond, and his reflection upon leaving jail and walking into the woods that "the State was nowhere to be seen" were probably inconceivable to average citizens of more hierarchical societies.[8] But Huck Finn and Jim on their raft, floating down a river a mile wide, away from the rigidity of slave laws, conventions, and institutions, could have understood Thoreau.

Yet this process was not simply a crude environmentalism. New Englanders and Virginians had different patterns of settlement that were modified not only by abundant land, but by immigration, expanding trade, and cultural expectations. The frontier and the culture were both vital in producing the result. Canada and Australia also had enormous vistas. It was not only differences in the land (such as the enormous desert areas of the interior of Australia, or the limited growing seasons of most of Canada), but the influence of values formed with different religious and political experiences, and without the historical break caused by a revolution. Edmund Burke realized the novelty of these circumstances when he asserted that the creation of an independent America meant "the appearance of a *new state*, of a *new species*, in a *new part of the globe*." Jefferson said no less when he argued that old humanity had been "crowded within limits either small or overcharged and steeped in vices which that situation generates," whereas in America a new chapter in the history of humanity was beginning. From the Puritans to the revolutionaries, the transcendentalists, and modern critics, there is a unifying theme of repudiation of stifling tradition for direct experience in an environment of choice. It is the freedom of the future rather than the bondage of the past.[9]

This material and cultural environment has produced a relatively rootless people: moving geographically, moving up or down socially, moving away from extended families, moving toward the illusion of personal independence. Already by 1847, the Argentine writer Sarmiento commented that "if God were suddenly to call the world to judgment He would surprise two-thirds of the American population on the road like ants."[10] Although the wilderness no longer exists, the American still desires to be free from close contact with others in a constricted environment. Consider the flight to the suburbs, the two million who visit the national parks each year, the millions of backpacking and camping enthusiasts, the ballads about truckers as modern cowboys, and the 110 million persons in individual cars who traveled 280 billion miles during the 1971 holidays.[11] Perhaps many of these people were attempting to escape from the hard complexities of modern urban life. Only the space and wealth of America could tolerate the tens of millions of private automobiles, rather than mass transit, or a landscape dotted with individual houses rather than apartment buildings. Scarcity and social density would have required a more communal perspective.

Because of these three factors, traditional authority, in the forms of a state church, the extended family, many comprehensive traditions, and a highly centralized and authoritative state, has not dominated the minds of Americans. Rather, as an "unsettled people," they have tended to organize themselves through loose structures into a "segmented society"—a "configuration of small social units," as Professor Wiebe has concluded.[12] American radicalism is an aspect of this heritage. Dr. Norman Ware generalized that, by the late 1880s, "the only bona fide American radical tradition was anarchy"; Lillian Symes and Travers Clement, in the 1930s, judged that "anarchism is undoubtedly the philosophy most native to the American temperament"; and, more recently, Dr. Staughton Lynd concurred that "American revolutionaries sought a society in which the state would wither away."[13]

It verges on banality to call these circumstances unique. In one sense everything is unique. But comparing our history with those of other societies may clarify both our similarities and our differences. When we look to Europe, for example, the basis for much of the political history of the past two centuries is rather meaningless for Americans. We have not experienced (or no longer remain conscious of elements of such a past) a crushed peasantry, a classical proletariat, feudal landlords, a formal aristocracy, a state church, an army caste, a struggle for the white male vote (a major issue for early European socialist parties), flaunted inequalities of wealth, or violent repudiations of basic democratic values (i.e., a return to absolute monarchy, feudal Catholicism, or Junker privileges). We have had a remarkable continuity as a relatively egalitarian culture. When walking the streets we see no ruins of feudal castles in the distance. Our written constitution and our political parties are the oldest of any major nation. The population is remarkably literate and mobile. We have never been severely humbled for long periods by war (with the exception of the South).[14]

This experience could be contrasted to that of one of our closest neighbors, Canada (Mexico would make an even more obvious comparison). Canada also had vast spaces and capitalism but with a different history: an emphasis on British loyalty, not rebellion; evolutionary change within traditions; the Catholicism and rigid institutions of Quebec; the Royal Canadian Mounted Police moving along with the frontier population to maintain order. Such a conscious preservation of traditional values has promoted both a self-identified conservative party (not a popular likelihood in the United States) and, in a far more class-conscious environment, a significant party for socialism.

Americans, however, praise change and liberation from institutional confines. There are political parties, but they generally lack the power to strictly discipline their members and officers. There are churches, but few would excommunicate a wayward believer. People feel free to offer the moral criticism of politics, economics, and society that is common in this culture. "The working class" has been further fragmented by immigration, race, ethnicity, religion, economic differences, and geographic and economic mobility. Individuals are usually concerned with individual needs. Though other structures dominate American life, they are curiously absent in much of American social criticism and literature:

One widely observed feature of present-day America is that the lives of most individuals are defined by their relations with an interlocking series of institutions—for example, government bureaus, churches, schools and universities, the armed forces, labor unions, chambers of commerce, farm bureaus...and, for most of us, that center of our daily activities, the office. But characters in the new fiction are exceptional persons who keep away from offices...and are generally as unattached as Daniel Boone....The characters likely to be treated at length are students of both sexes, young artists, writers, gentlemen on their travels, divorced or widowed mothers, gay boys, neurotic bitches...old women on their deathbeds, and preternaturally wise little girls.[15]

Our history has not encouraged the glorification of these institutions—they may be considered useful, but seldom august.

Such generalizations invite a list of exceptions, of course. But Tocqueville was correct when he observed that only God could see everything in its absolute particularity; people would have to be content with statements about the prevalent. The analyst of this culture is further justified by its relative cultural and political unity, which is greater than that of many Western countries such as Great Britain (with the Welsh, Scots, and Irish), northern and southern Italy, or contradictory Spain, without even discussing the severe tensions within many new nations, such as Zambia, which is the size of Texas but contains seventy-two distinct tribes or subtribes. Politically, it would be revealing to compare the rather homogeneous character of the American Congress with the legislatures of France, Italy, or Canada.

Nonetheless, any attempt to define an "American" anything is vulnerable to at least three shattering questions, based on, first, regional variations or exceptions—for example, that bane of Yankee history: "What about the South?" (others might add the Midwest, far West, or some other regional favorite in which they've specialized). A second question is based on racial or ethnic differences. Most commonly this means "What about blacks?" And third come class considerations, or, "You're just a petit-bourgeois escapist who doesn't understand the workers." Although the second and third objections may be allayed by my later examples from feminist and black radicalism, and illustrations will be drawn not only from the rarefied atmosphere of high culture but from popular consciousness, the first criticism is valid to the extent that, in such a vast nation, regional distinctions must be expected.

Most areas are not particularly troublesome for a symmetrical analysis. Models for my categories can easily be found not only in New England, but through the Midwest to California. The South, however, does not so easily fit into my structure. While it shares much of the same history, symbols, goals, and tacit agreements that bind other regions of America into a whole, its development has been exceptional in several regards. Its religious, social, and economic evolution has often diverged from national norms. Puritan and Quaker conscience had few Southern equivalents. Northern enthusiasm for an educated population (often for religious reasons) was infrequently found in the South, which lacked major school systems until after the Civil War. Although the South was not the intellectual Sahara Mencken once depicted, it has always possessed few educational centers.

Urban civilization has also been more generally developed in the North. Southern society, often begun around plantation nuclei and small towns, remained overwhelmingly rural. This has been significant for dissent: it is easier to control people when they are isolated on small farms, plantations, or villages. Cities, on the other hand, have often been disruptive forces.

Finally, the life of the South has been pervaded by the effects of slavery. Poor whites and poor blacks were seldom united by class interests and were often divided by race. (Northerners were not necessarily more tolerant; there simply were fewer blacks in the North until relatively recently, so it was not as crucial a consideration.) Immigrants, who might have added diversity to Southern society, avoided the South throughout most of the nineteenth and twentieth centuries. This parochialism was further reinforced when the system ended not because of internal reforms, but by outside imposition, when the South no longer had the space to expand its slave economy and conflicts with Northern free labor could not be avoided. The Civil War annihilated planter capitalism in one of the bloodiest social revolutions of the nineteenth century, killing more than 600,000 persons, burning much of the accumulated wealth of the region, and abolishing $2 billion in legal property—the slaves. This may have been the greatest expropriation of property before the Russian Revolution. Common hatred of the outsiders and inner racial hatreds were both powerfully reinforced. Southerners tended to become less optimistic and more inward-looking than most Americans. Although this Southern exceptionalism may be transformed during the coming decades of industrialization, migration into the area, urbanization, and unionization, this history has powerfully influenced the present.

For all these reasons (and, no doubt, more), while the background I have outlined for the North can be found in the South, it has been fundamentally modified. Although Southerners are Americans, they have a greater cultural emphasis on the family, history, religion, and local rights. Though the region has fostered most of the few truly "organic conservatives" in America, it contains fewer adherents of Burke than of Jefferson, laissez-faire economics, and the negative liberty of the Constitution. Activist government has been severely discouraged. It is also true, however, that radical critics have been less prominent. Though this "other South" has existed, its traditions have not been as vigorous as elsewhere: yeoman farmers and poor whites versus planters, Southern abolitionists, Populists, and others. Radicalism can be found, despite racism, malapportionment, one-party government, cries against radicals as "carpetbaggers" from the North, disfranchisement, repression, and popular intolerance. Militant religion, for example, has played a central role in the civil rights movement, labor struggles, utopian colonies, and Appalachian organizing. Some forms of individualist radicalism are more active here than anywhere else in the nation.[16]

This does illustrate, however, that there are inevitable problems when speaking of commonalities rather than particularities—categories rather than individuals. Still, it must be done to make sense of reality, and I maintain a tenacious grip on my schema, even if I have no Q-matrixes, regression coefficients, two-sector models, or even Beardian polarities. As Santayana once confessed: "I speak of the American in the singular, as if there were not millions of them, north and south, east and west, of both sexes, of all ages, and of various races, professions, and religions. Of course the one American I speak of is mythical; but to speak in parables is inevitable in such a subject, and it is perhaps as well to do so frankly."[17] Within this humbling limitation, it has been necessary to consider some of the basic components of our history. It is now time to struggle with another question: What politics, or antipolitics, have grown out of this environment?

PART II

JEREMIADS

Look not to legislatures and churches for your guidance, nor to any soulless *incorporated* bodies, but to inspirited or inspired ones.—Henry David Thoreau, "The Last Days of John Brown" (1860)

We "intellectuals" in America must all work to keep our precious birthright of individualism....*Every* great institution is perforce a means of corruption—whatever good it may also do. Only in the free personal relation is full identity to be found.—William James, *The Letters of William James* (1920)

The individual "citizen"...has about as much chance of determining his own fate as a hog dangling by one foot from the conveyor belt of a Chicago packing plant.—Dwight Macdonald, "The Root Is Man" (1946)

America...
Go fuck yourself with your atomic bomb.
I don't feel good don't bother me.—Allen Ginsberg, "America" (1956)

AN EXCLAMATION POINT

The often visionary rhetoric of much of American religion, capitalism, and expansion has often been frustrated by more limited realities. For some people, these high ideals have meant low expectations, expressed in the belief that corruption is common and that it is better to drop out, to be uninvolved. During the late 1960s, this heterogeneous group ranged from the presumably conservative "silent majority" to "acid heads." Many perfunctorily bow toward the old pieties. The frustration of others may be expressed in attempts to fulfill the ideals of America, and a few may be motivated in their denunciations by the realization that myths of equality and individuality have been thwarted or have become decadent in practice. Like Hebrew prophets who criticized *because* they were believers, some Americans may be moved by love or concern to offer a prophetic censuring of their society.

These critics cannot easily avoid the powerful influence of the physical and cultural past described earlier, which has fostered antiauthoritarin responses to accumulations of power and privilege. The most moderate political expression of these factors has been liberalism, which combines certain radical ideals with a fundamental concern for preserving the property relations of a capitalist system. Liberal reform, along with such other varieties of native radicalism as right and left libertarianism, will later be contrasted with European versions of social democracy and communism, often transplanted here without sufficient adaptation to the native soil and climate of opinion.

CHAPTER FOUR

LIBERALISM

Although liberalism did not receive its name until the early 1800s, it has always been one intellectual tendency of an expanding capitalism. Many of the basic assumptions of liberalism were expressed by the seventeenth-century Englishman John Locke in *A Second Treatise on Government* (1690). He asserted that humanity had originally been without government and was "by nature free, equal and independent." However, people limited their "perfect freedom" by forming governments that would preserve "lives, liberties and estates, which I call by the general name—property." The rising middle classes tended to favor the theory that the state was not based on medieval, organic values or on the absolutist principle of divine right, but that it was a social compact made with the consent of the governed. The activities of this government were limited, and a citizen agreed to obey only "so far as the preservation of himself and the rest of that society shall require." If a government habitually abused its powers, the citizen had the right of revolution.[1]

While Locke inherited much Puritan political theory, he emphasized temporal consent, not eternal right, and liberty, not power. A simple, economical, and minimal state was expected to maintain order so that the individual might be free to choose his own work, politics, religion, and manner of life. Society should be organized by individual incentives and individual responsibilities. Today we may regard these ideas as "self-evident" and "inalienable rights," but they were once considered radical nonsense. The alliance of the state and individual liberty was not found in the cultures of Rome, Greece, Israel, China—indeed not anywhere until, perhaps, the Renaissance and the Reformation in Europe. Condorcet, during the Enlightenment, was fully conscious that notions of privacy, personal freedom, and individuality were unprecedented.

This liberalism was steeled in many battles to overthrow forms of official coercion. By 1793, Jeremy Bentham argued that "the general rule is that nothing ought to be done or attempted by government: the motto or watchword of government on these occasions ought to be 'Be Quiet.' The request which agriculture, manufactures and commerce present to the government is as modest and as reasonable as that which Diogenes made to Alexander: 'Stand out of my sunshine.' "² Even when the necessity of the state was acknowledged, few wanted it to cast its shadow over their own lives.

Liberalism was thwarted elsewhere by intellectual and social barriers, but it became overwhelmingly dominant in the English New World. Here there were no major indigenous cultures, as in Mexico or Peru. There were no institutions or traditions that could powerfully inhibit the growth of liberalism. Although religion might restrict the activities of a Robert Keayne or a Samuel Sewall, it more often reinforced patterns of individual assertion. Consider the case of Benjamin Franklin (1706–90), the champion of self-help and the model American for a commercial civilization. If a man of Franklin's abilities had been born in England, he might have been reduced to being a literary hack (as was Daniel Defoe) or, if he had triumphed, he might have found a royal rank. In America he became a radical republican.

Franklin's developed ideal was a free and educated populace living in a vast marketplace of ideas and occupations. He acclaimed the freedom of American society from elites, political sinecures, and hordes of idle gentlemen ("golden hogs"). He equated hereditary aristocrats with something as absurd as "hereditary professors of Mathematicks." If a political office became too profitable, he felt it should be abolished or diminshed, since it might encourage corruption or pride in its holder. Farmers, he thought, were the only people who produced economic value and lived "innocent and virtuous lives." Public welfare encouraged idleness and "compelled the rich to maintain the poor."³ Furthermore, a state church was rejected as unnecessary and obnoxious, expensive government was repudiated, voluntary associations were endorsed, and the natural course of economic processes was favored over any kind of legislative interference. However, as a practical man, Franklin went no further than laissez-faire liberalism.

When traditional European authority challenged these American liberal values, it provoked a revolution. The British determination to maintain a standing army in the colonies at the end of the French and Indian War in

1763 was largely responsible for the following struggles over taxes, frontier defense, and the quartering of troops. These new burdens and the growing powers of the colonial administrators seemed unnecessary with the elimination of France's power in the New World. Many of the colonists feared the emergence of some tyranny more than actuality warranted. Disruption of their traditional liberties finally culminated in the Declaration of Independence, which forms a lengthy indictment of abuses of authority: taxes "without consent," use of mercenaries, "Swarms of Officers to harass our People, and eat out their Substance," compulsory support for the Church of England, impudent and expensive armies, limitations on trade, population, and territorial expansion of the colonies (including what was considered favoritism for Catholic Quebec), limitations on trial by jury, and dissolution of some elected governments.

Edmund Burke properly interpreted the American Revolution as a just response to the British attempt to impose strict outside discipline and costly regulation, violating local customs. Grievances generally were based on traditional fears of the destruction of political balance, especially by an encroaching military. While American history urged more local voice in governance, the colonies shared most of the cultural and ideological assumptions of eighteenth-century Englishmen.[4] These assumptions were given a more libertarian cast, however, by American physical and cultural circumstances. The Americans conducted the war itself with enormous difficulty because of the absence of a political center, rather unruly military forces, and fear of imposing taxes (although, conversely, this decentralization meant that the British had no single capital to seize and won no decisive battles with the scattered armies).

But even if the American struggle might be interpreted as a defensive or "lawful" one that demonstrated respect for proscriptive rights and traditions, its consequences were not conservative.[5] Future liberalism and radicalism were inspired when this nation was founded by subversion, treason, and armed struggle. The successful breaking of foreign, often aristocratic, ties (such as mercantilism) and many institutional continuities meant a powerful impetus to our sense of destiny, while conservative alternatives to a liberal interpretation of this future were generally unattractive. A British America might have perceived the colonial Puritans as negatively as the English do Cromwell and might have regulated the growth of capitalism or directed territorial expansion within orderly frameworks. The Revolution destroyed such models. Even values that persisted were likely to be vitally reinterpreted, such as conventional theories of natural law found in Puritan teachings in the North and common law in the South, beliefs in social contract expressed in covenant theology, and the ideal of a balanced government. These concepts were now expressed in a radical republic whose heroes were rebels, not loyalists, and revolutionary idealists, not builders. Separation—the Declaration of Independence—has been more renowned than reparation—the Constitution; Reformation was stressed, not the church.[6]

The major political manifestation of this was liberalism, which became the "official atmosphere" of America (to use Keats's term), or the public orthodoxy. As Willmoore Kendall defined the latter:

It is that tissue of judgments, defining the good life, and dictating the meaning of human existence, which is held commonly by the members of any given society, who see in it the charter of their way of life and the ultimate justification of their society. . . . [It] is that matter of convictions, usually enshrined in custom and folkways, often articulated formally and solemnly in charter and constitution, occasionally summed up in the creed of a church or the testament of a philospher that makes society The Thing it is and that divides it from other societies.[7]

The defeat of the Loyalists, and the flight of 100,000 to "Hull, Halifax or Hell" (including two-thirds of the living graduates of Harvard), debilitated American conservative thought, leaving few opponents to the ideal of liberation of individuals from the restraints of economic controls, political deference, and coerced religion. Although Kendall, a conservative, did not consider liberalism healthy for community, he could not deny that its pervasiveness in America often required our conservatives to invent their own "traditions" that relied upon Plato, Thomas Aquinas, Burke, or other individuals and movements that were extremely difficult to Americanize.

The liberal republic that was established was part of an international capitalist revolt against regulation marked also by the publication of *The Wealth of Nations* in the same year as the Declaration of Independence. During the coming decades Americans moved rapidly toward the realization of free choice within the marketplace. The franchise was expanded; the importing of slaves was halted by nearly all the Southern states; slavery was abolished by all of the North within a few decades; popular education was soon to be radically expanded; established religion began a rapid decline. The social ferment of the Revolution also prompted some of the first writing that advocated increased rights, or even equality, for women and blacks. The Revolution aroused expectations far beyond its initial goals.

In this sense the American Revolution did not cease in the 1780s but has been a continuing process. It has favored a society of constant change in the direction of its public principles of liberty, equality, and opportunity. Gunnar Myrdal once observed that "America, compared to every other country in Western civilization, has the *most explicitly expressed* system of general ideas in reference to human interrelationships."[8] The values it conserves are liberal or even radical. Since the Revolution, this intellectual system has formed one of the primary bonds holding American society together.

Such beliefs have functioned to reduce the need for institutional controls. Immediately after the Revolution, a nearly nonexistent government was established under the Articles of Confederation. Even the advocates of a stronger regime, however, were amazingly libertarian by European standards. *The Federalist* (#51) agreed that no humans were angels—including rulers—and that governments must be constantly scrutinized for arrogance. George Washington declared that "government is like fire—a dangerous servant—a fearful master." Washington, despite political and military threats from the British, Indians, French, and Spanish, refused to advocate a larger army for the new republic, for he was wary of its tyrannous nature. Jefferson also warned against the "wolfish" instincts of the state and offered the speculation that society without government ("as among our Indians") might be the happiest condition of humanity. Government was rendered dangerous by the negative elements of human character (what Madison called "a degree of depravity") and was generally made unnecessary by its more positive characteristics.

Although the Constitution was reluctantly adopted for the preservation of American property and trade, by the standards of that time it was extraordinarily limited. George Bernard Shaw would later aptly describe it as a virtual conspiracy against power. Authority was divided and subdivided, checked and balanced by every means. Even most of the founders probably shared Thomas Paine's hopes that "the more perfect civilization is, the less occasion has it for government, because the more does it regulate its own affairs, and govern itself."[9] Even when Americans clamored for public subsidies for canals and roads, they violently resented regulation. Alexander Hamilton discovered this when he dared to limit the absolute freedom of the unruly frontiersmen by taxing their liquor stills. He was immediately met by the Whisky Rebellion in 1794. Although the rebels were militarily defeated, they won their goal, the removal of the federal tax.

Aversion to institutional authority was a constant check on the aspirations of Hamilton, John Adams, and others. Their ideal of a central order was defeated by the intense localism of a nation of small farmers, small artisans, and small businessmen. The laissez-faire liberalism of these entrepreneurs did not glorify the state but humbled it to the rank of policeman and magistrate. The proper functions of government were to insure order and opportunity. Jefferson acquired the Louisiana Purchase so that it might be divided into small farms as a mainstay of freedom, and Jackson struck down the Bank of the United States in 1832 because it was a dangerous monopoly.[10]

This was the atomized America that Alexis de Tocqueville viewed in the 1830s. There was no memory of a feudal order or of any established in-

"The truth is that all men having power should be distrusted." James Madison

digenous aristocracy, and ownership of property flourished widely among
the common people. Tocqueville, as a European who was familiar with
stratified cultures that encompassed both princes and peasants, readily
perceived that the United States was a relatively simple class society in which
the bourgeoisie and its ideologies held power. For him, American radicals
and conservatives were likely to be Red Liberals and White Liberals—individualist critics and small government conservatives who could be viewed
as the right and left wings of a liberal bourgeois order.

But why didn't the infamous egoism of the Americans destroy this order?
In Europe, "aristocracy links everybody, from peasant to king, in one long
chain"; but in America "democracy breaks the chain and frees each link."
Why didn't this mean the collapse of society? When Tocqueville adopted
the term *l'individualisme* to describe American life, he realized that, in
Europe, the word would mean chaos, selfishness, and antisocial behavior.
There the ideal was integration into a community. But in America individualism was honored and each person was urged to depend upon
himself or herself.

Tocqueville originally feared that this egoism could lead to two extremes:
either anarchy would result or the terrified individual would flee to the
security of an authoritarian regime and mass conformity. But he finally concluded that while "anarchy does have a more terrible aspect in democratic
cultures than elsewhere," society was held together by its voluntary institutions and mores, and by the secular religion of democracy. The anarchic individualism of America was a necessary element of a complicated system of
egos, ideas, and institutions that limited the powers of each element. Tocqueville appreciated that democracy could both give enormous power to
some organizations and cause a frequent resentment against that power: "I
admire the way equality insinuates into the heart and mind of every man
some instinctive inclination toward political freedom, thereby preparing the
antidote for the ill which it has produced."[11] Curiously, the antidote of
anarchy, found in our "instinctive inclinations" to rebel against authority,
could lead to a balanced order.

"Anarchy," for Tocqueville and other nineteenth-century commentators,
had several meanings. A European could interpret the absence of any state
church, aristocracy, or powerful government as anarchy. A laissez-faire
liberal might even argue that the best society was anarchy plus a policeman
and a judge. In the almost bizarre words of one liberal politician, Carl
Schurz: "Here in America you can see every day how slightly a people needs
to be governed. In fact, the thing that is not named in Europe without a
shudder, anarchy, exists here in full bloom."[12]

For some, however, the process of liberation was incomplete. What a
European or Europeanized observer might interpret as anarchy had not gone
far enough for them. Discontented liberals were not convinced that laissez-

faire capitalism had been achieved. By the 1830s, a phenomenon was noticed that was labeled (somewhat derisively) "the universal reformer." Such a being was reputed to criticize everything on the basis of pure ideals: slavery, temperance, women's rights, moral reform, pacifism, education, and child-rearing. A radical worker like Seth Luther had complained in 1832 that the United States was only nominally a free country, since class distinctions continued to defy "that self-evident truth—ALL MEN ARE CREATED EQUAL." Some abolitionists had begun their assault on the prison of slavery. Women such as Sarah and Angelina Grimké argued that women were moral and responsible individuals who must speak their own consciences and assailed the "lust for domination" and "passion for supremacy" of the male sex. Margaret Fuller further attacked the anti-individualistic abstractions of Man and Woman in "The Great Lawsuit: Man *versus* Men. Woman *versus* Women" (1843). Elizabeth Cady Stanton modeled her feminist "Declaration of Sentiments" (1848) after the Declaration of Independence.[13]

These were militant liberals. While their opponents might reply that there was a divine economy in which delicate women, servile blacks, savage Indians, obedient children, and others must be part of a static hierarchy, critics appealed to the democratic goal that the individual should be free to achieve whatever he or she could in an enviroment of equal opportunity. They were representatives of an American tradition that has challenged such threats to personal freedom as state religion, predestinarian theology, the two Banks of the United States, slavery, "women's place," the Masons, "Wall Street," an elite military, "big business," centralized political parties, and the Catholic hierarchy.

Ironically, these individualist critiques have often been antipluralistic, if not authoritarian. Tocqueville first realized the paradox that American individualism expected allegiance to its general values and could respond with a cohensive intolerance toward real or imagined threats. Alternatives to individualism have often been met with a collective hostility. But even such authoritarianism, usually noninstitutionalized, has been compatible with anarchism. As we will see later, authority exists in anarchist theory, but it usually takes the form of public opinion rather than law, "restraining morals as inexorably as laws ever did anywhere" (as Jefferson portrayed his anarchist Indians).[14]

The ranks of this laissez-faire radicalism were decimated by the Civil War. Military struggle demanded government expansion and central authority far beyond that of the miniscule federal state of 1860, an unimpressive collection of post offices, several thousand troops, custom houses, and (Europeans snickered) a shabby capital in out-of-the way Washington. Neither the war nor its outcome could have been predicted: Why should Americans ferociously kill one another for anything so nebulous as "the preservation of the union''? The Civil War bloodily documented the strength of ideological bonds, which were far more durable than institutional churches (which shattered long before the war), fraternal orders, political parties, or the weak government itself. It had the fervor of a religious war, each side accusing the other less of treason than of heresy—the North "violating" the historic rights of property; the South rejecting principles of liberty and equality.

Emotional and economic forces that were released by the war enlarged the American state. Unchecked by either old conventions or Southern agrarian interests, government officials were eager to subsidize Northern businesses, erect a high wall of protective tariffs around Northern industries, welcome the cheap labor of immigrants (most of whom, before and after the Civil War, spurned the ethnically intolerant and economically backward South), and encouraged the stabilization of the currency and banks. While Americans cheered the heroic completion of a transcontinental railroad and other epic achievements, loud criticisms of industrial capitalism were also heard. Many Americans were irritated by phenomena that they had once considered the ills of Europe: sprawling urban slums near Park Avenue splendor, the depression that dragged on from 1873 to 1877, federal troops violently assaulting American workers, the first national strike in 1877 (luridly compared, by some, to the Paris Commune), the last days of cheap Western land, ever-increasing power by trusts and monopolies, mass organizations of the working class, and ostentatious signs of a moneyed elite that included the sudden proliferation of social registers, country clubs, and private schools.

American liberals of the late nineteenth century, with their traditional ideal of the free individual, were sometimes dismayed by such problems but were usually comforted by the thought that social evolution would find solutions without the intervention of the state. For support and solace, they often turned to the theories of Herbert Spencer, an Englishman who enjoyed an enormous vogue in America that culminated in a semiroyal reception during his 1882 visit. There were many reasons for the widespread popularity of his philosophy, which was reflected in the sale of 350,000 copies of his books from the 1860s to 1900. Spencer was "scientific"—nonreligious but not antireligious—trumpeted the inevitability of progress, had a comprehensive worldview, used a simple vocabulary, and had an "almost Anarchistic doctrine of the self-sufficiency of economic society."[15] In Spencer's own background were such influences as the Godwinian anarchism of Thomas Hodgskin and the Quaker and Nonconformist religion of his own family.

From his studies, Spencer had concluded that the state was founded during the ignorant, aggressive childhood of humanity, when society was maintained by force. As society matured, however, it became more differentiated into associations and individuals who combined for reasons of self-interest rather than external compulsion. Voting and politics were often "superstitions" of the past that should not be allowed to alter this progressive liberation, which could produce some magnificent (but at present unknowable) millennium. In the meantime, we should all recognize such universal axioms as self-interest, which requires the "law of equal liberty": "Every man has freedom to do all that he wills, provided he infringes not the equal freedom of any other man."[16] All who ignore this "law" are aggressors who ought to be repulsed or censured by the community, whether the aggressors are individuals or the state. Spencer actually entitled one of the chapters of his *Social Statics* "The Right to Ignore the State." This right existed when the state violated the Law of Equal Liberty by going beyond its only duty, which was to preserve order. He even speculated that the formation of voluntary associations to fulfill public needs might render the state entirely parasitic and worthy of abolition, just as the state church was superseded by individual churches that the individual could accept or reject.

Given these statements and implications, it was fundamentally false for the later historian Richard Hofstadter to state that Spencerianism was fundamentally ultraconservative," even while he conceded the antistatist quality: "it was almost anarchical, and it was devoid of that center of reverence and authority which the state provides in many conservative systems."[17] Spencer's work was not consciously conservative but represented one stage of liberal thought. Furthermore, the ideals of his system presented immense possibilities for what Hofstadter lightly dismissed as "radicalism on incidental themes." As we will discover in the following chapter, Spencerian liberalism had its counterpart in Spencerian radicalism.

However, Spencer and the American liberals seldom drew radical conclusions from their principles. They were content to admit that a limited state was required by humanity's imperfections. Nonetheless, men like E. L. Godkin and William Graham Sumner also left no doubt that it must be severely restricted to preserving civil peace and property, and that a free market should be the essential governor of society, whatever the consequences. They hoped that competition, unhampered by government-sponsored monopolies and restraints, would reach the complete utilization of resources and energies. Yet most champions of laissez-faire were not as cruelly blunt as Sumner, who once remarked that man had only one natural right: the right to make his way *out* of the world if he could not make his way in it.[18]

Most Americans preferred their laissez-faire aspirations framed with a few illusions, which were provided by Spencer. Others who were not convinced that the future promised an individualist paradise, thought that such might have existed in the past and developed a deep nostalgia for what they believed was a simpler and now lost America. Horatio Alger satisfied this need in more than one hundred novels that glorified the victory of virtuous and hardworking individuals over institutional barriers. By 1920 Americans had purchased seventeen million copies of this trite but pleasant formula.[19]

But many Americans, despite their enthusiasm for a fantasized past, or a hoped-for future, realized that the present required some type of collective action. The Main Street emporium was now stupendously overshadowed by national and international firms, and small farmers were competing with such bonanza farms as one of 75,000 acres in Minnesota that operated two hundred threshing machines. One labor leader, feeling endangered by corporate aggressiveness, cried out:

We are nourishing a serpent, fostering treason, giving aid and comfort to the enemies of society, welcoming an invader, assisting in the overthrow of free institutions and popular government, inviting a dictator, and laying the foundations of despotism. We are sowing the seed of revolution and may reap the harvests upon the bloody fields of civil strife or amid the groans and sighs of fettered slaves, bereft of manhood, wallowing in moral degradation, ignorance and vice, degraded from the exalted dignity of citizenship in a free and mighty nation to a condition of sycophantic dependence upon the despotic decrees of an aristocrat.[20]

Such melodramatic statements reflected—even if they magnified—the real drama of poverty, insecurity, and moral anguish within industrial America. For these critics, the trusts were "Europeanizing" America by creating "trust serfs" who could never be free. Both the demands of such conscience and social necessity began to transform the meaning of liberalism in America, just as the classic author of English liberalism, J. S. Mill, in later editions of his *Principles of Political Economy*, had confessed that he was no longer "charmed" by the gouging, pushing, and elbowing of the present order and longed for a more structured and humane economy. He moderately suggested high inheritance taxes for equalization, along with more sentimental hopes for producers' co-ops and "co-partnerships" in industry.

In America, Lockian solutions like "trust-busting" and muckraking articles about individual and group corruption were slowly replaced by agencies for business regulation. During the Progressive period from 1900 to 1916, and during the New Deal, laissez-faire liberalism was supplanted by welfare liberalism.[21] At the same time, the dominant varieties of extreme social criticism also changed, with anarchism being numerically replaced by syndicalism and utopian socialism becoming less significant than Social Democracy and Communism.

Today, liberalism is commonly defined as positive intervention by the state. One of the primary functions of activist government is to umpire competition and bargaining between various social and economic units. This interest-group liberalism has been dubbed "procapitalist syndicalism" (C. Wright Mills), "a kind of syndicalism based on organizing, balancing, and co-ordinating different functional groups" (William Appleman Williams), and "liberal-syndicalism" (the Schwendingers).[22] Its goal theoretically remains not the paternal state but the preservation and extension of the "marketplace" of opportunity and competition, whether for blacks through the civil rights movement or for women through the Equal Rights Amendment and reproductive self-determination (the right to choose: "voluntary motherhood"). Both old and new liberalisms preserve what Thurman Arnold once called "the folklore of capitalism": hostility for open class snobbery, limited respect for tradition, desire for constant improvement, fundamental optimism about progress, emphasis on individual effort, and a general trust in human goodness and the powers of practical reason. All of these beliefs have been nurtured by the apparent absence of rigid institutions in a constantly renovating capitalist system, creating the sense of continuous flux and immense possibilities. That this libertarian mythology is not always congruent with reality is a source of frustration and rebellion.

Many tensions also derive from the basic contradiction between the active role of the state and continued resistance to centralized power. Our public philosophy still tends to consider the individual, society, and the state as separate categories and distrusts institutional integration. American politics, reflecting this, is a checkerboard of entities. In the Chicago area, there are 2 states, 6 counties, 10 towns, 30 cities, 49 townships, and 110 villages, in addition to 235 tax districts, 400 school districts, and hundreds of political associations. This division of authority is moderate compared with that of metropolitan New York; a recent book was entitled *1400 Governments*. Centralized planning thus is limited even in the modern liberal state. The inability to act "efficiently" because of diffusion of power contributes to further devaluation of government.

Such government must suffer the further paradox of increasing public calls for the state to maintain or create opportunity along with growing public denunciations of bureaucracy. Basic reconciliation seems impossible. Liberation through education has meant more compulsory schooling (and, within that, the teacher as authority, rather than guide). Legislation for equal rights has created imperial courts and resented interference. Regulatory agencies to ensure competition have become adjuncts of the companies they are supposed to regulate. Labor unions that were intended to protect the rights of workers have become one-party, dictatorial bureaucracies. Other social services have reaped a harvest of criticism about the methods by which they were provided.

More generally, there is the paradox that though Americans seem to be an extremely political people, there is popular hostility toward professional politicians. There are numerous opportunities for some "voice" in national, state, city, and local elections, and on bond issues, recalls, initiatives, and referendums; yet James Bryce noticed that the actions of most politicians were not "within the horizon" of people's consciousness. When public misdoing is revealed, it reaffirms the common opinion that "it's only the politicians—what can you expect from the politicians?''[23] Even the president, who is accorded a certain aura because he is considered the direct spokesman for all the people, is most highly respected when he is seen as "superior" to politics. The bland Eisenhower, the idealistic Kennedy, the bumbling Ford, and the man-of-the-folks Carter have been trusted more than those presidents perceived as scheming manipulators—Johnson and Nixon.

By the late 1970s, left-wing liberalism had lost substantial public support, although many of its detractors were not "conservatives" so much as right-wing liberals. The content of the usual forms of liberalism had become similar to Fabian socialism, and a champion like Hubert Humphrey resembled the Social Democratic chancellor of West Germany, Helmut Schmidt. At this point, both the goals and the means of such liberalism may have changed. Liberation could have been displaced by regulation. Sidney Hook has complained bitterly of the emergence of totalitarian liberalism. The proposals of Senator Edward Kennedy and Governor Jerry Brown for two years of compulsory national service for young adults might properly qualify for such a label. Perhaps the growing public disenchantment with the illiberalism of welfare-state liberalism is also a sign that popular opinion, even if it has often demanded state action, has now come to resent the creation of "big government."[24]

CHAPTER FIVE

RIGHT LIBERTARIANISM

You see the beauty of my proposal is
It needn't wait on a general revolution.
I bid you to the one man revolution—
The only revolution that is coming.
—Robert Frost, *Build Soil*

There have always been opponents of the dominant liberalism who share many of its values but ridicule it as too moderate. While a liberal may chafe against the discipline of organization, these right libertarians move to restrict or even abolish conventional authority. When a liberal concludes that "there's truth on both sides" or "the truth lies somewhere between" two principles, the radical dismisses these subtleties. This militant laissez-faire liberalism can edge into moderate right libertarianism, which in turn can develop from Thomas Paine's fundamental critique of government (while accepting its present necessity) toward the complete antistatism of the Individualist Anarchists of the nineteenth century.

All varieties of right libertarianism assume an intimate link between personal freedom and property, praise "the market" as self-sufficient, and censure government for disturbing or constraining the natural liberty of individuals and voluntary associations. Whereas Locke conceded that some limited government was essential to preserve property, right libertarians suspect that government exists primarily to create and maintain "unnatural privileges" (such as monopolies) and is basically unproductive. They have been advocates of an extreme personalism of the entrepreneur unrestrained by the state. The interests of society would be realized not through government but by the free individual. This individual would be an exemplar of our competitive capitalist society: "the essential American soul is hard, isolate, stoic, and a killer," seeking to be "masterless."¹ Many of the capitalist radicals of the nineteenth century, for example, could be described as perfectionist egoists.² Transcendentalists, rationalistic theists, and many utopians envisioned a community of absolute laissez-faire. Emerson, Thoreau, and Whitman were, in different ways, such right libertarians.

All agreed that "reason is potentially perfect" in everyone. If Emerson was correct that "a man contains all that is needful to his government within himself," external power might only impede the realization of that potential. We should then develop the individual, not any institution; conscience, not the state; character, not politics. Emerson drew this conclusion when he asserted that "with the appearance of the wise man the State expires. The appearance of character makes the State unnecessary. The wise man is the State." (Anne Hutchinson would have used different words for much the same idea.) Thus, he counseled Americans to "give up the government, without too solicitously inquiring whether roads can still be built, letters carried, and title deeds secured when the government of force is at an end."³

But even the most extreme formulation of his radicalism did not disavow all authority, "merely" the government of force, or institutional power. The town meeting, as a free form of order, was acceptable to him. It was left to Thoreau, whom Emerson once described as a "born Protestant," to go beyond the declaration that the best government would govern not at all and actually secede: "Know all men by these presents that I, Henry Thoreau, do not wish to be regarded as a member of any incorporated society which I have not joined."⁴ Only if he had freely elected to assume the responsibilities of some organization could he be bound by its rules, just as Emerson later upheld the Harvard regulation for compulsory chapel (although this seemed inconsistent with his generally libertarian values). Emerson and Thoreau apparently believed that those who could not tolerate a group's discipline should either attempt to change its regulations or withdraw.

Thoreau's later fame grew not from the simple act of refusing a poll tax or from declaring his independence from most institutions, but from his marriage of Christian conscience and the Lockean right of revolution in his essay "Civil Disobedience," which was originally published as "Resistance to Civil Government." Nor was this theory separate from practice; it was embodied in his everyday life, far more than in Emerson's. According to a story that is apocryphal but still illuminating, a startled Emerson visited Thoreau in jail and asked "Why are you in there?" to which Thoreau replied, "Why are you out there?" Nonetheless, both men were thrilled by the direct ac-

From the *New Patriot*
(March–April 1971), p. 2.

tion of John Brown when he seized Harpers Ferry in 1859. Casting a slip of paper for some politician was trivial by comparison.

Their radicalism was not solely destructive, however, since they desired a new community. As Thoreau said, we can be bad subjects *and* good neighbors. Both took pride in the noble village of Concord, sought to discover humanity's ties to nature, and yearned for a democratic religion (once expressed as "not gods above men, but God in man"). Their individualism was not a model for personal isolation but evoked the universe of imagination within each human being. The universal was to be discovered within the particular.[5]

Whitman's egoism was the fullest achievement of this. He appealed to both Transcendentalists and empiricists with his vision of equality. Emerson endorsed the first edition of *Leaves of Grass*; Thoreau visited him and praised his lawless nature. Whitman's faith in a radically democratic society always perservered, despite his comments that politicians were like scum on top of a deep and pure ocean. His politics, however confused, could not be fully claimed by socialists, conservatives, or moderate liberals, any more than Emerson or Thoreau would be justly treated by such labels.

Like Emerson, Thoreau, and Whitman, the other critics of the 1800s seldom appealed to the state for action, favoring the ideal of individual liberation through free competition. This was reflected in the fame accorded to a man who was more systematically "extreme" than Emerson—Henry George. In 1879 he published a classic critique of monopoly, drawing upon his experiences as an impoverished young journalist who had witnessed both massive land speculation in California and the urban squalor of New York. *Progress and Poverty* catapulted him to glory, selling two million copies by 1905.

His book opened with the memory of the "virgin and rich" land of original America. Access to this resource was immediately restricted by a monopoly that George considered contrary to nature, private property in land. The earth, like the air, ought to be available to all. Instead, the owner could charge rent—an unearned income—or benefit from the increasing value of it as population grew, the economy matured, and technology advanced. Although this increment was created by society, it was exploited by the owner for his own gain. Land values and rents increased, reducing the profits of productive business, limiting salaries, braking the economy, and diminishing possibilities for employment. This was the essential cause of poverty in the midst of progress.

As a solution, George proposed that all rent be confiscated by the state. Owners of property could retain their deeds and the right to buy, sell, inherit, and bequeath land, but they could no longer receive unearned income from that land. This would eradicate speculation and wasteful uses of capital, applying this money, instead, to greater profits for business, larger paychecks for labor, increased production and consumption, and the eventual abolition of poverty and unemployment. "Society would thus approach the ideal of Jeffersonian democracy, the promised land of Herbert Spencer, the abolition of government."[6]

But George retreated from the brink of anarchy to propose a modest state that would be "the administrator of a great co-operative society...merely the agency by which the common property was administered for the common good."[7] It would collect rents and provide all necessary social services. The list of *unnecessary* functions was stunning: the army and the navy would be scrapped as expensive trifles and authoritarian threats to democracy. The diplomatic corps, as a model of European arrogance, was also expendable. Judges, laws, and officials would be severely reduced, and welfare programs would be eliminated.[8]

The governance of society would be essentially a product of the marketplace rather than of the actions of any bureaucracy. George was absolutely confident that while "regulation and restriction is itself bad...*laissez-faire* (in its full true meaning) opens the way to a realization of the noble dreams of socialism."[9] The state, in his society, was not a socialist planner, or even a liberal reformer. It was an occasional handyman who did fix-it jobs when problems arose: "If we do not believe in laisser-faire as it is generally understood, letting things alone, [we do believe that government should] clear the way, and then let things alone."[10] The less desirable aspects of capitalism would be modified by the propagation of a superior morality ("seek first the kingdom of God and His righteousness"), and as a last resort the government might be compelled to assume control of certain national monopolies, such as railroads, that endangered the public liberties by their power. However, he was unenthusiastic about this and other institutional checks, including unions of unskilled workers, which he compared to military regimentation.[11]

This was a fairly comprehensive right libertarian fantasy. Although George led and participated in some political actions, as did many of his followers, and though there were more than one hundred Single Tax clubs and even some colonies, his idealistic pleas smashed like a cheap toy against the massive material forces of his day. While Marx was somewhat premature in dismissing the book as "the capitalist's last ditch," he was emphatically correct in his evaluation of the Single Tax as another aspect of "bourgeois political economy," and "an attempt to save the capitalist regime." "Of course," Marx concluded, "this was not the meaning of the author, but the older disciples of Ricardo—the radical ones—fancied already that by the public appropriation of the rent of the land everything would be righted." The Single Tax was ultimately the "frank expression of the hate which the industrial capitalist feels for the landed proprietor who appears to him useless and superfluous in the system of bourgeois production."[12] Of course, it was somewhat misleading to call George a representative of industrial capital. Despite his appreciation of the complexity and interdependence of modern industrial society, he was essentially a spokesman for the petty bourgeois idealism of the past: Jeffersonian natural rights, Jacksonian antimonopoly, and the old liberalism.

A few who have trusted completely in the natural order of the marketplace have become explicit right anarchists. "Mind your own business" became the literal basis for an American anarchism. The egoism of private property combined with the religion of conscience to produce a thorough antimonopolism that was one logical culmination of what Tocqueville called our historic inclination to oppose bureaucratic power. Such an anarchist is, in one sense, the ultimate American.

In 1885 there were about eighty organized groups with seven thousand members.[13] Most of those within organizations, however, were of recent immigrant origin and tended to favor Anarcho-Communism and syndicalism. American radicalism of the nineteenth century is more clearly illustrated by a study of the Individualist Anarchists, especially focusing on their major philosophical spokesman, Benjamin R. Tucker (1854–1939).

Tucker was the most eloquent champion of a particular anarchism going back to Josiah Warren's 1833 newspaper the *Peaceful Revolutionist*. Like Warren, who once labeled his radical views "American Conservatism," Tucker was the conscious defender of historic principles. He was dogmatically consistent in carrying out the smallest implications of his heritage. As a friend once declared: "B. R. Tucker is an all-round man—Atheist, Anarchist, Egoist, Free Lover—not, like so many reformers, radical in one direction and reactionary in another." During the nineteenth century, he was the chief formulator of indigenous anarchism.[14]

His newspaper, *Liberty*, was the most intellectually consistent anarchist publication in the United States for more than a quarter of a century, from 1881 to 1908. In addition, his activities as a publisher, a translator, and proprietor of perhaps the largest radical bookshop of his day gave him some contemporary claim to being "the principal vendor of the 'reds' literature in the nation."[15] In 1899 he was invited to summarize his perspective at the Chicago Conference on Trusts, attended by governors or their representatives from thirty-four states, business and labor leaders, mayors, prominent social critics, and speakers for the largest farm organizations. His address, commending anarchism as the fullest realization of antimonopoly principles, was warmly received (one newspaper, with exaggeration, claimed that he had "painted the town red").[16]

Even his radical opponents conceded the value of parts of his work. Peter Kropotkin, the leading writer of Communist Anarchism, applauded his "criticism of the present State [as] very searching and his defense of the individual [as] very powerful." Emma Goldman, more directly his adversary, criticized his narrow and rancorous fear of communism but agreed that "he wielded a forceful pen and had done much to introduce his readers to some of the best works in German and French literature."[17]

Although general fame eluded him, his advocacy of all forms of progressive thought earned him some influence beyond rigid sectarians. He was warmly remembered by Walt Whitman—"I love him: he is plucky to the bone"—and was dubbed "a great American" by George Bernard Shaw. The patrons of Benj. R. Tucker's Unique Book Shop included Eugene O'Neill, who was fascinated by his comprehensive iconoclasm, saying that Tucker had deeply influenced his "inner self."[18]

It is through the life of Tucker that we can uncover the native roots of anarchism. The ideology he developed in the 1870s incorporated elements of radical Protestantism, Jeffersonian democracy, and Emersonian individualism, merging them with the laissez-faire liberalism of Herbert Spencer that was then in vogue. Until his death in 1939, he voiced the struggles and aspirations of the little entrepreneur, whether small farmer, artisan, or businessman. He called for the laissez-faire destruction of every monopoly, with the state as the worst of monopolies, creating or sheltering all other varieties of social, political, and economic privilege. He demanded an ultimate in democracy: "every man his own nation"; a complete Protestantism: "every man his own church"; and a classless society of equal opportunity, with all involuntary institutions abolished and replaced by a regime of contract.[19] This represented one extreme development of an early form of that middle-class philosophy, liberalism.

Benjamin R. Tucker, age 23

Tucker can be used to give life to these generalities. He embodied the anarchist influences of Protestant religion, physical environment, and business culture that were outlined earlier. By examining his spiritual and material background, we can provide some historical answers to the general questions, "What appeals did anarchism have to an American? Who were his teachers? Why and how did he become an anarchist? Who were his followers? And, not least, why did his movement fail?"

Benjamin Ricketson Tucker was born in the village of South Dartmouth, Massachusetts, on 17 April 1854, the son of a prosperous Quaker father and a radical Unitarian mother who could both claim descent from "two hundred years of Yankee stock." His class, environment, and religion were all crucial in defining his later radicalism.[20]

South Dartmouth was only a hamlet, but its horizons encompassed the islands of Polynesia, the Brazil Banks, "Off Hatteras," the arctic and tropic seas, and the waters around Japan, Australia, and Africa. This village was the home of several whaling entrepreneurs and was three miles from New Bedford, the self-announced whaling capital of the world. In 1857 New Bedford could boast half the entire American fleet of 655 ships. From 1849 to 1864 eight of those ships had Benjamin's father, Abner Tucker, as their managing agent or owner. His cosmopolitan capitalism was vividly illustrated by the unfortunate voyages of four of his ships: one sank off the coast of Brazil (1853; part of the cargo salvaged), one vanished in the middle of the Indian Ocean (1857; all lost), one was condemned in the harbor of Sydney, Austrialia (1859; cargo salvaged), and one was captured and burned by the Confederate cruiser *Alabama* (1863).[21]

In 1860 the Tucker family moved into the city of New Bedford, where Abner, desiring a more stable business, had expanded his grocery. New Bedford was then a flourishing community of 25,000. It was perhaps the wealthiest city, per capita, in New England and was one of the most socially and intellectually well-endowed towns of the entire region. In its streets, as Melville described them as early as 1850, mingled "green Vermonters and New Hampshire men" with dreams of whaling adventures, and "Feegeeans, Tongatabooarrs, Erromanggoans, Pannangians, and Brighggians."[22] Here was an exotic panorama of opulent homes with formal gardens, dark-dressed Quaker gentry, Queequeg selling embalmed New Zealand heads, and tall-masted ships with their many-colored flags representing each whaling firm. New Bedford was a complex city of the world; its wealth and diversity produced everything from polyglot boarding houses and brothels to some of the highest forms of rationalist religion. Possibly the New Bedford area could even be considered a microcosm of America, with its large foreign population, a sizable black community, numerous religions, a multitude of businesses like shipping and cotton mills, and nearby farms.

Within this society, both of Benjamin Tucker's parents were good nineteenth-century liberals. His mother, Caroline, had been raised by a "pronounced admirer'' of the individualism of Thomas Paine who had encouraged his daughter to achieve an intensive education, including a place in the first graduating class of Wheaton Seminary. Later she gained the nickname of Captain Tucker for her leading role in charity work, community reform, and social activities in the Congregational church. In her home she welcomed radical guests, the literature of social change, and the ideas of the new science and pseudoscience expressed by Darwin, Spencer, Buckle, Huxley, and Tyndall. The New Bedford *Signal* also praised Tucker's father as "a liberal-minded man, in religion as well as politics [who was] an acute reasoner upon the issues of the time."[23] The elder Tucker characterized his politics as those of a Jeffersonian democrat and was occasionally active in reform movements.

Benjamin, in this comfortable, book-laden environment, absorbed both many reform influences and the general class perspective of the petty bourgeoisie. This combination continued throughout his life, both in his career as a journalist and through his inheritance of $60,000, which allowed him to avoid many of the struggles of the lower classes. His training and circumstances permitted him to become an absolute individualist, while others had to compromise or join disciplined movements.

Besides his class, religion was a vital factor in his early formation. Much of his later atheism and antiauthoritarianism was an ironic outcome of a deeply rooted deism. His childhood church, the First Congregational, was the product of an earlier merger of two forms of religious radicalism, Quakerism and Unitarianism. Several of the most venerable members of the congregation were Quakers who had been disowned by their local meeting. There had been a struggle between the conflicting elements of Quakerism, some stressing the communal "discipline of the meeting" and others the "inner light" of personal conscience. The individualists, refusing to be bound by group control, had been driven from their meetinghouse into the local Unitarian church. They brought with them an ardent belief in the inner light dwelling in all men and women of all races (some Quaker "preachers" were women, and some Negroes attended the local meeting), a conviction that people were not destined to any fate but could exercise free will, and perhaps even a hinted hope of the perfectibility of humanity.[24] When Benjamin Rodman, one of the Quaker individualists, died in 1876 at the age of eighty-one, the local Unitarian minister recalled that Rodman had always called himself a Quaker, and that when he looked at the emancipation of the slaves and laissez-faire economics, he was fond of saying that "the whole world is turning Quaker."[25]

The Unitarian influence in the church was equally distinctive and permeating. It evolved from early New Bedford, which, as a center of Quakerism on the boundary between Puritan Massachusetts and Baptist Rhode Island, was "a natural home of nonconformist and polemic religion."[26] In such an environment, the local state church had become tolerant and "progressive," since to demand privileges, even if legal, would incur the wrath of most of the community.

Thus we find rationalist Unitarians and inner-light Quakers combined in the membership of one church, built upon ground donated to the Congregationalists by a Quaker, and preached to by the Reverend William J. Potter, a birthright Quaker who had rejected his traditional faith in 1851 as too concerned with a Calvinist sense of corruption and too little with the "brotherhood of all men." The life of Abner Tucker was actively involved in this heritage, not only as a member of the First Congregational Church, but as a Quaker who had been read out of his conservative meeting for marrying a Unitarian, Miss Cummings.

Benjamin had clear memories of "sitting steadily under the radical preaching" of the Reverend Mr. Potter, who rejected all dogmatic authority, whether of church organizations, scriptures, or creeds, and asserted individual freedom of belief.[27] The essence of this was captured in his 1871 address to the Harvard Divinity School. Potter centered on the fundamental contradiction between Protestant conscience and institutional authority. He asserted that the crucial principle of Protestantism was private judgment, citing the inner-light Quakers as an illustration of the full development of the authority of the individual. The Quaker element in Potter's congregation and his own Quaker beginnings and later rejection of the communal aspect of that faith would have prompted such a parallel. He further admitted that "the Roman Catholic is right when he says that the Protestant principle tends to the disintegration of the Church into churches and sects, and of these fragmentary churches and sects into individuals."[28]

But, in his 1871 lecture and in his everyday practices, he was convinced that chaos would not result from conscience. He believed in both the rational nature of religion and the existence of a natural religion that unified all other understandings of God. His goal was to convert his congregation to such an extreme rationalistic theism, and they responded with an eagerness that could have been anticipated from their church's origins. When he informed them in 1866 that he could no longer conscientiously administer the sacrament of communion, he had received a unanimous vote of confidence.

Potter was progressive not only religiously, but socially. He was not afraid to comment forcefully from his pulpit on public questions. In the 1860s and early 1870s (when Benjamin Tucker was often present), he frequently spoke, for example, in support of the Radical Republicans. Unlike the liberals of the New York *Nation* type, he never sought a reconciliation with the South by allowing the destruction of black rights, nor did he set an impossibly high standard for the Reconstruction governments. As he later evaluated the black-dominated legislature of South Carolina: "I was myself a frequent visitor in the Legislature that was in session in the winter and Spring of 1876, and I can honestly testify that it was usually a well-conducted body, and that I never found it in more confusion or doing more foolish things than I have often witnessed in the House of Representatives in Washington. This is not a very high standard, it is true, but it is enough for my argument.''[29] Such defenses of equal rights grew out of the religious convictions and abolitionist history of most of his congregation.

Potter's views were not an isolated phenomenon but were part of a small but significant movement among the religious intelligentsia who wanted a church consistent with their laissez-faire philosophy. During 1866–67, Potter was instrumental in forming the Free Religious Association. This was to be, in Potter's words, a "spiritual anti-slavery society" that would "emancipate" religion from the supernatural and traditional.[30] The FRA was more than an attack on the "creedbound conservatism" of the newly formed National Conference of Unitarian Churches. It was opposed to all Christian supernaturalism and affirmed the supremacy of individual conscience and individual reason. The anarchist possibilities in Free Religion will be analyzed a bit later.

For the moment, it must be said that the FRA's call for a "natural religion" was like an echo from the Enlightenment. As one scholar has concluded, the FRA "expounded a latter-day deism similar to the sentiments expressed by Paine in another era."[31] The FRA's message of the perfectibility of humanity, democratic faith in each person's worth, stress on natural rights, and affirmation of the efficacy of reason resounded in many prominent intellectuals. Dogma and emotion were shunned for a religion of reason.

The first public assembly in 1867 was almost like a modern community church or a kind of spiritual town meeting that covered most of the spectrum of "advanced thinkers": Progressive Quakers, liberal Jews, radical Unitarians, some Universalists, "come-outers," agnostics, Spiritualists, and scientific theists. All these voices found expression in the main journals of Free Religion, the *Radical* (1865–72) and the *Index* (1870–86), the latter having 4,500 subscriptions at its height. While the quantity of the FRA's audience may elude measurement, the quality was certainly high. The first person to pay his dollar to join, at the original meeting, was one of the main ideologists of American individualism, Ralph Waldo Emerson.

Radical religion also influenced the early years of Benjamin Tucker through his school, the coeducational New Bedford Friends' Academy. This was a classical institution that emphasized Latin and Greek to groom its students to enter Harvard or MIT. Its early Quaker control was soon shared by Unitarians, and by Tucker's time its main religious quality seems to have been a stringent training in individual responsibility. As the 1859 catalog announced: "the use of such external stimuli as prizes or rank is sedulously avoided."[32] There was some Quaker influence detectable in other controversies: in 1867 the trustees decided that military drill in the school was inconsistent with the intentions of the founders, and in 1875 they debated a resolution that would have banned patriotic speeches as contrary to the views of the early Quaker benefactors.

Benjamin was also able to hear, throughout the 1860s and 1870s, some of the most advanced religious and secular speakers of his day at the New Bedford Lyceum. Here, as elsewhere, expanded opportunities for leisure had often combined with a moral sense that found "elevating" topics of interest to the general public. Although the New Bedford Lyceum had somewhat degenerated by Tucker's time—as had lyceums in most places—slipping from Carl Bode's definition of a "town meeting of the mind" to an amusement arcade for mass democracy, it was still graced by examples of eloquence and intellect. Tucker later recalled being an "absorbed listener" to such orators and lecturers as Frederick Douglass, William Lloyd Garrison, Emerson, Wendell Phillips, Carl Schurz, George William Curtis, and Charles Bradlaugh. The young man especially idolized Phillips and praised his address at Garrison's funeral (1877) as the greatest speech of the greatest orator he had ever heard.[33] While later criticizing him for "keeping step with the army of authority" in the matters of Prohibition and tariffs, he believed that Phillips had always taken the correct position on equal rights for all races and classes.[34] Tucker's father had encouraged him to attend such meetings as abundant marketplaces of ideas.

Tucker's individualism, inbred by his home, school, and church, and his contempt for the classical curriculum, owing to the emphasis on science in his home and church, caused him to refuse to enter Harvard in 1870. At this time compulsory attendance at prayers was still enforced (and remained so until 1886), and a modern curriculum had not yet been introduced. Benjamin Tucker chose instead to enroll in engineering at MIT.[35]

By the age of eighteen, Tucker had gone through a dazzling array of causes, but without rejecting politics. In 1872, his father and he had formed a Greeley-Brown Club in New Bedford to support the Liberal Republican candidates against President Grant (they were dismissed as "a combination of Copperheads and kids"). The shabby failure of the campaign, and Tucker's perception that the courageous Greeley had been "whipped into his grave," contributed to his skepticism about elections.[36]

In 1872 Tucker moved to Boston and began studying at MIT when his time was not taken by plays, readings, concerts, reform lectures, and other activities that he regarded as more important. It was during the spring meeting of the New England Labor Reform League (NELRL) that he met the men who would crystallize his social and economic opinions. He was introduced to Josiah Warren (whom he would call "my first source of light"), the transcendentalist minister William B. Greene, and others. The NELRL was an eclectic assembly of reformers that had been founded at an 1869 convention. That gathering had included Wendell Phillips, Warren, Ezra Heywood, Andrews, Stephen S. Foster, William Henry Channing, and labor representatives of the Knights of Saint Crispin.

Most of these people were gentlemen labor reformers who preached against the evils of monopolies and corporations and extolled the virtues of the individual entrepreneur. Their opinions could be dismissed as "bourgeois sentimentality" or expressions of artisan enterprise made in ignorance of factory life.[37] It was certainly true that many of the labor reformers had a Jeffersonian yearning for the agrarian–small merchant heritage that was being overtaken by industrial capitalism. The programs of Warren, Spooner, or Andrews would have created an agrarian–small merchant society. For both the NELRL and the anarchists this demonstrated a kind of conservatism (a looking back to a more pleasant past): yet both knew that the workers had never received the whole value of their products in the past. The new society would require more than a copying or carrying out of old forms.

Most of the other varieties of labor organization in the late 1860s and early 1870s were as loosely structured and had as radical goals as the NELRL. First, there were the mass unions, such as the National Labor Union and the Knights of Labor. William H. Sylvis, president of the NLU from 1866 to 1872, struggled for an all-encompassing union, with producers' and consumers' co-ops, where all profits would go to the common people. This was to be accomplished by "agitation, education and legislation," not by strikes.[38] Since the NELRL, despite its antistatist views, occasionally dabbled in influencing legislation, they agreed with all of Sylvis's ideals. The primary difference was one of organization: the NLU had one, while the NELRL's annual conventional was a cluttered happening. But the Sylvis program, and his dream of "a nation of employers," was completely acceptable to these labor reformers.

The Noble Order of the Knights of Labor, founded in 1869, had a vision similar to that of the NLU and the NELRL. It stressed boycotts, rather than strikes. Its very name appealed to the chivalrous and religious sentiments of non-class-conscious workers. T. V. Powderly, who became the Grand Master Workman in 1879, repudiated the closed shop as coercive, opposed private ownership of land as contrary to God's creation (like Henry George), strongly objected to strikes as a form of violence, avoided politics, praised cooperation, and hoped for a capitalist society without classes. While the NLU and the Knights could easily be labled utopian, they did have the merit of attempting to deal with causes, not results.

A second type of organization was the labor party. In 1869 an Independent Party of workers "and friends" elected twenty representatives and one senator to the Massachusetts legislature. This may have prompted the formation of the nation's first Bureau of Labor Statistics in that same year and, in 1872, "the nation's first effective 10 hr. day."[39] The party's success was disappointingly ephemeral and resulted mainly in thick studies by the statistics bureau. For Tucker, there seemed no reason to place any hope or trust in labor parties.

The American branches of the First International—the International Workingmen's Association—made up a third variety of labor organization. One of those branches, Section 12, was led by S. P. Andrews and Victoria Woodhull. It was ejected from the International in 1872 for not having enough workers in its ranks. Actually, the socialists found this a convenient device to eliminate a group they disliked for its middle class and reformist constituency, whom Marx belittled as "bourgeois philanthropists." It was revealing that thirty-eight of the fifty American sections left the International in protest to form their own "International" in 1872—the same year that the association split between the Marxists and the Bakuninists. The bourgeois philanthropists and the Bakuninists had something in common: their rejection of central authority. The Reverend Samuel Johnson, a Free Religionist and social radical, said about the association and "Dr. Marx, its secretary" that he would "substitute the State for the Person" and amalgamate all business into one monopoly. The anarchists, too, refused all rule without individual consent, whether by corporations or classes.[40]

The fourth type of labor group then existing (other than broad reform alliances such as the NELRL and the Ten Hour and Eight Hour leagues) were the co-ops. Already in the 1850s, co-ops had been formed for sheep-raisers and cheese-makers, and later, they were established for the benefit of dairymen.

This was the rather idealistic labor environment that produced B. R. Tucker. Although he had become a convinced anarchist within a year after the 1872 NELRL conference and expounded his eclectic philosophy in the pages of the *Index* in 1873, he did not publicly declare his "label" until he began his newspaper in 1881. He began his career as a newspaperman and proofreader, by working on radical publications like the *Word*, editing the *Radical Review* during 1877–78, and working as a conventional journalist.

He also began his critique of many of his former associates as incomplete libertarians. Members of the FRA, for example, were religious radicals, but often social conservatives. They failed to apply the Protestant principle to society. If Walt Whitman was moved to write "obscene" poems, or if Victoria Woodhull wanted to take a new lover every night, why not? What was freedom if not the right to be different?

Some members of the FRA agreed with Tucker's logic that religious liberty and social liberty were inseparable. This was not surprising, since FRA discussions could easily drift toward radical topics or extreme conclusions, as we see in a cheery, if insipid, report of one meeting: "the 'Abolition of the State' proved a theme most fruitful of ideas and of a happy and delightful conversation."[41] It is significant that the devoutly religious member of the

FRA Sidney H. Morse praised Tucker when he was jailed for refusing to pay his poll tax in 1875. Morse argued that if we could no longer be taxed to maintain a church that we had not joined, why should we pay to uphold a state that we had not voluntarily endorsed? If the church could be replaced, why not government?[42]

Tucker added that Free Religion would be advanced by the abolition of the state because it was the state that mightily defended the orthodox mind through schools and tax benefits for the churches. Since the Free Religionists despised tax favors as reviving sectarianism that would otherwise have died and allowing authoritarian establishments like the Roman Catholic church to acquire vast property, they should therefore attack the state or be accused of having yet "to learn the logic of their own dissent."[43] Here we find a union of extreme Protestant and democratic individualism, speaking in an unfamiliar and strident voice the time-honored themes of personal conscience and consent of the governed.[44]

Democratic values, however, drove Tucker to the even more radical anarchism of repudiating God as the great anti-democrat. If God did exist, it would be necessary to abolish Him, since His existence might be a powerful argument for authority. When Tucker published Bakunin's *God and the State* in 1882, he advertised it as "Paine's 'Age of Reason' and 'Rights of Man' Consolidated and Improved." While few members of the FRA concurred, most had moved, however unconsciously, in this direction.

Francis Ellingwood Abbot, the editor of the *Index*, had already claimed that Christianity was inherently hierarchical and authoritarian and announced that he was a non-Christian theist. He hoped that the FRA would propound a "New Declaration of Independence" that would embody "the American idea": liberty. O. B. Frothingham, also active in the FRA, praised Luther as an admirable revolutionist who had transferred the focus of religious authority from the church to the Bible, from priests to the person. The old abolitionist and religious radical C. C. Burleigh had even democratized the Deity, replacing "Lord" with "Mister Jesus Christ." But once the old authority of church, priest, and Lord Jesus Christ was overthrown, it was difficult to reestablish order. Were there any boundaries to the democratic ego? Were there any limits to the sovereignty of individual conscience? Protestantism had become an ironic justification for atheism.

Capitalists and laissez-faire liberals, like Protestants, were also criticized for their inconsistency by radical individuals like Tucker. The principles of capitalism were assumed to encourage anarchy. Warren, Tucker, and others perceived the respectable Adam Smith as a distant ideological associate of anarchism because he had denounced such artificial privileges as primogeniture and monopolies, favoring competitive private enterprise. His work assumes the beneficence of business and the general corruption of government, although there are many scattered exceptions in *The Wealth of Na-*

tions that, if added together, would give an active role to the state. It is still revealing that Smith was a positive influence on the French anarchist Proudhon, the German anarchist Stirner (who translated some of his writings), and the American anarchists.[45]

They believed that Smith and capitalism promoted what Warren called "the sovereignty of the individual." Ideally, every person should be an equal competitor in the marketplace, whether male or female, black or white. Success should depend solely on personal merit. J. S. Mill, the classic writer of laissez-faire liberalism, while noting that there were "abundant differences in detail" between his views and those of Warren, adopted the term for his own use, and praised that "remarkable American, Mr. Warren."[46]

In 1873 Spencer used an analogous formulation, which he called the law of equal liberty. The state had no right to restrict a person, who was free to do anything—confined only by the "cost" of enhancing, maintaining, or diminishing his or her reputation, at the risk of public displeasure or with the hope of public approval. Following Locke's definitions of property, the individual owned himself, and whatever he had labored to produce. These were radical ideals when applied to social questions like women's liberation and black equality.

Anarchists like Tucker cited Mill, Spencer, and William Graham Sumner to prove that social evolution was inevitably producing greater individualization of society and the assumption of former state powers by voluntary associations. We should not be too amazed, then, by Richard Ely's comment that Spencer was among the writers "most familiar" to the American anarchists, or by the praise of Spencer by the *dynamiteur* Vaillant, Hapgood's remembrance of seeing a volume of Spencer's *Social Statics* in "an Anarchist salon" in Chicago, or Sacco and Vanzetti's later reference to Spencer as one of their teachers.[47] As we will soon discover, it was especially predictable that his writings were frequently admired by Tucker and his associates, although Tucker could fully endorse only Spencer's "The Right to Ignore the State" (which he printed separately as "an anarchist classic") and denounced some of his later writings as reactionary. While Tucker once asserted that Spencer was "as much of an Anarchist, if he only knew it, as Proudhon himself," he was aware that Spencer was almost completely ignorant about anarchism and expressed total contempt for it.[48] Tucker eventually placed his works in the category of "tendency" books: those that had a strong tendency toward anarchism but failed—by Tucker's standards—to understand the implications of their beliefs. Spencer, E. L. Godkin, Sumner, and other laissez-faire liberals were all declared guilty of retaining illusions about "the system of violence, robbery, and fraud that the plutocrats call 'law and order.' "[49]

For Tucker and most anarchists, the powers of any state, however limited, were crimes against individual liberty. First, they were not based upon valid contracts. The anarchists reasoned from Jefferson's phrase that "the earth belongs to the living" and Lincoln's "no one is good enough to govern another man without that man's consent" that the present should not be bound by the agreements of the past. Specifically, since all of those who had signed the Constitution were now dead, this moldy document should be null and void. It violated the supremacy of the present.[50]

Second, the state was a bastion of privilege, such as monopolies in patents, copyrights, legal benefits, limited banking, land restrictions, and tariffs. The anarchists were convinced that behind all the noble justifications of government was a sordid reality: "The Congressmen have gone home. Of course the treasury is empty and there is a big deficit for us to make good. Long live 'law and order'!"[51] This was parasitism on natural society, which could survive and prosper without it.

Third, the state was unjust because people were never given the choice of accepting or rejecting its powers. Thus, Lysander Spooner, a lawyer and abolitionist whom Tucker, Andrews, Morse, and Warren admired, speculated that if the principle that "taxation without consent is robbery" was valid for three million people rebelling against England, it was equally true for three people, or one.[52] S. P. Andrews, who wrote a book in the 1850s to interpret Warren's philosophy as "the final development of Protestantism, democracy and socialism," believed that Luther's principle of private judgment, combined with the individualism of democracy and the freedom from all exploitation of socialism required the annihilation of the elite power and privilege embodied in every state. For him, "genuine democracy is identical with the no-government doctrine."[53]

But how could such an ideal be achieved? Violent revolution seemed unlikely, although most anarchists had favored the South's right to secede from federal authority (even while advocating slave insurrections within the region), since their goal, the sovereignty of the individual, was the ultimate secession. In the North, Tucker had reenacted Thoreau's tax refusal to demonstrate, once again, that the essential foundation of government is force, and that this "political slavocracy" must be overthrown.[54]

Still, anarchists relied more on education than on nitroglycerine to demolish government. Tucker and the other anarchists generally hoped that just as public opinion had slowly abandoned the ideals of a king and an official church, the foundations of the state could also be undermined. This could not be accomplished by terror, since they accepted the Spencerian axiom that violence encouraged centralization. Enlightenment, however, would melt away the opposition. Anarchism would be irresistibly attractive if it were properly understood.

Meanwhile, alternatives to state functions should be built through schools, labor and commodity exchanges, cooperative banks, businesses, and labor unions, which many anarchists saw as "a crude step in the direc-

Courtesy of the New York Historical Society

Josiah Warren, cameo by Sidney H. Morse (left), and Stephen Pearl Andrews

tion of supplanting the State."[55] It was especially important that "strikes, whenever and wherever inaugurated, deserve encouragement from all the friends of labor. . . . They show that people are beginning to know their rights, and knowing, dare to maintain them."[56] Ultimately it might be possible to engage in massive civil disobedience, general strikes, and the systematic withdrawal of tax money from the state, causing it to collapse. But what then?

When people asked "What will replace the state?" the anarchists said, "this is akin to such questions as: If you abolish slavery, what do you propose to do with four million ignorant 'niggers'? If you abolish popes, priests and organized religion, what do you propose to do with the rude and vicious masses? If you abolish marriage, what do you propose to do with the children? etc., etc."[57] For anarchists, these were trifling details. Like Marx, they refused to predict the future, assuming that needs would be met by popular ingenuity. When society was freed from the bonds of the state, natural patterns of organization would spontaneously evolve. Until then, it was absurd to predict "A Complete Representation of Universal Progress for the Balance of Eternity."[58]

One myth about the anarchists can be dispelled, however. They have seldom envisioned anarchy as the abolition of all organizations. Instead, it would mean new forms of order, which some termed Jeffersonian anarchism or government-by-consent anarchism. S. P. Andrews pointed to such models as common nurseries, infant schools, and cooperative cafeterias. These would be more economical, efficient, and varied than tiny separate facilities. They would also assist in the abolition of "the unmitigated drudgery and undevelopment of the female sex."[59] Josiah Warren agreed that something like a common kitchen would be cheaper and more convenient and would "relieve the female of the family from the full, mill-horse drudgery to which they otherwise are irretrievably doomed."[60] Forms of economic production could also be enormously diverse. Andrews could imagine vast "combined houses" where a hundred or a thousand "may be engaged in the same shop, and still their interests would be entirely individualized."[61]

This would be a true "government by consent" where the necessary functions of society could be accomplished by voluntary associations. Then, if some individual, like a Henry David Thoreau, did not wish to join the fire protection company, he would not be required to do so. Of course, if his house caught fire, the company was also not under the slightest obligation to assist him. Or, if a person wanted protection (although, in a fully libertarian society, where all had been socialized to respect the rights of others, this should be an unlikely need), he or she might band together with others, pay in labor or subscriptions, and organize to meet their requirements. Thus, an anarchist police force!

This concept is likely to raise some objections. What about rivalries? Even if libertarians had achieved a general character of angelic tolerance, individuals and groups could have disputes or need defense from invaders. Most anarchists, however, were undismayed by such objections. They hoped that people would recognize, either by foresight or after an awkward period of conflict, that it was expedient to voluntarily limit the right of might, replacing it with a general acceptance of the necessity of equal liberty. Like all democrats, they assumed that people would be rational enough to realize what their best interests were and form social compacts and cultural restraints. Perhaps a dispute could be settled by a generally recognized association for adjudication, or by local juries.

Juries might consist of twelve persons whose names were drawn by lot from a wheel containing the names of all the citizens of the community. Service would be voluntary, although it could be expected for membership in any of the defense associations. The jury would "shape" the broad suggestions that would serve as anarchist "rules" to fit each individual case. Because the new regime would be one of contracts, not of laws, their primary activity would be to enforce the obligations that individuals had freely assumed. They would also have complete freedom to decide as their reason directed them any infraction against "the law of equal liberty" (that is, an unjustifiable invasion of another's rights). Being convicted of a crime could result in public censure, imprisonment, or even death. But anarchists agreed that "punishment is in itself an objectionable thing, productive of evil even when it prevents greater evil, and therefore it is not wise to resort to it for the redress of trivial wrongs."[62]

Other forms of nonstate governance were also possible. Aggressively anti-social people might be threatened with nonviolent sanctions, including boycott or exclusion from social life. This could replace physical coercion with more subtle forms of control, providing a reasonable substitute for formal government. Like the citizen of a small town who may fear gossip or ostracism more than jail for any wrongdoing, the self-conscious anarchist would be controlled both by principles and by the desire to cultivate favorable relations with others. If so, a pervasive natural order would result, with regulation accomplished by social pressure or norms rather than by force or institutional power.[63]

The boycott technique could take both positive and negative forms. It could be used to discipline or punish some persons or groups or to gain a larger objective. For example, race prejudice could be attacked by this method: "The Negroes of the South have the white people of that section in their power, and they can exercise that power without the commission of a single overt act." If they refused to associate with prejudiced whites—contributing their labor, consuming white products, showing respect or tolerance for them—though "radical antipathies" might persist, the power of the whites could be broken or at least controlled.[64]

The policy of boycott had been used successfully by Josiah Warren in his City of Modern Times on Long Island, in the 1850s. As one of his friends summarized this: "When we wish to rid ourselves of unpleasant persons, we simply let them alone. We buy nothing of them, sell them nothing, exchange no words with them—in short, by establishing a complete system of noninterference with them, we show them unmistakably that they are not wanted here, and they usually go away of their own accord."[65] But this was the ultimate sanction. An individual had to be belligerently offensive before the citizens of Modern Times were provoked. The village had some fame (and, among the respectable, infamy) for the political, social, and sexual diversity of its inhabitants. Nor were they all libertarians. Henry Edger, one of the few American disciples of a highly authoritarian Comtean positivism, lived at Modern Times and openly agitated for followers. He had a perfect right to believe whatever he wished, just as his neighbors had the perfect right to believe the opposite.

Still, one is somewhat uncomfortable with the rude justice of the boycott and similar forms of "government." George Orwell, in his writings on the Spanish Civil War, was respectful of anarchist ideals but feared that a totalitarianism of public opinion could result. He worried that the beliefs of the majority would be imposed upon everyone. Much earlier, Tucker had admitted that boycotters were no better than other human beings: they could "sometimes be cruel, sometimes malicious, sometimes short-sighted, sometimes silly."[66] There is undeniably a fervent element of moral crusade in such writers as Godwin, Proudhon, and Kropotkin. This could threaten spontaneity and diversity.

The American anarchists were aware of this hazard. Tucker had repudiated idealism because he feared its "invasive" possibilities. People should be free to be themselves. Warren had called fashion and habit the greatest obstacles to such liberation: "Fashion—more tyrannical than tyranny itself!. . . A power which controls all other controllable powers."[67] The anarchists, conscious of this danger, struggled for a society that respected peaceable "nonconformists."

They were convinced that such a permissive society was possible. They ridiculed the existing repression in laws, courts, and jails for denying that democratic hope. The continued existence of the state implied that "education goes for nothing; example goes for nothing; public opinion goes for nothing; social ostracism goes for nothing; increase of material welfare goes for nothing; decrease of temptation goes for nothing; health goes for nothing; approximate equality of conditions goes for nothing. . . . The Christian doctrine that hell is the only safeguard to religious morality [becomes the doctrine] that a hell on earth is the only safeguard of natural morality."[68]

"Hell on earth"—legal and economic coercion—was not necessary. People naturally wanted to associate with one another and could understand the utility of various forms of cooperation. Tucker, with his New Bedford background, recalled the lyceum (called by James Redpath, one of its chief promoters, a preeminently American institution), the Free Religion meetings, local congregations, and other forms of voluntary institutions like the later Chautauqua. His knowledge of the best qualities of Quakerism assured him that people could completely govern themselves without elected leaders. Each could follow his or her own light, even while forming communities of friendship and interest.

Similar groups could serve humanitarian needs. The anarchists were familiar with voluntary aid societies and agreed with Whitman that the spontaneous generosity of the masses was greater than the planned charity of the politicians. In 1870, for example, the Reverend Mr. Potter and Mrs. Abner Tucker had organized a $100,000 gift into a "Union of Good Works" to provide assistance to the unfortunate. These associations for economic and social problems were the model for an American socialism (as Tucker called it) where the individual retained the complete freedom to join or secede, while collective action was still possible.[69]

In essence, this merged Jefferson and Proudhon on the "sanctity" of contracts, the evils of large factories and large finance, the Enlightenment de-

The Haymarket massacre (1886). This portrayal, commonly believed, is historically inaccurate, since the orators had already begun to disband when a bomb was thrown.

testation of the sovereign state, and the aspiration for a world of equal individuals. Although the anarchists quarreled about the rights of property, they were unified by their radical attack on all privileges, on all semidemocracy. As Josiah Warren had commented: "The Democratic Idea, theoretically at the base of American institutions, has never been introduced into our military discipline, nor into our courts, nor into our laws, and only in a caricatured and distorted shape into our political system, our commerce, our education and our public opinion."[70] Given such "classically American" themes, it was understandable that Whitman subscribed to Tucker's anarchist journal, *Liberty: Not the Daughter but the Mother of Order*, and one scholar decided that "the political concept nearest to Emerson's 'ideal union in actual individualism' was the...American anarchism propounded by Josiah Warren, Stephen Pearl Andrews and Benjamin Tucker."[71]

By the turn of the century, however, this Olympian vision was apparently an abysmal failure. Public support for anarchism as an explicit ideology had almost vanished. The general public had first become conscious of anarchism in 1886 when a bomb killed seven policemen and wounded more than sixty others at a Chicago rally, and seven anarchists were condemned to hang. It rapidly became perceived as an alien cult of crime. This image was reinforced by Alexander Berkman's murder attempt on a representative of Andrew Carnegie in 1892, the assassination of President McKinley in 1901, killings of European royalty, and the dramatic strikes of the Industrial Workers of the World, founded in 1905. These were all considered evidence of the malignant nature of anarchism and justification for its repression.

Some have added that "the leadership" of the movement was also deficient. Tucker, for example, chilled many by his heartlessness and lack of broad sympathies. One critic declared that "he was so cold blooded a proposition that nobody can get acquainted with him. . . . He has a smile that looks nice outside, but, as one soon learns, is absolutely hollow and means nothing. He is courteous enough, but never seems interested, and is apparently glad when you're gone. If I were to invite him to dinner, I should expect him to sidestep the invitation by accepting indefinitely and then never speak of it again."[72]

He was certainly not a charismatic figure or a prosaic organizer, but he was a gifted controversialist who made severe tactical and philosophical errors (such as his endorsement of the Allies in World War I). Despite all this, however, anarchism did not fail because of such personal limitations. After all, every leader has flaws, and many of the adherents of anarchism were intelligent, sincere, and commendable people.[73]

Nineteenth-century anarchism failed primarily because it seemed archaic in the twentieth century. It withered at the same time that laissez-faire liberalism was generally abandoned for social engineering. Anarchists were no longer sustained by the hope that evolution was aiding their struggle. By 1908, even the die-hard Tucker had surrendered before the inescapable power of the modern corporation and state. He abandoned America for thirty years of silence in France, sadly confessing that the powers of the age were invincible and retreating into a whimsical acceptance: "I hate the age in which I live, but I do not hate myself for living in it."[74]

With the death of *Liberty*, the Individualist Anarchists no longer had a center or, it appeared, a future. Although scattered journals were published, there was no longer an audience or any major champion, and Anarcho-Individualism, as a conscious philosophy, nearly vanished for several decades. Nevertheless, there were almost spontaneous expressions of right libertarianism during the following years. Randolph Bourne, without studying any of the anarchist canon, also differentiated between the society and the state, condemned "the herd," and coined the classic phrase "war is the health of the state." This was an almost visceral radicalism, unconscious of intellectual predecessors. It was also reflected in the popular cynicism of the 1920s over being "manipulated" into the war by corporations and governments. Veblen spoke of an ideal "harmonious society of masterless men," and explicitly laissez-faire authors like Albert Jay Nock and John Jay Chapman wrote prolifically, although to limited audiences.[75]

Even during the repression of radicalism during and after World War I, some forms of moderate right libertarianism were successful. In 1919, for example, North Dakota established the first public bank in the United States. It was the offspring of a successful third party, the Non-Partisan League, into which the Socialist Party of North Dakota had merged. The bank, however, was neither quite capitalist nor quite socialist. It essentially relied upon the deposit of state revenues and sought to use public money for public needs. Although it was never allowed to open branch offices or to make personal and commercial loans, it was able to accept private savings and checking accounts and to make loans to farmers and students. The public bank was run by a three-member board of directors, all of whom were elected.

By 1977 it had returned $91,000,000 in profits to meet public needs, withstood criticism from vested interests, and been cited as a model during discussion of public banks in eight states and the District of Columbia. In 1975 the New York House passed a bill that would have created the second such bank in the United States, controlling the billions in New York funds and creating an immediate competitor to private banks, controlled by elites. Although this proposal was killed in the state senate, a degree of local, regional, and national discussion had begun and often pointed to the only existing experiment, the Bank of North Dakota.[76]

Several other experiments in right libertarianism could be cited from the bleak 1930s. It was during these years that a number of worker-owned plywood factories started in the Pacific Northwest, and others were added over the following decades. By the mid-1970s there were eighteen such factories, ranging from 80 to 450 worker-owners, each corporation grossing between $3 and $15 million a year. They collectively produced one-fourth of American plywood.

None of these businesses has been self-identified as socialist. Rather, the workers consider themselves entrepreneurs, or individual capitalists. They own a share in the business, elect the managers of the firm, and retain considerable control. By joining with other co-owners, they have created special benefits like dental and health care, gas at wholesale rates, lunches, and insurance paid for by "the company," along with greater concern for safety, 35 percent higher salaries, and job security in slack times.[77]

While other illustrations from this period could be drawn from the more exotic history of California, or prosaic co-ops and credit unions in the Midwest, right libertarianism was not the major form of radical activity during most of this century. Nonetheless, it remained an essential component of moderate social criticism because it was rooted in the existing relations of property. American history continued to resound with these cries: Government is parasitic! Down with taxes! The bureaucrats should all throw their briefcases into the Potomac! and—a perennial favorite—Politicians are all crooks! But militantly radical forms were uncommon.

It was somewhat unexpected, then, when the entire spectrum of right libertarianism became widely visible again in the 1960s and 1970s. The practical expressions of these sentiments in conventional politics might be George Wallace, representing many of the alienated of this period. He inveighed against the arrogant bureaucrat, the socialist egghead, the everpresent federal government, "the expert," and even "the establishment." Some commentators noticed that Wallace's appeal was not solely to racism but to a common resentment against being "ripped off" by those in power. This theme was also embodied in a 1970s group against court-ordered busing: Restore Our Alienated Rights (ROAR). In addition, one might even cite the remarkably "antigovernment" statements of Ronald Reagan during his various campaigns. Obviously a President Reagan would not have abolished the state, however. He might even have expanded its functions, as he did when governor of California. He and people like Senator Barry Goldwater were only moderate right libertarians but certainly were part of a particular tradition.[78]

Others drew more radical conclusions from the commonplaces of American mythology. Goldwater was a mild libertarian compared with Karl Hess, his onetime speechwriter, who evolved into anarchism. Ayn Rand, the individualist author, was a right-wing decentralist, while some of her followers yearned for statelessness. The Young Americans for Freedom was generally interpreted as a conservative organization; the Anarchist Caucus of YAF challenged this. It was the intention of all anarchists to create a society—in the words of some of kindred spirits in the 1960s—where everyone could "do his own thing." Those on the right were convinced that this was possible only through the ideal of a "free and humane market."

CHAPTER SIX

LEFT LIBERTARIANISM

And all that believed were together, and had all things common; And sold their possessions and goods, and parted them to all men, as every man had need.—Acts 2:44–45

And the multitude of them that believed were of one heart and of one soul: neither said any of them that ought of the things which he possessed was his own; but they had all things common.—Acts 4:32

[After the revolution] there will be no more jails, no courts, or police.

The White House will become a crash pad for anybody without a place to stay in Washington.

The world will be one big commune with free food and housing, everything shared.

All watches and clocks will be destroyed.

Barbers will go to rehabilitation camps where they will grow their hair long.

The Pentagon will be replaced by an LSD experimental farm.

There will be no more schools or churches because the entire world will become one church and school.

People will farm in the morning, make music in the afternoon and fuck whenever they want to.

—Jerry Rubin, *Do It!*

Militant liberalism and right libertarianism are both capitalist perspectives. A third vision of American radicalism does not strive to "fulfill" aspects of capitalism but desires to negate the entire system. While libertarians of the right despise the state because it hinders the freedom of property, left libertarians condemn the state because it is a bastion of property. While both have complained of institutional limits on individual development, the left libertarians—ranging from activists for community control, through commune-dwellers with only a confused philosophy, to explicit Anarcho-Communists and syndicalists—praise the full evolution of the individual within a community free of rigid structures.

Some of the roots of this critique are religious. At the dawn of our history, the Pilgrim colony at Plymouth had a community of goods. Many others have admired the godly life of sharing rather than the capitalist life of selfishness, the life of cooperation rather than competition. Some have attempted to purify society of greed, as Christ overturned the tables of the moneychangers, calling for a simple community governed by God's laws. As one early radical floridly expressed this idealism: "Plodding on the weary march of life, Association rises before [us] like the *mirage* of the desert. We see in the vague distance magnificent palaces, green fields, golden harvests, sparkling fountains, abundance of rest and romance; in one word HOME—which is also HEAVEN."[1]

In the nineteenth century, radical Christian communism (as opposed to Catholic monasticism) was as diverse as the Spartan celibacy of the Shakers and the relative moderation of the Reverend Adin Ballou, who was not convinced that communism was absolutely necessary to Christianize property. They were both ultra-Protestants who had separated from the corrupt, while agreeing that the unregenerate might still require the bonds of government. Ballou, however, was eloquently outspoken in his belief—later admired by Tolstoi in his antistatist years—that the absolute authority of God, not feeble human powers, must guide the everyday life of believers: "The *will of man* (human government) whether in one, a thousand, or many millions, has no intrinsic authority—no moral supremacy—and no rightful claim to the allegiance of man. It has no original, inherent authority whatsoever over the conscience. . . . When [human] government *opposes* God's government it is *nothing*; when it *agrees* with his government it is *nothing*; and when it *discovers* a new item of duty—a new application of the general law of God—it is *nothing*."[2] For Ballou, as for the Shakers, primitive Christianity had been corrupted by power. Many Protestants have suspected this, and a few have censured all human authority.

There have also been secular imperatives toward a community of property. One potentially explosive issue was perceived by Tocqueville in 1848. He warned that the inequitable distribution of property in a politically democratic society raised the specter that capitalism would be interpreted as an institution of elite privilege.[3] He might have added that, in theory, this could be a potent issue in the United States, since eminent domain was in the hands of the people, who had the common-law right to dispose of the nation's property, held in trust. But Tocqueville's fear was unrealized in America because most citizens have (by world standards) abundant property, and when they challenge the existing distribution it is usually with the intent of expanding their own "stake" in American capitalism.

More common arguments against private property have focused on the uncertainty and insecurity of capitalist life, even as modified by welfare capitalism. Fears of unemployment, change, rootlessness, meaningless work, or even a lonely old age are widely shared, and there is sometimes an intense nostalgia for the supposed warmth and stability of the small community and neighborhood life of an earlier era. For many this is passive sentimentality; for a few it becomes a basis for conversion to the alternative of communal security. They conclude that the individual should be motivated not by the simple rationalist functionalism of capitalist society but by a desire to be integrated into a whole. The individual should acknowledge his or her indebtedness to others for cultural, political, economic, and social life, just as the individual should not be separate from nature, conquering and "using" it, but should live in harmony with "natural" rhythms. Whether this unity is sought through religion, communes, sex, or drugs, it is the antithesis of the liberal atomism that has characterized so much of our history. Thus, it has been extraordinarily difficult to create models, since we cannot appeal to some American medievalism (as William Morris could romantically reconstruct European history) or to the peasant communes that were lauded by Proudhon and Kropotkin. Nonetheless, there has been a persistent history of communal ideals and attempts to realize them.

These forms of libertarianism also illustrated, like other varieties of anarchism, that they were not synonymous with chaos but upheld new types of authority. A Christian radical like Ballou denied in the 1830s that he was an "anarchist" in the stereotypical sense, because he hoped to substitute divine government for a fallible and usually contemptible human government, expressed in jails, wars, corruption, and imperfection. The latter depended upon cunning and physical force, while the former would be nurtured by persuasion and Christian love. Governance might occur through "neighborhood society by voluntary association," like town meetings. "If here and there a disorderly individual broke over the bounds of decency, the whole force of renovated public opinion would surround him and press in upon him like the waters of the ocean, and slight *uninjurious* force would prevent personal outrage in the most extreme cases." Ballou prayed that all of society would evolve beyond any need for compulsion. Whether this happened or not, he was certain that the Christian must behave as though the millennium had already arrived, refusing to support earthly power by voting, legislating, or fighting.[4]

Although Ballou was an active leader of a model village, Hopedale, the most renowned and thoroughgoing example of religious perfectionism was Oneida, New York, founded by John Humphrey Noyes in 1848. It was a theatrical, if not operatic, performance of the principles of left libertarianism. Earlier, Noyes had announced that true Christians were not only reformed, but reborn through belief. They had cast off all the chains of Satan and become universally emancipated as new Adams and new Eves. Being cleansed of every sin by God's grace, they could follow the invocation "Be ye therefore perfect, even as your Father which is in heaven is perfect." Under Perfectionism (as he called it), such external agents of law as churches and governments were obnoxious intrusions. As he informed William Lloyd Garrison in 1837:

I have subscribed my name to an instrument similar to the Declaration of '76, renouncing all allegiance to the government of the United States, and asserting the title of Jesus Christ to the throne of the world....I have renounced active co-operation with the oppressor on whose territories I live....I must either consent to remain a slave till God removes the tyrant, or I must commence war upon him, by a declaration of independence and other weapons suitable to the character of a son of God....My hope of the millennium begins...AT THE OVERTHROW OF THIS NATION.[5]

After this revelation, Noyes briefly published a journal, variously entitled the *Perfectionist and Theocratic Watchman,* the *Witness,* and the *Free Church Circular.* Finally, having gathered a band of disciples, he formed a covenanted society of saints, who submitted their lives and property to the care of the community. Oneida was to be a city on a hill, a beacon to a sinful world. Property was abolished as a sign of devilish egoism. More startlingly, monogamy was denounced as property in people and idolatry; it was to be replaced by "complex marriage"—the spiritual and physical union of all.

Order was sustained by committees, by the charisma of Noyes, by common beliefs, and by a remarkable practice (almost an ordeal) called mutual criticism. Members of the community were expected to submit themselves to occasional evaluation by a standing committee on criticism. If they were reluctant to volunteer, such an evaluation could be suggested or even required. The members of this committee rotated, so that someone might be a critic at one time and the object of criticism later. The panel analyzed the character of a person as he or she sat silent. Social virtues were thereby honored and reinforced, and arrogance was deflated by sharply honest words. It was, in effect, an anarchist form of government, supposedly combining the virtues of all other regimes with none of the vices of courts, police, or prisons. Noyes predicted that its use in families (children and parents criticizing each other), schools (students "grading" teachers), or in the general society would be strong medicine for a healthy order.[6] Today we might call this "feedback," sensitivity training, an encounter group, conflict resolution, or criticism/self-criticism.

Like most utopian colonies, Oneida was ultimately defeated by capitalist values. It could not transform the society around it—despite four decades of success—so it was slowly absorbed into that society. However, unlike most such groups, which were economically suffocated, Oneida's communism led to a prosperity that fed personal materialism. Today this amazing experiment has become another joint stock company, Oneida Silverware, just as some of the utopias of Iowa were divided into the individual farms or incorporated into the capitalist economy, as with the Amana refrigerator company.

Despite every failure, however, the ideal of a noncoercive community has never lacked advocates or an audience. This was most conclusively demonstrated in Chicago in the 1880's by the prominence of quasi-syndicalist elements within the local labor movement. By 1886, self-identified anarchists in that city published five journals (with a total circulation of about 30,000) and were the dominant force in the Central Labor Union, the major working-class organization. Although they were active in reform activities, such as the struggle for an eight-hour work day and wage increases, they hoped that their union work would be the embryo of a "workers' commonwealth." The *Alarm,* their English paper, identified the movement's aims as those of the 1883 Pittsburgh Manifesto:

First—Destruction of the existing class rule, by all means, i.e., by energetic, relentless, revolutionary and international action.

Second:—Establishment of a free society based upon cooperative organization of production.

Third:—Free exchange of equivalent products by and between the productive organizations without commerce and profit mongery.

Fourth:—Organization of education on a secular, scientific, and equal basis for both sexes.

Fifth:—Equal rights for all without distinction of sex or race.

Sixth:—Regulation of all public affairs by free contracts between the autonomous (independent) communes and associations, resting on a federalistic basis.

This promising movement was annihilated by 1886 when the anarchists were accused of throwing a bomb at a Haymarket Square rally, killing seven policemen and wounding more than sixty others. The blast and police gunfire also caused the death of ten workmen and the injury of as many as two hundred more. The press attributed the crime to foreign scum, "Red Flagsters," "Dynamarchists," and "Bomb Slingers." Eventually, four of the leaders of anarchism were hanged, one killed himself by exploding a fulminating cap in his mouth, and three were imprisoned. In 1893, Governor John Altgeld pardoned those three and condemned the entire proceedings as a judicial murder in which much of the prosecution evidence had been "a pure fabrication" and the jury had been packed. Nonetheless, the government had won a practical and symbolic victory by financially and emotionally draining the Left with legal attacks, by killing several of its major figures, and by convicting anarchism in the court of public opinion. Despite Altgeld's vindication of the men, most continued to perceive all explicit anarchists as firebrands and bomb-throwers.

Implicit anarchism, however, was another question. Forms of left libertarianism could be attractive to many Americans who feared the word anarchism. In the last decades of the nineteenth century, Henry Demarest Lloyd (1847–1903) and Edward Bellamy (1850–98) both outlined a cooperative commonwealth that would supersede capitalism. Their appeal to the conscience of the American public, combined with popular aspirations for freedom, attracted millions of readers.

Lloyd, the son of a Dutch Reformed minister, was early disturbed by the morality of capitalism and became a radical disciple of Jesus rather than Marx. His own comfortable wealth did not insulate his soul from the poverty of others. He became increasingly vocal as he grew older, although it is significant that he did not voice his concerns from any institution but spoke as an independent writer. Lloyd had shunned the ministry (regarding himself as too unorthodox), the law (which was "too technical and traditional"), and even the editorship of his own newspaper, which he could have afforded. Nor did he enter politics, saying that he wanted power, but "power unpoisoned by the presence of obligation." Instead, he was a free agent who defied even political commitments, cheerfully announcing that he was "a socialist-anarchist-communist-independent-cooperative-aristocratic-democrat."[7]

In *Wealth against Commonwealth* (1894), he launched his attack on monopoly with the Rousseauean assertion that "Nature is rich, but everywhere man, the heir of nature, is poor."[8] Inequality, enforced by the greed of capital, was thus a crime against nature, and especially against the immense potential of American life. His solutions, however, were grandiloquently amorphous. He hated pure competition as the ethic of the jungle. Government regulation of business might be both inadequate and dangerous, leading to further corruption by an already debauched state. Public ownership, while it might be required in the case of Standard Oil and other rapacious companies, was also to be feared, as possibly creating a power that would be insufficiently democratic and "intoxicate and harden its possessors." After viewing European ownership of some utilities and railroads, Lloyd was opposed to "central rule" by bureaucracies of any sort.

As an alternative to "business feudalism," state despotism, and liberal regulation, he suggested municipal control, mutual aid, and co-ops, applying the "cooperative methods of the post-office and the public school to many other toils." But his goal was not simply a controlled or "people's" capitalism (as some in the 1950s would have called it). His horizons were far more spacious: "We are to have much more. We are to have a private life of a new beauty...We are to be commoners, travellers to Altruria."[9] He apparently concurred with William Dean Howells's definition of the perfect society as a "purely voluntary association of kindred minds and tastes in a region of absolute altruism."[10]

For models, he turned both to the Bible and to modern experiments in local control, such as worker-owned factories and farms in England and Ireland, Swiss co-ops, and theories of "labor co-partnership." He defined democracy as the direct control of certain industries by the people, not by capitalists (even if regulated), not by bondholders, and not even by the state. Americans could work toward this program by developing a "new conscience" that would reinvigorate the old truths of Christian love. Education, instead of politics or class conflict, would lay the foundations for this just society.[11] In place of either the profits of the marketplace or the powers of the state, the future might hold exciting prospects for an association that was ideologically unified by a noncapitalist ethic and living by "the cooperative method."

Similar dreams of voluntary cooperation floated through most of the forty-two utopian novels that were published between 1883 and 1900.[12] Edward Bellamy was one of the rare exceptions who appeared to transcend our anarchist heritage, moving into a new world of planning. He shared much with other critics: a moralizing tone (his father was a Baptist minister), middle-class status, rejection of class struggle, and reliance on education. Yet his utopia was a disciplined order called Nationalism, where the state controlled all business, workers were drafted into an "industrial army" from the ages of twenty-one to forty-five, and the electorate was confined to retired members of the labor force. This authoritarian program was quite unlike anything I have described as left libertarianism. Later commentators have labeled his ideas everything from protofascism to state communism. Quite as important, his writings were wildly popular. His 1888 novel, *Looking Backward*, sold 400,000 copies by 1897, thrilled millions by its hopes for the future, and was likely the most talked-about social novel since *Uncle Tom's Cabin*. For a time, Nationalism was a catchword and a topic of heated debate. What was the meaning of this phenomenon?

Rather than immediately conceding Bellamy to the camp of authoritarian radicalism, let me consider the possibility that he did not define himself as an institutional disciplinarian and was not read as such by most of his followers. Perhaps we are distorting Bellamy by reading him through many of the experiences of our own time: war, prison camps, and mass regimentation.

First, Bellamy insisted that he was a Nationalist because he was an individualist. He opposed laissez-faire freedom, however, because it meant freedom only for a few. It was evident that the rich and the poor were unequal in rights, justice, power, and opportunities for personal development. Bellamy, on the other hand, promised liberation from the "slavery" and "prison" of present society, where only the wealthy held the keys of liberty.[13] Although Bellamy would require work, this was already necessary for all but parasites, without the redemptive returns of medical care, pleasant housing, nourishing food, shorter hours for the most onerous tasks, just wages, and a national labor exchange for those who sought jobs.

Once organized, his industrial army would not rely upon coercion, drill fields, barracks, guard-houses, drumhead courts, and firing squads. Indeed, workers, after a brief service, could refuse to work any longer, if they were willing to accept one-fourth to one-half pay for the rest of their nonworking lives. Bellamy's choice of the term "army" was awkward, although it did appropriately imply the limited liberty of the wage-worker in industrial civilization, whatever the social system. But his society, even at a crude level of operation, might have offered vastly more freedom for the average individual than any that then existed. He believed that the coming revolution would "declare every man forevermore independent of every other man and every woman of every man."[14]

Second, the Nationalist state was modeled on the post office, rather than on Prussian bureaucracy. His government was both "the august representative of all in general concerns, and everyone's agent, errand boy, and factotum for all private ends."[15] The image of an errand boy may have been

more precise than that of an august representative, since Bellamy naively expected a system that was "so logical in its principles and direct and simple in
its workings that it all but runs itself." Rather than a complicated structure
to direct and develop technology, production, and distribution, he supposed a simplified order, with equal wages, no army, navy, or police, few
judges, and—since the system was fundamentally perfect—no politicians.

Even centralization of production was not necessarily authoritarian, since
it offered a wider range of jobs to the worker and presented the possibility of
decentralizing industry and population centers as part of a general plan. His
fantasy of an almost rustic Manhattan of parks and fountains, with scattered
homes and businesses, undercuts his critics' image of Nationalism as one
monstrous factory under the constant eye of hordes of administrators. Overall, Bellamy was not entirely unjustified in claiming that "nationalism does
not propose a paternal government, but its logical and practical contradiction, a co-operative administration for the benefit of equal producers."[16]

Indeed, the Bellamyite state was not even the ultimate source of social
control, which was a series of common beliefs that formed a "religion of
solidarity." This was not an organized church, a leadership, or even a codi-
fied ideology, but an integral part of the culture, binding everyone and
everything into a semblance of an organic Anarcho-Communist society.
Bellamy offered the startling comparison that while European socialists
might tolerate inequalities of income and abuses of power by an elite,
Americans were more radically democratic and rejected all pompous bureaucrats.[17]

Third, this unity would not be forged by a Marxist party, a Populist party,
or a party of any sort. The currents of evolution were flowing toward the
revolution. Nationalism was visibly developing as business, labor, society,
and politics became more corporate. Although more than 140 Nationalist
clubs were formed by 1900, and newspapers were published, none of this
was essential to further the inevitable victory: "There never was, perhaps, a
reform movement that got along with less management than that of the Na-
tionalists. There has never been any central organization of the
clubs...While these clubs have been and are of the greatest use, and have
accomplished remarkable results in leavening entire communities with Nationalism, there has never been any special effort to multiply them or otherwise to gather the whole body of believers into one band."[18] The National-
ists were basically isolated from every national political party, since all were
flawed or insufficient. They trusted in natural growth toward their goals,
and prayed that this would be accompanied by a moral revolution or powerful revival of Christianity that would herald the final reformation, "The Republic of the Golden Rule."

This qualifies as passive millennialism rather than politics, differentiating
it from its closest European equivalent, Fabian socialism. The Fabians also

attacked both the efficiency and the morality of capitalism and urged the educated elite to prepare the way for a more rational society. Like Fabian bureaucracy, Bellamy's post office state certainly emphasized the bourgeois virtues: punctuality, thrift, temperance, regularity, uniformity, and efficiency. But Fabians would have regarded his ideals as fanaticism. By comparison, Bellamy is a reincarnated Puritan saint and they are easy going Anglicans; he is advocating eternal perfection and they, temporal reform. It was this moral absolutism that fascinated many, although even they may not have accepted his institutional mechanisms, just as those who had once lauded the sovereignty of God disparaged the institutions of man.

It is Bellamy's reliance on institutional power that compels us to the unavoidable conclusion that he is essentially outside the company of American libertarians. He removed every mediating force between government and the individual, justifying the horror of most American liberals and extreme libertarians that he had manufactured a monolith that would squash all spontaneity, and realize Tocqueville's nightmare that equality could destroy liberty.[19]

Genuine left libertarians have never accepted the confines of even such a model prison. With the radical individualists, they shared a hatred of structured authority and favored personal freedom within voluntary associations.[20] But they also had many class and political differences from the in-

John Humphrey Noyes
freedom within community

Emma Goldman
community within freedom

Courtesy of the Labodie Collection of the University of Michigan

dividualists. The editor of *Liberty* was typically pleased that his readers included bankers, lawyers, physicians, "one or two college professors," "a large number of journalists," "farmers by the score," "artisans of every sort," and "at least one policeman."[21] The Anarcho-Communist readers of the *Alarm* (1884–89), the *Rebel* (1895–96), *Mother Earth* (1906–17), or the *Blast* (1915–17) were far more likely to be from the masses. While the Individualists were seldom recent immigrants, the left libertarians were generally from other more tradition-bound and class-conscious societies. Whether they were anarchists when they arrived or became so here, they appealed to peasant, artisan, and proletarian traditions. Like Proudhon, Kropotkin, Bakunin, and the later Tolstoi, they drew much of their inspiration from visions of the "natural cooperation" of agricultural villages or the solidarity of workers. Even the middle-class anarchists of England usually favored the Communist Anarchism of Peter Kropotkin. Yet the American farmer was essentially a small businessman or land speculator, and few workers were class conscious. Capitalist and Protestant notions of egoism restricted the support for beliefs that had been formed in more communitarian cultures.[22]

These left libertarians sometimes adopted tactics, for example, that prompted severe hostility from the population. Anarchism first came to the attention of the general public in 1886 with a bombing in Chicago. Given the popular acceptance of the belief that peaceful change was possible, violence was condemned and anarchism was stereotyped as chaos. Berkman's attempt to assassinate an employee of Andrew Carnegie in 1892 (to the bewilderment or annoyance of most people, who could not understand politically motivated crimes) and the murder of McKinley in 1901 produced outrage against radicalism. Attacks on czars and kings might be acceptable, but an assault on the president, because of his aura of democratic election, was a severe error. The Individualists were united in their emphasis on education and passive resistance.

These separations in class and politics were exemplified by Tucker, a native-born individualist, and Emma Goldman (1869–1940), an immigrant communist. Although their censure of existing authority was in many ways similar, they presented radically opposed concepts of the new order. Tucker's goal was an anarchism of individuals and small groups; Goldman's, one of communes. In many ways it was the confrontation of bourgeois and proletarian. Voltairine de Cleyre, an Anarcho-Communist, perceptively noted that although Tucker was "a city man," he had never known "the oppression of the factory and mingled with workers' associations."[23] His middle-class New England gentility was another world from that of Emma Goldman, who had arrived in the United States, an impoverished Russian Jew, when she was eighteen. Unlike Tucker, she was educated in the clothing factory and the slums. When she heard about the

Chicago bombing, she was working sixty-three hours a week in a clothing factory in Rochester, New York for the grand sum of $2.50. The suffering of her early years was a powerful incentive in the evolution of the fiery orator, writer, and editor. Whereas the Boston *Globe*, in an article on the local radicals, could describe the Individualists as genial, polished, and refined, such terms were unlikely to fit the communists.[24]

During the last years of the nineteenth century and the early years of the twentieth, Tucker and the right libertarians were often adversaries of Goldman and the left libertarians. Nevertheless, they shared many of the same teachers and theories. Goldman agreed, for example, that "Herbert Spencer's formulation of liberty is the most important on the subject," and that Nietzsche and Stirner were allies in her own struggles: "If our society is ever to become free, it will be so through liberated individuals."[25]

Both rejected Marxism and conventional social democracy as the most oppressive forms of majoritarianism. Neither glorified "the masses." Goldman often complained of the ignorance and intolerance of the average American:

The mass itself is responsible for [the present order]. It clings to its masters, loves the whip, and is the first to cry Crucify! the moment a protesting voice is raised against the sacredness of capitalistic authority or any other decayed institution. . . . The Socialist demagogues know that as well as I, but they maintain the myth of the virtues of the majority because their very scheme of life means the perpetuation of power. And how can the latter be acquired without numbers? Yes, authority, coercion, and dependence rest upon the mass, but never freedom or the free unfoldment of the individual, never the birth of a free society.[26]

The Individualists and the communists also shared a common definition of the state as a coercive instrument created by elites to maintain the exploitation of "rank-and-file" Americans through laws, police, troops, and pleas for national loyalty. Goldman captured the typical anarchist sentiment when she entitled one of her essays "Patriotism: A Menace to Liberty."

Perhaps the bitterness of the confrontations between Tucker and Goldman is partially explained by these points of agreement. Each tended to view the other as a vicious heretic rather than as merely an ignorant unbeliever. Tucker despised the supposedly coercive quality of communist anarchism, while Goldman loathed the rampant selfishness of Tucker's brave new bourgeoisie. Goldman, unlike Spencer, Sumner, and Tucker, argued against the morality of competition, whereas they were fully satisfied with the amoral implications of business.

Much of Goldman's success was based on her call for a new moral community and for the rights of the individual within it to read and publish anything, to speak out, to be equal with all races and sexes, to practice birth control—to be free from any kind of force. She criticized America for failing to achieve its ideals of liberty and equality. Although her goals were fundamentally opposed to Tucker's, American symbolism was at least prominent in her social commentary. Many people were excited by her purist vision, just as William Dean Howells had acclaimed Kropotkin a saint and serialized his *Memoirs of a Revolutionist* in the *Atlantic Monthly*, or as Lincoln Steffens had agreed that direct action was superior to politics, and others had venerated Tolstoi.[27]

Few were converts, however. The enthusiasm of most was applied to liberal reforms. Roger Baldwin, entranced by the oratory of Goldman, built the American Civil Liberties Union, not an anarchist group. Others were limited to particular causes, such as free speech. Some were attracted to one aspect of anarchism, only to be repelled by some other issue. Goldman admitted that all forms of American radicalism were "crude" and "immature": "To the indefinite, uncertain mind of the American radical the most contradictory ideas and methods are possible. The result is a sad chaos in the radical movement, a sort of intellectual hash, which has neither taste nor character."[28] But if it had been possible to write a systematic statement of anarchist principles, it would have bound no one! Even this concern about theory ("abstractions") was excessive to Alexander Berkman, who broke away from *Mother Earth*, set up the *Blast*, and urged an even greater emphasis on action. Agitation, grass-roots organizing, consensus agreements, and spontaneous protest were counterposed to rational planning.[29]

The largest group to attempt to realize this impulse was the Industrial Workers of the World. It began with a colorful blaze of activity in 1905 and was still flickering in the 1970s. It was an outburst of anarchism in the Armerican working class, with such rousing slogans as "labor produces all, labor should own all." Claiming 100,000 members at its height, and influencing many more, it became a center of public discussion.

The IWW quickly became nonpolitical, arguing that "a kick on the job is worth ten at the ballot box." This direct action could include everything from violence—such as that portrayed in the song "Casey Jones," where a strikebreaker on the Southern Pacific in 1912 has an "accident"—to passive resistance to laws against soapbox orators by the simple expedient of filling the jails of a city like Seattle until it neared the brink of bankruptcy. The organization's insurrectionary character was also displayed in its refusal to sign contracts (asserting that the workers should be free to strike whenever they wished), its scorn for a well-paid labor bureaucracy as parasites on the workers, use of mass picketing, and refusal to create strike or benefit funds, relying instead upon contributions for particular struggles.

Given this intransigence, it is not surprising that many identified the IWW with the black cat of sabotage and willingly accepted the conservative definitions of IWW as "Irresponsible Wholesale Wreckers," "I Won't Work," and "I Want Whisky." Many others, however, were attracted to the group's idealism of "an injury to one is an injury to all" and to its vision of the perfect society.

In this new order, the IWW would have jettisoned the political state as dead weight. Since power should be in the workplace, not in legislatures, the just society would be a kind of syndicalism, or federation of unions. The citizen would vote where he or she worked, and the "government" would consist of a loosely allied council of workers whose "capital" would be wherever they were meeting. This transcended any conventional form of politics. One labor militant had this appreciative view: "The IWW's conception of a Republic of Labor, based on occupational representation, was a remarkable prevision of the course of development which must necessarily follow from the victory of the workers in this country."[30]

The IWW broke down because of internal divisions, external repression, and the ability of liberal society to absorb some of its secondary proposals. But even if the IWW had won union recognition and wage contracts, it might only have created stable, prosperous, and ultimately conservative unions. When industrial unionism prevailed in the 1930s—shorn of radicalism—it rapidly evolved into one of "the most effective means ever developed to discipline workers in the industrial plants and integrate a whole stratum of Americans into the system."[31]

This radical alternative was defeated not only by fair competition, however, but by court harassment (injunctions, indictments, bail, trials, fines, imprisonment) and by state-sponsored violence. The repression of libertarians was particularly severe during World War I, when they continued to ridicule the naive glorification of nation, patriotism, military honor, and world-conquering democracy. The individualistic and anti-authoritarian character of much of the indigenous radicalism had generally caused more irritation for the American government than German, French, or English radicals did for their states. While the German socialist party, the most prestigious Marxist group in the world, rushed to the defense of the German homeland, Eugene Debs, Emma Goldman, and most "Wobblies" refused to accept any grandiloquent verbiage about the war. Would the capitalists stand in the front lines?

The government responded to these taunts with such laws as the Sedition Act of 1918. This made it illegal to "utter, print, write, or publish any disloyal, profane, scurrilous, or abusive language about the form of government of the United States, or the Constitution of the United States, or the uniform of the Army or Navy of the United States." Under this and the Espionage Act several thousand people were indicted. Virtually the entire leadership of the IWW, for example, was paraded before the court in two monster trials in Chicago and Sacramento in 1917. With 250 defendants, this may have constituted one of the largest political trials in American history. Similarly, Eugene Debs was sentenced to ten years in prison, Big Bill

Haywood was crushed by a 20-year sentence and a $30,000 fine (he eventually fled to Russia), thousands were jailed, most critical publications were squashed by banning them from the mails, and many radicals felt at least some afflictions.[32] In a less brutal ploy to counteract the IWW's appeal, the government also sponsored unions for some workers, such as the Loyal Legion of Loggers and Lumbermen, and promoted some improvements in hours and wages (especially given the need for lumber and other materials in the war).

Emma Goldman, after her own arrest for forming the No Conscription League, counterattacked with a vigorous rebuttal: "We are greater patriots than those who shoot off firecrackers and say that democracy should be given to the world. By all means let us give democracy to the world. But at the present moment we are very poor in democracy. Free speech is suppressed. Free assemblies are broken up by uniformed gangsters.... Women and girls at meetings are insulted by soldiers in this 'democracy.'... How can we be generous in giving democracy to the world?"[33] She equated her activities with the Boston Tea Party and the American Revolution. Were these events "within the law"? She introduced Emerson and Thoreau as witnesses in her defense of the American liberties that had been won by revolution. She boldly claimed that her antimilitarism was more historically American than the views of her persecutors. It was a stirring defense of justice, but it failed to convince a judge and jury determined to convict nonconformity. Nor was prison the final indignity. Upon her release in 1919, Goldman, her longtime friend Alexander Berkman, and approximately 250 others were deported to Russia on the *U.S.S. Buford*, nicknamed by the press "the Red Ark."

By the end of that year, Debs was in jail, the IWW was being shattered, Goldman and Berkman had been exiled, and Tucker was secluded in Europe. America had temporarily rid itself of its noisiest libertarians. As many as 15,000 may have been arrested during 1917–19. And, once again, the radicals felt betrayed by the inconsistent libertarians, the liberals, who had been generally entranced by Wilsonian war idealism.[34]

During the 1920s, conscious varieties of left libertarianism did not flourish. For the Left, Marxism now seemed to be the philosophy of the future, and anarchism was usually considered a relic of a simpler epoch. There was a growing fascination with the red star of the Russian Revolution. Communists now had Marx, not Kropotkin, and many anarchists and syndicalists, such as William Z. Foster, James P. Cannon, and others formed new allegiances to the Communist Party. The socialism of Debs, the spontaneous anarchism of the IWW and the freewheeling radicalism of independent thinkers was replaced by sectarian squabbles over "scientific socialism." Was Bukharin a right opportunist? Was Trotsky guilty of left purism? As the radical intellectuals debated, most Americans turned away.

The IWW's "Wheel of Fortune" outlining the new order

The old radicals had been defeated by events; the new radicals were left alone.[35]

The IWW, the Stelton colony, and other libertarian groups persisted, but they were often splintered by controversies, much as Students for a Democratic Society was in the 1960s. Anarchist journals like the *Road to Freedom* lived in the past, reprinting articles by old personalities (Berkman, Goldman, Tresca, Lucy Parsons), trapped by a hopeless hostility to the present. Though the 1920s trial of Sacco and Vanzetti, two anarchists, attracted enormous attention, the defense was directed primarily by the Communist party, and the ideology of the men was never clearly explained. Their execution in 1927 cast a further shadow over libertarian hopes.

Prospects brightened with the Depression, but the beautiful scruples of anarchism could not survive everyday reality. Unemployed workers in the 1930s could not eat philosophy. While Americans have distrusted bureaucratic authority, they have also required pragmatic solutions to immediate, imperative needs. To them, both Emma Goldman and Herbert Hoover were crazy individualists. Goldman's "detestation of government might be regarded as placing her anomalously in the same part of the political spectrum as the gentlemen of the [right-wing] Liberty League, only on a more extreme position on its edge."[36] In theory they were opposites; in practice they had similar effects. Goldman's final years and the dreams of most anarchists were also darkened by the pall of defeat when Spanish anarchism was murdered by the late 1930s.

A few journals struggled on, some bohemians were attracted, dadaists, surrealists, and beats in the 1940s and 1950s continued the heritage, but the adherents had dwindled by the mid-1950s. Even most of the children of anarchists grew away from the faith. The younger members of an anarchist colony in New Jersey were sometimes caught playing cowboys and Indians, kings and queens, or even (in the 1940s) killing "Japs." It is understandable, then, that a scholar like George Woodcock concluded that anarchism, as a movement, had died by 1940.[37] Its continuing appeal was mainly to small elements of the middle class. A journal like *Retort* (1942–51) could interest such authors as Kenneth Rexroth, Paul Goodman, Saul Bellow, Alex Comfort, Sir Herbert Read, and Kenneth Patchen, but it could not entice the poor and skeptical "proletarians."

Does this mean that the work of the early anarchists had no social value? George Bernard Shaw gave one answer: they had been lively critics of the "balderdash" of official society. Shaw believed that an undogmatic "Fabian anarchism" could have made *Liberty* one of the best journals of social criticism in the United States.[38] While the anarchist critique suffered from the lack of conceptual sophistication and solid documentation, it had the virtue of asking more profoundly basic questions than most liberals or socialists. Anarchists challenged not only various policies and administrators, but the fundamental rationales for the state, patriotism, and conventional democracy. Shaw had praised "the Anarchist spirit as an element of progress" even in his rejection of "The Impossibilities of Anarchism." For all their flaws, they saw much that the complacent were blind to, or perceived only dimly. From their perspectives of anarchist egalitarianism, they had analyzed a world burdened by the political systems of "the master race," "the homeland of the revolution," and what they considered the pseudodemocracy of British and American elites. All government, to them, was exploitation. To labor under the shadow of the state, whether as a railway worker in Britain or in Russia, was equally remote from direct workers' control. As Emma Goldman had declared in 1937, anarchists continued to believe in "the old-fashioned idea that life without freedom is a monstrous delusion even if 'trains run on time' and 'our beloved comrade in the Kremlin has made Russia the most comfortable and joyous country in the world.' "[39]

Yet, by the 1950s anarchism was either forgotten or consciously shelved as archaic, reactionary, and quite out-of-date. Its cynicism about big business, big labor, and big government seemed to be an echo from the simpler society of earlier times. But the old radicalism was only dormant, not dead. The 1960s witnessed the revival of anarchism, not so much as a conscious ideology as an impulsive response to excessive authority. Joseph Conlin, in *The American Radical Press*, characterized the New Left as "reflexively anarchist." As such, it was quite within American traditions of rebellion. Many of the themes we have just discussed were vehemently repeated. Unjust authority was once again rejected, even to the extent of repudiating all authority. While capitalism has conquered such opponents as the IWW, it has consistently produced others. Anarchism was to reemerge as both a product and a criticism of the inconsistencies of America.[40]

CHAPTER SEVEN

STATIST RADICALISM

Who are you indeed who would talk
  or sing to America?
Have you studied out the land,
  its idioms and men?
  —Whitman, *Leaves of Grass*

🌿This brings us to the final dimension of American radicalism: traditional social democracy, communism, and other relatively authoritarian movements that rely upon coercive centers of state power (that is,
on involuntary collectivism) rather than on cooperative associations. All are
within modern trends toward industrial giantism, social, political, and
economic centralization, undemocratically controlled bureaucracies, and
ideological homogenization ("a party line"). People may be represented;
they may participate; but they do not directly control. Statist radicalism, in
every variety, is the antithesis of the libertarian goal, once expressed by Paul
Goodman as a "face-to-face society" where life would be "on a human
scale."

In the United States, every form of statist radicalism has been baffled by
at least one of four possible receptions. First, such a movement is likely to be
ignored. But if it has some popular appeal, it may suffer the second treatment, being converted into a handmaiden of liberalism. Third, it can be
swept away by right and left libertarian currents that wreck its structure.
Fourth, it might successfully defend itself, becoming a sterile sect.

The sad history of American Marxism has acted out several of these
fiascoes. It was initiated in the late 1840s by such men as Friedrich Sorge and
Albert Wedemeyer, who became the German-American leaders of an essen-

tially German-American movement. They and their compatriots behaved like priests who guarded the purity of the teachings from the corruption of "bourgeois consciousness" that permeated American society, including the workers. Few Americans were attracted by this Talmudic reverence; even fewer stayed—and many of these were purged from the First International with the connivance of Sorge and Marx.[1]

Engels, however, was appalled when they insisted upon conducting their public meetings in German! He complained that radicalism could not be imported, that it had to evolve naturally, perhaps drawing upon foreign sources, but using them for its own purposes. Engels was an early theorist of what Marxists would call American Exceptionalism. The uniquely rich lands and resources of America had been the foundation for a society where all classes had the broad philosophical and economic beliefs of a petty bourgeois or bourgeois ideology. Even to the lower classes, such norms as individual striving, the sanctity of property, voluntary associations, and cheap and efficient government appeared to be self-evident. Engels, sounding strangely like Tocqueville in his analysis, was moved to make this comment in 1895: "It is remarkable, but quite natural, how firmly rooted are bourgeois prejudices even in the working class in such a young country which has never known feudalism and have grown up on a bourgeois basis from the beginning.... The worker also imagines that the traditionally inherited bourgeois regime is something progressive and superior by nature and for all time, not to be surpassed."[2] As long as the economic order remained fairly prosperous and there were some opportunities for most people, European-style socialism was killed at the roots. While a society based upon scarcity might demand sharing—if necessary, after revolution—America seemed to offer something for everyone, either now or in the future. Both the working class and the bourgeoisie were mesmerized by possessive individualism.

Engels was more sensitive to these historical and cultural forces than the average Marxist, but he and later analysts of Exceptionalism still concluded that American society would eventually follow the "laws" of economic evolution, so that the proletariat would cease to be procapitalist, embrace social democracy, and move toward the abolition of property.

Both the schematic analysis and the classical outcome of Marxism were first revised, in this country, by Daniel De Leon. When he joined the Socialist Labor Party in 1890, only two members of the central committee spoke English, and he rapidly became convinced of the necessity of (in his words) "nativizing" the party. The SLP was Americanized by a version of left libertarianism. De Leon speculated that the United States, as an advanced capitalist society, could immediately enter the world of stateless com-

Courtesy of The Socialist
Labor Party

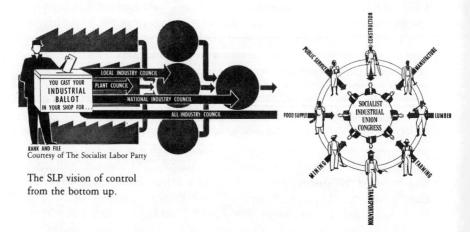

RANK AND FILE
Courtesy of The Socialist Labor Party

The SLP vision of control
from the bottom up.

munism, in which the political system would be replaced by "socialist industrial unionism," a federation of unions that governed things rather than
people.[3]

To achieve this, De Leon advocated some means that were compatible
with anarchism—such as revolutionary unions—and others, such as politics,
that were not. His ideal party had the final goal, however, of abolishing
itself. It would serve its function of educating the workers, agitating them,
and organizing them to build a new society. It would then cease to exist.

In the new society, organization would be based upon industrial representation, rather than on political divisions like cities or states. People would
vote for local and regional representatives of their professions or interests.
Such delegates would democratically plan and coordinate production and
distribution, and they would be subject to immediate recall if their consti-
tuents were displeased. Although De Leon characterized his "industrial
government" as a state, it bears clear resemblances to syndicalism.

Although De Leon was a rare innovator in American Marxism, his influence was poisoned by a bitterly dogmatic style. He ridiculed all reforms,
describing them as "the tapeworm of immediate demands" and as mere
ambulance service on the industrial battlefield. In 1900, the SLP repudiated
twenty-one reforms that had been in its platform, leaving one plank: total
revolution immediately. As one of De Leon's followers later said, "Why
wash garbage before you throw it in the can?" Party work was conducted in
such an atmosphere of ideological purity, refusal of alliances with other
radicals, and extreme centralization. Some critics referred to De Leon as the
pope of the American Left, and his legacy ossified into a virtual church that
cherishes the truths of "Marxism–De Leonism." The libertarian elements of
this perspective were incomplete even during De Leon's lifetime but were

later to be entirely submerged, just as Lenin, alive, was a genuine revolutionary but the embalmed Lenin is now displayed to uphold the Russian status quo.

De Leon's grim sectarianism prompted its opposite in 1901, the Socialist Party of America. The austere discipline of the SLP, along with its veneration of Marx, was repudiated as a "Prussianism" that was worthy of a Germanic rather than an American party. Instead, the SPA became a virtual circus of Bellamyites, leftover Populists, remnants from the American Railway Union, Christian Socialists, and other varieties of reformers and revolutionaries. Throughout its main history during 1900–1920, it reflected the usual American pattern of politics, which would later be called in Europe "the Popular Front." The SPA consisted of many state and ethnic federations and a galaxy of uncontrolled, privately run, do-it-yourself publications. Despite various complaints that the party was a "machine" (it is revealing that this is no praise in highly industrialized America), in fact, "every socialist tended to be his own party."[4]

This antipathy toward institutional authority, which is a hallmark of anarchism, was embodied in the evangelical leader of the party, Eugene V. Debs. Although he was given the party's nomination for the presidency five times, he remained more of a spokesman for the gospel of socialism than a party administrator. As a left libertarian, he never sat on the executive committee of the SPA, nor was he a delegate of any of the party conventions. Despite his renown as a leader, he found it impossible to organize his own faction within the SPA and was constantly manipulated by those who could. This intensified his disdain of authorities, provoking him to say that he was "willing to be charged with almost anything, rather than being a leader."[5] He justified this "prejudice against officialdom and dread of bureaucracy [on the grounds that] the natural tendency of officials is to become bosses."[6] The national officers of the SPA were not angelic exceptions, and he publicly corrected them for intolerance and careerism, hoping that criticism and the rotation of jobs would forestall bureaucratization.

The program of the party, like its leadership, was often rather disorganized. In 1900, some members harked back to schemes for utopian colonies, proposing that the State of Colorado be colonized, with an eye to capturing the local government and making it a model. The early party was a menagerie of heterogeneous ideologies, although, even from this beginning, there was also a tendency toward homogenization. Members were forbidden to support *any* capitalist politicians (although expulsion was unlikely for such an offense). European notions of ideological unity were present, if not dominant. Although the SPA attempted to become a genuinely

American radical party, it continued to speak socialism with a slightly German accent, to write some English publications that read as though they had been translated, and to appeal too frequently to the authority of foreign theorists, foreign parties, and foreign ideologies. Yet the SPA became sufficiently attuned to national needs to become one of the most popular of American radical groups. By 1912 it had received nearly a million votes in the presidential election, had put 1,200 members in public office, had 118,000 dues-paying members, claimed up to one-third of the ballots for the leadership of the American Federation of Labor, and was supported by 5 English dailies and 262 English weeklies.

This effort to be indigenous, and its relative success, involved the party in a fatal contradiction. In theory, the SPA was more than a reform party. In practice, it was at the forefront of reforms that patched up capitalism. It advocated a Department of Labor, progressive taxation, women's suffrage, minimum wages, factory inspection, unemployment insurance, agricultural supports, and the right to unionize. John Spargo magnificently symbolized its goal as "communism in economic opportunity." The more liberal the party became, the more successful it was; the more successful it was, the more liberal it became. "By 1912, it could be described as the left wing of the progressive movement."[7] The SPA either stimulated liberals to implement reforms to prevent "red revolution," or it popularized repairs that diminished its own appeal. Its primary function, despite its own definition as a replacement for capitalism, was to assist, during a critical period, in the transition to a different form of liberal society. Many in the party were unhappy with this historical task.

As an umbrella organization, the SPA was especially vulnerable to collapse. With the outbreak of the war and the Russian Revolution, the party was weakened by ideological dissension and torn by government repression. The leadership of the SPA, overwrought by constant harassment and fearful of growing communist influence, defended the moderate programs of the party by expelling more than half its members! This spectacular repudiation of basic democracy left the Social Democratic movement split into a dogmatic socialist party and a dogmatic communist party that frequently expended most of their energies in fratricidal denunciation of one another.[8]

Later, the Reverend Norman Thomas restored the SPA to a "liberalized" Social Democracy, while he personally achieved public respect as a fervent moral critic and agitator. He was skeptical that idealism could ever be fully realized in institutions and, as a pacifist, denied that coercion should be used for human liberation. As he frankly confessed in his Socialist party application in 1918: "Perhaps to certain members of the party, my socialism would not be the most orthodox variety. As you know, I have a profound fear of the undue exaltation of the state and a profound faith that the new world we desire must depend upon freedom and fellowship rather than upon any sort of coercion whatever.''⁹ This was in startling contrast to the little Lenins, little Trotskys and little Stalins of the later Communist movement, or even to the social engineering of some of the New Dealers. As Norman Thomas replied to the belief that Franklin Delano Roosevelt had carried out the generous goals of socialism: "Yes, he carried them out in a stretcher." Nevertheless, it is also true that liberal reforms, during the Progressive era and the New Deal, stabilized capitalism and underwrote its claims of superiority.

By the late 1970s, the heirs of the SPA were the Democratic Socialist Organizing Committee (which labored within the Democratic Party), the Social Democrats, USA (who rubber-stamped anyone that unions endorsed, including a bland, right-wing senator in 1976, Henry Jackson), and a somewhat more orthodox Socialist Party—USA (which ran an independent candidate for the presidency but was only slightly to the left of Senator Hubert Humphrey). The National Secretary of DSOC summarized the dilemma of Social Democrats: "We conceive of ourselves as a loyal but critical section of the mass movement of the existing left in the United States—which is unfortunately a liberal, not a socialist mass movement."¹⁰ If the Democratic party is the "mass party" of the "left," that is where Social Democrats should be, pushing it farther in what they define as a leftward direction.

The Communist party, despite its militant origins as a party composed mainly of foreigners, eventually had a similar career. At first it seemed doomed to isolation as the bastard child of the American Left and the Soviet Union. By the late 1920s, it had expelled its right and left wings, both of which had argued that Marxism had to be adapted to local conditions. As a member of the left Communist party, James Cannon, reasoned in 1923: "The American movement has no counterpart anywhere else in the world, and any attempt to meet its problems by the simple process of finding a European analogy will not succeed. The key to the American problem can only be found in a thorough examination of the peculiar American situation. Our Marxian outlook, confirmed by the history of the movement in Europe, provides us with some general principles to go by, but there is no pattern, made to order from European experience, that fits American history.''¹¹

This advice was ignored. What followed was a fruitless struggle to plant "democratic centralism" in the American soil, complete with scientific theory, Leninist party, and the dictatorship of the proletariat (Cannon, when he embraced Trotskyism, did little better). From its earliest years, the Communist party was not a native radical party but a local sect of Soviet communism. When the Soviet Union condemned Bukharin, his American followers were ousted; when the Soviet Union tossed Trotsky overboard, the CPUSA took its cue. It had ceased to be an independent organization, voluntarily surrendering its will. The party generally drifted with the current, knowing its position essentially by its political relation to the USSR, not by what it always called "the science of Marxism."

This negative fact had a briefly positive influence in the 1930s, although the negative finally overwhelmed the positive. Before 1935, the CPUSA had copied the USSR's policy of deriding both liberals and non-Communist radicals as hidden "social fascists" and implied the imminent storming of capitalism for the creation of a dictatorship of the proletariat. When this divided the opposition to Nazism and aided its victory, the USSR sensed grave dangers and retreated from this indefensible position. Communist parties were now urged to form "united fronts" of all progressive forces to "defeat fascism." Although fascism was scarcely a threat in the United States, the American Communist party dutifully obeyed, and efforts to build an independent socialist party languished. Rather, Communist party energies were concentrated on the defense of President Roosevelt against Republican reactionaries (after his rehabilitation from the ranks of the social fascists), and on enthusiastic participation in union organizing, student movements, antifascist publications, black struggles, and other activities of militant reform. The CPUSA became a liberal party—at least in programs—whose motto was "Communism is twentieth-century Americanism."

This has often been casually dismissed as a bizarre and fraudulent episode in American radicalism. On the contrary, many leaders, members, and supporters of the Communist party were convinced that this was not merely a tactical move to create protective coloration for the party or to build some Trojan horse, but a genuine effort to acclimate communism to the United States. They made a remarkable, though flawed, attempt to demonstrate that they were legitimate heirs and modern representatives of historic values.

First, they made severe errors in their forms of analysis. Because the Popular Front emphasized the immediate utility of history, the CPUSA rushed into a polemical use of patriotism without defining what should have been (by its Marxist values) the most elementary issue about any historical event: What economic and class forces were involved? Instead of analyzing the essence of earlier movements, the party concentrated on surface similarities, using ideas as weapons or instruments for particular jobs and losing the overall perspective and depth. Thus, while it may be true that working-class movements can draw lessons from middle-class movements, it is not self-evident that "the Communist Party carries forward the democratic elements of Jefferson [and] Paine."[12] Thomas Jefferson was not Karl Marx; Paine was not Lenin; bourgeois revolution was not proletarian revolution; laissez-faire radicalism was not a transition to state communism.

Because of this failure to establish the nature of such conflicts as the American Revolution, the CPUSA necessarily committed many other errors.

It published eulogistic commentaries on Thomas Paine (the very model of a petty bourgeois radical), Thomas Jefferson (a laissez-faire liberal), Benjamin Franklin (the quintessential entrepreneur), and even George Washington. The Communist party attempted to transform these middle-class leaders into proto-Communists rather than merely saying that they were progressive, in many ways, in their own time. In fact, the CPUSA offered excuses for their limitations. Thus, George Washington would have been more humane if he had been better informed, and Paine would have been a Jacobin if only he had been more fluent in French. Samuel Adams was praised without any real understanding that he was, both religiously and economically, a reactionary (that is, a Calvinist and a mercantilist).[13] Benjamin Franklin received the astonishing title of "the forerunner of Marx" (Carl Reeve) because he was the first to define wage labor and value (Sam Darcy) and because of his "profound understanding of private property" (J. Mindel). Granville Hicks surpassed this with a comparison of Franklin and Lenin, noting that both were idealists who were tactically flexible. This was undiluted romantic nonsense, leading to an article in the theoretical journal of the CPUSA avowing that "in America, only the workers and democratic forces can draw new strength from the ideals of Benjamin Franklin.[14] These peculiar writings, flatulent oratory on the Fourth of July and Thanksgiving, and Browder's placing a portrait of Washington in his office next to that of Lenin were representative of a profound theoretical confusion between liberal and Marxian radicalism.

Second, these ideals would have required that the Communist party abandon its Marxist-Leninist form of organization. This was partially recognized, but only superficially accomplished. In 1944 the CPUSA become the Communist Political Association, an event accompanied by the enthusiastic singing of the "Star-Spangled Banner." Many members and leaders of the party believed that the postwar period would be one of economic, social, and political advance, and that the Communists could work most effectively as a pressure group rather than as a Marxist-Leninist party. Earl Browder, the leader of the Communist party, asserted that American capitalism was deeply rooted, vigorously adaptable, and still progressive: "We 'Reds' and 'Bolsheviks' have much more confidence in the strength of capitalism in this country than has, for example, Herbert Hoover"! The CPUSA, assuming the hardy longevity of this basic system, transformed itself into "a non-party organization of Americans which [carries] forward the tradition of Washington, Jefferson, Paine, Jackson and Lincoln, under the changed conditions of modern industrial society."[15]

Communist party practice, however, condemned its theories. There was no spirited internal democracy, and the party was also open to the charge of manipulation or conspiracy by obscuring its own presence within various popular front groups and liberal activities.

These problems were not obvious at first, and the CPUSA achieved its widest influences as a vanguard of radical liberalism. But when the USSR suddenly changed its policies in 1939, 1941, and 1944, the party felt obligated to follow, destroying most Americans' trust in its independence. Thus, in May 1944 there was unanimous party support for the Popular Front. By July 1945, after a condemnation by Jacques Duclos of the French Communist party (and, by implication, Stalin), there was overwhelming opposition. The impetus for this change came from Duclos, not because of internal party debate. While there had been some discussion within the leadership, none of this had been aired in public, and much of the membership was dismayed and began to drop away.[16]

By the late 1940s and early 1950s, most Americans justifiably responded with complete cynicism to the CPUSA's claim that it was the champion of the best heritage of our society. Because of the absence of party democracy and because of ideological and practical inconsistency, Communist party oratory about radical continuity was not believable. John Gates, the editor of the *Daily Worker*, later realized that though Debs had been villified by the government and condemned to Atlanta Penitentiary, he had nonetheless received one million votes for the presidency in 1920. Debs was often perceived as an advocate of civil liberties and an opponent of unjust wars. Gates asked why the CPUSA—which was, in theory defending many of the same principles—lacked such popular enthusiasm. He concluded that Communist party statements had been fundamentally dishonest and had isolated the party from the American public. Gates understood that party leaders like Betty Gannett and V. J. Jerome were living in a fantasy world when they said: "We have only to look about us, at ourselves and our comrades throughout this country, to see how organically we are part of the American working class; how we look, speak, act, and feel with the American people, because we are *of* the people." As Gates later responded to J. Edgar Hoover's book *Masters of Deceit*, the Communists had ultimately deceived only themselves by trying to speak in American terms while maintaining alien principles.[17]

Of course, this difficulty has not been restricted to American Communism. It was the French socialist Leon Blum who first remarked that the Communist party was a foreign sect—neither indigenous nor internationalist, but the local representative of a specific country, the USSR. Such past criticisms may have contributed to the French Communist party's announcing, in February 1976, that it now wanted "communism under French colors," "a socialism for France." Santiago Carrillo, the head of the Spanish Communist party, agreed that "for years, Moscow was our Rome. The Great Revolution was our Christmas. But today we have grown up." The British, Italian, and Yugoslavian parties have also tried to combine communism with local traditions, as have many communists in the Third World.[18]

By these definitions, the American Communist party has never grown up. Throughout its history, it has patterned itself on Russian specifications. In one period it will be extremely purist, repudiating national history and denying all allegiances to other groups and classes. Or it may oscillate from this left sectarianism to what an orthodox Marxist might call right opportunism, which resembles liberalism or Fabian socialism in its emphasis on moderate reforms, broad alliances, and pragmatic theory. In either case, the final vision of American Communism has usually remained that of the Soviet Union and eastern Europe. The United States government has played this theme for its full value, combining propaganda with physical repression to complete the isolation of the party from any significant influence.[19]

If this is so, why has the Communist party survived, like so many other ideological relics? It attracts some of those who condemn the imperfections in American society and feel the need for a new totality or community, because Soviet communism seems a practical, working model. Also, its stated goals of equality, justice, and a "new socialist man" have great moral and humanist appeal. Howard Fast once called Marxism and the Communist party his God, Granville Hicks praised "the moral judgements of Marxism," and Richard Wright said that "it was not the economics of Marxism, nor the great power of trade unions, nor even the excitement of underground politics that claimed me," but the sense of brotherhood that the party represented.[20] It would be simplistic to argue that most party members have been dupes or fools manipulated by conscious frauds. For many, the party is considered idealism in action. This has probably added more to its ranks than the science of Marxism-Leninism, just as disillusionment caused by the reality of the party has continually thinned its membership.

By the late 1960s both Communism and Social Democracy essentially functioned as reform movements. The Communist party, in the era of detente, had rechristened the *Daily Worker* as the more pleasantly innocuous *Daily World*. Its contents more closely resembled the liberalism of the *New York Times* than the Marxism of Lenin's *Iskra*. The party glorified the "law and order" found in Soviet cities, refused to support the Equal Rights Amendment (as a threat to laws that gave special privileges to women), upheld the sanctity of the home against the sexual revolution, frowned upon the "anarchism" of the New Left, and advocated the creation of an "antimonopoly coalition" that would expand popular control of the economy.[21]

Authoritarian parties of other ideologies, such as Trotskyism, have also been profoundly subverted by the empiricist culture in which they live. They have usually attempted to gain some success by subordinating theory and planning to direct struggles. This has invariably led not to revolution but to reform. Of course there have always been dogmatic exceptions: small enclaves of Maoism, pure Trotskyism, straight De Leonism—an entire spectrum of abstract, mechanical, and Jesuitical radicals.[22]

While there are still American radicals who behave like moths fluttering about the luminaries of foreign movements, these are leaders without followers, radicals of America who are not American radicals. The American public, workers included, remain skeptical of labor parties, socialism, Communism, elites, experts, and comprehensive rational theories. It has been mainly the intelligentsia, rather than the common people, who have been drawn in this direction. Intellectuals, who are fond of orderly interpretations and define progress as ever-greater specialization of function and hierarchies of authority, have regularly diagnosed the healthy suspicion of all systems as "anti-intellectualism." Insofar as the intellectual has been a consistent enemy of the anarchist disposition of much of our culture, this charge is certainly true.[23] But it is correct to judge this "anti-intellectualism" a sign of backwardness, if not infantilism (as Irving Babbitt once proclaimed)? Political experience, not ideas, has perennially revived American antipolitics.

Our native radicalism has ignored neither these failures nor the splendid idealism of Paine, Robert Owen, Marx, and many others. The critical traditions of America have drawn upon Europe, just as Christianity would be unimaginable without the "foreigner" Christ, the American language without the English language, or our Anglo-Saxon politics without the Anglo-Saxon heritage. Religious, political, economic, and social experiences from others have been grafted unto our inherited radicalism, rooted in the American environment. More exotic species, however, have withered or died in the clumsy attempt to transplant them.

Finally, when someone argues that socialism, for example, has failed in the United States, it should be asked, of course, whether it has really succeeded anywhere. There are many interpretations of such countries as the USSR and China as state capitalist systems. Authoritarian communism can be analyzed as a left-wing consolidation of capitalism, just as fascism is a consolidation from the Right. Under communism, the individual capitalist is replaced by the collective capitalist (the state), the division of labor remains the same, alienation persists, "scientific management" is exalted, efficiency, productivity, and capital accumulation are prime virtues, and whatever expands the productive capacity of society is considered "historically progressive." Consider a recent description of a Russian factory where the main work area was dominated by a gigantic poster of Lenin ("Lenin is eternally with us") surrounded by such thrilling banners as "Every day of shock labor is a stride toward communism" and "Discipline is the precondition of success." Or the North Korean newspaper that proudly informs us of speed-up campaigns to meet higher production quotas. It would be more reasonable to call this state capitalism and a new form of oppression than radical liberation.

The vague boundaries of these concepts will make some uneasy (others may find them a thicket), but technical rigor would not have served the interests of truth. Since everyday life is a jumble of ideas, circumstances, and sentiments, any claim to "retrospective symmetry" should be viewed with intense cynicism.[24] Although there are main currents in American criticism, they do not represent unidimensional continuums that have flowed smoothly through the centuries. A right libertarian in economics might urge the repression of free trade in ideas. A left libertarian who favored an open discussion of values could still advocate a planned economy. Liberals and authoritarian radicals may share right or left libertarian ideas. A Populist might simultaneously have laissez-faire fantasies and programs for government regulation; a Jacksonian radical could endorse the slogan "every man his own entrepreneur" and support left libertarian concepts.[25]

To underscore these variations on my theme, we might glance at feminist and black radicalism, which participate in the general pattern but differ in their usually greater collective consciousness, based upon race or sex.[26] While Martin Luther King, Jr., and Gloria Steinem could be interpreted as militant liberals, they have been distinguished by a sense of group identity (derived from group oppression) far stronger than that of the typical white liberal. Among blacks, even right libertarian projects share this sense of collectivity, whether expressed in Marcus Garvey's showy but disorganized Universal Negro Improvement Association, the increasingly probusiness, mild, and respectable Nation of Islam (a functional equivalent to Puritanism and the temptations of success), or "black capitalism." The Black Panthers, on the Left, stressed community control—"intercommunalism." not internationalism. Authoritarian black radicals, on the other hand, often recited the same texts as whites (like Stalin on the national and colonial questions, or Mao on the Third World), but they may also indulge in Pan-African sentimentality, such as the enthusiasm of W. E. B. DuBois for Nkrumah, dictator of Ghana. "Black power," of course, can mean anything from cultural affirmation and interest-group politics to "psychological emigrationism" ("we have to live here but we are not Americans"), or calls for physical separation into a black nationalist state, either within the United States or elsewhere. So, again, there is a complex interaction with American ideals—of affirmation, despair, and rejection. But whatever the specific commitment, general black cynicism about politics is at least as great as the average white American's.

Feminism has the same spectrum: the National Organization of Women (which is essentially liberal, working toward equal opportunity in the job marketplace, along with control over one's own body, such as "voluntary motherhood''), feminist businesses and co-ops (sometimes right), feminist communes and collectives (perhaps left), and feminist authoritarians within such publications as *Women in Revolution* (Spartacist League) and *Battle Acts* (published by Women of Youth against War and Fascism, a semi-Trotskyist group).

Thus, despite the reality of diversity, there have been some continuities. Each of these forms of criticism has a definite mode of operation, core, or center of gravity. That is what I have attempted to define.

It might be argued, of course, that many of the ideals discussed have been stranded by the currents of social and technological evolution—that they are the ''obsolete'' but colorful dreams of romantic reactionaries. Such a thesis is contradicted by the continual reemergence of each of these forms of radicalism from every defeat, apparently satisfying some cultural imperatives. Most recently, the crises of the 1960s revived all types of American libertarianism, right, liberal, and left, with authoritarian critics, as usual, a distant fourth. Once again, rebellious people challenged institutional power. As in the past, American society naturally generated the antidote to a destructive conformism, whether the academic ''machine'' at the University of California at Berkeley (''Student at UC: Do Not Fold, Spindle, Mutilate or Bend''), the military ''machine,'' or the political ''machine.'' Anarchism's rejection of monopoly and modern bureaucracy was the living spirit of the ad hoc structures of most of the New Left and the general anti-authoritarianism of the youth movements of the 1960s and the first years of the 1970s. It was the renewal of old traditions, further evidence that the black flag has been the most appropriate banner of the American insurgent.

PART III

REVIVAL AND REFORMATION, 1960–77

Come out of her, my people, that ye be not partakers of her sins, and that ye receive not of her plagues.—Revelations 18:4

I never made no social contract with you.
—Tuli Kupferberg, the Fugs (a rock band)

O beautiful for specious guise,
For livid napalm flame,
For chemicals that wipe out crops
And those that kill and maim.
   America, America
   Defending liberty,
   Maintaining calm
   In Vietnam,
   You'll keep it safe for me.
 —"America the Beautiful as It Might Be Sung by Premier Ky," *Industrial Worker*, 1971.

THE BEGINNING OF ANOTHER CYCLE

Subterranean anarchist currents once again surfaced in the 1960s. The crises of that period broke the confidence that America had solved its problems, and, as social criticism emerged and evolved, the black flag was once again unfurled. We will sketch its initial impulse in the 1950s, the creation of a broad critical movement in the 1960s, its differentiation into right and left tendencies, and its final shattering into various anarchist splinters. These ranged from Anarcho-Capitalists who desired the organization of society solely on the basis of "the free market" to Anarcho-Communists who sought an individualized society of decentralized communes. The essentially middle-class character of both of these anarchisms will be analyzed and illustrated.

We must begin with this basic question: Why wasn't the radical upsurge of the 1960s fundamentally channeled into, directed, and amplified by any existing organization like that of the 1930s? First, the old Left aroused little more than disdain or antiquarian interest. The Communist party was still in the gutter, where it had been thrown by the Hungarian Revolution of 1956, Krushchev's exposé of Stalin, its own bureaucratic ossification, the ravages of McCarthyism, and the policy of Popular Frontism that severely limited an already microscopic public profile. Clearly, general skepticism about the Communist party and the USSR discouraged any immediate return to the

Depression rhetoric of Marxism-Leninism. Other groups of the old Left were seen as equally absurd relics of a contemptible past. The Socialist Party of America, for example, had become a tiny club composed primarily of intellectuals who frequently rubber-stamped liberal Democratic candidates.[1]

Second, if Stalin and other left icons were smirched, so was the image of Roosevelt; most of New Deal liberalism seemed quite as blemished. The Western occupation of the Suez in 1956 disturbed many who had not expected this from any of the nations of the self-identified free world. Within the United States, the Montgomery bus boycott of 1956, and the beginning of a whole new struggle for civil rights, revealed the painfully incomplete achievement of the American dream of equality. Attacks by the United States government against socialist Cuba—including Adlai Stevenson's defense of the Bay of Pigs invasion and Kennedy's support for that venture—alienated some American progressives. For others, the violent death of Kennedy seemed to symbolize corruption in our culture.

By the mid-1960s, then, the stage was set for a confrontation between the egalitarian, pacifist mythology of official America and the realities of race conflict, burgeoning military budgets, the rediscovery of poverty, malnutrition, and neglect among millions, economic uncertainty, and—the most dramatic bombshell in American intellectual life—the Vietnam theater of the absurd. Here, especially, masses of people were "radicalized" by the disparity between official versions of the idealism and morality of state policy and the Saigon sordidness of brothels, bars, black markets, and moneyed, dictatorial elites. Those who had turned to Lyndon Johnson in 1964 as a champion of peace felt the sting of betrayal. There was a growing disillusionment with the center of the consensus.

At home, increasing numbers from the Right, liberal center, and Left believed that state interference with the individual was becoming excessive. The critics emphasized different problems, including a standing army, secret police, legalized morality in sex, drugs, and other private areas of life, a military-industrial-scientific elite, a propaganda machine, and a rapidly centralizing government. For some, growing distrust of the federal government combined with antimilitarism and anti-industrialism to make all systems suspect of retarding people's full development. This anarchistic reaction was fundamentally opposed to centralized authority in all forms, and, while this was a common response to power in many industrialized countries in the 1960s, it took its most capitalist and individualist pattern in America. The apparent moral insolvency of all the old institutions generated an anti-institutional "movement," a New Left, a decentralist Right, and a "counterculture."

These discordances between the official and the actual on such questions as the war annoyed and angered many Americans and resulted in the revival of American left and right versions of the liberal "philosophical method" noted by Tocqueville. This prompted numerous fascinating evolutions, such as the development of a Taft and Goldwater supporter into an Anarcho-Capitalist. Karl Hess concluded that the power realities of Vietnam had stripped the government of any claim to morality. The war, he said, must "remind all conservatives that whenever you put your faith in big government for any reason, sooner or later you wind up as an apologist for mass murder."[2] Only corporate liberalism was less rejuvenated. Its complicity in supporting an increasingly unpopular war and the growing belief that it had failed to solve basic social problems limited its appeal to the new reformers and radicals of the 1960s. It was within this nourishing context of the revival of social and political controversy that all forms of American anarchism, limited for decades by the reform successes of state liberalism to various immigrant groups and small, isolated, and often bitter journals living in the past, made a startling reappearance in major expressions of youth culture, black protest, the New Left, and dozens of explicitly anarchist papers and groups.[3]

At first the new and immature movement expressed itself in broad general concerns, such as draft resistance and black liberation, not as a consistent, self-conscious, structured phenomenon. It rapidly became more coherent in theory and more diverse in its activities. The Montgomery bus boycott of 1956 and the following sit-ins and other forms of direct action had already convinced many that such tactics were more effective in commanding respect for blacks than the old techniques of politics and legal cases. Later, it was generalized by some that government promises in all areas would have to be secured by popular organization and action and that legalistic types of protest were neither sufficient nor perhaps essential to achieving full democracy. Thus, Abbie Hoffman, who had worked in the civil rights movement in Georgia and Mississippi in the early 1960s and had been beaten and battered, came to the treacherous end of this legal and  moral route when he was indicted in the "Chicago Conspiracy Trial" under a provision of the Civil Rights Act of 1968! Similar frustration by others over broken or perverted government promises, humiliation at physical abuse during the period of nonviolent action, state suppression of the militant Black Panthers, and numerous persecutions led to increasing cynicism about federal and state politics and greater emphasis on community control and self-defense.[4]

Similarly, the anticonscription movement, the early Students for a Democratic Society (SDS), and radical liberals progressed from counseling and canvassing to draft refusal, acts of civil disobedience such as the Berrigans' burning of draft records, and general interpretations of the roots of conscription and other oppressions in capitalism, militarism, and imperialism. The liberalism of the founding document of the SDS, *The Port Huron Statement* (1962) and its 1964 presidential slogan "part of the way with LBJ,'' were replaced with a thoroughgoing radicalism. The defeat of reform liberals such as Eugene McCarthy, the spectacle of the Chicago Democratic Convention—which Jerry Rubin called the Fort Sumter of the youth culture—and several political trials (Spock, the Berrigans, Chicago Conspiracy, the Black Panther cases) further destroyed the credibility of New Deal/Fair Deal liberalism. Lyndon Johnson and Hubert Humphrey were reviled as mass murderers. Many on the Left sought an alternative with Eugene McCarthy—and then experienced contempt for his ineffectual politics. Many also praised Robert Kennedy and were embittered by his death. The New Left, as Christopher Caldwell might have argued, was so bourgeois that it might advocate McCarthy one day and Marx the next; in its spontaneous, nontheoretical radicalism it was typically anarchist.

In short, the new social critics tended to become anti-institutional. The "love generation," bred in a period of prosperity and embodying a new ethic of abundance, could not accept any of the old rhetoric of either communism or the New Deal liberalism that effectively advocated the supremacy of the absolute majority. The efficient, orderly utilitarianism of the "consensus" side of liberalism—noted already by Tocqueville—was rejected for an emphasis on individual experience. The old Left had never endorsed the personalism of drugs such as marijuana; also, it had shied away from sexual experimentation and all mysticism.

This was the anarchism of the affluent young, free from the stultifying experiences of industrial workers and accustomed to immediate gratification. These were the young who would have agreed with D. H. Lawrence that the revolution should be made not for seriousness but "for fun," not for the working class but "so we can all be little aristocracies on our own."[5] While there were and continued to be urban and rural communes, consciousness-raising groups, and similar minor social efforts, the youth culture had been primarily communal in some of its symbols and ideals, but not usually in organization and practice. There was no Community party of youth culture, only an unorganized community of affection, a personalist politics of direct, simple, and natural styles of language, dress, hair, and life. For this youth culture, progress was not defined as more efficiency, more money, or more manipulation, but as a freer life. This desire for freedom was expressed in music, the underground press, guerrilla theater, and happenings.[6]

Our next logical question is, How was it possible to organize such obviously anarchist impulses? The structural forms of this increasingly self-conscious and coherent youth libertarianism were certainly found in some black power elements, with their direct action, antielectionism, and group autonomy, but most especially in the SDS (1959) and in major elements of the rightist Young Americans for Freedom (YAF, 1960). Of these last two, it was the New Left that gave the decentralism, antielitism, individualism, and sensualism of the new social critics its primary political forms. SDS was initially an agglomeration of radical democrats, assorted liberals, pacifists, and socialists aroused by inequities in race relations, income, housing, politics, and education. It rapidly became socialist in rhetoric and anarchist in practice after the Vietnam buildup in 1964 and the insufficiency of civil rights laws and "antipoverty wars" without community organizing, direct action, and a broadly socialist perspective.

This frustration with liberal politics resulted in the polarization of SDS into various decentralist and authoritarian elements. Most, however, used the centralist language of Marxism-Leninism in a sort of radical one-upmanship ("redder than thou"). In 1969, SDS ceased to be a national organization of 70–100,000 supporters and shattered into a number of sects. These consisted mainly of the Workers-Students' Alliance (Progressive Labor: Maoist), and two groups of anarchoactivists that had little ideology and claimed to be Leninists, the Revolutionary Youth Movements I and II. The last two became the Weathermen, who engaged in such street actions as "smashing the glass of the ruling class." When the Maoist-controlled SDS abandoned the group's previous anarchism, its following abandoned it.

The destruction of the open, all-inclusive SDS did not mean the destruction of either the New Left or the youth culture. Rather, new forces were liberated from now-sterile organizations and combined with other agents in society to form various "liberation" fronts for women, gays, Chicanos, and others, or added to the vigor and sophistication of research and publishing groups like the North American Congress on Latin America, Pacifica Studies Center, Concerned Asian Scholars, Union for Radical Political Economics, and the New England Free Press. Some of these groups were intellectual, some were anti-intellectual, but all were decentralized. Even those that advocated Marxism were in the awkward position of Marxism-without-a-party (Lenin would have frowned). Much of the New Left retained what Staughton Lynd had once called the spirit of Thoreau and what Carl Oglesby believed was Emersonian individualism.[7] The ego and ideas of the New Left fled from any disciplined framework.

Also in 1969, forces like those that destroyed the largest New Left party disrupted the largest association of right-wing youth, the Young Americans for Freedom. The struggle between the old, individualist Right and the new statist, anticommunist Right within YAF exploded under the cumulative pulls and pressures of the sixties. This horde of ideological furies included the Vietnam War, debates over the supposedly increasing statism of the nationalistic welfare-warfare state, a decline of any major fear of a red menace within the United States, the correct interpretation of American domestic problems, and sharp disagreements over the validity of American and European forms of conservative theory. In the New Left, the debate had been

Marx and Mao versus Joe Hill and Gene Debs. On the Right, it could have been described as Burke versus Jefferson. Despite YAF's early definition, in the Sharon Statement, as an antistatist society of liberty, it was soon dominated by the largely urban Catholic mass base that had been created by Joseph McCarthy and the anticommunism of the 1950s. This New Right tendency had earlier become more elegantly articulate with the founding of the *National Review* in 1955, a journal expressing ideas essentially opposed to the classical liberalism of the Foundation for Economic Education and its publication, the *Freeman*. The exemplars of the two groups have been nearly antithetical. The heroes of the old libertarian right were Jefferson, Paine, Garrison, Spencer, Mencken, Robert Taft, and the Herbert Spencer of today, Ayn Rand. This tradition included the Anarcho-Individualism of Spooner and Tucker from the nineteenth century. The New Right, however, admired Hamilton (seldom influential before), Burke, Bonald, some European Catholic conservatives, and other frequently foreign authoritarians. One conservative, Peter Viereck, dismissed most of the New Right theorists as "hothouse Bourbons and czarist serf-floggers." The old Right of laissez-faire, free enterprise, rugged individualism, "noninterference" abroad and civil liberties at home, had generally not accepted conscription, vast military spending, NATO, the Truman Doctrine, the Korean War (opposed by Herbert Hoover, Howard Buffett, and Joseph P. Kennedy), and the Vietnam War. The new, vehemently anticommunist Right has seldom been rooted in any major American philosophical tradition, but responded primarily with instincts similar to those found in Know-Nothingism and other "paranoias," as described by Richard Hofstadter. It represented an aggressive foreign policy, a basic acceptance of such national economic controls as wage and price restrictions and import quotas, frequent repression of civil liberties in favor of legalized moral codes, and, all around, a rather disciplinarian culture. The old Right claimed that most of this is really "un-American."[8]

During the 1969 convention, to the accompaniment of such competing chants as "Fuck the Draft"/"Kill the Commies" and "Sock it to the State"/"Sock it to the Left," YAF split into several factions. Although a few self-described libertarian conservatives continued to write for the *National Review* and to work within YAF, the decentralists who had urged the abolition of conscription, freer drug laws, sympathy for student rebels, antistatist critiques of all governments (including both the United States and the USSR), and a moderate foreign policy either were purged or seceded from YAF. Many of the rebels joined new coalitions such as the New York Libertarian Alliance and the Society for Individual Liberty. These were to be plagued by the instability of their diverse constituency, which included several varieties of Objectivists, free marketeers. Stirnerites, Spencerians, Anarcho-Communists, Anarcho-Syndicalists, and others. From this split in

YAF, and the provocative comment by a major Anarcho-Capitalist, Dr. Murray Rothbard, that whereas twenty years ago he was regarded as an extreme right-wing Republican, he was now considered an extreme New Leftist, we can see the essential validity of one Marxist evaluation: "many college kids find the transition from Republican to anarchist much less difficult than may be imagined."[9] This is true because of the middle-class, "American" character of this form of libertarianism.

The collapse of SDS and YAF, and the forces that caused their disintegration, also prompted an amazing explosion of explicitly anarchist journals. Whereas there were only four notable, or at least noticeable, American publications in 1960—the *Catholic Worker, Industrial Worker, Manas,* and *Views and Comments*—and a few others before 1969, after this date we see the emergence of several dozen.[10] Under the generally acknowledged rubric of "libertarianism," these new and explicit anarchisms differentiated themselves with such terms as Anarcho-Capitalist, Anarcho-Communist, Anarcho-Individualist, Anarcho-Marxist, autarchist, Christian Anarchist, extreme classical liberal, free enterprise utopian, individualist, libertarian conservative, natural law anarchist, Objectivist, syndicalist, voluntarist, and, one might note, other labels. Since their anarchism usually arose out of their experience of American life, not through reading and study, and since any reading would reveal that anarchism was vague and divided into a three-ring circus of factions, the anarchists inevitably disagreed about who they were, what they wanted, and how they were going to get it.

Despite this diversity, we can categorize all anarchists as essentially left-wing libertarians who champion the growth of the individual within a community (Anarcho-Communists, Christian Anarchists, and most Anarcho-Pacifists) and right-wing libertarians (Anarcho-Capitalists, and ultraindividualists) who are more egoistical and stress the individualism of the unregulated marketplace. Since the social ethic of America is not communal but is based on a private world of personal fulfillment and satisfaction (the self-made man, not social man), it is not surprising that what I call right-wing libertarianism was the predominant element of the new, explicit anarchism. Whereas the major English journals were the Anarcho-Communist *Freedom* and *Anarchy*, the main American voices were the *Individualist* and the Society for Individual Liberty. As two Englishmen commented on right-wing libertarianism in England: "In three words, there ain't much, at least in comparison with America."[11] While the explicit anarchists have been politically marginal, they are not necessarily intellectually marginal, since they represent certain vital aspects of American culture. This was recognized in the 1960s by articles in the *National Observer*, the *New York Times*, *Ramparts*, and *Playboy*, by reprints of European and American anarchist classics, and by a certain revived notoriety for the term. This prominence included the traditional and simple-minded application of it to bombings, riots, campus disorders, the failure of "gun control," new political trials under old "criminal syndicalism" and "criminal anarchism" laws, and even insipid books in praise of anarchism (as Emile Capouya said of one of them; "this twelve dollar book contains about ten cents worth of recognizable anarchism"). There was also sudden publicity for the major and often middle-aged libertarian theoreticians. Before this public attention, Dorothy Day had once lamented that "whenever the *New York Times* refers to me, it's as a 'social worker.' Pacifism and anarchism are just dismissed."[12] Beginning in the late 1960s, the principles and presence of anarchism (however defined) were more likely to get a public hearing.

CHAPTER EIGHT

OLD VISIONS OF THE NEW WORLD

When anarchism received such a hearing and was closely listened to, it was quickly apparent that its right- and left-wing manifestations were extreme exaggerations of the common "philosophical method" of liberalism. We have already seen these elements inherent in the specific responses of the indigenous right, left, and youth culture to the tensions of the 1960s. Further examination will reveal two characteristics shared by most of the critics: first, the middle-class nature of them and their audience and, second, the educational and nonviolent forms of their analysis and programs. Within these dimensions, the old Right and the New Left had many similarities; it was in many of their ultimate goals that they fundamentally differed.

It is not difficult to document the first point, that the main social component of this new social criticism was white middle-class youth. The 1960s equivalents of the petit bourgeois native anarchists of the late nineteenth century—Tucker, a bookstore owner, editor of a small newspaper, and commercial publisher, or Henry Bool, a furniture-store proprietor—were students, intellectuals, and college-trained professionals. Thus, one could often see well-dressed students, economists, historians, psychoanalysts, writers, and lawyers at Ayn Rand gatherings, and one major directory concluded that the typical semianarchist and anarchist journal was "started by a college student [who], in addition to being editor and publisher, writes most of the material. . . .Many of the libertarian periodicals are published on campus or aimed at a student audience."[1] The writers and readers for such journals were equally bourgeois. The portly Dr. Rothbard, an economics professor, and Leonard Liggio, an instructor in history, embodied the middle-class, academic form and content of most anarchist criticism. Theorists who were not formally academic, such as the late Paul Goodman (who did have a Ph.D. in English) were seldom proletarian, but were poets, novelists, essayists, or cultural commentators. Only a few renegade political intellectuals such as Karl Hess had come close to corporate power. This former business executive, speech writer, and major literary contributor to the 1960 and 1964 Republican party platforms converted traditional Republicanism into radicalism. In his mind, local control, individual liberty, and criticism of centralized power, communism, militarism, and "foreign meddling" were amplified into Anarcho-Capitalism.[2] Even the IWW and other labor-oriented groups had come to consist mainly of students, hippies, dropouts, and a few surrealists rather than of workers.[3] It should be expected, given this middle-class constituency, that anarchism has been mainly middle class in methods of socioeconomic analysis, plans for action, and, in many cases, goals.

Like bourgeois analysis generally, anarchist thought is ahistorical and non-traditional, lacking any systematic appreciation of continuity and reference to the evolution of the present from the past than can be found in both European conservatism and Marxism. The anarchists agree with Jefferson that "the earth belongs to the living" and are indifferent to the past, to most of their own heritage, and to a consideration of present problems as historical problems. Bourgeois society has only an inchoate sense of history, which is found in the small set of historical pieties that it occasionally alludes to and in such spontaneous responses to the social anxiety of the 1960s as the comprehensive reissuing of anarchist classics by Bakunin, Kropotkin, Proudhon, and all the American anarchists, with a few references to them as anticipating the modern criticism of the highly institutional society. However, while a few critics, such as Dwight Macdonald, may refer to our "anarchist tradition from Benjamin Tucker up to the Wobblies," or an Anarcho-Capitalist may assert that the basic concepts of Objectivism are found in "the writings of the nineteenth century anarchists Benjamin Tucker and Lysander Spooner," most commentators, including anarchists, will do little more than refer to this tradition.[4] The Anarcho-Capitalists, who had more of a historical sense, did occasionally cite past anarchists like Spooner and Tucker as "the forefathers of modern libertarianism," but only a few individuals like Murray Rothbard, in *Power and Market*, and some article writers were influenced by these men.[5] Most had not evolved consciously from this tradition; they had been a rather automatic product of the American environment.

The Anarcho-Capitalists *usually* ignored what they regarded as the anti-quated Anarcho-Individualism of the nineteenth century. Other libertarians offered only the most meager of generally nostalgic comments on the past, such as Paul Goodman's praise for the Articles of Confederation government, or Ayn Rand's somewhat romantic view of the beauties of nineteenth-century laissez-faire capitalism. However, the Left and the Right shared certain pieties about the past, including a common admiration for the work of Samuel Adams, Paine, and Thoreau, the antigradualism of Garrison, and the struggles of militant abolitionism. Though the Left and Right might differ somewhat on the choice of historical events or heroes, they were united by the American desire for a natural society found in the often-cited Declaration of Independence. A New Leftist would have objected to little, if anything, in this version of the Declaration by a YAF group:

Whenever any form of government becomes destructive of these ends (life, liberty and the pursuit of happiness), it is the Right of the people to alter or abolish it, and to institute new government....When a long train of abuses and usurpations (Draft, drug laws, military industrial complex, police terror, taxation, imperialism, censorship, sex laws and government), pursuing invariable the same object evinces a design to reduce [the people] under absolute despotism, it is their right, their duty, to throw off such government, and to provide *New Guards* to their future security.[6]

Both groups wished to throw off the government of the state for the government of society or voluntary organization, that is, a "participatory democracy." The radical egalitarianism and natural society perspective of the Declaration is essential to the official ideology of America. As Tucker commented in 1882, "it is probably the most 'communistic' document that ever obtained popularity among good 'law-and-order' people."[7] American social criticism is often based on the inability of American society to achieve its aspirations. The historical sense found here might be called "natural rights presentism," a vague feeling of historic commitment.

The second major bourgeois element of this analysis is its nonclass and noninstitutional approach. Unlike the explicit consciousness of European conservatives of the heritage of their class, their church, and their traditions, or the sociohistorical analysis of Marxism, the American critic talks grandly of ill-defined "exploiters" or "oppressors" and the vast "people," not the proletariat, all usually within the narrow context of specific cases rather than continuities. While some left and right anarchists have seen their origins in the rebellion of small producers, whether peasants or craftsmen, against the nation, the state, and the factory system, and may even see their own present movement as essentially middle class, they generally perceive their constituency not as mainly one class but as "discontented elements in all layers of the population."[8] In this regard it is fully representative of the non-class-conscious nature of existing American society.

In this analytical world of either indignant moralism or appeals to the natural rights of people, with its tendency to see society as personalities or groups rather than institutions, it could be predicted that such methods of analysis would produce equally personalized, atomistic concepts of organization and action. These would usually exclude such collective means as politics, in the sense of an organized party or parties, and labor unions. The problem of organization has become imperative since the collapse of the nineteenth-century libertarian belief that anarchy would be the natural product of evolution. Although a modern argument could assert that industrial evolution has made anarchy technologically possible, or that statist society will ultimately break down of its own weight, neither of these claims is likely to convince the skeptical nor to be suddenly realized. In response to their embarrassing inadequacy in fulfilling the necessity for some agency to promote anarchism, the anarchists of Left and Right resorted to makeshift schemes for alternative institutions: private schools, co-ops, day-care centers, women's centers, discussion groups, libertarian alliances, and affinity groups. Despite such activities, it was difficult even for the anarchists to believe that their emphasis on the transformation of the consciousness and life of the individual (what Robert Frost called the one-man revolution) or upon the living patterns of small groups could really be expected to overthrow the state and bring about anarchy. This basic quandary—finding and physically organizing its constituency—remained a problem for both left and right libertarians.

Since they found it a Sisyphean labor to construct an effective anarchist organization, the anarchists usually directed their primary energies into a traditional liberal enterprise: educating the public. Just as Tucker believed in "the omnipotence of truth" in the 1870s, contemporary anarchists have faith in the peaceful powers of reason rather than in insurrection. Paul Goodman was a "typical" activist who did not fight, disrupt, or violently refuse but was simply a quiet man who wrote curt letters to editors and engaged in Gestalt therapy. One of the largest Anarcho-Capitalist groups, the Society for Individual Liberty (SIL), was primarily known for its information services in literature, speakers, films, and reprints. This genteel approach, naturally enough, can evoke the support of most middle-class people. For example, John William Ward, a scholar of Jacksonian America, applauded the antistatist vision of the early anarchists, their rejection of categories for individual cases, and their repudiation of terrorism and most violence for education. It is only when this emphasis on education failed to produce any basic structural changes that some of the critics, such as the Weathermen in the late sixties, became frustrated and embittered and turned to destructive forms of direct action.[9]

But for the most part the anarchists have always concentrated their energies on producing a revolution by ideas, through magazines and meetings similar to those of Tucker and Goldman. This activity is stimulated by a belief in the vast powers of education and in the capacity of the average intellect to be rational. Such activity would be quite impossible for someone who agreed with William Graham Sumner's estimate that the common people lived perfectly instinctive lives, "just like animals." The whole bourgeois democratic ethic, revealed here in education, makes the content of such journals as the *Catholic Worker* or the *Industrial Worker* resemble the concerns and responses of the *Nation* or some other liberal publications. Thus in early 1960 the *Catholic Worker* was involved in the Sobell case, Polaris missiles, ROTC on campus, torture in Spain, walks for peace, antinuclear testing, civil rights, and civil disobedience. In 1971 the *Industrial Worker* spoke extensively on welfare rights, workers' defense, the power of the FBI, Indians, conglomerates, and women's liberation. To be sure, the *Catholic Worker* yearns for Christian Anarchism as a solution, and the *Industrial Worker* offers some kind of workers' control, but they are remarkably like the liberal press in their immediate concerns.

This emphasis on nonviolent means, whether education, meetings or actions, was common to the civil rights movement, the early New Left, most of the old Right, and, in theory, most of American society. It was the Vietnam War that politicized this pacifism for many and caused some to reject it. As Dr. Mulford Sibley has concluded, a consistent pacifism requires a radical social philosophy, probably anarchism, socialism, or communism, based upon pacifism's principles of nonviolence, limited organization, local autonomy, emphasis on the individual and small groups, and no coercion or exploitation, A number of pacifist journals have had such tendencies, such as the *Catholic Worker*, *Liberation*, *OUR GENERATION against Nuclear War*, *Peace News*, *Peacemaker*, *WIN Peace and Freedom through Nonviolent Action*, and the *War Resisters'* League Newsletter, and several anarchist groups and individuals have been explicitly pacifist.[10]

The similarities of analysis and proposed courses of action between the Left and Right libertarians once generated some hope of an alliance. Whereas the New Right, the old Left, and corporate liberalism denounced the new social criticism as impractical and excessive, or condescendingly called some of its aspects lovable but absurd, its "leaders" and membership occasionally considered some form of cooperation between the individualists and the communalists. Carl Oglesby, once head of SDS, was aware of the resemblances between the old Right and the New Left that caused a YAF chapter at the University of Kansas to become an SDS chapter, or a YAF leader in 1966 to speculate on the possibilities for a "genuine rapport between the libertarian Right and the New Left." Rothbard had early claimed that the terms Left and Right were becoming "increasingly obsolescent" and acted on this theory by editing a journal entitled *Left and Right*, joining the coalition Peace and Freedom Party in 1968 and speaking at coalition meetings such as the 1970 Festival of Liberation in California, which in-

cluded such commentators as Paul Goodman, LeFevre, and the right-wing
psychoanalyst Thomas Szasz. Other right libertarians published in left journals, such as Leonard Liggio as an associate editor of *Leviathan* and contributor to the *Liberated Guardian*, and there was some collaboration between various journals.[11]

The factions could unite under the individualistic demand for an end to
all regimentation and coercion, to be replaced with every person running his
or her own life (much like Tucker's hope of "every man his own government"), variously termed "participatory democracy" or laissez-faire.
Within this goal, the Left and Right could work on tax and draft resistance,
black liberation, radical government decentralization, anti-imperialism,
antirepression, and an ultimate society based on voluntary association.
However, though the two factions might equally denounce the present
"neo-fascist state" (a remark by YAF leader Anderson) and might seem
analogous in their activities, there were severe disagreements over the questions of private property and the laissez-faire capitalist system. The individualist right consisted essentially of "radical capitalists" (the MIT group
called itself Rad Caps), who were antimonopolist but certainly not anti-
business. The Right could not accept such aspects of the New Left as the end
to private property, which they saw as the basis for individual liberty; the SIL
letterhead makes the stark declaration: "Life, Liberty and Property; One
and Indivisible." Nor would the Right tolerate an end to the wage system,
buying and selling, and the roles of employer and employed. The Right
demanded, as had Tucker, only a "fair wage" for labor (without accepting
his labor theory of value), competition, and hierarchical social and economic
relations. Compared with New Left individualism, there was a harshly
possessive, antisocial quality here, illustrated by one of Rand's heroes
dynamiting a public housing project because it wasn't built precisely to his
specifications, or by Rand's expressions on "the virtue of selfishness."[12]

These were not merely differences among the life-styles of the new
radicals. The drugs, sex, literature, and dress of the Left represented a more
thoroughly humanist and utopian socialist vision than that of the Right. The
leftist search was for a multiracial, culturally pluralist, bisexual community
of affection, consisting not of capitalist competitors but of brothers and
sisters. The Anarcho-Capitalists more fully incorporated the bourgeois personality and culture: the interiorization of repression ("self-restraint," "the
one-dimensional man"), the total destruction of the extended family, an
emphasis on the production and consumption of goods rather than the
humanist enrichment of life, and a negative concept of liberty solely as
freedom from compulsion. These contrasting definitions of the content of
absolute liberty were reflected in the choice of historical and contemporary
allies. The Anarcho-Capitalists looked back to the old traditions of classical
liberalism, hoped that YAF and Objectivism would continue to exist as

bridges to "the freedom philosophy," and some even suggested an alliance with the radical Right, "many of whom are populist, isolationist, anti-monopoly, and hate the 'communist' US government."[13] The New Leftists, on the other hand, generally admired such historical activists as John Brown or William Lloyd Garrison, saw little systematic American tradition with which they could identify, and felt an immediate empathy with the struggles of oppressed black and white peoples at home and with the socialist and national liberation movements, especially of the Third World.

We may justifiably conclude from this overview of how some explicit anarchists looked at the world, what flaws they saw, their proposals for change, and their manner of attempting change that anarchist criticism was not some temporary youth fad but an integral element of American culture that will remain as long as the United States is a liberal, middle-class society. The desire for freedom from government restraint, often to gratify one's own immediate desire with little operative concern for the long-term common good, is primarily a "bourgeois ego trip" in its faulty analysis, failure to define and organize its own social base, and inability to provide the effective means for the achievement of its ideals. Still, it must be acknowledged that this anarchism can be considered one plausible culmination of Enlightenment and Protestant traditions of individualism, democracy, and personalized humanism. The same spontaneous criticisms have occurred among dissatisified Americans in the past: witness Populist indignation at bigness, the Individualist Anarchists' disgust at the incomplete application of Spencerian liberalism, the revulsion of the immigrants Berkman and Goldman against the inadequate realization of American mythology, anarchist and classical liberal criticisms of the Philippine Insurrection resembling those directed against Vietnam, or the similarities between the direct action, stirring songs, and decentralized organization of the IWW and the civil rights movement. We should not disregard the perennial flowering of such criticisms of power and idealistic demands for a personal politics of individual fulfillment simply because (as Karl Hess remarked) the petals appear to be red and black instead of formally red, white, and blue.

In the future, it seems reasonable to assume that, just as the demands of corporate capitalism have transformed classical liberalism and the old Right, explicit anarchism may also undergo a metamorphosis. By 1970 the "conservative" Nixon had requested huge government subsidies for railroads and aircraft companies, manipulated interest rates, and imposed wage and price controls. Hubert Humphrey, Lyndon B. Johnson, Nixon, and William Buckley all agreed that modified, non-laissez-faire capitalism was basically sound and needed only secondary reforms. To respond to this intensifying institutionalization of advanced capital, anarchism should also develop more corporate forms of perspective, as it partially did with the Anarcho-Syndicalism of Hess or the Anarcho-Communism of Bookchin and the

Match. But, by and large, the conscious anarchists of the early 1970s were still well described by Emerson's 1867 discussion of the party of the future: they, also, were "fanatics in freedom: they hated tolls, taxes, turnpikes, banks, hierarchies, governors, yea, almost laws."[14]

Even if these forms of anarchism became more coherent, it is unlikely that any of them could offer more than a symbolic threat to the American state, rather like the anarchist Beat candidate for president in 1960, or the Yippies' "festival of life" countering the "Demo convention of death" in 1968.[15] However, though anarchy may never succeed as anarchy, it is still valuable as a general critique of the failures and myths of official liberal society, providing, in some cases, workable alterations, though not alternatives. The most widely known anarchist was the late Paul Goodman, who was an improvisor, a pragmatist, an inspirer—perhaps, one should say, a utopian liberal. He once described himself as a "conservative anarchist" because of the fundamental practicality of his proposals and was primarily criticized by other intellectuals for the extreme idealism of his systematically rational projects.[16]

The new criticism of the 1960s was partially ignored, and the rest was either absorbed by reforms or dissipated by repression, constituting the dominant liberal pastiche of candy and coercion. On these two aspects, Dr. Dubofsky has said that the young radicals could have prepared for their future by studying the rise and effective demise of the IWW. Another commentator, Irwin Silber, has noted that the cultural revolution of the young often provided no more than a sensualism that debilitated the will of its practitioners for the harder labor of radical social change or created new gimmicks for patching up capitalism. "Think of the way in which the American Left, no matter what its intent, has performed the socially useful task of engendering the ideas and agitation for very useful social reforms (social security, unemployment insurance, etc.) which have become a cornerstone of the capitalist state.[17] This has been the principal function of the American Left to the American middle class. It essentially develops elaborate expositions of many bourgeois values—while zealously proclaiming itself to be antibourgeois—and the bourgeoisie may finally act, usually constructively and minimally, when the disparity between the real and the ideal becomes too discomforting.

It is true that the ambiguously anarchistic tendencies of middle-class America are seldom expressed in the complete conclusions of formal anarchism. Tocqueville saw "anarchy" as the extreme of freedom that counterposed the extreme of servitude; neither extreme is attained, each is the antidote of the other. The average, practical American, though generally not an admirer of the state, would probably agree with George Bernard Shaw that the state is "like bad weather in winter.... When we have done our best in the way of overcoats, umbrellas, and good fires, we have to put up with the winter; so, when we have done our best in the way of Democracy, decentralization, and the like, we must put up with the State.''[18] But in the mind of that person, and certainly in the minds of other thinking people, there may be the vague, undefined vision of the spring of anarchy.

CHAPTER NINE

THE FUTURE OF THE RADICAL PAST

Nor for the past alone—
for meanings to the future.
  —Walt Whitman

Shall we conclude with a worldly sigh that the more things change the more they remain the same? The historian often creates this impression by exhaustively cataloging his information within certain traditions. But the patterns of the past are not some inescapable iron cage. History also instructs us that new conditions may present new opportunities or dangers that can transform or replace old principles and practices. While there have been thematic continuities, distinctive traits, and continuing predicaments in our indigenous radicalism, there are no simple formulas of repetition. What cultural projections can be made, then, by a daring, or perhaps foolish, historian?

The essential nature of American protest, in the likely future, will continue to be profoundly influenced and shaped by religion, environment, and capitalism. Of these, religion has demonstrated an unexpectedly hardy persistence, given the common assumption of intellectuals that God would wither away in the modern scientific world. Instead, by the late 1970s the percentage of adults attending church was higher in the United States than in any other Western nation. A 1977 publication by Gallup, *Religion in America*, noted that 42 percent of adults went to a church or synagogue in an average week, seven out of ten called themselves church members, six out of ten said that religion was ''very important in their lives,'' and many believed that religion would expand its influence in the coming decade. In fact, church membership and attendance began an upturn after nearly two decades of decline. While Catholicism was less successful—with 55 percent of Catholics attending services in 1976 compared with 71 percent in 1964, it remained true that in America Catholicism, like other faiths, was far stronger than in Europe or Latin America, where a typical Catholic might only be baptized, married, and buried in the church. Despite these institutional affiliations, however, Tillich's characterization of Americans as "nominalists by birth" probably remained true: American theologies (as formal systems) continued to be underdeveloped, dogmatism had been severely challenged by ecumenism (the democratic revolution in religion), and the "ultimate power" for most religions was not the theological schools or church headquarters but the local congregation.

But institutional health—Churchianity—cannot be used as the sole measure of the powers of religion. It must not be forgotten that many of the 96 percent of the population that defined themselves as religious were members of no institutional church. Indeed, the end of the 1970s was especially marked by the dramatic emergence of experiential and noninstitutionalized forms of religion. Gallup concluded that one out of eight Americans was attracted to various forms of mysticism (like Transcendental Meditation) or aspects of the "human potential movement" (including biofeedback techniques or encounter sessions). Many of these free spirits seemed to regard the organized churches as repressive institutions and echoed the themes of the Transcendentalists for simple religion (whether of Jesus or Buddha), nature (back to the land), small society, limited technology, "feeling" rather than reason, and spontaneity instead of convention.

Thus religion, in every sense, maintains a major and even pervasive influence in our culture, expressed through churches, the banalities of United States presidents, the ethical fervor of reform activities, the moralizing of columnists, some of the indignation of the State Department, or the opinions of the average person on the street.

In 1976 this living tradition was most startlingly manifested—for Europeans—by the political campaign of a "twice-born" Baptist, Jimmy Carter. Foreigners were frequently disturbed that an evangelical Christian whose sister was a faith healer could be a serious candidate for the leadership of a vital nation of the industrial West. Many Americans, however, were searching for a moral revival after the debacle of Watergate. The career of Richard Nixon had glaringly highlighted the flaws in our moral rhetoric, both in the disjunction between his words and his actions (the seamier side of this heritage) and in some of the principled criticism of him, reaffirming that all people are moral agents responsible for their actions, that no one is above the law. The ethical condemnation of Nixon contributed to the crumbling of his defenses of legitimacy and his flight in disgrace. Nevertheless, that such an episode could occur was unsettling. For large numbers, the evangelical immediacy of Carter's promises ("I'd never lie to you"), his somber sincerity, and his "attacks on Washington" for its corruption and insenstivity to human needs were deeply attractive.

Other idealists, however, were dismayed by the vagueness of his comments and programs, especially members of strong institutional faiths, such as Catholicism, or religions with a strong sense of historical continuity, like Judaism. As one Catholic writer observed:

His attacks on Washington are in striking correspondence with the roots of the historical evangelical movement, with its deep distrust of and frequent attacks on the hierarchy of the church. Washington has become the Babylon of Carter rhetoric and the bureaucracy the agency of the Antichrist....He faces the problem that Catholicism stands, at least to some degree, in opposition to his distrust of institutions. Mr. Carter has not yet achieved a St. Francis' understanding of the role of hierarchy in the Church, and he has little understanding, either, of the traditional Catholic view of the nature of the Church.[1]

It was also paradoxically true that this evangelical Christian later became the chief administrator of an enormous bureaucracy, with powers extending throughout the world, an anomaly rather like combining the functions of oracle and accountant, or like Isaiah, after castigating the mighty of the earth, becoming king. Yet in America it happens.

Once elected, Carter appealed to the spiritual imagination of America. He proclaimed in his inaugural address that human rights ought to be absolute and created a foreign policy that emphasized universal human rights, not the power politics or game theory that many believed had characterized the Nixon-Kissinger years. Whereas the Russian representative to the United Nations Commission on Human Rights was Valerin Zorin, prominent in justifying the invasion of Czechoslovakia, Carter appointed a militant liberal, Allard Lowenstein. A vociferous critic of American foreign policy in the 1960s and early 1970s, Lowenstein had achieved the noble rank of seventh on Nixon's list of enemies. Unlike Zorin, who was an apologist for everything his country had ever done, Lowenstein could admit errors and imperfections, while legitimately arguing that he had always personally upheld the ideals of justice above the mere preservation of order. It was unimaginable that the Russian or Chinese governments would have appointed such an independent-minded critic to represent them.

American radicals, however, have generally responded to such idealism with unmitigated contempt. Just as Watergate was seldom reported in the racical press until the later stages (it was, after all, a predictable illustration of capitalist depravity and decline), moral pronouncements of the United States government are scornfully dismissed without any significant attempt to praise their positive aspects, insist upon the realization of official goals, or demand consistency. Even though government claims may be hypocritical, pretentious, or chauvinist, American radicals have confused a realistic analysis of them with cynicism. Foreign policy is simply added to the monotonous litany of crimes, exposés, and denunciations that fill the radical press, with seldom one constructive word. This depressing chronicle has never inspired the enthusiastic allegiance of Americans. Although such criticisms may be motivated by high ideals, they are frequently unrelated to common beliefs and are even less often positively expressed.

Any radical movement, to be popular in the United States, must draw upon the biblical language of rebirth, liberation, purification, and dignity. Martin Luther King, Jr., spoke of "the blessed community" to be achieved by "truth force" and "love force." It was such appeals to conscience that explained much of the power of King, the antiwar movement of the 1960s, various battles for civil rights, the aura of Robert Kennedy, and support for Cesar Chavez of the United Farm Workers. American radicals have often acted as prophets or (in Daniel Aaron's phrase) "men of good hope," but modern concern for "scientific socialism" and realistic radicalism have suppressed these calls for spiritual fulfillment, which ironically shrinks the definition of radicalism to the virtually capitalist value of the widest possible consumption. This is an arid utilitarianism compared with the vision of a just society, based upon the reverence for each person's life that is still a deeply rooted faith among us and one source of reform awakenings and conversions to activism.[2]

The second factor—environment—may have abruptly changed by the late 1970s. America began as a utopia for those in search of God or gold. As John Locke crystallized the image of Eden: "In the beginning, all the world was America."[3] Many settlers were attracted by the chance for a new beginning, financial or spiritual or both. "America was promises"—here were rich potentialities for a truly "new world" away from "the dead kings and remembered sepulchres."[4]

This environment insured some freedom, opportunity, and diversity. John Cotton could honestly justify the expulsion of dissenters from Puritan Boston with the claim that, given the immensity of the land, banishment was not confinement but enlargement, freeing the individual from what he or she regarded as "the burden and bondage" of social rules.[5] Space was a solution to many social problems. Americans have often feared the end of this frontier solution, whether it was the barrier of the mountains in colonial days, the Great American Desert in the mid-1800s, or the officially announced "end of the frontier" in the 1890s. For all of its history, the United States has been an expanding society.

This American frontier is not yet physically exhausted. It is true that, after three and a half centuries of settlement and struggle, America is now a land of fences rather than open spaces, filled with hundreds of millions of citizens. If Thoreau looked to Oregon today, he would see mighty dams on his flowing rivers and growing cities in his forests. But, compared with much of Europe, Asia, Latin America, and Africa, America is still distinctive for having so many places—as Gertrude Stein once said—where nothing is rather than something is. We remain an unusually nomadic people; almost half our population changes residence each five years. While many do not go more than five miles, during 1970–76 almost 1.5 million established new homes in Florida, and more than 400,000 each went to California and Texas.[6] Intellectually, Americans also cherish the ideal of openness, expressed in the New Frontier (now a state of mind rather than a region) and in the official inaugural book for Jimmy Carter: *A New Spirit: A New Commitment; A New America.*[7]

Although land is unlikely to be an immediate problem, the limitation of resources could be a severe shock to our way of life. In the early 1970s we continued the squandering of the earth we have indulged in for centuries. We drove weighty gas-and-oil-guzzling cars (the average European car weighed 2,700 pounds; the average American car, 4,100 pounds); we lived in overheated houses, unlike people in other countries, who kept warm in the winter primarily by wearing more clothing; we worked in monstrous buildings without natural ventilation (requiring energy both to heat and to cool); we bought ''necessities'' that most of the world considered luxuries; we threw away hundreds of millions of bottles, cans, newspapers, and magazines, thoughtless of the possibilities of recycling; we flew in half-empty planes; and we fed our pets a diet better than that of half the world's people. Americans have been called the spoiled children of the Western world, living in a throwaway society of convenience foods, household gadgets, fancy wrappers, nonreturnable bottles, and other waste. We have adopted a creed like that of the Great Gatsby, who ''believed in the green light, the orgiastic future.'' But by the late 1970s the green light may have turned yellow. President Carter, in his energy message of 21 April 1977, gave notice that Americans could be expelled from the Eden of cheap energy, that ecology was not a pastime limited to bird watchers, backpackers, and similar exotics. After his speech to Congress, which was greeted with polite silence, broken by several restrained handclaps, the members got into their wastefully inefficient limousines and were driven away. But this is a problem that cannot be driven away from; a day of reckoning is inevitable for the consumptionist habits of Americans. The stripped, plundered, and decimated earth cannot bear our present technology and standard of living. As Mahatma Gandhi once remarked: ''The earth provides for every man's need, but not for every man's greed.''[8]

Our history of expansion has not prepared us for a sense of limitation, whether of spaces or resources. We are accustomed not to living with problems but to solving them (through reason, money, technology, or force) or, sometimes, evading them. The room for these options is shrinking, as the conservation of natural wealth, urbanization, and the rise of socialism abroad may inevitably end the epoch of unrestrained American appetites. If so, what effect would this have on the "possessive individualism" so common among Americans?

Perhaps one response was found in the 1976 enthusiasm for a tune called "Convoy." This song, which described a thousand-truck convoy speeding through toll booths, breaking laws, and evading the police, was part of a fad glorifying truckers as an independent people with a "cowboy-like freedom."[9] Will there be a cultural lag before values catch up to socioeconomic realities, or will the old values force some modification of those realities? An attack on basic living standards could, of course, produce social convulsions. Would a society of scarcity, of limitations, lead to frustration and rebellion? Would radicalism be reflected in outbursts of individualism or in new collective forms of consciousness? What would optimism and progress mean if not "more and better"? One barrier to radicalism has been our passive belief in progress—that the past has seen improvement and so will the future. Can this faith in the furture survive? Clearly, the new world garden may no longer be a sanctuary for American innocence.

Paradise has not been lost, however, for American capitalism. Compared with that of any other nation, the United States business civilization has uniquely comprehensive foundations in raw materials, capital, labor force, and markets. The influence of this capitalism is everywhere in our culture. On one hand, it fosters an American narcissism of private property: my home, my wife or husband, my children (Robert Owen called the bourgeois family a den of selfishness), my property, my needs, and my career. Yet it also produces a kind of self-denigration. The worker in a factory or an office is specialized in a few tasks, has little or no voice in decision-making, is competing with others (it's every man for himself and, now, every woman for herself), seldom perceives his or her role in a larger context, and knows little about the final product. Both of these aspects are further enhanced by job mobility and insecurity; during 1965–70, one out of three workers changed jobs, a phenomenal rate compared with that of Japan, Sweden, England, France, the USSR, or any other industrialized nation.[10] The cumulative effect is to discourage collective consciousness, while at the same time reducing the individual to a standardized unit in homogenized mass production, mass society, mass culture. In brief, "the lonely crowd."

There are many ways that social discipline is now maintained essentially by self-discipline (ideology rather than the police). Those employed, for example, usually see themselves as "earning their way" in society, or "paying their dues," and contrast their productivity and independence with the parasitic state dependence of those who are on welfare. There is no basic sense of solidarity with other common people. While American public assistance programs are less extensive and generous than those of Europe, our population is generally more hostile toward the poor, viewing them as a separate group rather than as part of "the public" and condemning them as personally responsible for their plight. As citizens of the richest country in the world, we apparently resent those who, presumably, have failed to realize their opportunities. Our "welfare crisis," then, is in many ways ideological rather than financial.

George McGovern discovered this in 1972 when he essentially proposed a minimum income to replace welfare payments and was greeted with vehement opposition. The majority clearly favored Richard Nixon's motto of "workfare, not welfare" and his plea during the 1972 inaugural address that "in our lives, let each of us ask not just what will government do for me, but what can I do for myself?" As a foreign writer observed: "In Britain, an increase in public assistance is likely to be taken as an indication that something is wrong with the other policies of the welfare state. A rise in the welfare rolls in America denotes that something is wrong with the recipients."[11]

While the employed worker frequently considers himself superior to those on welfare, he often recognizes the limits of his own independence. The worker is forced to a *partial* knowledge of collectivity by constant reminders of his or her limitations in an office, factory, or government job. The individual may also be constrained by his union, which has its own institutional dues and disciplines. Few can dream of "escaping" to become their own employers in an economy that is tending toward oligopoly. In 1975, two hundred corporations controlled two-thirds of the manufacturing output of the United States, and the income of General Motors alone was greater than the gross national product of most of the nations of the world. All these limitations on typical people may, however, be resented.[12]

Frustrations have been partially relieved, and egoism has been gratified, by consumerism. So far, the general successes of capitalism have reduced tensions in the past and nurtured individual hopes for a better life in the future. American abundance has been a surrogate for socialism, focusing our attention on what William Dean Howells called "the smiling aspects of life." In 1977, the United States with 6 percent of the world's population, possessed half the world's wealth, consumed about 60 percent of the world's yearly mineral production, and used one-third of the world's energy, at the same time that 25 percent of its industrial capacity remained idle. Our consumption of energy has been doubling every ten years since 1945. This dynamic of our civilization negates most attempts at conservation and restriction.

Courtesy of Community Press Features

Instead, the individual consumer is constantly urged to buy, to eat, to wear. Instant credit underwrites a "have-it-now" ethic of self-seeking and self-gratification, making us children of egoism rather than restraint. We are further bound to capitalism by long-term installment payments and mortgages. Marx was not thinking of these chains when he announced that this was all the workers had to lose by rebellion! Explicit radicals are likely to be feared as threats to *our* property, whether our homes, our cars, or our savings. Even a strike might endanger the individual's entire accumulated aspirations. Collective organizations, such as trade unions, have further strengthened our bondage to the individualism of consumption, with George Meaney and other labor leaders praising "our American capitalistic system."[13] Capitalism, then, appears to us as a society of choice, quite unlike the regimentation of existing socialist cultures. It has meant that we live longer, in more comfortable housing, with a more satisfying diet and superior entertainment. We naturally view the market as freedom and the consumer virtually as Emerson's "imperial self."

The emergence of the welfare state has often reinforced, rather than restricted, this egoism. Central planning can support individualism: tax write-offs for individual homes, road-building schemes that favor personal transportation, private retirement funds, and expansion of credit. Even Social Security is premised on individual contributions rather than an outright grant by the state. Although Social Security taxes are fantastically regressive, falling heavily upon those least able to pay, there is little, if any, debate on their validity. They are passively assumed to be just. And although the government bureaucracy has grown, to administer pensions and other programs, public respect for government has not.

But by the late 1970s it was possible that capitalism might no longer be able to balance these contradictions. An expanding society could build on credit, youth, and the future, but what happens when opportunities shrink, debts must be paid, the median age changes from twenty-eight in 1970 to a projected forty in 2030 (with fifty-two million on Social Security), and when what has been defined as progress (such as more and more cars) might no longer be feasible or even desirable? In 1977 millions had exhausted their unemployment benefits, the jobless rate was 20 percent among those sixteen to nineteen years old, and 50 percent among black teenagers. In a highly technological society, what jobs would there be for "common labor"? There might even be a "human surplus" of highly skilled workers. These people, in a society based on an ethic of success, could be social dynamite. The historian Carl Degler has accurately concluded that so long as Americans can believe in Horatio Alger, Karl Marx will be "just another German philosopher." Has Horatio Alger finally declined into a feeble old age?[14]

But the systematic teachings of Marx will be an unlikely replacement. Most existing models of Marxian socialism also assume that whatever expands the productive capacity of a society is progressive, and they inculcate a "communist attitude" toward work that is a functional equivalent to the role the Puritan work ethic played in motivating and disciplining significant elements of our population. Today, in American society, the basic issue is not more production. Material accumulation is widespread enough so that we could now discuss distribution of what exists and the quality of present and future life. More people are likely to ask "why sacrifice enjoying myself now by yoking myself to a mortgage or other obligations?" In the early 1970s, less than one-third of the population agreed that they could easily accept being "bossed around."[15] Furthermore, the reliance of conventional Marxism upon state solutions is incompatible with basic elements of this culture.

When conflicts between American ideology and reality have stimulated demands for action, our anarchist suspicion of formal orthodoxies and institutionalized power contributes to inaction and confusion. If government does grow, this is seldom regarded as a healthy sign of public service but is seen as a cause of concern, like cancer. The disjuncture between the real power of the American government and the public's interpretation of it is becoming severe. On one hand, there is the reality that state and federal expenditures account for almost 40 percent of the GNP, that government employs two-fifths of all professional, technical, and related workers (and indirectly employs many more), owns 760,000,000 acres of land and 405,000 buildings, and rents 54,000 more structures. Few Americans repudiate most of the functions of this government, including unemployment insurance, Social Security, food stamps, Medicare, relief, and a host of other benefits. There are further imperatives for the state to become a comprehensive planner (foul air, impure water, inadequate housing, urban decay, unemployment, and others).

At the same time, American life resounds with criticism of government, despite the fact that American tax rates are far lower than those of Europe. Americans generally agree with Shelley's sentiment that politics is "a desolating pestilence" or the anarchist comment that politics is the science of theft. Freedom is still generally interpreted as freedom from government, and communal controls and restraints are more resented in America than, let us say, Great Britain, where there is "much greater public trust of government," more respect for politicians, and "a greater willingness to believe in the probity of government however disagreeable its actual policies."[16]

Here, the exposés concerning Watergate, the CIA, the FBI, and other agencies, along with the excesses of the so-called imperial presidency, seemed to intensify the antipolitical opinion that was so eloquently expressed by Thomas Paine two centuries ago: "Society in every state is a blessing, but Government, even in its best, is but a necessary evil; in its worst state, an intolerable one.''[17] Leaders have adapted to this suspicion of parasitism and to Americans' hostility toward clear expressions of authority by participating in an elaborate etiquette of deference. President Eisenhower, in the 1950s, proudly stated that he was ''no politician,'' and, more recently, both President Ford and President Carter have presented folksy images. It has been good politics to deny being a politician. Every major presidential candidate in 1976 agreed that the federal bureaucracy had become incomprehensibly large, inefficient, and excessive. Candidates for other offices have sometimes appealed to this resentment, such as Senator Harry Byrd placing a copy of the federal budget on a block and chopping at it with an ax.

The public response to these problems has been less vigorous, often being restricted to querulous complaints, apathetic participation, or just ''dropping out.'' For many, politics has become a spectator sport. They have said: ''There's little use in writing to public officials because they aren't really interested in the problems of the average man,'' and ''people like me don't have any say about what the government does.''[18] Why vote? In the 1972 presidential election, George McGovern received 22 percent of the eligible votes, Richard Nixon received 33 percent, and 45 percent abstained. A 1972 Harris Poll rated public confidence in the leadership of Congress at 21 percent; in 1976, a *Time* magazine survey gave Congress an overall positive rating of 27 percent and the executive 13 percent. In the presidential election of 1976, 40 percent of the possible voters were not affiliated with either of the major parties, and the actual voters were the smallest percentage of those eligible in twenty-eight years. Although the new addition of eighteen-year-old voters must be mentioned, it remains true that *much* of the population has a general lack of interest, if not diffuse hostility, toward the expense, irrelevant programs, and alleged incompetence of existing politics. In one survey, 66 percent of those who had gone to the polls doubted that their vote had any significance.

This alienation creates strains in the functioning of democratic political institutions. Jimmy Carter, for example, was elected by many of the people who were most disenchanted with conventional politics: large numbers of youths, blacks, the poor, women, blue-collar workers, and critical liberals. Lou Harris, the pollster, recorded the common responses of these people: ''We don't count''; ''most people with power try to take advantage of you''; ''Washington is out of touch''; and ''we are left out of things.''[19] In the past it has been easier for the institutions to ignore such original supporters than to satisfy their needs. This, however, must further increase their cynicism, despair, and, perhaps, anger.

Pessimism about the powerful is not limited to politics. In business, two studies conducted during 1975–76 found majorities for ''employee control of United States corporations.''[20] Wildcat strikes were steadily increasing, and many workers harbored violent grievances against union bureaucrats as well as company managers.[21] While "law and order" was lauded during most of the 1960s and 1970s, the law as an abstraction was more respected than were the courts or the police as institutional enforcers. Even television programs with policemen as heroes were notorious for their physical violence, reckless car chases, and macho stars rather than for the solemn majesty of justice. As this book has argued, these spontaneous feelings can be called traditional.

In such a confused, uncertain era, basic political terms like conservative, liberal, and radical are difficult to define. When NBC claimed that the majority of Americans labeled themselves "conservative" in 1976, one exasperated analyst refused to accept the term: "In today's muddied political vocabulary, the nearest definition of conservative, in the popular mind, probably is 'anti-government, or anti-politician.' "[22] Despite such an appropriate caveat, let us be bold enough to return to our categories of liberal critics, right libertarians, left libertarians, and statist radicals. Although American radicalism, like American religion, is divided into myriad sects and movements, there are still major denominations.

In the late 1970s, as before, much of American criticism was a hopeful extension of liberalism or an angry rejection of it. Proponents continued to uphold a "bargaining society" where the politician negotiated alliances of special interest groups, often in single-issue coalitions, for the promotion of social equality and economic progress.[23] Just as American liberals had once feared the undemocratic, unresponsive authority of the Federalists, the "slave power" and the "predatory" robber barons of the late nineteenth century, modern crusaders like Ralph Nader or Senator Gaylord Nelson attacked Exxon, General Motors, IBM, and the military-industrial complex. While they recognized that the tycoon of the past had irreversibly become a team player, they condemned these combinations as threats to "free enterprise." In Nelson's words: "Americans, ever suspicious of concentrated political power, have permitted concentrations of economic power to develop, substantially unchallenged, that would make a Roman emperor gasp."[24]

But these liberals are vulnerable, both within their own consciences and within their constituencies, to the obvious charge that the utopian ideals of life, liberty, and the pursuit of happiness have remained unfulfilled promises for millions, and that the future might be one of stagnation and regression rather than future liberation. American idealism feeds both liberalism and its opponents by educating us for hope and disappointment. Imagine a ghetto black listening to the proposals of the War on Poverty and the Great Society, watching glamorous ads on television, hearing commercial hucksters on radio—What do all the expectations finally produce? The reality is likely to be unemployment, poverty, crime, drugs, welfare, and a bleak tomorrow. Yet our history, during this century alone, has seen a Square Deal, a New Deal, a Fair Deal, a New Frontier, and a Great Society.

Such attempts to institutionalize our ideals cannot avoid another danger-ous contradiction. While reform movements have contributed to Tocque-ville's "irresistible revolution" toward equality, they have also built up cen-tralized bureaucracies that have drawn a fusilade of criticism for elitist ar-rogance or, at the very least, undemocratic indifference. When Elliot Richardson, a liberal Republican, resigned as director of Health, Education, and Welfare in the early 1970s, he made the astonishingly radical criticism that "the legislative process has become a cruel shell game, and the service system has become a bureaucratic maze, incomprehensible, and inacces-sible."[25] We are caught in an impossible ideal: we want a society that in-sures equality but does not "interfere" with our own lives; a welfare state that "provides a sense of community without really bothering anybody." And our insistence can have a disintegrating effect on government by foster-ing "a pitiful disregard for implementation, incoherent administration and unrealistic expectations."[26]

This profound dilemma is still a fundamental element of American liber-alism. While the 1970s saw reaffirmations of corporate liberalism, which emphasized government regulation of business—such as Nader's call for "taming the giant corporations" with an employee bill of rights—the period was more significant for the emergence of people who called them-selves "new liberals" or populists. They stressed voluntarism rather than regulation, individual action in place of state intervention. Some were like echoes from an earlier stage of history, such as ex-Senator Fred Harris, who emphasized old-fashioned trust-busting to create greater opportunities for little people, local activism, and volunteer projects. This drew upon a rich heritage. Tocqueville, for example, was one of the first to realize the unique role of voluntary committees and local initiative in our culture, which, he said, constituted "a mighty third force" that was separate from both the state and business. During 1973–74, an estimated 37,000,000 persons volunteered for various activities, donating $14,000,000,000 worth of free labor. American philanthropy, which involves millions of donors, is also famous.[27]

While many of these models were rooted in the past, most of the new liberals were not champions of laissez-faire, "populism," or New Deal social engineering. This group, responding to the apparent limits of recent capitalism and public irritation with big government, combined an earlier pessimism about government spending and regulation with a concern for the preservation of natural resources. Such politicians as governors Brown of California, Carey of New York, Dukakis of Massachusetts, Grasso of Con-necticut, and Byrne of New Jersey spoke of reduced government functions, self-help, efficiency, a plain life, welfare as charity, not right, "austerity" in state expenses and (perhaps) stable or reduced taxes. As Brown expressed this: We must adopt a "politics of lowered expectations" suitable for "an era of limits." Finally, even the president, usually the prophet of American optimism, asserted in his inaugural address that "more is not necessarily better" and that "even our nation has its recognized limits." While this sober realism was profoundly subversive of the American dream of ever-higher standards of living and security, this politics seemed to satisfy most of the public and the corporations. As Governor Dukakis promised: "We're starting to run this state as a business, because we want to keep your business."[28]

This new liberalism, with its critique of big government and (more delicately) big business, had some charm for moderate libertarians of both the Right and the Left. In 1976, for example, the former leader of SDS, Tom Hayden, praised Harris and Brown and announced that "the radicalism of the '60's is the common sense of the '70's." Many right libertarians also felt a certain identification with the new liberalism, which was sometimes reciprocated. Thus, Governor Brown of California was one of the admirers of E. F. Schumacher, whose book *Small Is Beautiful* sold over one million copies by the late seventies. Schumacher's religious appeals, emphasis on technology rather than politics, criticism of bureaucracies, and pleas for individual self-criticism and action were extremely attractive to many Americans. He further endeared himself by asserting that he was not a radical but was merely seeking to recapture the past, with its simpler life of small ownership and community responsibility.[29]

But whereas the new liberals and the moderate libertarians may have deplored much of centralized authority, the new indigenous radicals, of both the Left and the Right, have tended to reject it. Such radicals generally agreed with Theodore Roszak that "politics is the organization of power, and power is the enemy of life." Since the most obvious form of organized power is the state, all libertarians share an absolute skepticism about its functions. As a right libertarian book summarized these doubts, shared by the Left:

An increasing number of people are beginning to suspect that government actions are the cause of our social ills. . . . Nearly everyone is against *some* governmental actions, and an increasing number want to cut the size of government. . . . There are even a few who have come to believe that it is not just *certain* governmental activities, nor even the size of the government, but *the very existence of government* which is causing the problems.[30]

As an alternative to government, right libertarians continue to present "the doctrine of self-interest," or "enlightened egoism," that Tocqueville perceived in American culture. Competition in a free market would presumably create temperate, cautious, and (again, in Tocqueville's words) "self-controlled" citizens.[31] Right libertarians, or radical capitalists—as Ayn

Rand once called herself—glorify a kind of utopian individualism. They exaggerate our understanding of people as units of production, with those who are on welfare, poor, or retired commonly regarded as less valuable members of society.

These right libertarians continue to range from decentralists who propose education vouchers as a substitute for compulsory education, and the trust-busting of multinational corporations, to Anarcho-Capitalists. In 1976 most of the less fanatical supported the Libertarian party, which polled 183,000 votes, making it the largest third party, surpassing the combined totals for the Communist party, Socialist Workers' party, Socialist party, and Socialist Labor party (although Eugene McCarthy, who ran as an independent, exceeded this number). The Libertarian party, founded in 1971, proposed to "legalize freedom" and "get government off our backs" by some of the following actions:

Greatly reduce the size, power and expense of government.
End government prying into citizens' private affairs.
Repeal all "victimless crime" laws.
Repeal special interest legislation for business and labor.
End foreign entanglements, including any involvement in the Middle East, and
  bring U.S. troops home.[32]

Another right libertarian group that combined some of the appeals of the old Right and the New Left was the People's Bicentennial Commission (PBC), founded in 1971. It grew out of earlier attempts to construct a movement that expressed a "revolutionary nationalist," "Americanist," "radical patriotic," or "red, white, and blue Left."[33] The organization sought to reclaim an American heritage of individualist radicalism, citing Thomas Paine, not Chairman Mao, and using the "Don't Tread on Me" flag of the American Revolution, not the red banner of the National Liberation Front. Rather than looking to the models of peasant guerrilla war, the PBC established a radical identity that was rooted in this culture. As they quoted Benjamin Rush from 1787, "The American War is over, but this is far from the case with the American Revolution. On the contrary, only the first act of the great drama is at a close."

The PBC led its first national demonstration in 1973, in the Boston Tea and Oil Party, drawing 25,000 persons by official count. For the demonstration, and in later work, the PBC made these parallels between the 1770s and the 1970s: First, it argued that the enemy was still the same—centralized, monopolistic power. In the 1770s it had been George III: in the 1970s it was Richard Nixon and the imperial presidency. In the 1770s the colonists had fought against the East India Company, called the first multinational cor-

Courtesy of the People's Bicentennial Commission

poration. In the 1970s it was the oil companies, the twenty-four largest corporations that employed nearly five million persons, and the enormous federal bureaucracy. So the PBC called for the impeachment of the president and tossed oil drums into Boston Harbor instead of tea crates. The group was trying to ask basic questions of popular control that are vital in any age, proving that the American Revolution was not a dead event.

Other major issues in the 1770s had been unjust taxation, which was compared with the modern employee's working two and a half hours of each eight-hour day to pay the government while some multimillionares pay little or no income tax. In addition there were skyrocketing inflation, high-salaried bureaucrats catering to special interests, and the leaking of secret government papers showing corruption and deceit in the highest offices. These problems were not all in the past.

By 1976 the PBC had 10,000 members, a staff of eighteen, and a budget of $250,000, with the national director, Jeremy Rifkin, being paid a grandiose $85 a week. Decisions at the Washington, D. C., office were reached by consensus, and local groups were completely autonomous, like committees of correspondence. The primary efforts of the groups were educational: a speaker's bureau, a guerrilla theater group, a newspaper called *Common Sense*, and many pamphlets, such as one comparing the PBC with the official bicentennial, *The Tory's Program/The Patriot's Program*.

Through these activities, the PBC condemned both socialism and capitalism, using such terms as "corporate aristocrats," "authoritarian fiefdoms," and "economic royalty." In their Declaration of Economic Independence, they called for a decentralized and democratic economy—that is, for worker's control. They cited a 1975 poll in which Americans were asked if they would prefer working in a business owned by outside investors, by the state, or by the workers. More than 66 percent answered that they approved of a firm owned and managed by workers.

The old Left generally dismissed the PBC as petty-bourgeois individualism, asserting that such forms of direct democracy as self-management in the workplace or town meetings were archaic in a time of pervasive centralization. One Marxist, writing in the Maoist-influenced *Guardian*, characterized the group this way: "In general, PBC represents a cautious (i.e. deliberately not militant) populism, which yearns for the days of early developing capitalism minus the atrocities against Blacks and Indians. In the end, its program is utopian and idealistic, and bears little relation to the people's real struggles against monopoly capitalism."[34]

But who are "the people"? While most radicals speak only to other radicals, the PBC sold its publications to more than two thousand libraries and five thousand schools, distributed sixty-five thousand copies of a pamphlet through the National Council of Churches, had radio announcements on more than seven hundred stations, and spoke to such diverse audiences as left rallies, the American Library Association, the Campfire Girls, and some chapters of the Veterans of Foreign Wars. None of the "mass parties" of contemporary radicalism have reached so many people.[35]

Of course it is possible to criticize the PBC on many grounds. It is true that any ideal from the eighteenth century cannot be understood literally today. The original meaning is in its own time. Still, ideals of all kinds are commonly redefined and reinterpreted. While the original revelations of Judaism, or Catholicism, or Protestantism may no longer be literally applicable (thus we ignore the biblical injunction "thou shalt not suffer a witch to live"), such faiths remain living ideological forces *because* they have been constantly revised. In this sense, the PBC could legitimately claim that it was carrying out the unfinished business of the American Revolution, while the statist Left is obviously incompatible with the decentralist, antiauthoritarian and laissez-faire radicalism of this tradition.

After the Bicentennial, the PBC transformed itself into the People's Business Commission, to continue publishing a newspaper, encourage local organizing around tax resistance and reform, and raise other issues of community control, some of them reflected in its first book—*Own Your Own Job: Economic Democracy for Working Americans*. It does not advocate trust-busting but argues for popular control *within* the workplace, which it contrasts with both the arrogance of big business and the "unresponsive, self-serving bureaucracy" of conventional socialism. The new PBC pledged to continue its criticism of hereditary and corporate privilege, based on the principles of equality and opportunity expressed in the first American Revolution.[36]

Left libertarians also persisted into the 1970s, representing half of the original paradox of Puritanism that united "the exaltation of the individual and the search for a perfect community."[37] As capitalism continued to destroy a society based upon the extended family, tradition, and sense of community, replacing it with one organized strictly by functional roles (the classic models of *Gemeinschaft* and *Gesellschaft*), the need for security and meaning in a transient, unstable society urged some to seek a community that would consciously or unconsciously realize the biblical injunction, "Let no man seek his own, but every man another's wealth" (1 Cor. 10:24). This had been the text for the first sermon at Plymouth.

Left libertarians have interpreted this ideal community to be voluntary and uninstitutionalized. There must be no barriers to spontaneous action, direct revelation, intuitive truth. One Catholic writer has rather unexpectedly summarized this intellectual and emotional demolition of inflexible structures: "The greatest enemy of human happiness in the world today, as well as the most serious obstacle to the development of social justice, is the soulless, musclebound, dim-witted dinosaur called the corporation—and it doesn't much matter if it makes cars, sells books, tries to teach children, negotiates with management, or purports to preach God's word; nor in fact does it matter very much whether it calls itself capitalist or socialist.[38]

This community would be knit together, as a single body, by the antiego-ist beliefs of "belonging," "sharing," "closeness," and "warmth"—all re-jecting what Emma Goldman called the property morality of capitalism. The linear model of disciplined production would be replaced by a genera-tive one marked by self-cultivation, natural growth and regulation, living for the "now" rather than for tomorrow. As Dorothy Day commented in *The Long Loneliness* (1952): "We have all known loneliness and we have learned that the only solution is love and that love comes with community."

The community of left libertarians includes simple decentralists and mili-tant anarchists: commune dwellers (some wanting to "retribalize" society), the Catholic Workers, IWW, Marxist-Humanists, Council Communists, Free Socialists, Free Communists, Mutualists, Libertarian Marxists (like Daniel Guerin), and advocates of workers' management. Beyond their com-mon bonds of hostility toward private property and the dream of a noncoer-cive community, they have had wildly diverse beliefs concerning the realiza-tion of their utopias.

Those who live anarchism as a life-style, rather than as a philosophy, have the least organization. A sense of the universal may be achieved by rather privatistic means: drugs, personal religion, small groups, and meditational techniques. Drugs, for example, may alter personal consciousness, be-coming the radical equivalents of the more common forms of escapism, such as alcohol and tranquilizers (Miltown, Equanil, Pacidyl, Noludar, Librium, and Valmid). In this sense, anarchism as life-style becomes an unconscious satire on the average American, by combining expressions of cultural Pro-testantism and capitalist egoism. As one sociologist has observed, "Doing your own thing often meant exploiting other people sexually and emotion-ally, taking other people's property, and keeping oneself in such a state of chemical or sensory stimulation that nothing but the most superficial rela-tionship could be maintained. Incapable of effective organization, self-indulgent, lacking in character and loyalty, the instinctual anarchists often provided a parody of liberalism rather than an alternative to it."[39] The bizarre careers of Abby Hoffman and Jerry Rubin as marketable celebrities and vain supermen illustrate that left libertarians cannot easily transcend their sociocultural context. The cry for direct personal experience can destroy community more easily than reconstruct it.

Theories of organization have been more prominent among intellectually committed radicals, such as the School for Living, *News and Letters*, or the Catholic Worker movement. The latter is especially remarkable, given its formal allegiance to the Catholic church even while its founding light,

Dorothy Day, has resolutely identified herself as a "Catholic anarchist." Although the Catholic Workers have never hesitated to criticize all institutions as imperfect, the church—even when a "harlot"—remains their mother and they the loving children. By the late 1970s, more than eighty-five thousand copies of their newspaper were distributed each month (as they had been since 1933), gaining it a unique role in our Catholic Left and a singular status in world anarchism.[40]

While my interpretive categories are elastic enough to encompass most groups, I confess that the Catholic Workers seem to be in another dimension. They are both left libertarians, in practice, and—by their commitments—institutionalized anarchists. Perhaps this is a wondrous anomaly that I should leave to the meditation of others, fleeing back to rationality. However, the day-to-day life of this movement answers some of the seeming paradoxes of its success in this self-centered culture. It praises the ideal of personal responsibility (with Day complaining that people should not glorify her as a hero but should discover the heroic within themselves), urges the church to "liberate" itself from its earthly riches, appeals to the conscience of all (including the wealthy), and does its good works through decentralized facilities (soup kitchens, used-clothing rooms, hospitality houses, and farms). From those it helps, it demands no ideological pound of flesh; no one has to toe any party line before being granted Christian kindness. Still, despite these "explanations," if it did not exist I would have thought it impossible.

Only slightly less unlikely would be the combination of several of these tendencies into a single organization. Nonetheless, this also occurred when the New American Movement (NAM) was founded in 1972 as a virtual recreation of the pluralistic Socialist party of Eugene Debs before World War I and of the similar chaos of the early SDS. Its original goals clearly resembled those of SDS: "decentralization of decision-making, an end to bureaucratic rule, and the participation of all people in shaping their own lives and the direction of society." It was a coalition that envisioned a multisectional movement, with separate caucuses for women, blacks, and others, with many classes and interests, but all within a broader socialist context. By the late 1970s, historic tensions were obvious, as many Marxists left, accusing NAM of "localist," antileadership, petty-bourgeois "New American opportunism," while, at the same time, another portion moved toward running as Democrats in primaries and, in other elections. Old patterns were repeating themselves.[41]

Authoritarian radicalism, meanwhile, has occasionally admitted that most of American radicalism has sought to realize the offical ideology rather than overthrow it (as with Chartism in England or Social Democracy in Germany); yet it maintains that the limits of this capitalist reform will inevitably be reached. Then, "objective conditions" will require a model of revolution

Photograph by Bob Fitch

"Our problems stem from our acceptance of this filthy, rotten system."
—Dorothy Day

similar to those of other nations: a centralized and consolidated single party creating a centralized and consolidated national state.

A vital beginning in this task is, of course, a "correct theory." Authoritarian radicals have usually become colonists of some other culture, isolating themselves from any contamination by the local traditions of liberalism, or right and left libertarianism. Instead, the reader of a Maoist newspaper is likely to be lectured that the American worker has a "deep thirst for Marxism-Leninism-Mao Tsetung thought," along with a burning hatred for all "petty wrecking, splitting, phrasemongering opportunist influences."[42] Comrades, we should all be "marching toward" the dictatorship of the proletariat "under the glorious banner" of the vanguard party of Marx/Lenin/Stalin/Mao/Trotsky and others, in constant combat with the social fascists and social imperialists. For most readers, following these adventures in obscurantism and sectarian conceit, it is probably tempting to shout "Curb your running dogs!"

The product of this theory is usually a vanguard party that venerates everything from Moscow or Peking as divine revelation, imposes an iron discipline on its membership, and readily expels and slanders all dissidents. Such a party invariably behaves as the omniscient guardian of a childlike, benighted populace. These judgmental and condescending practices reinforce the American conviction that socialism means control, manipulation, regimentation, a Kafkaesque bureaucracy, and a hypocritical language of Newspeak.[43]

This ignorance of America is the fundamental error of all centralist creeds, and the basis for their unique failure here, quite unlike their success elsewhere in the world. These groups usually know more about Albania than America and bombard each other with manifestos on the class struggle in Ethiopia. By the late 1970s, "objective conditions" had at least temporarily changed. One could no longer argue that free land, immigration, or an evergrowing prosperity were the sources of contemporary defeat. As a left libertarian newspaper taunted its critics:

How much "riper" must "objective conditions" become? We have an ongoing depression with huge unemployment; world capitalism in a deep crisis; a decaying major party system; corruption and scandal in low and high places reaching to the forced resignations of the vice-president and president complete with impeachment proceedings; exposures of the CIA and FBI; urban rot, collapsing social services, rising crime, unworkable schools, inadequate medical care; not to mention the Vietnam war and the profound impact of the struggles against it.[44]

Nor can repression be used as an argument. Was McCarthyism more severe than the concentration camps of Hitler, executions by the Chilean junta, or torture in Iran? Anyway, that was a quarter of a century ago. No, it should be clearer by now that three and a half centuries of history will not disappear overnight. Furthermore, "objective conditions" cannot be naively separated from subjective ideas and feelings, since we "see reality" through such inherited social responses and express "objective reality" through traditional forms of language.

What, then, are the hallmarks of indigenous radicalism? First, its essence has consisted not of ideas or formal traditions, but of sociocultural experiences, "habits," or responses; in brief, the resistance to institutional authority. This has been, paradoxically, the historical continuity of an ahistorical, untraditional anti-institutionalism. American radicalism has always lived in the world of immediate sensation. Its criticisms and programs are "now." Emerson spoke as the voice of direct revelation, defying the walls of every "prison" of the stultifying past, while Marx, from a more history-and-class conscious society, believed that even when radicals imagined that they were "engaged in revolutionizing themselves and things, in creating something entirely new, precisely in such epochs of revolutionary crisis they anxiously conjure up the spirits of the past to their service and borrow from their names, battle slogans and costumes in order to present the new scene of world history in the time-honored disguise and this borrowed language" (*The Eighteenth Brumaire of Louis Bonaparte*). Thus, Marx was in direct opposition to the anarchist spontaneity of Emerson, and concomitantly, of American culture.

But this anarchist tradition has not been conscious of itself as a tradition, which has contributed to much of the confusion of American radicalism. Rather than learning from both accumulated wisdom and the contradictions of the past, American radicalism has always lived in the eternal present of childlike innocence. Its speech has usually been the infantile or adolescent expression of a cluster of assumptions ingrained in our society, never formulated as a conscious philosophy. At times this has allowed a powerful immediacy, but more often it prevents radicalism from perceiving its place within this culture, critically reappropriating from our heritage a clear and native identity. Instead we find uncertainty and occasional retreats to artificial constructs imported from elsewhere or mechanically developed without a concern for evolution. Marx criticized Feuerbach, saying that "the point is not to understand the world but to change it." In contrast, American radicals have been *too* occupied with changing the world and not enough with understanding it. What activist has followed Marx's example of studying for twenty years in the British Museum? Yet American radicalism shares this flaw with a society that values activism above thought and pragmatism before planning, abandoning all tradition that has no direct utility in contemporary life.

Second, this anarchist impulse is not merely intellectual Luddism or nihilistic negation. Rather, it often takes the form of an idealism about the powers of humanity, freed from church, state, party, and other institutions that restrict the realm of genuine choice. This could be called a moralistic affirmation, since it almost approaches a millennialist belief in a potential democratic idyll, when Tocqueville's "irresistible revolution" will culminate in a society of absolute equality, abolishing all the class and sexual limitations of the past. In this utopian vision, a constantly changing democracy would trust the abilities and conscience of the average person to create a happy life, if liberated from institutional exploitation. This may be sentimentality, but it is a genuinely American daydream.

Third, in organization an American radicalism can learn less from the electoralism of social democratic parties or the unitary models of Marx and Lenin than from the revolutionary federalism of the anarchists. An elite party may have been appropriate in Russia or China, but such an organization is not going to overthrow the enormous American bourgeoisie or the American "Kulaks." Rather, a mass democratic movement would be necessary to fundamentally reorganize this society. It would have to be based upon local units (caucuses, community projects, or committees) that would be sensitive to local problems, such as tenant questions, consumer issues, health care, power structure research, co-ops, newspapers, and free schools. It would be doing things that involved people's everyday lives. It could not arrogantly dismiss the middle class. It would have to avoid the flagrant abuses of democracy that occur in almost all workers' parties and states. In brief, it would be a living model of the new society: decentralized, nonauthoritarian, "liberated."[45]

For our models, we cannot rely ultimately upon the deus ex machina of foreign revolutions but must contemplate the potentialities of our own society. We are not required to reproduce the oppressive standardization of economically primitive societies. The United States is already an advanced industrial order; it has vast opportunities for a pluralistic future. Our realistic motto could be "Let the machines do the work." Automated trains, printed circuits, prefabricated houses, automobile factories with only a few workers, the application of computers to production, machines that plow, machines that dig, and machines that build other machines could all be liberating. Machines should be workers, rather than workers' becoming machines. These are unprecedented possibilities. The dreariness of Chinese poverty and official orthodoxy, or the unamusing satire on socialism of the Russian version of *Animal Farm* is not for Americans. Authoritarian radicalism merely offers new versions of this old joke: "Under capitalism, man exploits man. Under communism, it's just the reverse."[46]

Our homegrown radicalism is an alternative to both traditional socialism and capitalism. It has liberal, right, and left ideological ancestors, who have been described in this book. However, an ecumenical radicalism could both conserve and expand these historic principles while learning from foreign experiences that are compatible with advancing an American libertarian revolution. This meeting ground might include the Paris Commune of 1871, Russia during 1905 and 1917–21, Spain during 1936–39, Hungary in 1956, Algeria in the early 1960s, France in 1968, Chile in the 1970s, and Portugal in 1975. Libertarian theories could also be analyzed, such as syndicalism, Anarcho-Communism, Oscar Lange's "market socialism" of the 1930s, the idea of the general strike, cooperative movements, the "ultraleft" critique of Leninism, and the Council Communism of Karl Korsch, Anton Pannekoek, Herman Gorter, Paul Mattick, Serge Mallet, and André Gorz, along with existing models in West Germany, Scandanavia,

Israel (kibbutzim), Algeria, and Yugoslavia. From all of this, we may find answers to what Bakunin called the greatest problem of radicalism, "to integrate individuals into situations which they can understand and control."[47]

Let me sketch the possible outlines of this. People might be organized by local units, electing delegates (if representation could not be avoided) with limited mandates that could be immediately revoked. "Managers" of all sorts would be directly accountable, and their actions would be subject to initiative, referendum, and recall. Technicians and specialists would still be necessary, but their status would be transformed. It would not be enough for the workers to decide *what* to do, and then have the technicians tell them *how* to do it. Rather, the workers would be involved in the original discussions about both the what *and* the how.

Each person would be able to vote where he or she works or is active, on all issues of significant concern. Such elections would occur when necessary, since in the era of television, radio, and rapid communication, there should be instantaneous democracy rather than the relic of elections by calendar date. Participation would mean greater experience and thus, in a general way, greater competence. Since an individual would presumably have the option of refusal and a socially minimum guaranteed income, this "democracy" would not violate libertarian principles.

This could function in the following way: auto workers might vote for people to speak for their particular shop, for others who would be general representatives for their factory, for industrywide stewards, and members of a central council of labor that would be necessary for discussion, statistics, and the coordination of production. The workers would have direct, continuous control over their representatives. Delegates for general community interests should sit on all these committees to speak for those who did not work (including the young and the aged) and to criticize activities that might be racist, sexist, concerned only with local profit, or harmful to the overall community, such as air and water pollution. Similar values would apply to housework (Charlotte Perkins Gilman once suggested collective laundries, dining areas, child-care and cleaning facilities), schoolwork (with "self-teaching" and the "self-managed child"), or office work.

This system could be given many names: "ad-hocracy," "pluralist commonwealth," "regional socialism," "institutionalized individualism" (with the institutions really being normative orders), voluntarist socialism, "cooperative and creative individualism," or "individualist socialism." Even today, there are some working models in various groups and activities. Though they are small and disorganized, they go beyond the rhetoric of democracy to day-to-day reality, attempting to realize the IWW dream of "building the new society within the shell of the old.[48]

While the historian cannot predict the outcome of our libertarian sensibility, it is possible to indulge in one social prophecy: we can say (with Marx) that all people, including Americans, enter the future backward, looking toward the past, judging today and tomorrow at least partially by the standards of yesterday. Certainly the American radical, among others, cannot lightly ignore centuries of experience. Social criticism, to be effective, must be rooted in its own environment. Although it may domesticate some foreign influences, it must speak with a plain American vocabulary, urging American goals, to be achieved by American methods. For radicals to deny their own past is to insure their future defeat.

NOTES

Overview

1. Ralph Waldo Emerson, "The American Scholar," in *Emerson's Works*, pp. 83–115 (Boston: Houghton Mifflin, 1883).

2. A panoramic survey is found in "The State" (articles by Morton Fried, Frederick Watkins, and—on stateless societies—Aidan Southall), in *International Encyclopedia of the Social Sciences*, 15:143–69 (New York: Macmillan and Free Press, 1968) (including bibliographies). Consider also: Lucy Mair, *Primitive Government* (Baltimore: Penguin, 1964); Lawrence Krader, *Formation of the State* (Englewood Cliffs, N.J.: Prentice-Hall, 1968); George Woodcock, *Anarchism* (Cleveland: Meridian, 1961); and James Joll, *The Anarchists* (New York: Grossett and Dunlap, 1964). As a rule, stateless societies have been socially and intellectually homogeneous, not diverse. Whether this would describe an anarchist America is another question.

3. Norman J. Ware, *The Labor Movement in the United States, 1860–1895: A Study in Democracy* (New York: Appleton, 1929), p. 304 (italics added). Some of the key literature on dissent is reviewed by Marvin Gettleman in "American Radicalism: A Bibliographical Survey" (*Stacks*, a publication of the libraries of the Polytechnic Institute of Brooklyn, no. 24 [March 1970]) and, more recently, in Milton Cantor's *The Divided Left: American Radicalism, 1900–1977* (New York: Hill and Wang, 1977).

Logical bookkeepers may realize that my enterprise begins with several ironic debits, such as providing a system to anarchy, being more conscious of antecedents than most anarchists, and using a foreign term in my analysis of indigenous radicalism. But these have all been convenient abstractions, and so they have been used.

4. Quoted by Richard Drinnon, in "Thoreau's Politics of the Upright Man," *Anarchy*,

no. 26 (April 1963), p. 121. Few anarchists, even those as explicit as Paul Goodman, have been consistent. Many have been capable of returning to a basic liberalism, such as members of the New Left working for Eugene McCarthy while retaining a more radical rhetoric. Dorothy Day illustrated this indifference to rational order when she rebuked Dwight Macdonald for a criticism: "Really, Dwight, you've known me long enough not to expect me to be consistent!" (quoted in Dwight Macdonald, "Revisiting Dorothy Day," *New York Review of Books* 16 [28, January 1971]: 19).

Despite these particularistic realities, consult Max Weber for a classic commentary on the value of "synthetic constructs," in *The Methodology of the Social Sciences*, ed. Edward Shils and Henry A. Finch, pp. 89–92, 93–94, 97–99 (New York: Free Press, 1949). Those who are searching for a more systematic definition of "radical" might refer to the (in my opinion) unnecessarily elaborate discussion by Egon Bittner in *International Encyclopedia of the Social Sciences* (13: 294–300). The reader should not neglect, however, the word "reflections" in my own subtitle. This will not be a physics of politics or an Euclidean geometry of anarchism. While I have attempted to write in plain English rather than Sociologese or Socspeak, I have nothing to impart of catechismal or mathematical clarity.

5. Ferdinand Toennies, *Community and Society [Gemeinschaft und Gesellschaft]* (East Lansing: Michigan State University Press, 1957); Maurice Stein, *The Eclipse of Community: An Interpretation of American Studies* (Princeton: Princeton University Press, 1960); Joseph Gusfield, *Community: A Critical Response* (New York: Harper and Row, 1975); Richard Brown, *Modernization: The Transformation of American Life, 1600–1865* (New York: Hill and Wang, 1976).

6. *The Quest: History and Meaning in Religion* (Chicago: University of Chicago Press, 1969), p. 9.

7. Sydney Ahlstrom, *A Religious History of the American People* (New Haven: Yale University Press, 1972), p. 124.

8. Edmund Burke's image of Puritanism, drawn in "On Conciliation with the Colonies" (1775), in *Speeches and Letters on American Affairs*, p. 93 (London: Everyman's Library, n.d.).

9. Robert Wuthnow, *The Consciousness Reformation* (Berkeley: University of California Press, 1976), p. 111; Alex Inkeles, "American Perceptions," *Change* 9 (August 1977): 27.

10. Yehoshua Arieli has documented many of these elements in his book *Individualism and Nationalism in American Ideology* (Cambridge, Mass.: Harvard University Press, 1964), along with Eric Hobsbaum's remark that "what distinguishes the various members of the ideological family descended from humanism and the Enlightenment, liberal, socialist, communist or anarchist, is not the gentle anarchy which is the utopia of all of them, but the methods of achieving it" (Hobsbaum, *The Age of Revolution, 1789–1848* [New York: Mentor, ·1962] p. 287). Judith Shklar has also commented that "anarchism" was one of the "cardinal traits" of the Enlightenment thought readily accepted in America (*After Utopia* [Princeton: Princeton University Press, 1957). It is significant that the first statement of philosophical anarchism, William Godwin's *Political Justice* (1793), is rooted in this liberalism.

11. Henri Peyre, "The Study of Literature," in *The Cultural Migration: The European Scholar in America*, pp. 28–29 (Philadelphia: University of Pennsylvania Press, 1953).

12. Henry Pachter, "On Being an Exile," *Salmagundi*, nos. 10–11 ("The Legacy of German Refugee Intellectuals"; entire issue, fall 1969–winter 1970), p. 33; S. M. Lipset and Richard Dobson, "The Intellectual as Critic and Rebel: With Special Reference to the United States and the Soviet Union," *Daedalus* 101 (summer 1972): 137–98; Roger Asselineau, "The Impact of American Literature on French Writers," *Comparative Literature Studies* 14 (June 1977): 119–34.

13. Quoted by Richard Kostelanetz, in "The Prevalence of Paul Goodman," *New York Times Magazine*, 13 April 1966, p. 100. Goodman's anarchism was an extreme affirmation of this belief in the creative capacities of common people.

14. William Holmes McGuffey, *McGuffey's Newly Revised Eclectic Fourth Reader* (Cincin-

nati: Sargent, Wilson and Hinkle, 1853), p. 205. This dream of a community of equal opportunity has been examined (and ridiculed) by H. Mark Roelofs: "The demands of Americans for a universal and unqualified recognition of a natural equality. . . voice an impossible ideal, one so wholly opposed to social structures as to be anarchistic" (*Ideology and Myth in American Politics* [Boston: Little, Brown, 1976], p. 71).

15. Lawrence Goodwyn, *Democratic Promise: The Populist Movement in America* (New York: Oxford University Press, 1976).

16. Saul Alinsky, *Rules for Radicals* (New York: Random House, 1971), p. 196.

17. James Baldwin, "The Male Prison," in *Nobody Knows My Name*, pp. 152–62 (New York: Dell, 1961).

18. John Holt, "Deschooling Society," *Reason*, Vol. 3 (April–May 1971).

19. 1855 preface to *Leaves of Grass*, ed. John A. Kouwenhoven (New York: Modern Library, 1950), p. 452. Despite his frequent loathing of the "smell" of politics, he always concluded that "the people" were purer than their institutions.

20. Harry Kelly, *Mother Earth* 2 (February 1907): 559. For modern discussions of the membership of the new radicalism, see Fred Gordon, "A Class Analysis of the Radical Student Movement" (Boston: New England Free Press, n.d.); "The Class Background and Orientation of the New Left" (Boston: New England Free Press, n.d.); James R. Allen and Louis J. West, "Flight from Violence: Hippies and the Green Revolution," *American Journal of Psychiatry* 125 (1968): 366 (On Haight-Ashbury); and David Whittaker and William Watts, "Personality Characteristics of a Nonconformist Youth Subculture: A Study of the Berkeley Non-Student," *Journal of Social Issues* 25 (April 1969): 72–73.

21. William Z. Foster, *Toward a Soviet America* (New York: Coward-McCann, 1932). For a literary expression of this idea, read Jack Parker's "Two Flags," in *New Pioneer* 2 (July 1933): 6–7 (a descendant of Betsy Ross sews a new flag—red, with a hammer and sickle).

22. James Weinstein, letter, *New American Movement* (newspaper), April 1972. By this purist standard, feminists or blacks, also seeking a historical identity, could discover few if any "perfect" models, since even a Frederick Douglass did not understand the dialectic, and Elizabeth Cady Stanton was insufficiently liberated. For such a pathetically negative interpretation of the Bicentennial, see Rusty Conroy's "'76 Fest Masks War Threat, Profits," *Guardian*, 21 January 1976, p. 9. Dimitroff once characterized such ultraleft views as "national nihilism."

23. Several examples are cited in a pamphlet representing the "revolutionary nationalist" position: John Rossen, "Toward a New Patriotism" (Cicero, Ill.: Johnny Appleseed Patriotic Publications, 197?). Further comments can be found in Susan Sontag, *Trip to Hanoi* (New York: Farrar, Straus and Giroux, 1968); John Schaar, "The Case for Patriotism," *New American Review*, no. 17 (May 1973), pp. 59–99, and John Rossen, "Toward a Socialist Redefinition of Patriotism: A Proposal," *In These Times* 2 (21–27 September 1977): 17. Perhaps, however, our "patriotic radicalism" is antinationalistic. It is certainly skeptical about embodying idealism in institutions. Consider the implications of Schaar's despair: "Today our skepticism about all notions of disinterested, public-regarding behavior is so thoroughgoing that the patriot can hardly appear. We are inclined to regard all professions of disinterested and altruistic motive as the blandishments of a charlatan or the intrigues of a schemer" (p. 74).

24. Quoted in *In These Times* 2 (14–20 September 1977): 17.

25. "Toward a Post-Scarcity Society: The American Persepective and S.D.S." (Chicago: Radical Decentralist Project, mimeographed, May 1969), p. 9. T. W. Adorno, a onetime German exile, concurred in the importance of absorbing this history: "It is scarcely an exaggeration to say that any contemporary consciousness that has not appropriated the American experience, even if in opposition, has something reactionary about it" (Adorno, "Scientific Experience of European Scholar in America," in *The Intellectual Migration*, ed. Donald Fleming and Bernard Bailyn, pp. 369–70 (Cambridge, Mass.: Harvard University Press, 1968). The response of the old Left within America has been *unreflective* opposition.

26. "The Whole of Poland Is on Strike Today," *Fifth Estate* (Detroit) 11 (August 1976): 10;

recent issues of *China Reconstructs* and *China Pictorial*; Michael Albert, *What Is to Be Undone?* (Boston: Porter Sargent, 1974). It is equally true, of course, that workers in these societies have greater job security, health care, and other guarantees that have alleviated much of the cruelty of a society based fundamentally on personal aggrandizement. A fuller discussion of these concepts can be found in my essay "For Democracy Where We Work: A Rationale for Self-Management," in *Reinventing Anarchy*, ed. David DeLeon and others (London: Routledge and Kegan Paul, 1978).

27. Read *The Failure of a Dream? Essays in the History of American Socialism*, ed. John Laslett and S. M. Lipset (New York: Anchor Books, 1974), and *The Socialist Idea: A Reappraisal*, ed. Leszek Kolakowski and Stuart Hampshire (London: Weidenfeld and Nicolson, 1974). The original title for the 1973 London conference—"What Is Wrong with the Socialist Idea?"—had been modified to "Is There Anything Wrong with the Socialist Idea?" Most commentators, however, identified readily with the first formulation.

Chapter One

1. "Every aspect of [Puritan literary] style betrays a consuming involvement with 'me' and 'mine' that resists disintegration. We cannot but feel that the Puritans' urge for self-denial stems from the very subjectivism of their outlook, that their humility is co-extensive with personal assertion" (Sacvan Bercovitch, *The Puritan Origins of the American Self* [New Haven: Yale University Press, 1975], p. 18).

2. T. H. Breen, *The Character of the Good Ruler: A Study of Puritan Political Ideas in New England, 1630–1730* (New Haven: Yale University Press, 1970), p. 47.

3. This provocative thought is from John Quincy Adams's "The New England Confederacy of MDCXLIII" (1842), *Collections of the Massachusetts Historical Society*, 3d ser., vol. 9 (Boston: Freeman and Bolles, 1846), p. 202. Background for such issues can be found in John C. Bennett, *Christians and the State* (New York: Scribner's, 1958); George Lee Haskins, *Law and Authority in Early Massachusetts* (New York: Macmillan, 1960); and Darrett Rutman, "The Mirror of Puritan Authority," in *Puritanism and the American Experience*, ed. Michael McGiffert, pp. 65–79 (Reading, Mass.: Addison-Wesley, 1969).

4. Roger Williams, *The Complete Writings of Roger Williams*, 7 vols. (New York: Russell and Russell, 1963), 3:96, 124–25; 7:189–90, 201, 218, 268. Williams was less radical than the Puritans, however, when he insisted that an ungodly ruler should not be overthrown.

5. Cushing Strout, *The New Heavens and New Earth: Political Religion in America* (New York: Harper and Row, 1974), p. 20.

6. Cited in Charles M. Andrews, *The Colonial Period in American History* (New Haven: Yale University Press, 1936), 2:55. Although a Catholic anarchism is theoretically possible from the same Christian tradition of the superiority of natural law over temporal rule (and was realized in the career of Dorothy Day and the Catholic Worker movement), this has been extraordinarily rare. Institutional restraints have usually controlled such impulses.

7. Thomas Hutchinson, *The History of Massachusetts from the Earliest Settlement Thereof in 1628 until the Year 1750*, 3d ed. (Boston, 1795), 2:439.

8. Edward Johnson, *Wonder-Working Providence* (New York: Barnes and Noble, 1967 [1654]), p. 127.

9. Winthrop, quoted in Charles Francis Adams, ed., *Antinomianism in the Colony of Massachusetts Bay, 1636–1638* (Boston, 1894), pp. 157–58. Winthrop was not surprised by the evolution of the dissenters: "Mrs. Hutchinson and those of Aquiday island breached new heresies every year. Divers of them turned professed Anabaptists, and *would not wear any arms*, and *denied all magistracy among Christians*, and maintained that there were not churches since those founded by the Apostles and evangelists, nor could any be, nor any pastors, nor seals administered but by such" (Winthrop, *The History of New England from 1630 to 1649*, ed.

James Savage, 2 vols. [Boston, 1825], 2:38). Major studies include Emery Battis, *Saints and Sectaries* (Chapel Hill, N.C.: Institute for Early American History and Culture, 1962), and David Hall, ed., *The Antinomian Controversy* (Middletown, Conn.: Wesleyan University Press, 1968).

10. Barclay, *An Apology for the True Christian Divinity*, 14th ed. (Glasgow, 1886 [1678], p. 35; he also refers to conscience as the throne of God). William Perkins, who was widely admired, summarized this ambiguous definition of authority: "We must be a law to ourselves; We must be voluntaries, without constraint, freely yielding subjection to the will of God" (discussed in David Little, "Max Weber Revisited: The 'Protestant Ethic' and the Puritan Experience of Order," in *The International Yearbook for the Sociology of Religion* 3 [1967]: 105, 109). But what is God's will? Who has certain knowledge, except one who has *experienced* it? Perhaps a black spiritual answered this: "Do what the spirit say do."

11. *The Writings of William Penn*, ed. Frederick B. Tolles and E. Gordon Alderfer (New York 1957), p. 110.

12. Edwin Bronner, *William Penn's "Holy Experiment"* (New York: Temple University Press distributed by Columbia University Press, 1962), p. 108; Murray Rothbard, "Individualist Anarchism in the United States: The Origins," *Libertarian Analysis* 1 (winter 1970): 14–28; Murray Rothbard, *Conceived in Liberty*, 2 vols. (New Rochelle, N.Y.: Arlington House, 1975); Eunice Minette Schuster, "Native American Anarchism: A Study in Left-Wing Individualism," *Smith College Studies in History* 17 (October 1931–July 1932): 5–197; A. J. Beitzinger, "Theological and Religious Background," in *A History of American Political Thought* (New York: Dodd, Mead, 1972), pp. 31–112 (he has a fine sense of the contradictions between order and conscience); and Alan Tully, *William Penn's Legacy* (Baltimore: John Hopkins University Press, 1977).

13. *The Testimony of the President, Professors, Tutors and Hebrew Instructor of Harvard College against the Reverend George Whitefield, and His Conduct* (Boston, 1744), p. 14.

14. *Autobiography of Peter Cartwright, a Backwoods Preacher*, ed. W. P. Strickland (New York: Carlton and Porter, 1857), p. 409.

15. Quoted by Perry Miller, "Emersonian Genius and the American Democracy," in *Nature's Nation*, p. 168 (Cambridge: Harvard University Press, 1967).

16. Emerson, quoted in "The American Proposition: A Permanent Revolution in the Affairs of Men," *Fortune*, February 1951, p. 68; Thoreau, "A Plea for John Brown" ("He was the most American of us all"), in *The Works of Henry David Thoreau*, ed. Brooks Atkinson (New York: Modern Library, 1950), p. 429. Although Emerson and Thoreau might not have assented, many critics have further argued that since human nature is flawed (or, as the Puritans said, depraved), we cannot be trusted with *any* power. This is a stunning reversal of the conservative axiom that government is required because of depravity.

17. Consult *Nonviolence in America: A Documentary History*, ed. Staughton Lynd (Indianapolis: Bobbs-Merrill, 1966).

18. Channing, "The Moral Argument against Calvinism" (1809), in *The Works of William Ellery Channing*, pp. 459–68 (Boston: American Unitarian Association, 1875). (Channing, I might note, was an enthusiastic reader of the English protoanarchist William Godwin). European Catholic views are often clarifying: Jacques Maritain, *Reflections on America* (New York: Scribner's, 1958), and Father R. L. Bruckberger, *Image of America* (New York: Viking, 1959). It is also significant that systematic theologians, political theorists, and philosophers have been conspicuously absent from our culture, as though this spirit defied all structures.

19. Alcott, *Non-Resistant*, 19 October 1839, p. 4; William O. Reichert, "The Rebel as Anarchist: Come-Outers and Non-Resistants," in *Partisans of Freedom*, pp. 36–51 (Bowling Green, Ohio: Popular Press, 1976).

20. Eisenhower, quoted in Maurice Klain, "'Politics'—Still a Dirty Word," *Antioch Review* 15 (winter 1955–56): 457 (Klain allows Philip Graham, a Washington publisher, to draw a

reasonable conclusion: "[Our derision produces] a fantastic system in which we treat our politicians as unsavory characters while we charge them with preserving our civilization").

For an unenthusiastic interpretation of such perfectionist tendencies, see Irving Kristol, "Utopianism in American Politics," in *On the Democratic Idea in America*, pp. 127–49 (New York: Harper and Row, 1972). There are abundant illustrations of human government being menaced in the name of "the government of God" in Lewis Perry's *Radical Abolitionism: Anarchy and the Government of God in Antislavery Thought* (Ithaca: Cornell University Press, 1973).

21. Studies on the general interrelations of political and religious culture include William Lee Miller, "American Religion and American Political Attitudes," in *Religious Perspectives in American Culture* ed. James Ward Smith and A. Leland Jamison, pp. 81–118 (Princeton: Princeton University Press, 1961): T. Scott Miyakawa, *Protestants and Pioneers: Individualism on the American Frontier* (Chicago: University of Chicago Press, 1964): S. M. Lipset, "Religion and Politics in America," in Robert Lee, *Religion and Social Conflict* ed. Robert Lee and Martin Marty, pp. 69–172. (New York: Oxford University Press, 1964); William McLoughlin, "Pietism and the American Character," *American Quarterly* 17 (summer 1965): 163–86. Note also the characterization of C. Wright Mills by Ralph Miliband, a Marxist: "There is in Mills a not very dormant anarchist" (Miliband, "Mills and Politics," in *The New Sociology*, ed. Irving Louis Horowitz, p. 82 [New York: Oxford University Press, 1965]).

Chapter Two

1. Karl Polanyi has written one of the most illuminating studies on the emergence of this radically new order: *The Great Transformation: The Political and Economic Origins of Our Time* (Boston: Beacon, 1957 [1944]).

2. Max Weber rejected the belief that capitalism had always existed and that forms of it could be found in the history of both Jews and Catholics. First, Weber commented that profit-seeking was not enough to qualify one as a capitalist: "The unchaining of the economic interest merely as such has produced only irrational results; such men as Cortes and Pizarro, who are perhaps its strongest embodiment, were far from having an idea of a rationalistic economic life" (*General Economic History* [New York: Collier, 1961], p. 261). Second, he remarked that those aspects of early Jewish business that could qualify as more developed had been "speculative pariah-capitalism" that had not created any of the business forms necessary for capitalism as a modern system: stocks, industrial labor, bills of trade, the legal forms of capitalism, and other vital institutional and intellectual innovations. Although Jewish merchants might have diffused these forms, and Catholics such as the Medici, the Fuggers, or Jacques Savary may have been prominent commercial people, they did not build a new society. The controversies surrounding these issues are summarized in two useful anthologies: David Landes, ed., *The Rise of Capitalism* (New York: Macmillan, 1966), and M. J. Kitch, ed., *Capitalism and the Reformation* (New York: Barnes and Noble, 1968).

3. William Taylor has depicted, in *Cavalier and Yankee* (New York: Braziller, 1961), the Southern mythology that evolved by the nineteenth century. The South had supposedly been settled by Cavaliers or Normans, who created an agrarian slaveholding democracy of warriors and gentlemen modeled after Athens, whereas Northern society was alleged to have been founded by Roundheads or Saxons who had manufactured a businessmen's Sparta. Because of the various factors I mention in the text, Northerners came to see Southerners as dissolute, whereas Southerners in turn saw Yankees as money-mad Puritans. David Bertelson has also compared a "North" built on Puritan and Quaker blueprints of a new and purer world with the less ambitious bases of Southern civilization (*The Lazy South* [New York: Oxford University Press, 1967]). Whatever the legitimacy of these historical images, James McBride Dabbs made the irrefutable observation, in *Who Speaks for the South?* (New York: Funk and Wagnalls,

1964), that it was impossible to indoctrinate the slaves in "the Puritan ethic" of "the holiness of work." References to Protestant influences also occur in the classic study by W. J. Cash, *The Mind of the South* (New York: Knopf, 1941), and in Edmund S. Morgan's "The Labor Problem in Jamestown, 1607-18," *American Historical Review* 76 (June 1971): 595-611. Several of these interpretations are lucidly stated, and affirmed or dismantled, in C. Vann Woodward's "The Southern Ethic in a Puritan World," *William and Mary Quarterly*, 3d ser. 25 (July 1968): 343-70.

4. Thomas Hooker, *A Survey of the Summe of Church-Discipline* (London, 1648), p. 188.

5. John Winthrop, *Winthrop's Journal "History of New England,"* 1630-1649, ed. J. K. Hosmer (1908), 1:134, 325; 2:20.

6. *The Diary of John Hull, Archaelogia Americana* (Boston, 1857), 3:215.

7. Perry Miller, *The New England Mind: From Colony to Province* (Cambridge: Harvard University Press, 1962), p. 51.

8. For more thorough definitions and histories of this concept, read Richard Michaelson, "Changes in the Puritan Concept of Calling or Vocation," *New England Quarterly* 26 (September 1953): 315-36; Stephen Foster, "Wealth: The Calling, Capitalism and the Problem of Prosperity," in *Their Solitary Way*, 99-126 (New Haven: Yale University Press, 1971), and Michael Walzer—who, despite his many erroneous comments on Weber, correctly notes the considerable Puritan emphasis on the moral and social virtues of work—in *The Revolution of the Saints* (Cambridge: Harvard University Press, 1965).

9. *Wonder-Working Providence of Sions Saviour in New England,* ed. W. F. Poole (Andover, 1867), pp. 173-74.

10. A few scholars have concluded that the Puritans tended, if not in theory certainly in practice, to equate poverty with sin and wealth with grace. See Christopher Hill, "William Perkins and the Poor," in *Puritanism and Revolution*, pp. 215-38 (London, 1958), and his "The Poor and the Parish," in *Society and Puritanism in Pre-Revolutionary England*, pp. 259-97 (London, 1964). The official ideology was accurately stated, however, by the Reverend John Cotton: "No man can certainly discern the love or hatred of God to himself or others, by their outward events or estates" (*A Brief Exposition on the Whole of Ecclesiastes* [Edinburgh, 1868], pp. 96-97).

11. Bernard Bailyn evaluated this incident in his introduction to *The Apologia of Robert Keayne: The Self-Portrait of a Puritan Merchant* (New York: Harper Torchbooks, 1965), also found as "The Apologia of Robert Keayne," *William and Mary Quarterly*, 3d ser., 7 (1950): 568-87. Another monograph by Bailyn provides the most comprehensive social context for this trial: *New England Merchants in the Seventeenth Century* (Cambridge: Harvard University Press, 1965). Stephen Foster has reasoned that this was not a simple struggle between "medieval farmers" and "modern merchants" (*Their Solitary Way*, pp. 119-20). Nevertheless, Foster provides evidence that each group tended to use "old" or "new" notions depending upon their general economic interests. Thus he asserts that the "cure" for such wage and price litigation was to be found in "more merchants, more markets, better roads, and fewer shortages—in brief, in economic growth" ("in brief," a dynamic capitalist system!). He further admits that "as the economy of the coastal regions improved, the 'just price' retreated westward." That is, capitalism broke free from strict community controls.

12. William Bradford, *The History of Plymouth Plantation, 1620-1647*, ed. Worthington C. Ford, 2 vols. (Boston, 1912), 1:55n. Babbette May Levy analyzed the ideological difficulties of prosperity in her "Success: The Puritan High Road to Damnation," in *Preaching in the First Half Century of New England History*, pp. 40-59 (Hartford, Conn.: American Society for Church History, 1945). Similar riddles perplexed many of the Quakers, Baptists, and Huguenots, all of whom were disproportionately active in American business life.

13. Quoted in Herbert Schneider, *The Puritan Mind* (Ann Arbor: University of Michigan Press, 1958), p. 78; Sebastian de Grazia, *Of Time, Work and Leisure* (New York: Twentieth Century Fund, 1962), p. 257.

14. *Manifesto of the Communist Party* (Peking: Foreign Languages Press, 1968), pp. 34–35. A century and a quarter later, such problems were "discovered" in a faddish book by Alvin Toffler, *Future Shock* (New York: Random House, 1970).

15. Peter Kropotkin, *Kropotkin's Revolutionary Pamphlets* (New York: Dover, 1970 [1927]), p. 64.

16. Baltimore *Sun*, 12 January 1976, p. 2; Jefferson as quoted by Edmund Morgan, in "The Puritan Ethic and the American Revolution," *William and Mary Quarterly*, 3d ser. 24 (January 1967): 3–43. Informative writings on the myths of success are Moses Rischin, ed.; *The American Gospel of Wealth: Individualism and Beyond* (Chicago: Quadrangle, 1965); Irwin G. Wylie, *The Self-made Man in America* (New Brunswick: Rutgers University Press, 1954); John Cawelti, *Apostles of the Self-made Man* (Chicago: University of Chicago Press, 1965); Richard Weiss, *The American Myth of Success* (New York: McGraw-Hill, 1971).

17. Baltimore *Sun*, 4 September 1972, p. 1.

18. James Petras has a realistic appraisal of this situation in "The Myth of the Decline of U.S. Capitalism," *Telos*, no. 28 (summer 1976), pp. 181–87.

19. Kay Lehman Schlozman, "Coping with the American Dream: Maintaining Self-Respect in an Achieving Society," *Politics and Society* 6, 2 (1976): 241–63, esp. p. 256.

20. "East Coker," in *Four Quartets*, p. 16 (New York: Harcourt, Brace, 1943).

21. For a comparison between Emerson and Marx on the effects of capitalism, read *The American Disciples of Marx* by David Herreshoff (Detroit: Wayne State University Press, 1967), pp. 11–30 (the quotation used is from p. 18). Emerson once lamented: "How insular, and pathetically solitary, are all the people we know" ("Society and Solitude," in *Works* [Boston, 1904], 1:9).

Of course, it might also be demonstrated—as I will attempt to do later—that all industrial societies, whether capitalist or communist, have failed to solve these problems.

22. In order: a receptionist, from Studs Terkel, *Working* (New York: Avon, 1974), p. 57; a union president, in Terkel, *Working*, p. 261; an auto worker, quoted in Peter Herman, "In the Heart of the Heart of the Country: The Strike at Lordstown," in *The Rise of the Worker's Movements*, ed. Root and Branch, p. 51 (New York: Fawcett, 1975). See also André Gorz, ed., *The Division of Labour: The Labour Process and Class Struggle in Modern Capitalism* (Atlantic Highlands, N.J.: Humanities Press, 1976).

23. Trotsky, *My Life: An Attempt at an Autobiography* (New York: Scribner's, 1930), p. 271. The phrase "golden chains" was forged by Daniel Bell in his essay "Work and Its Discontents" (New York: League for Industrial Democracy, 1970). Melvin Kohn, in *Class and Conformity* (Homewood, Ill.: Dorsey Press, 1969), presented the thesis that lower-class children were more likely to be actively indoctrinated with the ideas of middle-class respectibility because it was something to be achieved rather than assumed. Joan Huber and William Form, in *Income and Inequality* (New York: Macmillan, 1973), agreed that most people were convinced that success was based on personal responsibility.

24. Elinor Langer, "The Women of the Telephone Company," *New York Review of Books*, vol. 14 (12 and 26 March 1970). One study concluded that even limited experiments in "participation" increased productivity by 10 to 70 percent (Department of Health, Education, and Welfare, *Work in America*, 1973).

25. John D. Rockefeller, III, *The Second American Revolution* (New York: Harper and Row, 1973), pp. 7–8, 16.

26. Ibid., pp. 20, 29–30, 164, 167, 179, 194. Rockefeller is one of many critics, from Emerson to David Reisman or William Whyte, who reserve their highest approval for the self-conscious individual. Reisman, in *The Lonely Crowd* (New Haven: Yale University Press, 1950), lauded "the autonomous individual," and Whyte, in *The Organization Man* (New York: Simon and Schuster, 1956), rejected the "social ethic" of the organization for personal conscience. Individual success is the American ideal.

Chapter Three

1. Archibald MacLeish, "America Was Promises" (1939), in *Collected Poems* p. 359 (Boston: Houghton Mifflin, 1963). Space, of course, is interpreted differently by various societies, as Edward T. Hall, an anthropologist, has demonstrated in an insightful cross-cultural study: *The Hidden Dimension* (Garden City, N.Y.: Doubleday, Anchor, 1969).

2. William Bradford, *Bradford's History of Plymouth Plantation, 1606–1646*, ed. William T. Davis (New York: Scribner's, 1908), p. 106; Harry W. Ward, *Statism in Plymouth Colony* (Port Washington, N.Y.: Kennikat Press, 1973). This document was not originally designated a "compact" (a term that was not applied to it until 1793), but was called merely "an association and agreement."

3. Quoted in Vernon Louis Parrington, *Main Currents in American Thought* (New York: Harvest ed., Harcourt, Brace, 1954 [1927]), 1:127–28. Perry Miller gathered further evidence that the presence of the frontier could unsettle order. He quoted such worthies as Increase Mather, in 1677, complaining that "people are ready to run wild into the woods again and to be as Heathenish as ever, if you do not prevent it," and a lament by one minister before the General Court in 1705: "[People] bid defiance, not only to Religion, but to Civility itself" (*The Puritans*, ed. Perry Miller and Thomas Johnson, 2 vols. [New York: Harper and Row, 1963], 1:17, 17n). This subject is, of course, a minefield of controversies. A representative selection of the literature on one "frontier thesis," Frederick Jackson Turner's, has been collected by Ray Allen Billington in *The Frontier Thesis: Valid Interpretation of American History?* (New York: Holt, Rinehart and Winston, 1966).

4. Hector St. John De Crèvecoeur, *Letters from an American Farmer* (New York: Dutton, 1926 [1782]).

5. *The Complete Writings of Thomas Paine*, ed. Philip Foner (New York: Citadel, 1945), 2:453.

6. Bayard Rush Hall (trained at Union College and Princeton Theological Seminary; went to Indiana in 1823), *The New Purchase; or, Seven and a Half Years in the Far West* (Princeton: Princeton University Press, 1916), p. 321 (a man passing his house supposedly observed: "Thar's whar the grammur man lives that larns'em Latin and grandlike things. Allow we'll oust him yet!"); Thoreau, "A Yankee in Canada," in *The Writings of Henry David Thoreau*, 20 vols., 5:16–17, 68 (Boston: Houghton Mifflin, 1906); Perry Miller, *Nature's Nation* (Cambridge: Harvard University Press, 1967).

7. Thoreau, "Walking," in *The Writings of Henry David Thoreau*, Riverside ed. 11 vols., 9:251–304, esp. p. 251 (Boston: Houghton, Mifflin, 1884–1894): "the most alive is the wildest!"

8. Such motifs are developed by R. W. B. Lewis in *The American Adam* (Chicago: University of Chicago Press, 1955) and in Laurence Veysey's *The Communal Experience: Anarchist and Mystical Counter-Cultures in America* (New York: Harper and Row, 1973). Nature worship and "transcendental individualism" are combined in Thoreau and Emerson, as in the later beats and hippies, who were also attracted to Oriental religion that promised a sense of the whole, yet, in American hands, led to personal withdrawal and self-sufficiency.

9. Jefferson to Joseph Priestly (1801), quoted in Daniel Boorstin, *America and the Image of Europe* (Cleveland: Meridian, 1960), p. 19. Thus, Norman O. Brown unfavorably contrasts the suffocatingly small spaces of Europe with the symbolic and physical openness of America that has been powerfully liberating. For him, America is the sense of potentiality for a new beginning: [Here, it is] possible to think about what it would mean to bring an end to that nightmare which is history" (interview, in *Voices and Visions*, ed. Sam Keen, pp. 32–33 [New York: Harper and Row, 1974]).

10. D. F. Sarmiento, "Travels in the United States in 1847," in *A Sarmiento Anthology*, trans. S. E. Grummon, ed. A. W. Bunkley (Princeton: Princeton University Press, 1948), p. 207.

11. The last figure is cited in George W. Pierson, *The Moving American* (New York: Knopf, 1973), p. 14. See also Stanley Elkins, "Institutional Breakdown in an Age of Expansion," in *Slavery*, pp. 27-37 (Chicago: University of Chicago Press, 1959). Leo Marx, *The Machine in the Garden* (New York: Oxford University Press, 1964); Morton and Lucia White, *The Intellectual versus the City* (Cambridge: Harvard University Press, 1964); Roderick Nash, *Wilderness and the American Mind*, rev. ed. (New Haven: Yale University Press, 1972); Peter Schmitt, *Back to Nature: The Arcadian Myth in Urban America* (New York: Oxford University Press, 1969); and Peter N. Carroll, *Puritanism and the Wilderness* (New York: Columbia University Press, 1969).

12. Rowland Berthoff, *An Unsettled People: Social Order and Disorder in American History* (New York: Harper and Row, 1971); Robert Wiebe, *The Segmented Society: An Introduction to the Meaning of America* (New York: Oxford University Press, 1975).

Some essentially materialist explanations for the political ideas of most Americans are Daniel Boorstin, *The Genius of American Politics* (Chicago: University of Chicago Press, 1953); Louis Hartz, *The Liberal Tradition in America* (New York: Harcourt, Brace, 1955); and David Potter, *People of Plenty* (Chicago: University of Chicago Press, 1954). While none of these writers is "consciously materialistic," each provides such an interpretation for the general absence of political theory in America. In brief, they agree that prosperous America had no need to write any political philosophy. Life required only the popular liberal dogmas that Tocqueville encountered in the 1830s. The few exceptions have been prompted by severe crises: *The Federalist* (the basic issue of government), *Disquisition on Government* (slavery), and liberal reform works published during the Great Depression of the 1930s.

13. Norman Ware, *The Labor Movement in the United States, 1860-1895: A Study in Democracy* (New York: Appleton, 1929), p. 304; Lillian Symes and Travers Clement, *Rebel America: The Story of Social Revolt in the United States*, introduction by Richard Drinnon (Boston: Beacon, 1972 [1934]); Staughton Lynd, *The Intellectual Origins of American Radicalism* (New York: Pantheon, 1968), p. 163. Lynd, however, shuns the term "anarchy," and avoids a discussion of individualism, restricting "the radical idea" to "a way of life at once free and communal." This perspective is too narrow, encompassing only what I define as left libertarianism.

Erwin C. Hargrove has speculated that the American Right emphasizes an individualism of property, while the Left stresses an individualism of persons, both of which tend toward anarchy ("On Canadian and American Political Cultures," *Canadian Journal of Economics and Political Science* 32 [August 1966]: 107).

14. C. Vann Woodard has edited a volume of cross-cultural essays, of varying quality, in *The Comparative Approach to American History* (New York: Basic Books, 1968). R. R. Palmer, in his broad-ranging work on the revolutionary era of bourgeois ascendency in the West, commented that " 'aristocrats' in America had less to lose, and 'democrats' had less to complain about" (*The Age of Democratic Revolution*, 2 vols. [Princeton: Princeton University Press, 1964], 2:510).

15. Malcolm Cowley, *The Literary Situation* (New York: Viking, 1954), p. 47. It could also be said of most later fiction, movies and television programs that institutional realities were often minimal. Erik Erikson might have interpreted this as an illustration of our love for "adolescent plasticity," so radically opposed to any society based upon tradition (*Children and Society* [New York: Norton, 1950]). Consider also Richard Chase's *The American Novel and Its Tradition* (New York: Doubleday, 1957).

16. Grady McWhiney, *Southerners and Other Americans* (New York: Basic Books, 1973); Carl Degler, *The Other South: Southern Dissenters in the Nineteenth Century* (New York: Harper and Row, 1974); John Shelton Reed, *The Enduring South: Subcultural Persistence in Mass Society* (Chapel Hill: University of North Carolina Press, 1975); and Edward Guinan, ed., *Redemption Denied: An Appalachian Reader* (Washington, D.C.: Appalachian Documentation, 1976). A comprehensive study on Southern radicalism remains to be written.

17. George Santayana, *Character and Opinion in the United States* (New York: George Braziller, 1955), pp. 94-95.

Chapter Four

1. John Locke, *A Second Treatise on Civil Government*, ed. Thomas I. Cook (New York: Hagner, 1947). Locke, however, was not a democrat. By "the people" he meant the elite or, as we might say, "the people who count." Perhaps the basic definition of American liberalism is Louis Hartz's *The Liberal Tradition in America* (New York: Harcourt, Brace, 1955). Like Hartz, I will be using "broad terms broadly." If I defined liberalism or many other words more precisely than I do, they would no longer be something that actually existed. Unlike Hartz, however, I emphasize the individualism rather than the conformity that Tocqueville noticed.

Other basic histories of liberalism include Frederick Watkins, *The Political Tradition of the West* (Cambridge: Harvard University Press, 1948), which is heavily influenced by Cold War concepts; and W. D. Grampp, *Economic Liberalism* (New York: Random House, 1965). Richard Ashcraft has an analysis of the social origins of liberalism in "Marx and Weber on Liberalism as Bourgeois Ideology." *Comparative Studies in Society and History* 14 (March 1972): 130-68. C. B. Macpherson has essays on liberalism in *The Real World of Democracy* (Oxford: Clarendon, 1966). The standard reference for changes in American laissez-faire is Sidney Fine's *Laissez-Faire and the General Welfare State: A Study of Conflict in American Thought, 1848-1895* (Ann Arbor: University of Michigan Press, 1956). A lament for the collapse of this old liberalism was composed by Arthur Ekirch in *The Decline of American Liberalism* (New York: Atheneum, 1967).

2. Quoted in *The Future of Capitalism: A Symposium* (New York: Macmillan, 1967), though Bentham, who could be wildly contradictory, sometimes said the opposite. For an orderly, brief exposition, see Guido de Ruggerio, "Liberalism," in *Encyclopedia of the Social Sciences*, 9:435-42 (New York: Macmillan, 1933), along with Harold Laski's article "Liberty" (ibid., pp. 442-47) and Isaiah Berlin's *Four Essays on Liberty* (London: Oxford University Press, 1969), p. 129. Laski asserted that English liberalism began with "the antithesis of the individual and the state."

3. Benjamin Franklin, *Letters and Papers of Benjamin Franklin and Richard Jackson, 1753-1785*, ed. Carl Van Doren (Philadelphia: University of Pennsylvania Press, 1947), pp. 34, 35. This reference, directed against the English Poor Laws, was written in 1753. For another, in 1789, see *The Writings of Benjamin Franklin*, ed. Henry Albert Smyth, 10 vols. (New York, 1905-7), 5:122-27, and "On the Price of Corn, and the Management of the Poor," ibid., 5:534-39.

4. David L. Jacobson, ed. *The English Libertarian Heritage* (Indianapolis: Bobbs-Merrill, 1965); Bernard Bailyn, *The Ideological Origins of the American Revolution* (Cambridge: Harvard University Press, 1967).

5. S. M. Lipset has studied the Revolution's impact on American values by comparing them with Canadian opinions on authority, political systems, religious sentiments, class relations, and education. He concluded that the United States was a far more "leftist" or "populist" culture ("Revolution and Counter-revolution: The United States and Canada," in *Revolution and Counter-revolution*, pp. 31-63 [New York: Basic Books, 1968].

6. Dr. August Nigro, "Separation and Reparation in Classic American Literature" (presented at an NEH seminar in the Sociology Department of the University of California, Berkeley, on 25 May 1977). There was to be no centennial for the Constitution, and Lincoln and others have dated our founding from 1776, not 1789.

7. Frederick Wilhelmsen and Willmoore Kendall, "Cicero and the Politics of Public Orthodoxy," *Intercollegiate Review* 5 (winter 1968-69): 84-85.

8. Gunnar Myrdal, *An American Dilemma* (New York: Harper and Brothers, 1944), p. 3.

An independent Marxist, Leon Samson, recognized that this "Americanism" functioned as a kind of substitute socialism. So long as most Americans equated freedom, equality, and opportunity with "free enterprise," socialism would be defeated. Radicals, he said, would have to demonstrate that socialism would fulfill "the American way of life," not annihilate it. Samson's work is intelligently outlined in Frank Warren's book *An Alternative Vision: The Socialist Party in the 1930's* (Bloomington: Indiana University Press, 1974), pp. 54–69.

9. Paine, *The Complete Writings of Thomas Paine*, 2:408; Jefferson letter to James Madison (1787), in *The Papers of Thomas Jefferson*, ed. Julian P. Boyd, 2: 2:92–93 (Princeton: Princeton University Press, 1955); Jefferson, letter to Edward Carrington (1787), ibid., 11:49; Washington, quoted in William O. Douglas, *A Living Bill of Rights* (New York: Doubleday, 1961), p. 10; *The Federalist*, ed. Jacob E. Cook (Middletown, Conn.: Wesleyan University Press, 1961).

10. Paine "Common Sense" (1775), in *The Works of Thomas Paine*, p. 294 (New York: Wm. Wise and Company, 1924); Jefferson, First Inaugural, in *The Writings of Thomas Jefferson*, ed. A. A. Lipscomb and A. E. Bergh, 20 vols., 3:320–21 (Washington, D.C., 1905). Jefferson, in practice, was not always as libertarian as his theories, a flaw that was documented by Professor Leonard Levy in his *Jefferson and Civil Liberties* (Cambridge, Mass.: Harvard University, 1963).

11. Alexis de Tocqueville, *Democracy in America*, trans. George Lawrence, ed. J. P. Mayer (Garden City, N.Y.: Doubleday, Anchor, 1969), pp. 508. 667–68. For a systematic statement and evaluation of this unifying "culture religion," consult my article " 'The Dogma of the Sovereignty of the People': De Tocqueville's [*Religion*] *in America*," *Journal of Church and State* 14;2 (1972): 279–95.

12. Later to Malwida Von Meysenbug, in *Speeches, Correspondence, and Political Papers of Carl Schurz*, ed. Frederick Bancroft, 1:8 (New York, 1913). Progressive elements of the rising middle classes of Europe often turned to America as a successful model of a middle-class culture. Especially in England, Benthamites, Chartists, Dissenters, Radicals, and some early socialists were frequent admirers of the American cause, looking upon the United States as a vanguard nation in much the same way that some later radicals viewed the Soviet Union. Several excellent studies on the relationship between the American and British progressive middle classes are Howard Mumford Jones, "The Radical Republic," in *O Strange New World: American Culture, the Formative Years*, pp. 273–311 (New York: Viking, 1964); G. D. Lillibridge, *Beacon of Freedom: The Impact of American Democracy upon Great Britain, 1830–1870* (Philadelphia: University of Pennsylvania Press, 1954); David Crook, *American Democracy in English Politics, 1815–1850* (Oxford: Clarendon, 1965), which makes vital qualifications of much of Lillibridge's analysis; and Henry Pelling, *America and the British Left: From Bright to Bevan* (New York: New York University Press, 1957). Early French commentaries on the United States are treated in René Remond, *Les Etats-Unis devant l'opinion francais, 1815–1852*, 2 vols. in one (Paris: A. Colin, 1962).

13. Seth Luther, quoted in "Was This Nation Born in Revolution?" (Washington, D.C.: People's Bicentennial Commission, 1974?), p. 8; Keith Melden, "Forerunners of Freedom: The Grimké Sisters in Massachusetts, 1837–38," *Essex Institute Historical Collections* 103 (July1967): 223–49. Melden attributes much of the unexpected discussion about women's rights to expanding education, changes in the work force, and organizational experience gained in benevolent and charitable groups. American feminism was the first to emerge in the modern world as a separate movement.

14. Jefferson to Edward Carrington (1787), in *The Papers of Thomas Jefferson*, 11:49. Although Jefferson's society could ostracize antidemocratic heretics, and in that sense be repressive, it was also a model of radical liberalism. In one of his most "extreme" letters, he outlined a decentralist paradise based on ward government: "Divide the counties into wards of such size that every citizen can attend, when called on, and act in person. Ascribe to them the government of their wards in all things relating to them exclusively. A justice, chosen by

themselves, in each, a constable, a military company, a patrol, a school, the care of their own poor, their own portion of the public roads, the choice of one or more jurors to serve in some court...will relieve the county administration of nearly all of its business, will have it better done, and by making every citizen an acting members of the government, and in the office nearest and most interesting to him, will attach him by his strongest feelings to the independence of his country, and its republican constitution" (from a letter to Samuel Kercheval, written on 12 July, 1816, in *Free Government in the Making*, ed. Alpheus Mason, pp. 369, 371–72 [New York: Oxford University Press, 1949]).

American responses to several institutionally authoritarian movements are studied by David Brion Davis in "Some Themes of Counter-Subversion. An Analysis of Anti Masonic, Anti-Catholic and Anti-Mormon Literature," *Mississippi Valley Historical Review* 47 (September 1960): 205–24. The same themes are easily found during the Red Scare of the 1920s and the anti-Communism of the 1950s.

15. Yehoshua Arieli, *Individualism and Nationalism in American Ideology* (Cambridge: Harvard University Press, 1964), p. 332. For a superb summary of his influence in America, see Richard Hofstadter, "The Vogue of Spencer," in *Social Darwinism in American Thought*, pp. 31–50 (New York: George Braziller, 1959). Other aspects of his work are analyzed in Jay Rumney, *Herbert Spencer's Sociology* (New York: Atherton, 1966) and John David Peel, *Herbert Spencer: The Evolution of a Sociologist* (London: Heinemann, 1971).

16. Herbert Spencer, *Social Statics* (New York: Appleton, 1913), p. 55. In theory, Andrew Carnegie and a Slovak worker in one of his mills should have equal rights. Clearly, this doctrine favored the Carnegies.

17. Hofstadter, *Social Darwinism in American Thought*, p. 7.

18. Edward C. Kirkland, *Business in the Gilded Age* (Madison: University of Wisconsin Press, 1952), p. 40; *Essays of William Graham Sumner*, ed. A. G. Keller and M. Davie (New Haven: Yale University Press, 1940). Sumner was not a typical liberal: he was no optimist, did not envision continual progress, denied equality, and insisted that increases in the population, combined with limited resources, required a more or less animalistic struggle for survival.

19. Richard Wohl, "The 'Rags to Riches' Story: An Episode of Secular Idealism," in *Class, Status and Power*, ed. R. Bendix and S. M. Lipset, p. 394 (New York: Free Press, 1953). Richard Weiss added this evaluation: "Correctly understood, Alger is not a representative of his time, but a nostalgic spokesman of a dying order. Of middle-class rural origins, he was always an alien in the industry-dominated society of his adult life" (*The Age of Industrialism in America*, ed. F. C. Jaher, p. 305 [New York: Free Press, 1968]). John Sproat also criticizes "the politics of nostalgia" in *"The Best Men": Liberal Reformers of the Gilded Age* (New York: Oxford University Press, 1968).

20. John E. Hayes, general secretary and treasurer of the Knights of Labor, in *The Chicago Conference on Trusts, 1899* (Chicago: Civic Federation of Chicago, 1900), p. 338.

21. Philip Foner and James Weinstein have disputed the origins of "the new liberalism" in a series of conflicting essays: Weinstein's criticism of Foner in "Gompers and the New Liberalism, 1900–1909," *Studies on the Left* 5 (fall 1965): 94–105 Foner's rejoinder, ibid., 6 (March–April 1966): 71–75; and Weinstein's conclusion, ibid.: 76–9. Weinstein's interpretation is fully developed in *The Corporate Ideal in the Liberal State, 1900–1918* (Boston: Beacon, 1968).

22. Mills, "The Labor Leaders and the Power Elite," in *Power, Politics and People*, pp. 108–9 (New York: Ballantine, 1963 [1954]). Williams, *The Contours of American History* (New York: World, 1961), pp. 358–60; Herman and Julia Schwendinger, "Liberal-Syndicalism," in *The Sociology of the Chair*, pp. 121–29 (New York: Basic Books, 1974).

23. *American Commonwealth* (New York: Macmillan, 1914), 2:241. As a European, Bryce was also amazed at the freedom of the American press to "paint the faults of politicians in strong, not to say exaggerated colours" (p. 245).

The Supreme Court has been one of the few institutions to be treated with a certain reverence because it has been perceived as the interpreter (however fallible) of the societal truths embodied in the Constitution and, beyond that, "natural law." Its legitimacy is less as a historical institution than as the visible representative of invisible verities.

24. In Europe, liberalism has generally retained its traditional meanings, with the philosophical exception of the "organic liberalism" of T. H. Green and L. T. Hobhouse. Nevertheless, in practice, what Americans consider "liberalism" would usually be termed "socialism." Fritz Machlup comments on this cultural gap in "Liberalism and the Choice of Freedoms," in *Roads to Freedom*, ed. Erich Streissler, pp. 117–46. (New York: A. M. Kelly, 1969).

Chapter Five

1. D. H. Lawrence, *Studies in Classic American Literature* (New York: Viking, 1964). p. 64; Michael Colacurcio, "The Symbolic and the Symptomatic: D. H. Lawrence in Recent American Criticism," *American Quarterly* 27 (October 1975): 486–501.

The substance of extreme laissez-faire liberalism is condensed in this description: "The community is a fictitious *body* composed of the individual persons who are considered as constituting, as it were, its *members*. The interest of the community then is what?—The sum of the interests of the several members who compose it" (Jeremy Bentham, *An Introduction to the Principles of Morals and Legislation*, ed. J. H. Burns and H. L. A. Hart [London: University of London, Athlone, 1970], p. 12).

2. John L. Thomas, "Romantic Reform in America, 1815–1865," *American Quarterly* 17 (winter 1965): 658.

3. Emerson, "Politics" (1844), in *The Complete Essays and Other Writings of Ralph Waldo Emerson*, ed. Brooks Atkinson, p. 430 (New York: Modern Lilbrary, 1940); *Journals of Ralph Waldo Emerson*, ed. E. W. Emerson and W. E. Forbes (Boston: Houghton, Mifflin, 1909–14), 3:200; 5:302–3; *The Letters of Ralph Waldo Emerson*, ed. Ralph Rusk (New York, 1939), 1:412–13. Emerson and others are placed in their historical setting by R. Jackson Wilson's essay "The Plight of the Transcendental Individual" (*In Quest of Community*, pp. 1–31 [New York: Oxford University Press, 1968].

4. Henry David Thoreau, *Walden*, and *Civil Disobedience* (New York: Airmont Publishing Company, 1965), p. 246; Emerson, "Thoreau," in *The Works of Ralph Waldo Emerson*, 5 vols., 3:381 (New York: Charles Bigelow, 192?).

5. Richard Drinnon, "Thoreau's Politics of the Upright Man," *Anarchy*, no. 26 (April 1963), pp. 117–28. Thoreau, however, was more emotionally expressive, more sensitive about nature, and less willing to live for tomorrow.

6. Henry George, *Progress and Poverty* (Garden City, N.Y.: Garden City Publishing Company, 1926), p. 453.

7. Ibid., p. 454.

8. Henry George, "The Functions of Government," in *Social Problems*, pp. 171–93 (Garden City, N.Y.: Doubleday, 1912) (it was, in rank of importance, chap. 17); Henry George, "The Man *versus* the State," in *The Complete Works of Henry George*, 5:65–71 (Garden City, N.Y.: Doubleday, Page and Company, 1911).

9. Preface to 4th ed., *Progress and Poverty* (New York: Robert Schalkenbach Foundation, 1935), p. xvii.

10. Henry George on Edward Bellamy, *Standard*, 28 September, 1889.

11. Albert Jay Nock, *Henry George* (New York: Morrow, 1939); Charles Barker, *Henry George* (New York: Oxford University Press, 1955); Steven B. Cord, *Henry George: Dreamer or Realist?* (Philadelphia: University of Pennsylvania Press, 1965); and Edward Rose, *Henry George* (New York: Twayne, 1968).

12. Marx to John Swinton, 2 June, 1881, in "Unpublished Letters of Karl Marx and Friedrich Engels to Americans," trans. and ed. Leonard Mins, *Science and Society* 2 (spring 1938): 227; Marx and Engels, *Selected Correspondence* (New York: International, 1935), pp. 394–96.

George Bernard Shaw humorously claimed to have instantly recognized the Americanness of Henry George the first time he heard him lecture: "He spoke of Liberty, Justice, Truth, Natural Law, and other strange eighteenth century superstitutions, and he explained with great simplicity and sincerity the views of the Creator who had gone completely out of fashion in London the previous decade and had not been heard of there since" (quoted in Charles Barker, *Henry George*, p. 376). It may reflect the more thoroughly bourgeois nature of American culture that most of the English who were deeply influenced by George evolved into socialism, whereas most of his American followers either lost themselves in laissez-faire reveries or were (like Louis Post, later a federal official under President Wilson) effectively absorbed into the new liberalism.

13. Morris Hillquit, *Loose Leaves from a Busy Life* (New York, 1934), p. 4. Other sources agree. For background, read James J. Martin, *Men against the State: The Expositors of Individualist Anarchism in America, 1827–1908* (Colorado Springs: Myles, 1970 [1953]).

14. George Schumm, "Benjamin R. Tucker—A Brief Sketch of His Life and Work," *Freethinker's Magazine* 11 (July 1893): 439; Warren, quoted by Joseph Dorfman, in *The Economic Mind in American Civilization*, 5 vols., 2:674 (New York: Viking, 1946–195?).

15. "Only Books That Teach Anarchy Are Sold in This Sixth Avenue Shop," New York *Herald*, 12 April 1908. This honor was really deserved by Charles Kerr of Chicago.

16. Tucker, "The Attitude of Anarchism toward Industrial Combinations," in *The Chicago Conference on Trusts, 1899*, pp. 253–61 (Chicago: Civic Federation of Chicago, 1900). Some press reactions can be found in the Tucker files at the Labadie Collection of the University of Michigan.

17. Peter Kropotkin, "Anarchism," *Encyclopaedia Britannica*, 11th ed. (New York: Encyclopaedia Britannica, 1910), 1:917; Emma Goldman, *Living My Life*, 2 vols., 1:232 (New York: Knopf, 1931). Lucy Parsons, the wife of anarchist A. R. Parsons, who was hanged in 1887 for his supposed complicity in the 1886 Haymarket "riot," generously concurred with George Schilling's evaluation: "It was not until after Benjamin R. Tucker, of Boston, issued his *Liberty*—which I have always regarded as an epoch in the intellectual progress of the movement—that the principle of voluntary association, in contradistinction to State control, began to make systematic converts" (quoted in Michael R. Johnson, "Albert R. Parsons: An American Architect of Syndicalism," *Midwest Quarterly* 9 [January 1968]: 199).

18. Whitman, quoted in Horace Traubel, ed., *With Walt Whitman in Camden* (Boston: Small, Maynard and Company, 1906), 1:350; Shaw, quoted by his official biographer, Archibald Henderson, in *George Bernard Shaw: Man of the Century*, p. 178n (New York: Appleton-Century-Crofts, 1956). In the 1930s, Shaw reaffirmed that he had "a warm regard for Benjamin, and have lost no opportunity of publicly expressing it" (*Free Vistas*, ed. Joseph Ishill, 2 vols., 2:302 [Berkeley Heights, N.J.: Oriole Press, 1937]. The same volume contains H. L. Mencken's estimate that Tucker was "a man who deserves a great deal more fame than he has got" (p. 273). For O'Neill's contact, see Louis Shaeffer, *O'Neill: Son and Playwright* (Boston: Little, Brown, 1968), pp. 102–5, 122–23, 135, 139, 260, 339.

19. These quotations are from the man whom Tucker later called his "first source of light," Josiah Warren (*Practical Details* [Princeton, Mass.: Cooperative Publishing Company, 1872], p. 75). I have used the term anarchist to denote all those who believed in the possibility of a stateless society, whether or not they ever adopted this single word to describe themselves. The term was not commonly used by complete antistatists in America until the 1880s.

20. I am indebted to Mrs. Nina Regis, genealogical librarian of the Free Public Library, New Bedford, Massachusetts, for information on the Tucker family.

21. Alexander Starbuck, *History of the American Whale Fishery, to the Year 1876*, 2 vols.

(New York: Argosy-Antiquarian, Ltd., 1964), and "The Gentle Anarchist of Ste. Devote," *Bulletin: Old Dartmouth Historical Society*, New Bedford (Winter, 1961), p. 4.

22. Herman Melville, *Moby Dick*, ed. Harrison Hayford and Herschel Parker (New York: W. W. Norton, 1967), p. 37. Richard Engler has also written a useful essay: "A Crowded Coast: New Bedford," in *The Challenge of Diversity*, pp. 3–42 (New York: Harper and Row, 1964).

23. Reprinted in the *Word* 8 (August 1879): 3. Benjamin Tucker was to identify the anarchists as "simply unterrified Jeffersonian Democrats" (*Liberty* 5 [10 March 1888]: 3). When he became editor of *Liberty*, he was reminded of Jefferson's comment that if he had to choose between a society without government and a society without newspapers, he would prefer the former.

24. T. D. Seymour Bassett, "The Quaker and Communitarianism," *Bulletin of the Friends' Historical Association* 43 (1954): 84–99; Frederick Tolles, "New Light Quakers of Lynn and New Bedford," *New England Quarterly* 32 (September 1959): 291–319; "Reminiscences of Quakerism" (semifictional), *Chambers' Journal of Popular Literature*, 3d ser., 13 (5 May, 1860): 284–86; "New Bedford," *Harper's Magazine* 21 (June 1860): 1–19.

25. William J. Potter, "In Memoriam," *Index* 7 (19 October, 1876): 499.

26. Steven T. Byington MS. on Tucker, 1939, Labadie Collection, University of Michigan; Daniel Ricketson, *History of New Bedford* (New Bedford: Daniel Ricketson, 1858); William J. Potter, MS. history of the First Congregational Society of New Bedford "As Illustrative of Ecclesiastical Evolution" (Old Dartmouth Historical Society, New Bedford); Leonard Ellis, *History of New Bedford* (Syracuse, N.Y.: D. Mason and Company, 1892).

27. Tucker, in Emanie Sachs, *"The Terrible Siren": Victoria Woodhull, 1838–1927*, pp. 236–66, esp. p. 241 (New York: Harper's, 1928). This autobiographical fragment, besides being a charming account of his seduction by Victoria and his following status as her "boy lover," has extensive information on his early life. Further background is provided by "Boston Radicals," in the Boston *Sunday Globe*, 5 April, 1891; Paul R. Frothingham, in *Heralds of a Liberal Faith*, ed. S. A. Eliot, 3 vols., 3:303–8 (Boston, 1910–56); and an article on Potter in the *Dictionary of American Biography*.

28. Potter, "The New Protestantism: Its Relation to the Old," *Radical* 9 (September 1871): 113.

29. Potter, "The South Carolina Negro," *Index* 7 (2 November, 1876): 523. Local abolitionist activity is summarized in Daniel Ricketson's *History of New Bedford*, p. 252, and Roman J. Zorn's "The New England Anti-Slavery Society," *Journal of Negro History* 42 (July 1957): 157–76.

30. Potter, *The Free Religious Association: Its Twenty-five Years and Their Meaning* (Boston, 1892), pp. 8–9. This follows the pattern I mentioned in the Introduction: as Quakers and Unitarians became institutionalized and traditional, a libertarian reaction was generated against the increase of authority. The basic work on the FRA is Stow Persons's *Free Religion* (New Haven: Yale University, 1947). Tucker's own memories can be found in a letter to the Reverend E. Stanton Hodgin, reprinted in the New Bedford *Sunday Standard*, 12 June 1927, and in an article, "Tucker Hailed as Paul of Anarchistic Gospel," ibid., 22 May 1927. For tangible proof of Tucker's early commitment to Free Religion, see his 1872 pledge of one hundred dollars to the *Index*. Final payment was made in 1876 (*Index* 7 [1876], "Cash Receipts," p. 605).

31. Sidney Warren, *American Freethought, 1860–1914* (New York: Columbia University Press, 1943), p. 111. Paine, one of the deistic heroes of many of the Free Religionists, had once asserted: "My own mind is my own church" (*Thomas Paine: Representative Selections*, ed. Harry Clark, p. 235 [New York: American Book Company, 1944], which reminds me of Warren's remark). Like both the Free Religionists and the anarchists, Paine was "very bourgeois" and believed that "freedom...meant a combination of individualistic religion and individualistic freedom of trade" (Herbert Schneider, "American Enlightenment," in *History of American Philosophy*, p. 71 [New York: Columbia University Press, 1946]). See also Joseph L.

Blau, "American Enlightenment," in *Men and Movements in American Philosophy*, pp. 36–72 (New York: Prentice-Hall, 1952).

Before the creation of the FRA, protoanarchists like Lysander Spooner and Josiah Warren had appealed to deistic traditions. Spooner composed two pamphlets in 1834 and 1836 called *The Deist's Immortality* and *The Deist's Reply*, and Warren expected that Enlightenment reason, proving the sterility of government, would "melt away all political systems" (*Word* 1 [July 1872]: 1). Arthur Schlesinger, Sr., has also argued, in his little book *The American as Reformer*, that the two vital stimulants to reform in America have been the attempts to achieve Enlightenment ideals (such as the "all men are created equal" of the Declaration of Independence) and the humanitarian principles of the Christian religion. Much of this was found in the FRA.

32. Quoted in John M. Bullard, *Friends' Academy, 1810–1960* New Bedford: Reynolds-DeWalt, 1960, p. 107. See also Thomas R. Rodman and John Tetlow, *Centennial History of Friends' Academy* (New Bedford, 1876) and catalogs and circulars from the academy in the New Bedford Public Library.

33. Benjamin R. Tucker to Ewing C. Baskette, 11 October, 1935 (Baskette Collection, University of Illinois. Speakers during this period were verified by Richard C. Kugler, director of the Old Dartmouth Historical Society (New Bedford) in a letter dated 12 February, 1969.

34. *Liberty* 1 (1 April 1882): 1.

35. The religious rules of Harvard were typical for that day. When Ezra Cornell and Andrew White founded the strictly secular Cornell University in 1867, they were subjected to a storm of clerical abuse. Furthermore, university education tended to ignore or dispute much of modern science. In 1883, Charles Francis Adams had delivered a stinging address to the Harvard Phi Beta Kappa for the failure of the university to teach more than "a superficial knowledge of two dead languages." For Tucker's later objections, see *Liberty* 1 (12 November 1881) and *Liberty* 3 (26 December 1885): 1.

36. Tucker, letter to the editor, New Bedford *Sunday Standard*, 24 September 1924, and his essay in Sachs, "The Terrible Siren," p. 241. For further comment, read *Liberty* 9 (26 November 1892), p. 1. Greeley was one of his models for a radical editor when he began his own newspaper in 1881.

37. John R. Commons and others, *History of Labor in the United States* (New York: Macmillan, 1918), 2:138–39. For a discussion of the NELRL and its "sentimentalist credo," see David Montgomery, in *Beyond Equality: Labor and the Radical Republicans* (New York: Knopf, 1967), pp. 411–14. Gerald Grob, in *Workers and Utopia* (Evanston, Ill.:Northwestern University Press, 1961), divides the labor movement into two groups, reform unionists and trade unionists, and states that the former (like the NELRL) sought to restore the supposed past independence of the worker.

38. William H. Sylvis, *The Life, Speeches, Labors and Essays of William H. Sylvis*, ed. James C. Sylvis, p. 276 (Philadephia: Claxton, Remsen and Haffelfinger, 1872).

39. Commons and others, *History of Labor*, 2:141.

40. Johnson, "Labor Parties and Labor Reform," *Radical* 9 (November 1871): 241–65 (for Wendell Phillips's outraged repudiation of much of Johnson's commentary, see pp. 389–90); Marx, "American Split," in *Documents of the First International*, 5 vols., 5:323–32 (London: Lawrence and Wishart, n.d.).

41. *Index* 5 (1 January 1874); F. E. Abbot, "The Work of Free Religion," *Index* 6 (25 November 1875): 558; F. E. Abbot, "The Spirit of 1876," *Index* 7 (30 March 1876): 150. Many FRA members also met extreme individualists like Ezra Heywood, S. P. Andrews, and Josiah Warren at meetings of the Radical Club. See *Sketches and Reminiscences of the Radical Club*, ed. by Mrs. John T. Sargent (Boston: James R. Osgood, 1880).

42. *Index* 6 (9 December 1875), p. 580. See also his letter in *Word* 4 (February 1876): 3. Herbert Spencer verged on a similar conclusion: "Thanks to the growth of the Protestant

spirit...we have ignored the State [regulations concerning a person's faith and form of worship]—wholly in theory and partly in practice. But how have we done so? By assuming an attitude which, if consistently maintained, implies a right to ignore the State entirely" ("The Right to Ignore the State," reprinted in *Rampart Journal of Individualist Thought* 1 [winter 1965]: 71.

43. *Liberty* 8 (4 June 1892): 4. The radical individualism of the FRA may validate a later comment that was quoted by Martin Luther King, Jr.: "A religion that ends with the individual, ends" (King, *Stride toward Freedom* [New York: Harper, 1958], p. 90).

44. Tucker, "Do Liberals Know Themselves?" *Liberty* 1 (4 February 1882): 1. While God was also denied as an unscientific abstraction (that is, based on a transcendental leap of intuition rather than on empirical verification), Tucker admitted that anyone had a right to believe in one God or many gods so long as others were not compelled to pay similar homage.

45. Tucker, *Instead of a Book, by a Man Too Busy to Write One* (New York: B. R. Tucker, 1893), p. 5; Tucker, letter entitled "The Sin of Usury," *Index* 4 (23 October 1873), p. 423, with a reply by F. E. Abbot.

46. J. S. Mill, *Autobiography* (New York: Holt, 1874), p. 256.

47. See Richard T. Ely, *The Labor Movement in America* (New York: Crowell, 1886), 245 ff.; Hutchins Hapgood, *The Spirit of Labor* (New York: Duffield, 1907); James J. Martin, "Victor S. Yarros Delineates the Spencerian Influence," in *Men against the State*, pp. 232–37 (De Kalb, Ill.: Adrian Allen Associates, 1953).

Some of Spencer's works, such as *Man versus the State*, have even been advertised by the Anarcho-Communist press. For example, see the back pages of P. J. Proudhon, *The General Idea of the Revolution in the Nineteenth Century* (London: Freedom Press, 1923). In 1921, Sacco and Vanzetti also listed Spencer as one of their teachers, along with Tucker, Proudhon, Kropotkin, Bakunin, Stirner, and others. While showing few powers of differentiation, their referrences appear to be genuine (letter to Governor Fuller, in Osmund Fraenkel, *The Sacco-Vanzetti Case*, p. 148 [New York: Knopf, 1931]. See also Nicola Sacco and Bartolomeo Vanzetti, *The Letters of Sacco and Vanzetti* (New York: Viking, 1928).

48. *Liberty* 1 (10 December 1881): 1.

49. Tucker, *Liberty* 10 (28 August 1894): 1.

50. "NATURAL RIGHTS versus Governmental Usurpation" (quotations from Jefferson), *Word* 3 (October 1874): 1. Although Jefferson's remark is, strictly speaking, related only to primogeniture, it was certainly reinterpreted by others.

51. B. R. Tucker, *Liberty* 7 (7 March 1891): 1. He further remarked that "when people begin to hate their governments, they will begin to love one another" (*Liberty* 9 [24 September 1892]: 1). The only comprehensive anarchist study of nationalism is Rudolf Rocker's *Nationalism and Culture* (Los Angeles: Rocker Publications Committee, 1937). By and large, early anarchists like Tucker and Goldman seldom wrote elaborate tomes on their major concepts. Proudhon composed disjointed treatises, but Kropotkin was very unusual, in the nineteenth century, as a systematic anarchist thinker. For additional commentary, see my essay "Anarchism on the Origins and Functions of the State: Some Basic Notes," in *Reinventing Anarchy*, ed. David DeLeon and others (London: Routledge and Kegan Paul, 1978).

52. Quoted in Herbert L. Osgood, "Scientific Anarchism," *Political Science Quarterly* 4 (March 1889): 9–10 n.

53. Stephen Pearl Andrews, *The Science of Society*, no. 1 (New York: T. L. Nichols, 1854), p. 39.

54. Some of the "no-government" implications of radical abolitionism have been outlined and analyzed by Eunice Schuster, in "Native American Anarchism: A Study in Left-Wing Individualism" (*Smith College Studies in History* 17;3 [1932]: 61–70, 79–80), Stanley Elkins's "Institutional Breakdown in an Age of Expansion," in *Slavery*, pp. 27-37 (Chicago: University of Chicago Press, 1959, and Lewis Perry, in *Radical Abolitionism: Anarchy and the Govern-*

ment of God in Antislavery Thought (Ithaca: Cornell University Press, 1973). The career of Lysander Spooner, for example, was primarily based on a consistently radical application of this antistatist abolitionism. Sketches of his pre- and postwar anti-institutionalism are found in Aileen Kraditor's *Means and Ends in American Abolitionism* (New York: Pantheon, 1969) and George Frederickson's *Inner Civil War: Northern Intellectuals and the Crisis of the Union* (New York: Harper and Row, 1965).

55. Tucker, *Liberty* 1 (10 June 1882): 3. Their definitions of a union resembled Proudhon's voluntary associations of workers, Emerson's "beneficent socialism," Spencer's joint-stock companies, and other forms that rejected compulsory dues, discipline, and numerous officers.

56. Tucker, *Liberty* 1 (15, April 1881); 1. It is revealing that while the antistatists were generally sympathetic to the workers in the Great Strike of 1877, many of the most prominent Free Religionists displayed intense hostility. See *Index* 8 (20 September 1877): 452.

57. Tucker, *Liberty* 1 (1 October 1881): 3. He once confessed that it was easier to demonstrate why he was not anything else than to tell why he was an anarchist: "Archy once denied, only Anarchism can be affirmed. It is a matter of logic" ("Why I Am an Anarchist," *Twentieth Century Magazine* 4 [29 May 1890]: 5–6).

58. Tucker *Liberty* 3 (3 June 1885): 4.

59. S. P. Andrews, *The Science of Society*, no. 2 (New York: T. L. Nichols, 1854), pp. 179–81.

60. Warren, *Equitable Commerce* (New York, 1852), p. 69. A prominent historian of religion, Franklin Littell, has criticized Warren, saying that "the patriarchal principle, especially when reinforced by religious sanctions, worked better than philosophical anarchism as a social cement" ("The Problem of Authority," introduction to Charles Nordhoff, *The Communistic Societies of the United States* [New York: Schocken, 1971], p. xx). Aside from the possible objection that most Americans would not find the image of "social cement" an attractive one, Littell's interpretation is flawed by inaccurate information (such as the statement that Utopia and Modern Times were short-lived), and in the apparent assumption that all anarchists repudiated all authority.

61. Andrews, *Science of Society*, no. 2, p. 49. While this implied craft labor, not factory jobs, he was not merely an archaic spokesman for a simpler agrarian and petty capitalist period. None of the major anarchists repudiated modern technology. Godwin, in the 1790s, had eloquently expressed the possibility that machines could liberate people for a fuller life. He made the fantastic prediction that the members of a properly functioning society would work a half-hour every day! Warren and Andrews more modestly estimated that two hours of daily labor might provide all necessities. Kropotkin was also confident that mechanization could free men and women from innumerable tedious and degrading tasks.

62. Tucker, *Liberty* 11 (8 February 1896): 5. One scholar has contrasted Tucker's "moral egoism" with the "asocial solipsism" of a German ultraindividualist whom Tucker greatly admired, Max Stirner. Tucker honored the limitations of a society of contracts, with absolute respect for the rights of others and with many forms of popular will as law (R. W. K. Paterson, *The Nihilistic Egoist, Max Stirner* [London: Oxford University Press, 1971], pp. 128–30).

Kropotkin was fearful that defense associations would be the seed for recreating the state, but he offered no realistic alternative for defending anarchism. His criticisms are scattered throughout *Kropotkin's Revolutionary Pamphlets*, ed. Roger Baldwin (New York: Dover, 1970 [1927]—such as pp. 173–74, 297).

63. E. A. Ross, an American academic, made this distinction in his early work, *Social Control* (1901), which drew many examples from the American frontier. The anarchist possibilities of this were mentioned by John Ellerby in "Anarchism and Social Control" (*Anarchy*, no. 32 [October 1963] p. 321).

64. Clarence Lee Swartz, "The Solution of the 'Negro Problem,'" *Liberty* 15 (December 1906): 47.

65. Quoted in John B. Ellis, *Free Love and Its Votaries* (New York: U.S. Publishing Company, 1890), p. 398 (this book's information on Modern Times is more reliable than its interpretations). One inhabitant characterized the town's philosophy this way: "We are Protestants; we are Liberals" (p. 386).

Modern Times prospered for more than a decade, but like most utopian ventures it was disintegrated and digested by the larger social order that surrounded it. It could not escape from such effects of the Civil War as conscription and inflation, and the growing financial and population pressures of its socioeconomic environment.

66. Tucker, *Liberty* 14 (April 1903): 4. A century before Orwell, the conformist dimensions of American mass culture had been studied by Tocqueville, who warned of "the tyranny of the majority." Indeed, the politics of much of *Democracy in America* frequently resemble the anarchism of *Homage to Catalonia*.

67. Warren, *Equitable Commerce*, p. 117.

68. Tucker, *Instead of a Book*, pp. 57–58.

69. Leonard B. Ellis, *History of New Bedford*, p. 602. Mrs. Abner R. Tucker was also the 1891 president of another voluntary society for charity, the women's group of the New Bedford Fort Society, which aided the families of seamen (p. 601). As an aside, it might be noted that her son coldly denied altruism as a motive for benevolence. He was certain that all people were charitable only when it gave them egoistic gratification. Kropotkin, on the other hand, assumed that compassionate "mutual aid" was an essential element of human nature.

Another parallel to anarchist forms of organization was the Free Religious Association. Reverend Potter outlined a structure that was "designedly free and spontaneous in its plan" (*Proceedings at the First Annual Meeting of the Free Religious Association* [Boston: Adams and Company, 1868], p. 5). O. B. Frothingham heartily endorsed this: "Not long ago I heard the Free Religious Association violently assailed because it did nothing but talk. This is true: it never pretended to do anything else" (Frothingham, "Free Religious Association," *Unitarian Review* 31 [May 1889]: 394).

70. Quoted in James J. Martin, "Josiah Warren," *Liberation* 2 (December 1957): 11. Tucker asserted that "the most perfect Socialism is possible only on the condition of the most perfect individualism" (*Liberty* 8 [16 July 1892]: 2).

71. Yehoshua Arieli, *Individualism and Nationalism in American Ideology* (Cambridge: Harvard University Press, 1964), p. 283. Tucker denied that Emerson became less individualistic and more "statist" in his declining years. For quotations of Emerson's "anarchism," see Tucker, "Emerson, the Reformer," *Liberty* 1 (13 May 1882): 3–4.

Whitman's subscription can be verified by examining the index references to it in the volumes of Horace Traubel's *With Walt Whitman in Camden* (various publishers). See also "Leaves of Grass," *Liberty* 1 (26 November 1881): 3, and Tucker's "The Whirligig of Time," New York *Herald* (Paris ed.), 23 November 1930. As early as 1877, Tucker's *Radical Review* had lauded Whitman in a thirty-five-page appreciation by the Reverend Joseph Marvin, and a scattering of congratulatory comments by Morse. When *Leaves of Grass* was banned in Boston in 1881, it was Tucker who risked prosecution by noisily defying this act. Whitman realized that Morse, Tucker, and others considered him a near-anarchist, but he looked upon them as fanatics, even if admirable fanatics.

72. Allen L. Benson to Herman Keuhn, 23 April 1908 (Houghton Collection, Harvard).

73. General information is found in "The Sage of Ballard Vale" (Steven Byington), Boston *Daily Globe*, 15 October 1967, p. 18; "The Death of George Schumm," *Nation* 153 (20 September 1941); James J. Martin, *Men against the State*, pp. 237–50.

It was astonishing that both Peter Kropotkin, the leading theoretician of Communist Anarchism, and Tucker, the leading Individualist Anarchist, indentified with the Allies. They urged the destruction of Prussian Germany as the mother of reaction (Tucker, letter, *Instead of a Magazine* 2 [15 September 1915]: 22–23; Tucker, New Bedford *Standard*, 15 September 1922).

But this should be placed in the context of the general collapse of international radicalism: Merle Fainsod, *International Socialism and the World War* (Cambridge: Harvard University Press, 1935).

74. Tucker to Ewing C. Baskette, 7 November 1934 (Baskette Collection, University of Illinois); Tucker, "State Socialism and Anarchism" (London: Fifield, 1911), p. 29. His career is analyzed in greater depth in my dissertation, "The American as Anarchist" (University of Iowa, 1972), which includes a list of his translations and publications, along with a discussion of such contributors to *Liberty* as George Bernard Shaw and Vilfredo Pareto.

75. Randolph Bourne, *Untimely Papers* (New York: Huebsch, 1919); Albert Jay Nock; *Jefferson* (New York: Hill and Wang, 1960 [1926]); idem, *Our Enemy the State* (New York: Free Life, 1973 [1935]); and idem, *Henry George* (New York: Morrow, 1939); John Jay Chapman, *Collected Works*, 12 vols. (Weston, Mass.: M and S Press, 1970); Michael Wreszin, *The Superfluous Anarchist: Albert Jay Nock* (Providence, R. I.: Brown University Press, 1971); John Flynn, *As We Go Marching* (New York: Free Life, 1973 [1944]).

76. James E. Rowen, "North Dakota's Answer—A State-Owned Bank," *In These Times* (clipping, ca. April 1977, p. 7); qualified by reader's letter, ibid., 1 (20 April 1977): 17. Given the circumstances, Rowen's use of "state-owned" is not entirely appropriate.

77. Paul Bernstein, "Run Your Own Business: Worker-Owned Plywood Firms," *Working Papers for a New Society* 2 (summer 1974): 24–34. Some of these corporations were influenced by the cooperative traditions of Scandanavian immigrants, adapted to American needs.

78. David Montgomery, "What's Happening to the American Worker?" (n.p.: Radical America, early 1970s), pp. 16–19; "Reagan Mines Anti-Government Lode," Baltimore *Evening Sun*, 11 January 1976, pp. 1–2.

John C. Calhoun was another curious example of a conservative whose principles led toward the weakening of central institutional authority. Calhoun sought to protect local rights by formulating his theory of concurrent majorities: no law passed by the general public would be valid until the special interest it affected would concur. Although he attempted to limit this procedure to basic laws, it could easily provoke a dangerous question: why can't minorities *within* a special interest also have a veto? If so, Calhoun's ideas would have immobilized, if not annihilated, practical government.

Chapter Six

1. John Humphrey Noyes, quoted in Everett Webber, *Escape to Utopia: The Communal Movement in America* (New York: Hastings House, 1959), p. 222. Standard references include: Arthur E. Bestor, *Backwoods Utopias: The Sectarian and Owenite Phases of Communitarian Socialism in America, 1663–1829* (Philadelphia: University of Pennsylvania Press, 1950); Donald Drew Egbert and Stow Persons, eds., *Socialism in American Life*, 2 vols. (Princeton: Princeton University Press, 1952); Richard Fairfield, *Communes U.S.A.: A Personal Tour* (Baltimore: Penguin, 1972); Robert Fogerty, ed., *American Utopianism* (Itasca, Ill.: F. E. Peacock, 1972); William Hinds, *American Communities and Co-operative Colonies* (Chicago: Kerr, 1908); Robert Hine, *California's Utopian Colonies* (New Haven: Yale University Press, 1966 [1953]); Mark Holloway, *Heavens on Earth: Utopian Communities in America, 1680–1850* (New York: Dover, 1966 [1951]); John Humphrey Noyes, *History of American Socialisms* (New York: Dover, 1966 [1870]; Ron Roberts, *The New Communes: Coming Together in America* (Englewood Cliffs, N.J.: Prentice-Hall 1971).

2. An 1839 speech, quoted in Leonard Krimerman and Lewis Perry, eds., *Patterns of Anarchy* (Garden City, N.Y.: Doubleday, 1966), p. 143; Count Leo Tolstoy and the Reverend Adin Ballou, "The Christian Doctrine of Non-Resistance," *Arena* 3 (December 1890): 1–12.

3. Quoted in J. Hampden Jackson, *Marx, Proudhon and European Socialism* (London: English Universities Press, 1957), p. 73.

4. Adin Ballou, *Christian Non-Resistance* (Philadelphia: J. Miller M'Kim, 1846), pp. 229–33.

5. William Lloyd Garrison, *Life of William Lloyd Garrison* (Boston: Anti-Slavery Office, 1845), pp. 145–48 (emphasis in the original).

6. [John Humphrey Noyes], *Mutual Criticism* (Syracuse, N.Y.: Syracuse University Press, 1975 [1876]); William Hinds, *American Communities* (New York: Corinth, 1961 [1878]), p. 135; Maren Lockwood Carden, *Oneida: Utopia to Modern Corporation* (Baltimore: Johns Hopkins University Press, 1969). Noyes and his followers, despite their unusual conclusions, had many roots in conventional revivalism. The evangelist William Miller, for example, had proclaimed in 1831 that the kingdom of God would be established in 1842. Noyes should be contrasted, however, to both social moderates and more repressive forms of religious communism, including Shakerism and (at first) Mormonism.

7. Quoted in Caro Lloyd, *Henry Demarest Lloyd, 1847–1903; A Biography*, 2 vols. 1:39–40, 301 (New York: Putnam's, 1912).

8. Lloyd, *Wealth against Commonwealth* (New York: Harper and Row, 1894), p. 1

9. Lloyd, ibid., pp. 534–35. Note that he uses the word "anarchy" in the stereotypical sense on p. 496.

The definitive biography was written by Chester MacArthur Destler: *Henry Demarest Lloyd and the Empire of Reform* (Philadelphia: University of Pennsylvania Press, 1963). The ramshackle term "empire" is well chosen: it was an ideologically diverse realm, neither an absolute monarchy nor a modern nation state.

10. Howells, "Equality as the Basis of Good Society," *Centruy Magazine* 51 (November 1895): 67.

11. Consider such remarks as these: "Someday, we will supersede politics by education" and "the ordinary political methods of voting and campaigning make it impossible for the real will and the real interests of the people to come forth" (in Caro Lloyd, *Henry Demarest Lloyd*, 1:296). By 1903, he did "feel as if the time were coming when every one ought to find some political means to work out our salvation," but he never found his own political deliverance (quoted in Destler, *Henry Demarest Lloyd*, p. 502).

12. Utopian literature of this period is discussed in Vernon Louis Parrington, Jr., *American Dreams: A Study of American Utopias* (Providence, R.I.: Brown University Press, 1947). One alternative to both the pro-state and anti-state theme was presented by Kenneth Roemer: In many utopias "government bureaucracies were given tremendous powers so that utopians might eventually enjoy an idealized Jeffersonian anarchy" (*The Obsolete Necessity: America in Utopian Writings, 1888–1900* [Kent, Ohio: Kent State University Press, 1976], p. 174).

13. Bellamy, "How I Wrote 'Looking Backward'" (1894), in *Edward Bellamy Speaks Again*, p. 219 (Kansas City, Mo.: Peerage Press, 1937).

14. "Fourth of July, 1892" (1892), ibid., p. 206.

15. Bellamy, *Equality* (New York: Appleton, 1934), p. 58. Bellamy honored not only this democratic tradition, but the cultural taboo against the word socialism. He boldly asserted that he was vindicating the rights of private property by making each citizen a stockholder in "one great business corporation," the national trust. The state then becomes "the Great Capitalist" (see *Looking Backward* [Cambridge: Harvard University Press, 1967], p. 127, and Bellamy, "'Looking Backward' Again," *North American Review* 150 [1890]: 360–61).

16. Bellamy, "Some Misconceptions of Nationalism" (1890), in *Edward Bellamy Speaks Again*, p. 128.

17. Bellamy, introduction to *Socialism: The Fabian Essays* (Boston: Brown, 1894), pp. ix–xviii.

18. Bellamy, "The Progress of Nationalism in the United States," *North American Review* 154 (June 1892): 746.

19. Arthur E. Morgan, *Edward Bellamy* (New York: Columbia University Press, 1944) and

Sylvia Bowman, *The Year 2000: A Critical Biography of Edward Bellamy* (New York: Bookman Associates, 1958). Both are eulogies.

20. Max Baginski, "Stirner: The Ego and His Own," *Mother Earth* 2 (May 1907): 142–51; Max Nettlau, "Anarchism: Communist or Individualist?—Both," *Mother Earth* 9 (July 1914): 170–76.

21. B. R. Tucker, "Are Anarchists Thugs?" *Liberty* 13 (January 1899): 3–4. This was first printed in the New York *Tribune*, 4 December 1898. English anarchism—with some comparisons to American varieties—was portrayed by Henry Seymour in "The Genesis of Anarchism in England" (*Free Vistas*, ed. Joseph Ishill, pp. 119-39 [Berkeley Heights, N.J.: Oriole Press, 1937]) and by George Bernard Shaw, "The Impossibilities of Anarchism" (London: Fabian Society, 1893). Shaw contrasted the individualism of Tucker with the communism of Peter Kropotkin, as the two major schools of anarchist theory. Elsewhere, he somewhat unfairly observed that a reader would seldom learn from such "modern Anarchists" as Kropotkin, Spencer, and Tucker that the workers were "seething in horror and degradation whilst the riches of the proprietors was increasing by leaps and bounds" (Shaw, "The Transition to Social Democracy," in *Fabian Essays*, p. 177 [London: Walter Scott, 1899]). Anarcho-Communists (including Kropotkin) and syndicalists tended to be more sensitive.

22. For a Marxist critique of American anarchism as an extreme liberal "atomistic individualism" and "petty bourgeois revolutionism," read Albert Weisbord, *Conquest of Power*, 2 vols., 1:225-36 (New York: Covici-Friede, 1937). During the nineteenth century, European commentators like William Morris and Prince Kropotkin had noted that Individualist Anarchism found significant support only in America.

23. Voltairine de Cleyre, *Selected Works* (New York: Mother Earth Publishing Association, 1914), p. 111. It should not be forgotten, however, that both the labor organizers and socialists of his time were often middle class. Samuel Gompers, head of the AFL, was arrested only once in his lifetime, in 1879, for talking to a picket. As he looked back on this experience: "That was one of the most uncomfortable days I have ever spent, sitting there in the dirt and filth and vermin, surrounded by men of unclean bodies and minds who used only vile language. Fortunately for the effect on me, there was only one day of it" (Gompers, *Seventy Years of Life and Labor* [New York: Dutton, 1925], 1:122-23). For a stark contrast with the early industrial environment of Emma Goldman, see Richard Drinnon's *Rebel in Paradise* (Chicago: University of Chicago Press, 1961). Goldman despised both Tucker and Gompers as middle-class cowards.

24. "Boston Radicals—As Mild-Mannered Men and Women as Ever Scuttled the Ship of State," Boston *Sunday Globe*, 5 April 1891. Some contemporary comments on the "elegance" of Tucker's newspaper were made in the *Irish World* 24 (21 July 1894): 4 (which refers to "Mr. Benjamin Tucker, the cultured Anarchist of Boston"); *Donahoe's Magazine* 46 (November 1901): 441–47; and a letter by Carl Nold to Agnes Inglis, 6 January 1933, in the Labadie Collection of the University of Michigan ("It had become fashion to listen to his talks 'among the better class of society.' Thus, he and his friends got the nick-name of 'The Parlor Anarchists.' "). Of course, similar comments could have been offered about the virtual salon that later formed around Goldman's *Mother Earth*.

Read also: Voltairine de Cleyre, "Anarchism," in *Selected Works*, pp. 115-16, and the editor's introduction [Clarence Lee Schwartz] to B. R. Tucker, *Individual Liberty* (New York: Vanguard, 1926), pp. v–vii.

25. "What I Believe" (1908), in *Red Emma Speaks*, ed. Alix Kates Shulman, p. 35 (New York: Random House, 1972): Goldman, *Anarchism and Other Essays* (Indore, India: Modern Publishers, 195?), p. 42. Spencer's books were also found in many of the "libraries" of IWW locals.

26. Goldman, "Minorities versus Majorities," in *Anarchism and Other Essays*, p. 70. Authoritarians like Edward Bellamy were usually condemned, while laissez-faire critics like Henry George were often commended.

27. Lincoln Steffens, "Liberty in the United States" (originally given at the Paterson Free Speech Protest Meeting, 5 January 1913), *Mother Earth* 8 (December 1913): 332–34. Roger Baldwin, one of the founders of the ACLU, also admired Kropotkin for his sublime ideal of a cooperative society. In 1927, he edited a collection entitled *Kropotkin's Revolutionary Pamphlets* (New York: Dover, 1970 [1970 introduction by Baldwin, v–viii; 1927 introduction, pp. 1–12]).

28. Emma Goldman, "Syndicalism: Its Theory and Practice," *Mother Earth* 7 (January 1913): 373. To illustrate, Kropotkin cites the following range of people in his 1905 essay on anarchism, praising them as forerunners: William Lloyd Garrison, Thoreau, Emerson, Whitman, J. S. Mill, and Spencer (*Revolutionary Pamphlets*, p. 299).

29. Alexander Berkman, "An Intimate Word to the Social Rebels of America," *Mother Earth* 10 (December 1915): 328–30.

30. James P. Cannon, "The I.W.W." (New York: Pioneer, 1956), p. 29. Cannon, during his long lifetime, was an IWW member, a founder of the Communist party, a major organizer of the American Trotskyist movement, and a comprehensive militant. In keeping with classical Marxism, he believed that after the successful establishment of communism, the state would "wither away."

31. Paul Buhle, "New Perspectives on American Radicalism," *Radical America* 2 (July–August 1968): 51. Recent studies on the IWW have been usefully outlined by Buhle in "The Wobblies in Perspective" (*Monthly Review*, June 1970, pp. 43–53) and William Preston, "Shall This Be All? U.S. Historians versus William D. Haywood et al." (*Labor History* 12 [summer 1971]: 435–53).

32. The history of this repression is documented in a study by H. C. Peterson and Gilbert Fite, *Opponents of War, 1917–1918* (Madison: University of Wisconsin Press, 1957) and William Preston's *Aliens and Dissenters* (Cambridge: Harvard University Press, 1963).

33. Quoted in *The Agitator in American Society*, ed. Charles Lomas (Englewood Cliffs, N.J.: Prentice-Hall, 1968), pp. 110–11.

34. When Robert Minor (a well-known cartoonist who was then less well known as an anarchist) sent powerful dispatches from Russia during 1918–19 condemning the arbitrary and ruthless policies of the Bolsheviks, American liberals actually became more receptive to their regime. They had previously feared that the Bolsheviks were anarchists and that order had broken down in Russia (Christopher Lasch, "The Bolsheviks as Anarchists," in *The American Liberals and the Russian Revolution*, pp. 127–57 [New York: Columbia University Press, 1962]).

35. Terry Perlin, "Anarchism in New Jersey: The Ferrer Colony at Stelton," *New Jersey History* 89 (1971): 133–48; Paul Buhle, "*The Road to Freedom*: Anarchism in the Twenties," *Libertarian Analysis* 1 (winter 1970): 50–55; Fred Thompson, comp., *The I.W.W.: Its First Fifty Years* (Chicago: Industrial Workers of the World, 1955), pp. 127–201 (for the years 1919–55). The IWW also split in 1924 between the centralists and decentralists.

36. Editor's introduction to Emma Goldman, "Was My Life Worth Living?" *Harper's Magazine* 170 (December 1934): 52.

The anarchist's fervent commitment to the Spanish Revolution of the 1930s is recaptured in a book edited by Sam Dolgoff, *The Anarchist Collectives: Workers' Self-Management in the Spanish Revolution, 1936–1939* (New York: Free Life, 1974). Journals of this period are analyzed in "Anarchist Publications," in *The American Radical Press, 1880–1960*, ed. Joseph Conlin, 2:371–429 (Westport, Conn.: Greenwood, 1974) (IWW papers are included in 1:95–113; *Catholic Worker* 2:457–71; *Spanish Revolution* 2:481–86). These publications were: *Free Society* (1921), *Road to Freedom* (1924–32), the *Clarion* (1932–34), *Man!* (1933–40), *Vanguard* (1932–39), *Challenge* 1938–39), *Why?* and *Resistance* (1942–52), *Politics* (1944–49; of related interest), *Views and Comments* (?), *Retort* (1942–51), and the *Catholic Worker* (1933–present), along with scattered IWW items. An example of religious anarchism is outlined in William D. Miller's *Dorothy Day and the Catholic Worker Movement* (NewYork: Liveright, 1972) and Ammon Hennacy, *The Book of Ammon* (Salt Lake City?: Hennacy, 1965). Subterranean influences are uncovered in a book on the beats of the 1950s: Lawrence Lipton, *The Holy Barbarians* (New York: Messner, 1957).

37. Laurence Veysey, *The Communal Experience: Anarchist and Mystical Counter-Cultures in America* (New York: Harper and Row, 1973), p. 176; George Woodcock, "Anarchism Revisited," *Commentary* 46 (August 1968): 59.

38. Shaw, *Liberty* 12 (1 August 1896): 6–7. For Shaw in *Liberty*, see "What's in a Name?" 3 (11 April 1885): 7; "Shutting Up an Individualist," vol. 4 (30 July 1887); "Economic Theories of Interest," 5 (24 September 1887); "How Capitalists Make Their Capital," 5 (8 October 1887): 6; and "The Municipal Theatre Absurdity," 12 (1 August 1896).

39. Goldman, letter to the editor, *New York Times*, 4 July 1937. The anarchists could be criticized, however, for failing to appreciate degrees of exploitation among the various systems. Thus, Goldman somewhat extravagently decided that while "Fascism... is repudiated and fought by the progressive elements of every country, America alone has given fascism social standing and recognition" (Goldman, "America by Comparison," in *American Abroad,* ed. Peter Seagoe, p. 180 [The Hague: Servire Press, 1932]).

Libertarian Marxists like Karl Korsch, Paul Mattick, and other "Council Communists" were generally less superficial. They attempted to renew the Marxian critique, arguing that the "once revolutionary and anti-statist ideology" of Marx had undergone a transformation during the assumption of state power similar to "the transformation of revolutionary, anti-statist Christianity into the official religion of the Roman state" (Korsch, "The Crisis of Marxism" [1931], *New German Critique* 1 [fall 1974]: 10). But such people had little influence in the 1930s Left, although they produced three journals in America: *Council Correspondence, Living Marxism,* and *New Essays.*

40. Keith Melville, "The Anarchist Response," in *Communes in the Counter Culture*, pp. 114–33 (New York: Morrow, 1972); Michael Lerner, "Anarchism and the American Counter-Culture," in *Anarchism Today*, ed. David Apter and James Joll, pp. 43–69 (New York: Doubleday-Anchor, 1972); Benjamin Barber, *Superman and Common Men: Freedom, Anarchy and Revolution* (New York: Praeger, 1971); Judson Jerome, *Families of Eden: Communes and the New Anarchism* (New York: Seabury, 1974); *Communities: A Journal of Cooperative Living*, no. 24 (January–February 1977); Wilson Carey McWilliams, *The Idea of Fraternity in America* (Berkeley: University of California Press, 1973); Joseph R. Conlin, ed. *The American Radical Press, 1880–1960*, vol. 2 (Westport, Conn.: Greenwood Press, 1974), p. 372.

Chapter Seven

1. Hans Gerth, *The First International—Minutes of the Hague Congress of 1872* (Madison: University of Wisconsin Press, 1958), p. 195–99, 263–68.

2. Letter to F. Sorge, in Marx and Engels, *Letters to Americans, 1848–1895* (New York: International, 1953), p. 243. Approximately the same analysis was later offered by Victor Berger (called "the American Bernstein") and Morris Hillquit ("the American Kautsky"). Both understood the central importance of history: "The feeling of class distinction in America, at least among native workingmen, has not the same historic foundation that it has in Germany, France, or England. There the people were accustomed for over a thousand years to have distinct classes and castes fixed by law" (Berger, *Appeal to Reason*, 8 July 1903). "Paradoxical as it may sound, our very democracy has mitigated against the immediate success of Socialism. The American workingmen have never had to struggle for attainment of their political emancipation, as their disenfranchised brothers in most other countries have" (Hillquit, "Problems and Prospects of American Socialism," New York *Call*, 5 December 1909).

3. Morris Hillquit, *History of Socialism in the United States* (New York: Funk and Wagnalls, 1910), p. 359.

Carl Reeve, a Marxist-Leninist, criticized De Leon for his "semi-syndicalism" (*Life and Times of Daniel De Leon* [New York: Published for the American Institute of Marxist Studies by the Humanities Press, 1972], pp. 105–18). A De Leonist critique of Reeve is printed in the *Collector's Exchange* (Grand Rapids, Mich.), no. 9 (November 1975), pp. 11–14. De Leon refused to call himself an anarchist or a syndicalist, and possessed a meager knowledge of their writings. For example, he falsely accused Benjamin Tucker of pacifism and of advocating voluntary committees that would be autocratically run(!). Furthermore, De Leon dismissed most of the European theorists with superficial mockery, such as his sole reference to Malatesta: "As to Malatesta, the least said of him the better" ("Socialism versus Anarchism" [New York: New York Labor News, 1970], pp. 49, 49 n, 54-55). Nevertheless, he qualifies as a left libertarian for his rather nonstatist definitions of "government."

Another early Marxist who revised the received teaching was Laurence Gronlund. In his *Cooperative Commonwealth* (1884), *Our Destiny* (1890), and *The New Economy* (1898), he moved toward left liberalism by insisting that the progressive middle class would lead any transformation, stressing the patriotism and morality of his ideals and urging respect for the rights of property.

4. H. Wayne Morgan, introduction, *American Socialism, 1900-1960* (Englewood Cliffs, N.J.: Prentice-Hall, 1964), p. 4. It would be instructive to compare the American and German socialist parties of this period. The latter, while containing many intellectual and structural divisions, was far more unified than anything practicable in America.

Although I am convinced of the differences, John Spargo (once a member of the National Office of the SPA) attributed the limited success and later failure of the party to its "Germanic dogmatism." He was partly motivated, however, by his fury at the SPA's antiwar stand in World War I and his subsequent resignation ("The German Domination of American Socialism and Its Consequences," in *Americanism and Social Democracy* [New York: Harper and Brothers, 1918], pp. 159-85).

5. "The Canton, Ohio Speech" (1918), in *Writings and Speeches of Eugene V. Debs*, p. 417 (New York: Hermitage Press, 1948).

6. "Sound Socialist Tactics" (1912), in *Writings and Speeches*, p. 355. He was reprimanding the SPA central committee for its decision to investigate the ideological purity of the *International Socialist Review* and other publications, and for its persecution of the IWW. Its censorious proceedings were characterized as un-American.

7. Ira Kipnis, *The American Socialist Movement, 1897-1912* (New York: Columbia University Press, 1952), pp. 423-29. While modifying Kipnis, James Weinstein agreed that "the sophistication and ability of those in power to move to the left in the face of real, imminent, or anticipated threats from radicals circumscribed the space within which revolutionaries could act" (Weinstein, *The Corporate Ideal in the Liberal State*, [Boston: Beacon Press, 1968] p. 138). By 1920 the SPA had declined, partially because of the reforms that had been instituted to stabilize capitalist society.

8. Debs, after great indecision, favored the SPA because of its democratic values. While in prison, he had written that "socialism and prison are antagonistic terms"—and he also found the Communist party too confining (E. V. Debs, *Walls and Bars* [Chicago: Socialist Party, 1927]). He is also remembered, of course, for his utopian outburst: "While there's a soul in prison, I am not free!"

9. Quoted by Michael Harrington in his review of W. A. Swanberg's biography of Thomas, *New Republic* 176 (1 and 8 January 1977): 24.

10. Jack Clark, *In These Times* 1 (5-11 January 1977): 22. Michael Harrington first made this thesis fashionable among some intellectuals, although he later retracted his claim that certain elements within liberalism and the labor movement necessarily constituted "an invisible social democracy," whether or not they were conscious of this status.

11. Quoted in Theodore Draper, *American Communism and Soviet Russia* (New York: Viking, 1960), p. 82.

12. "The Revival of the Communist Party" (preamble to the constitution of the CPUSA), *New Masses* 56 (August 1945): 5. It is even more astonishing that this was written *after* a purging of "revisionists" from the organization.

13. Consult the introductions and selections from the following works, all of them published by International in New York: James S. Allen, ed., *Thomas Paine* (1937); Philip Foner, ed., *Thomas Jefferson* (1943); Philip Foner, ed., *George Washington* (1944); Samuel Sillen, ed., *William Cullen Bryant* (1945); Elizabeth Lawson, ed., *Samuel Adams* (1946); and Philip Foner, ed., *Franklin Delano Roosevelt* (1947). For a recent attack on "the absurdity of turning eighteenth century mercantile liberals into twentieth century populist-socialists," read Harry Chotiner's "The American Revolution and the American Left" (*Socialist Revolution*, no. 21 [April–June 1976], pp. 6–28).

14. J. Mindel, "Benjamin Franklin," *Political Affairs* 26 (May 1947): 471–80; Sam Darcy, "On Benjamin Franklin" (letter), *New Masses* 30 (27 December 1938): 19; Carl Reeve, "Benjamin Franklin—Champion of Democracy," *Communist* 18 (July 1939): 594–605; Granville Hicks, "A Great American," in *Granville Hicks in the New Masses*, ed. Jack Alan Robbins, p. 369 (Port Washington, N.Y.: Kennikat Press, 1974): Francis Franklin, "July 4th—Birthday of American Democracy," *Communist* 17 (July 1938): 630–41; Claude G. Bowers, Earl Browder, and Francis Franklin, *The Heritage of Jefferson* (New York: Worker's School, 1943).

15. Preamble to CPA, quoted in Earl Browder, "The Road Ahead" (New York: Worker's Library, 1944), p. 27; Browder, "Is Communism a Menace?" (New York: Worker's Library, 1943), p. 31. To place these theoretical deficiencies into a larger context, see Paul Sweezy, "The Influence of Marxian Economics in American Thought and Practice," in *Socialism and American Life*, ed. D.D. Egbert and Stow Persons, vol. 2 (Princeton: Princeton University Press, 1952); William Appleman Williams, *The Great Evasion* (Chicago: Quadrangle, 1964): and Paul Buhle, "Marxism in the United States," in *Towards a New Marxism*, ed. Bart Grahl, pp. 191–215 (St. Louis: Telos Press, 1973).

16. Jacques Duclos, "On the Dissolution of the Communist Party of the United States," *Daily Worker*, 24 May 1945. The later othodoxy is well expressed by Gil Green in "The Browderite Conception of History," *Political Affairs* 28 (October 1949): 65–84.

General background for this commentary can be found in David Shannon, *The Decline of American Communism* (New York: Harcourt, Brace, 1959); Irving Howe and Lewis Coser, *The American Communist Party* (New York: Praeger, 1962); Joseph Starobin, *American Communism in Crisis, 1943–1957* (Cambridge: Harvard University Press, 1972); Al Richmond, *A Long View from the Left* (Boston: Houghton Mifflin, 1973); and Philip Jaffe, *The Rise and Fall of American Communism* (New York: Horizon, 1975).

17. Betty Gannett and V. J. Jerome, "On Patriotism and National Pride," *Political Affairs* 33 (October 1954): 28–35; John Gates, *The Story of an American Communist* (New York: Thomas Nelson, 1958), pp. 141–42.

18. "A Show of Independence," *Newsweek* 88 (12 July 1976): 33–34; Leon Blum, *For All Mankind* (New York: Viking, 1946).

19. Earl Browder, *The People's Front* (New York: International, 1938), p. 86. Read James Weinstein, *Ambiguous Legacy: The Left in American Politics* (New York: New Viewpoints-Franklin Watts, 1975), and a libertarian socialist critique by Ronald Radosh, *Nation* 222 (17 January 1976): 55. As two libertarians of the 1930s remarked: "[The CP] made the Society of Jesus look like a college Liberal Club in comparison. It was a church, not a movement, and a church which operated under the thumb of a college of cardinals four thousand miles away" (Lillian Symes and Travers Clement, *Radical America* [Boston: Beacon, 1972; 1st ed. 1934], p. 372). However, Steven Murdock has demonstrated that the CPUSA was not utterly centralized,

by his essay on one state party: "California Communists—Their Years of Power," *Science and Society* 34 (winter 1970): 478–87.

20. Howard Fast, *The Naked God* (New York: Praeger, 1957); Granville Hicks, *Part of the Truth* (New York: Harcourt, Brace, 1965); Richard Wright, in *The God That Failed*, ed. Richard Crossman pp. 115–62 (New York: Harper and Row, 1949).

21. Zoltan Deak, ed., "Americans against Monopolies" (New York: Paine-Whitman Press, 1976), a rather indiscriminate collection that allies Thomas Paine and the CPUSA because both are enemies of monopoly capitalism. Such a union of individualist radicalism and state communism is clearly fated to miscarry. Communist party attempts to "capitalize" on the Bicentennial suffered many of the same errors as the Popular Front, although there was greater sensitivity to the historical gap.

22. One example of liberal reform within the Trotskyist movement would be the Socialist Worker's party and its creation of the largest "umbrella" antiwar group, the National Peace Action Coalition. Some studies of the history of American Marxism: Daniel Bell, *Marxian Socialism in the United States* (Princeton: Princeton University Press, 1967), criticizes it for being "in" but not "of" this culture; David Herreshoff, *The Origins of American Marxism* (New York: Pathfinder, 1973 [1967]; Tim Wohlforth, *The Struggle for Marxism in the United States* (New York: Bulletin Book, 1971), a lament against the "populist, petty bourgeois" nature of American radicalism. Problems of socialist organization are summarized in my article "Whatever Happened to an American Socialist Party? A Critical Survey of the Spectrum of Interpretations," *American Quarterly* 15 (Dember 1973): 516–37.

23. Richard Hofstadter, though regarded as an iconoclast by many, nevertheless embodied several of these conventional pieties in *Anti-Intellectualism in American Life* (New York: Knopf, 1963).

24. John P. Roche, "American Liberty: An Examination of the 'Tradition' of Freedom," in *Origins of American Political Thought*, ed. J. P. Roche (New York: Harper, 1967), 1:17.

25. Edward Pessen, *Most Uncommon Jacksonians: The Radical Leaders of the Early Labor Movement* (Albany: State University of New York Press, 1967). The Populists were another rainbow coalition.

26. Contemporary movements have been dissected in the journal *Black Scholar* and by Carol Ehrlich in her incisive pamphlet "Anarchism, Socialism and Feminism" (Baltimore: Research Group One, 1977).

The Beginning of Another Cycle

1. The ideology of the 1950s and early 1960s is discussed in Chaim Waxman, ed., *The End of Ideology Debate* (New York: Funk and Wagnalls, 1968).

2. Karl Hess, quoted in "From Far Right to Far Left," by James Boyd, *New York Times Magazine*, 6 December 1970, p. 69. Hess later called his vision of a society organized on the basis of voluntary groupings "syndicalism." A provocative example of an earlier left-wing odyssey can be found in Dwight Macdonald's "Why I Am No Longer a Socialist," *Liberation* 3 (May 1958): 4–7. Macdonald abandoned Marxism because of the failures of Russian socialism and came to believe in the usually reactionary nature of the proletariat, the need to preserve property in order to defend freedom, and the ideal goal of anarchism ("no coercive institutions"). It should be stressed, however, that the new radicals of the 1960s were *not* consistent. Many originally favored the state-sponsored social engineering of New Deal liberalism. Later, when this was decisively rejected, the New Left split into anarchist and authoritarian factions.

3. Karl Shapiro, "On the Revival of Anarchism," *Liberation* 5 (February 1961): 5–8; Paul Goodman, "The Black Flag of Anarchy," *New York Times Magazine*, 14 July 1968, pp. 10–11 + .

4. Martin Duberman offered an insightful comment on the incipient anarchism of the New

Left and many black liberation groups of the 1960s in "Anarchism Left and Right," *Partisan Review* 33 (fall 1966): 610–15.

5. D. H. Lawrence, "A Sane Revolution," quoted in epigraph, Richard Neville, *Play Power* (New York: Random House, 1970).

6. "Youth Culture," *Radical America*, vol 3 (November 1969), entire issue; Murray Bookchin, "The Youth Culture: An Anarcho-Communist View," in *Hip Culture* (New York: Times Change Press, 1970), pp. 51–63.

7. Even during the first days, when most SDS members claimed that the group accepted no ideology (an attitude that could be very anarchistic), some members realized that the basic approach was anarchical (see Tom Good, "Ideology and SDS," *New Left Notes* 1 [5 August 1966]: 5). Jack Newfield, in a perceptive history, declared that anarchism (along with pacifism and socialism) was one of the main tendencies of the New Left (*A Prophetic Minority* [New York: New American Library, 1966]). Other major references include Massimo Teodori, ed., *The New Left* (Indianapolis: Bobbs-Merrill, 1969), probably the most comprehensive anthology; Kirkpatrick Sale, *SDS* (New York: Random House, 1973); Harold Jacobs, ed., *Weatherman* (Berkeley: Ramparts, 1970); and a reasonable Marxist critique of the limitations of the New Left that is somewhat conscious of the limitations of the Old Left, Gil Green's *The New Radicalism: Anarchist or Marxist?* (New York: International, 1971).

8. Peter Viereck, "The Philosophical 'New Conservatism,' " in *The Radical Right*, ed. Daniel Bell (New York: Doubleday, Anchor, 1964), p. 189; Murray Rothbard, *The Betrayal of the American Right* (Berkeley: Ramparts, 1972). Although Rothbard sentimentalized some of the old Right (for example, Taft really argued that the United States should have been "firmer" in Korea, advocated aid to reactionaries like Chiang Kai-shek, and demanded that all Communists be purged from the American government), he significantly contributed to understanding the differences between the old and new Right.

9. Robert Carson, "On Future Developments in the College Left," *Monthly Review* 21 (March 1970): 56. One of the major documents from this convention, written by the Anarchist Caucus, is "The Tranquil Statement," reprinted in Henry Silverman's anthology *American Radical Thought* (Lexington, Mass.: Heath, 1970), pp. 266–73. The split, which disrupted most of the California, Pennsylvania, Virginia, and New Jersey chapters, created numerous "alliances," newspapers, and even an attempt to found a Libertarian Press Association. A sympathetic account is found in Jerome Tuccille's *Radical Libertarianism: A Right-Wing Alternative* (Indianapolis: Bobbs-Merrill, 1970). Tucille's book was itself a major illustration of the schism in American conservatism, a status that was recognized in Lowell Ponte's review in the influential journal of the youth culture, *Rolling Stone* (no. 71 [26 November 1970], p. 44).

10. For my comments on contemporary anarchism, I have examined most issues of the following anarchist or laissez-faire papers published during 1960–73: the *Abolitionist* (Verona, N.J.), *Anarchos (New York), Black Mask* (New York), *Catholic Worker* (New York), *Comment* (New York), *Commentary on Liberty* (Philadelphia), *Good Soup* (New York), *Hard Core News* (Houston), *Individualist* (Silver Springs, Md.), *Industrial Worker* (Chicago), *Invictus* (Los Angeles), *Left and Right* (New York), *Libertarian American* (San Antonio), *Libertarian Analysis* (New York), *Libertarian Connection* (Los Angeles), *Libertarian Forum* (New York), *Libertas* (Santa Ana, Calif.), *Life and Liberty* (New Jersey), *Manas* (Los Angeles), *Match* (Tucson), *New Banner* (Columbia, S.C.), *NYLA: News for Libertarians* (New York), *Protos* (Los Angeles), *Radical Libertarian* (Winchester, Mass.), *Rampart Journal of Individualist Thought* (Larkspur, Colo.)., *Rap* (formerly *Pine Tree*; Santa Ana, Calif.), *Right On* (Bronx, N.Y.), *SIL News* (Philadelphia), *Rebel Worker* (Chicago), *Red Sky, Blue Sky* (San Jose, Calif.), *Thorn* (Ann Arbor, Mich.), *Vanguard* (and a street handout, *Tool*; Cleveland), and *Views and Comments* (New York). Since it has been impossible to discover the full publication dates for all now defunct journals, I have omitted such information.

Other valuable references: *Alternative Press Index* (Baltimore, 1969–present); Bell and

Howell Press Syndicate, *Underground Newspapers Microfilm Collection* (series); *Directory of Libertarian Periodicals* (Brighton, Mich.), substantially limited to Anarcho-Capitalists; Friends of Malatesta (Buffalo, N.Y.), Libertarian-Anarchist Book Service (New York), Libertarian Book Club (New York), Libertarian Enterprises (Richmond, Va.), The Society for Individual Liberty (Philadelphia) and the Solidarity Bookshop (Chicago).

11. Chris Tame and Mark Brady, "Libertarianism in England," *Libertarian Connection*, no. 22 (10 September 1971), p. 17. We can see that this has been true in the past from such works as Eunice Schuster's *Native American Anarchism* (1932) and James J. Martin's *Men against the State* (1953). In 1970, the national total of extreme libertarians may have been about 10,000. SIL had about 130 clubs with 1,400 paid members, and the California Libertarian Alliance had about 1,000 members. The largest circulation libertarians were Ayn Rand, on the Right, whose novels have sold more than 3,000,000 copies, and the *Catholic Worker* on the Left, with a monthly press run of 85,000.

12. Dorothy Day, interview in *Protest: Pacifism and Politics*, ed. James Finn, p. 382 (New York: Random House, 1967). The new critical environment either stimulated new ideas in older people or brought new publicity for their old ideas: Murray Bookchin (born 1921), Dorothy Day (1897), Paul Goodman (1911), Karl Hess, (1923) Carl Oglesby (1935), Murrary Rothbard (1926), and Karl Shapiro (1913). Thus, after a life of general obscurity, the fifty-year-old Goodman "was embarked on the odd but grateful episode of being a Student Leader" (Goodman, *Five Years: Thoughts during a Useless Time* [New York: 1966], p. vii). For some stereotyped images of the time, see James Buchanan and Nicos Devletoglu, *Academia in Anarchy* (New York: Basic Books, 1970); Sidney Hook, *Academic Freedom and Academic Anarchy* (New York: Cowles, 1970); T. R. B., "A Bullet in the Computor," *New Republic* 158 (20 April 1968): 6; and "Is the U.S. Drifting toward Anarchy?" *U.S. News and World Report* 63 (4 December 1967): 50–52. For Capouya's comment, read his critique of William Powell's *Anarchist Cookbook*, in *Commonweal*, 94 (12 March 1971): 17; and, for an illustration of a contemporary "anarchy" trial, Frank Donner, "The Epton Anarchy Trial" (of a Maoist!), *Nation* 201 (15 November 1965): 355–58, 372.

Chapter Eight

1. David Haviland and Stanley Lieberman, eds., *A Directory of Libertarian Periodicals* (Brighton, Mich.: Haviland, 1971), pp. 1–2. On the West Coast, a paragon of this bourgeois background was Robert LeFevre, a former real estate operator, restaurateur, and newspaper editor who founded the radical laissez-faire Rampart College, later situated above the First Western Bank in Santa Ana, California (Michael Engler, "Mr. LeFevre's Remarkable College," *California Sun*, July 1971). This occupational background was similar to that usually found among earlier European anarchists: Ferrer (education), Kropotkin (geographer, agronomist), Morris (arts and crafts), Pelloutier (labor and civil rights lawyer), Proudhon (writer), E. Reclus (geographer), and Max Stirner (schoolteacher).

2. Although the former importance of Karl Hess as a Goldwater Republican has been challenged ("The Sudden Eminence of Karl Hess," *National Review* [29 December 1970], pp. 1388–89), Stephen Shadegg found him a significant member of a small team constituting Goldwater's brain trust (*What Happened to Goldwater?* [1965], p. 196), Theodore White concluded that he was among those "who made up the candidate's inner group" (*The Making of the President, 1964* [New York: Atheneum, 1965], p. 118), and John Kessel refers to him as "the chief speechwriter who traveled with Goldwater during the campaign" (*The Goldwater Coalition* [Indianapolis: Bobbs-Merrill, 1968], p. 134).

3. Jerry [no further indentification], "Are We Real Workers?" (letter to the editor), *Industrial Worker*, vol. 67 (January 1970); report of the Twenty-ninth Annual Convention, ibid., pp. 4–5.

4. Dwight Macdonald, "Why I Am No Longer a Socialist," *Liberation* 3 (May 1958): 7. This is a limited perspective, since American anarchism arose before Tucker and has continued, both as a conscious movement and as an inherent social element. Macdonald may have sensed this, since he later comments on the instinctive anarchism of Americans. For Tuccille's remark on Objectivism, see *Radical Libertarianism: A Right-Wing Alternative* (Indianapolis: Bobbs-Merrill, 1970), p. 5 (there were no actual direct relations; they were alike because both are bourgeois). The agitation of the 1960's also prompted, among other things, the reprinting of many libertarian classics, such as the Arno Press series "The Right Wing Individualist Tradition in America," along with at least some bibligraphies in libertarian papers: Holley Cantine, "The Individualists," *A Way Out* 23 (October 1967): 8–10; Herbert Roseman, "An Unorthodox Bibliography," *Modern Utopian* 2 (September–October 1967): 36; *Win* 7 (1 March 1971): 20. Consider the initial statements for such organizations as the New England Libertarian Alliance, which claimed the goal of uniting the work of Bakunin, Proudhon, Tucker, Mencken, and Ayn Rand (prospectus).

5. Roy Childs, *SIL Services Bulletin* (winter 1970), p. 2; Harrison Drake, "Remember Lysander Spooner," *Invictus*, no. 7 (1970). The only real continuities were the few remaining Individualist Anarchists from another era, such as the eighty-year-old Laurence Labadie. The works of these men were still occasionally available. Ayn Rand, who could easily be seen within older traditions of liberalism, American natural rights philosophy, and Individualist Anarchism, made little reference to any of these traditions. For an authorized version of the origins and substance of Objectivism, see Nathaniel and Barbara Branden, *Who Is Ayn Rand?* (New York: Paperback Library, 1964). The basic critical work is William R. O'Neill's *With Charity toward None* (New York: Philosophical Library, 1971). Rand scorned Objectivist Anarchists as "hippies of the right" who had misunderstood her.

6. "The 'Tranquil Statement,' " reprinted in *American Radical Thought*, ed. Henry Silverman, p. 273 (Lexington, Mass.: Heath, 1970). An example of a similar quote can be found on the address page of *Commentary on Liberty* 6 (September–October 1969).

7. Tucker, *Liberty* 2 (9 December 1882): 2 (of course, he refused to acknowledge any "God-given" rights). The early radicals' view of the Declaration was summed up by Abram Walter Stevens, an admirer of the pioneer anarchist Josiah Warren: "Prophetically, if not actually, every person and every institution in this land is free. Historically and logically we are committed to freedom" (*Index* 6 [17 June 1875]: 282). The only institutions that Stevens, Warren, Tucker, and Spooner could accept within this logic were "free institutions," that is, voluntary associations.

8. Murray Bookchin, "Anarchy," *Win* 7 (15 May 1971): 22. Bookchin, a Communist Anarchist, Paul Goodman, a pragmatic, "Left-liberal" anarchist, and Leonard Liggio, an Anarcho-Capitalist, all agreed on the initial class origin of anarchism among the lower-middle-class petty bourgeois, although Anarcho-Communists laid a greater stress on the peasantry. For a view of anarchists as "very often small-scale business people," see Arthur Uloth, *Anarchy* (London), no. 74 (April 1967), pp. 114–16.

9. Tucker, *Index* 8 (18 January 1977): 36; John William Ward, "Violence, Anarchy, and Alexander Berkman," *New York Review of Books* 15 (5 November 1970): 25–30; George Novack, "Marxism versus Neo-Anarchist Terrorism" (New York: Pathfinder, 1970). for a perceptive criticism of Novack's Marxism—which virtually rejected terrorism on principle, quite unlike Lenin's assessment that terror was on occasion the most appropriate form of action—see "Terrorism and Communism," *Spartacist*, no. 17–18 (August-September 1970).

10. Mulford Q. Sibley, "Pacifism: The Rejection of Violence," in *Power and Civilization*, ed. David Cooperman and E. V. Walter pp. 499–513 (New York: Crowell, 1962). Sibley could apparently make the confused claim that anarchism is both an "eddy in the current of modern pacifism" and "extremely important" because he was concerned with pacifism in general, not only Western pacifism but also Hindu and Buddhist forms. This allowed him to say that most

of pacifism is "other-worldly" and therefore not dedicated to creating a perfect society. However, his own definition for Western pacifism, his concepts of what a pacifist society *should* be like, and the errors he commits about anarchism—such as his implication that Berkman was always violent, that most pacifists could not accept the anarchopacifism of DeLigt, and that "anarchy" (undefined) would be a poor setting for pacifist life—leads one to conclude that Sibley is most correct when he asserts the element of anarchism inherent in Western pacifism. The War Resisters International embraced, as one of its affiliates, the journal *Anarchisme et Nonviolence* (*War Resistance* 2 [1969]: 18). The stable counseling groups for conscientious objectors, like the American Friends' Service Committee or the Central Committee for Conscientious Objectors, abjure any extreme politics, unlike the militant Committee for Nonviolent Action. Some young members of the IWW, such as David Harris, have been pacifists, as have some individualists such as Robert LeFevre. For one Anarcho-Capitalist appreciation of the similarities, see David Rosinger, "The WRL Conference," *Abolitionist* 2 (November 1971): 6–8.

11. Herbert Roseman, "A Collaboration: *The Modern Utopian* and School for Living's *A Way Out*," *Modern Utopian* 2 (October–November 1967): 41; Murray Rothbard, "Liberty and the New Left," *Left and Right* 1 (autumn 1965): 35–67; Thomas Anderson (executive secretary of the Michigan YAF), "Letter from the Right," *New Left Notes* 1 (8 July 1966): 3–4. These favorable comments should be contrasted with those of David Keene, "Libertarian into Anarchist," *National Review* 22 (6 October 1970): 1065–66 ("only a handful of kooks and gatecrashers" who "side with America's enemies"), and Phillip Abbot Luce, "The World of Lysander Spooner," *New Guard* 11 (January–February 1971): 37–39.

12. Ayn Rand, *The Virtue of Selfishness: A New Concept of Egoism* (New York: New American Library, 1965); Tony Lang, "Karl Hess Is Aflame with the Idea That Every Man Can Run His Own Life," *Washington Post Sunday Magazine*, 6 December 1970; Ronald Hamowy (editor, *New Individualist Review*), "Left and Right Meet," *New Republic* 154 (12 March 1966): 16.

13. "What Is to Be Done?" *Abolitionist* 2 (August 1971): 2; Donald Ernsberger, "YAF and the New Right: A Self-Criticism," *Commentary on Liberty* 4 (March 1968): 2; "Polarization," *Libertarian Forum* 2 (15 October 1970): 1, 3, 5; Mike Marotta, "Why Libertarianism?" *Vanguard* 1 (September 1971): 26–32.

14. Emerson, "Historic Notes of Life and Letters in New England," in *Works* (Boston: Houghton Mifflin, 1883), vol. 10, p. 309. For an example of one individual who claimed to have outgrown his initial anarchism and become a Marxist (a trend in the American Left during the late 1960s, accelerating its sectarianism and alienation from the mass of American society), see Peter Joseph, "Letter," *Liberation* 15 (January 1971): 33. The early 1970s produced a new radical prolet-cult with a gaudy array of Marxist-Leninist-Maoist and Stalinist groups. This appeared to be a dazzling American example of the combination of centralist verbiage and wild, decentralist squabbling sects; it seemed to be anarchism waving a red flag.

15. Bill Smith, "Three Men on a Horseback" (on the beat phenomenon), *New University Thought* no. 22 (autumn 1962): 73–80; Lorraine and Fredy Perlman, "Chicago: August, 1968," *Black and Red*, no. 2 (October 1968), pp. 1–45 (commentary and documents).

16. Nat Hentoff, "Village Anarchist," *Reporter* 29 (18 July 1963): 54–55; Michael Harrington, "On Paul Goodman," *Atlantic* 216 (August 1965): 88–91. The Anarcho-Communists frequently scorned him as a reformer: George Molnar, "Meliorism," *Anarchy* (London) 8 (March 1968): 76–83, reply by Ross Poole, pp. 83–87; Kingsley Widmer, "American Conservative Anarchy," ibid., 1, 4, new series (1971): 14–19.

17. Irwin Silber, "The Cultural Revolution: A Marxist Analysis" [pamphlet] (New York: Times Change Press, 1970), p. 11. This is actually rather un-Marxist, since any structural reforms were probably adopted not because of "ideas and agitation," but because of the imperatives of the depression.

18. George Bernard Shaw, "The Impossibilities of Anarchism," Fabian Tract no. 45 (London: Fabian Society, July 1893), p. 23. Shaw divided anarchism into two schools, represented by the individualism of Tucker and the communism of Kropotkin, and criticized both.

Chapter Nine

1. James M. Powell, "A Medieval View of Jimmy Carter," *America* 135 (23 October 1976): 250.

2. Robert Bellah, "American Civil Religion in the 1970's," in *American Civil Religion*, ed. Russell Richey and Donald Jones, p. 271 (New York: Harper and Row, 1974); Bruce Douglas, "Socialism and Sin," *Christian Century* 93 (1 December 1976); 1072-76; Royal E. Shepard, Jr., "Manifesto for the New Liberal Church," *Christian Century* 93 (6 October 1976): 837-39; "Christians for Socialism in the United States," *Radical Religion* 3, 1 (1976): 52-54 (the goal is not a "privileged bureaucracy" under socialism, but "liberation from physical, social, economic, political, cultural and spiritual bondage"); "Organized Religion's Rise after a Decade of Decline," San Francisco *Examiner* 10 April 1977, pp. 1, 8: "A Matter of Interest" (editorial), *Catholic Worker* 43 (March-April 1977): 2; Charles Y. Glock and Robert N. Bellah, eds., *The New Religious Consciousness* (Berkeley: University of California Press, 1976); *Religion in America: Gallup Opinion Index, 1977-78* (Princeton, N.J.: American Institute for Public Opinion, 1977).

3. Quoted in Robert O. Mead, *Atlantic Legacy* (New York: New York University Press, 1969), epigraph.

4. Archibald MacLeish, *America Was Promises* (New York: Duell, Sloan and Pearce, 1939), pp. 1-2.

5. John Cotton, "A Reply to Mr. Williams His Examination; And Answer to the Letters..."(1647), *Publications of the Narragansett Club*, 1st ser., 2 (1869): 18-19.

6. San Francisco *Examiner*, 24 November 1976, p. 2. A 1977 article attempted to reinterpret these data by claiming that moves are not disruptive because reintegration is rapid, the distance is seldom great, and previous friendships can be maintained by the use of cars and telephones. The authors conclude that "far from suffering the loss of intimacy, movers can draw upon people from both the old and the new neighborhoods." They admitted that some groups find relocation more painful: the poor, elderly, minorities, women and children (that is, the majority!). Such a thesis could also demonstrate, however, that relations between neighbors and ties to communities are superficial in America. What intimate human contacts can be sustained by telephone? Reintegration may be quick, but at what level? Furthermore, the authors agree that there is a powerful nostalgia for the good old days of the warm small-town community. They correctly label this a delusion that has little historical basis; yet the existence of such a dream is itself significant. Our capitalist society does not satisfy this yearning. See Claude Fischer and Ann Stueve, "Homeward Bound: Exploding the Myth of Mobility," *California Monthly* (originally printed in *New Society*), (March 1977), p. 3.

7. Advertisement, San Francisco *Examiner*, 17 January 1977, p. 7.

8. Gandhi, quoted in *California Living*, supplement to San Francisco *Sunday Examiner and Chronicle*, 3 April 1977; San Francisco *Chronicle*, 21 April 1977, pp. 1, 10, 24; Seymour Melman, *Our Depleted Society* (New York: Holt, Rinehart and Winston, 1965); Richard Hofstadter and S. M. Lipset, eds., *Turner and the Frontier Thesis* (New York: Basic Books, 1968); Frank Fraser Darling, *Wilderness and Plenty* (Boston: Houghton Mifflin, 1970).

9. "The Trucker Mystique," *Newsweek* 87 (26 January 1976): 44-45. See also Jane Stern,

Trucker: A Portrait of the Last American Cowboy (New York: McGraw-Hill, 1975).

10. San Francisco *Examiner*, 9 February 1977, p. 2.

11. Hugh Heclo, "The Welfare State: The Costs of American Self-Sufficiency," in *Lessons from America*, ed. Richard Rose, p. 270 (New York: John Wiley, 1974); "Americans Don't Like the Poor," San Francisco *Examiner* 18 February 1977, p. 10. Welfare payments could be compared with the overwhelming acceptance of veterans' benefits, which are "earned."

12. Paul Jacobs, *The State of the Unions* (New York: Atheneum, 1963); B. J. Widick, *Labor Today* (Boston: Houghton Mifflin, 1964); Jeremy Brecher, *Strike!* (San Francisco: Straight Arrow Books, 1972); Stanley Aronowitz, *False Promises* (New York: McGraw-Hill, 1973); J. Zerzan, "Organized Labor versus 'The Revolt against Work,' " in *Unions against Revolution*, pp. 47–62 (Chicago: Black and Red, 1975); Studs Terkel, *Working* (New York: Pantheon, 1974).

13. See *The Future of Capitalism: a Symposium* (New York: Macmillan, 1967), p. 27.

14. Norman Macrae, "The New American Dilemma: A Nation of Entrepreneurs Seems to Have Lost Its Way," *Atlas* 23 (January 1976): "The Greying of America," *Newsweek*, 28 February 1977, pp. 50–52, 55–58 (in 1790 more than half the population was aged sixteen *or younger*!); "Teenage Unemployment Reported at 20 Percent," *Weekly People* 86 (18 December 1976): 1.

15. Daniel Yankelovich, *Work in America: Report of the Special Task Force to the Secretary of Health, Education, and Welfare* (Cambridge, Mass.: MIT Press, 1972), p. 44.

16. L. J. Sharpe, "American Democracy Reconsidered," *British Journal of Political Science* 3, 1–2 (1973): 17.

17. "Common Sense" (1775), in *The Works of Thomas Paine*, p. 294 (New York: Wm. Wise and Company, 1924); "The Bureaucracy Explosion," *Current*, no. 186 (October 1976), pp. 3–10. For a general perspective on American hostility toward power, see John Bunzel, *Anti-Politics in America: Relfections on the Anti-Political Temper and Its Distortions of the Democratic Process* (New York: Knopf, 1967).

18. Anonymous quotations, from Harold L. Sheppard and Ned Q. Herrick, *Where Have All the Robots Gone? Worker Dissatisfaction in the 1970's* (New York: Free Press, 1972), p. 32; Reg Murphey, "The Voters Mood of Discontent," San Francisco *Chronicle and Examiner*, 31 October 1976, sec. B, p. 2.

19. Lou Harris, "Distrustful Public a Carter Headache," San Francisco *Examiner*, 3 January 1977, p. 2; Donald Warren, *The Radical Center: Middle Americans and the Politics of Alienation* (South Bend, Ind.: Notre Dame University Press, 1976); James D. Wright, *The Dissent of the Governed: Alienation and Democracy in America* (New York: Academic Press, 1976). Warren specifically denies that expressions of individualism are inherently reactionary, praising them as healthy responses to arbitrary bureaucracies.

20. Ernest B. Furgurson, "The Mood of America in 1976," Baltimore *Sunday Sun*, 4 January 1976, K-1; *Common Sense* 4, 1 (January 1976): 2.

21. William Serrin, *The Company and the Union*, 2d ed. (New York: Knopf, 1974), pp. 233–36; "Wildcat: Dodge Truck, June, 1974" (Detroit: Black and Red, n.d.); Ken Weller, "The Lordstown Strike" [1971] (London: Solidarity, n.d.).

22. Ernest Furgurson, "How the Politicians Adapt to an Anti-Politician Mood," Baltimore *Sunday Sun*, 25 January 1976, K-5.

23. Robert Dahl and Charles E. Lindblom, *Politics, Economics and Welfare* (New York: Harper, 1953), pp. 333–34.

24. Quoted in *Economics: Mainstream Readings and Radical Critiques*, ed. David Mermelstein (New York: Random House, 1973), p. 85.

25. Quoted in Richard Cornuelle, *De-Managing America: The Final Revolution* (New York: Random House, 1975), p. 7. Or meditate on this plea by a justice of the Supreme Court: "We must realize that today's Establishment is the new George III. Whether it will continue to adhere to his tactics, we do not know. If it does, the redress, honored in tradition, is revolu-

tion'' (William O. Douglas, *Points of Rebellion* [New York: Vintage, Random House, 1970], p. 95).

26. Heclo, ''The Welfare State,'' pp. 278, 280.

27. ''The Volunteers,'' San Francisco *Examiner*, 18 January 1977, pp. 17–18 (The United Way gives a De Tocqueville award for distinguished volunteer service). While some forms of this populism, such as that of Saul Alinsky, have elements of community control, they are essentially liberal in their pragmatic ''realism.'' See the debate between Frank Ackerman and Harry Boyte in *Socialist Revolution* (no. 35 [September–October 1977], pp. 113–29).

28. Paul Jacobs, ''Nothing for Everyone: Brown's New Politics,'' *Mother Jones* 1 (July 1976): 24–28, 59 (see also the following essay by Sid Blumenthal, ''Less Is Better in Massachusetts, Too,'' p. 29); *Militant* 40 (30 January 1976): 5; John C. Bennett, ''America's Shift from Revolution to Counterrevolution,'' *Christian Century* 93 (9–16 June 1976): 561–64; Jimmy Carter, inaugural address, San Francisco *Examiner*, 21 January 1977, p. 7; ''What Is a Liberal—Who Is a Conservative? A Symposium'' (entire issue), *Commentary* 62 (September 1976); George Cabot Lodge, *The New American Ideology* (New York: Knopf, 1976), calls for a change from individualism to ''communitarianism,'' somewhat like that portrayed in Daniel Bell's *The Cultural Contradictions of Capitalism* (1976). Bell suggested the model of a ''public household'' based on a sophisticated balance of all groups.

29. Chuck Fager, ''The Genesis of Small Is Beautiful'' (interview), San Francisco *Bay Guardian*, 3 March 1977, pp. 4–5; Jules Witcover, ''Fred Harris: Wooing the Left,'' *Progressive* 40 (Janaury 1976); Tom Hayden, ''Fred Harris: A Populist with a Prayer,'' *Rolling Stone* 8 May 1975; Nelson Blackstock, ''What Makes Tom Hayden Run?'' *Militant* 40 (30 January 1976): 23. Some basic commentaries on liberalism: Robert Paul Wolff, *The Poverty of Liberalism* (Boston: Beacon, 1968); Arnold S. Kaufman, *The Radical Liberal: New Man in American Politics* (New York: Atherton, 1968); Theodore J. Lowe, *The End of Liberalism* (New York: Norton, 1969); H. Mark Roelofs, ''The Adequacy of America's Dominant Liberal Ideology,'' *Bucknell Review*, 18 (fall 1970): 3–15; Alan Ritter, ''Anarchism and Liberal Theory in the Nineteenth Century,'' *Bucknell Review* 19 (fall 1971): 37–66; Theodore J. Lowi, *The Politics of Disorder* (New York: Basic, 1971); Jerome Mileur, ed., *The Liberal Tradition in Crisis* (Lexington, Mass.: Heath, 1974), along with several articles and comments on ''corporate liberalism'' in *For a New America*, ed. James Weinstein and David Eakins (New York: Vintage, 1970?, pp. 46–161 and *A New History of Leviathan*, ed. Ronald Radosh and Murray N. Rothbard (New York: Dutton, 1972).

30. Morris and Linda Tannehill, *The Market for Liberty* (New York: Arno, 1972), p. 2. See also Theodore Roszak, ''The Disease Called Politics,'' in *Seeds of Liberation*, ed. Paul Goodman, p. 450 (New York: George Braziller, 1965); Robert Nozick, *Anarchy, State and Utopia* (New York: Basic Books, 1975); ''A Free Society Is Built One by One,'' *LeFevre's Journal* 3 (winter 1975): 6–7; Murray Rothbard, *For a New Liberty* (New York: Macmillan, 1973); Tibor R. Machan, ed., *The Libertarian Alternative* (Chicago: Nelson-Hall, 1974); Irving Kristol, ''What Is a 'Neo-Conservative'?'' *Newsweek*, 19 January 1976, p. 17.

Christopher Lasch was correct, I think, when he said that ''in American radicalism, power and authority are [frequently] defined as the source of evil. Politics then becomes non-politics'' (review of Paul Goodman's *People or Personnel* in *Commentary* 40 [November 1965]: 116).

31. ''How the Americans Combat Individualism by the Doctrine of Self-Interest Properly Understood,'' in *Democracy in America*, ed. J. P. Mayer, pp. 497–500 (New York: Harper and Row, 1966).

32. ''The Libertarian Party: It's about Time'' (Washington, D.C.: Libertarian Party National Headquarters, n.d.).

33. John Rossen, letter, *New American Movement* 1 (April 1972): 2, 13. Rossen had earlier published a journal called the *New Patriot* and edited an anthology that was reissued as *The Little Red, White and Blue Book: Revolutionary Quotations by Great Americans* (New York:

Grove, 1969). For his links to the PBC, read *How to Commit Revolution American Style*, ed. Jeremy Rifkin and John Rossen (Secaucus, N.J.: Lyle Stuart, 1973).

34. Rusty Conroy, "'76 Fest Masks War Threat, Profits," *Guardian* (21 January 1976): 6.

35. Calvin Trillin, "Parallels," *New Yorker* 49 (21 January 1974), 67 ff. Representative publications from the PBC (no date): "The Light in the Steeple: Religion and the American Revolution"; "We Hold These Truths: The Declaration of Independence as a Living Document"; "The Tree of Liberty: The Revolutionary Tradition in America Today"; "Declare Your Independence from Big Business."

36. *Common Sense*, vol. 4 (January 1976); Jeremy Rifkin, "The People Are Passing Us By," *Progressive* 39 (October 1975): 13–14; *People's Business*, vol. 1, no. 1 (1977), and Jeremy Rifkin, *Own Your Own Job* (New York: Bantam, 1977). Rifkin is unjust to state socialism, which does insure steady employment, medical care, education, and other benefits that a large number of Americans do not enjoy.

37. Sacvan Bercovitch, *The Puritan Origins of the American Self* (New Haven: Yale University Press, 1975), 176.

38. Father Andrew Greeley, in a symposium, "What Is a Liberal—Who Is a Conservative?" *Commentary* 62 (September 1976): 66.

39. Robert N. Bellah, "Religion and Polity in America," *Andover Newton Quarterly* 15 (1974/75): 121. The diligent student might turn to some of the following writings: Glenn Meredith, "Some Thoughts on Anarchist Culture," *Black Star* 1,1 (1975): 4–5; Richard Fairfield, *Communes: A Personal Tour* (Baltimore: Penguin, 1972); Rosabeth Kanter, ed., *Communes* (New York: Harper and Row, 1973); Andrew Rigby, *Alternative Realities* (London: Routledge and Kegan Paul, 1974). Various critical schools are defined in their publications: "About Ourselves," *Solidarity Newsletter*, no. 11 (spring 1975), p. 2 (also "Malaise on the Left," pp. 1, 4); "Workers' Councils and the Economics of Self-Management" (Philadelphia: Solidarity, 1974); Paul Cardan, "Redefining Revolution" (London: Solidarity, early 1970s edition); "Principles of Association," *SRAFederation Bulletin for Anarchist Agitators*, no. 49 (December 1975); "How We Can Do It," *Industrial Worker* 69 (March 1972): 6–8; Root and Branch, *The Rise of the Workers' Movements* (New York: Fawcett, 1975); Greg Calvert and Carol Neiman, *A Disrupted History: The New Left and the New Capitalism* (New York: Random House, 1971); Daniel Kramer, *Participatory Democracy: Developing Ideals of the Political Left* (Cambridge, Mass.: Schenkman, 1972); and many studies on workers' control, such as Jaroslav Vanek, *The Participatory Economy* (Ithaca: Cornell University Press, 1971), and Howard Wachtel, *Workers' Management and Workers' Wages in Yugoslavia* (Ithaca: Cornell University Press, 1973).

40. *The Green Revolution: A Voice for Decentralism*, vol. 32 (December 1975); "Marxism vs. Anarchism" (editorial statment), *Internationalism*, no. 8 (December 1975), pp. 19–21; "Who Are We?" *News and Letters* 21 (Janaury–February 1976): 11; Raya Dunayevskaya, *Marxism and Freedom*, 3d ed. enl. (London: Pluto Press, 1971 [1958]); and Dunayevskaya, *Philosophy and Revolution* (New York: Dell, 1973).

I could locate only one foreign model that might vaguely resemble the Catholic Workers: B. J. Miller, "Anarchism and French Catholicism in *Esprit*," *Journal of the History of Ideas* 37 (January 1976): 163–74.

41. NAM preface to Harry Boyte and Frank Ackerman, "Revolution and Democracy" (Minneapolis: NAM, 1972); "New American Movement" (Chicago: NAM, 1976?); John Judis, "New American Movement, 1975," *Socialist Revolution*, no. 26 (October–December 1975), pp. 117–42; "Convention Papers, 1975" (Chicago: NAM, 1975); G. William Domhoff, "Why Socialists Should Be Democrats," *Socialist Revolution*, no. 31 (January–February 1977), pp. 25–36; "An Electoral Strategy," *California Discussion Bulletin* (NAM), January 1976.

42. *The Call: Political Newspaper of the October League* 4 (January 1976): 14.

43. Irwin Silber, "Fan the Flames," *Guardian* (Silber has been the long-time editor) 28 (21

January 1976): 18; *Revolution* (organ of the Central Commitee of the Revolutionary Communist Party, USA—formerly Revolutionary Union), vol. 1, no. 4 (5 January 1976); *Challenge: The Revolutionary Communist Newspaper* (Progressive Labor Party), vol. 12 (21 August 1975); *Young Spartacus*, no. 38 (December 1975 [read all about RSB, SWP, YSA, CAR, NSCAR, RU and RCP!]); "Perspectives for the American Revolution; Revised Resolution of the Worker's League" (New York: Labor Publications, 1974); and "The Debris of Marxism" (panel discussion), in *Dissent, Power and Confrontation*, ed. Alexander Klein, pp. 237–81 (New York: McGraw-Hill, 1971).

44. Editoral, *In These Times* 1 (2–8 February 1977): 24.

45. "On Organization" (Chicago: Radical Decentralist Project, mimeographed, May 1969). One historical model was invoked by an SDS slogan of 1966: "Turn America into a town meeting" (*New Left Notes*, vol. 1 [June 1966]).

46. For some typically condescending statements by two Marxists, read Eric Hobsbaum, "Reflections on Anarchism," in *Revolutionaries: Contemporary Essays* (New York: Pantheon, 1973), pp. 82–91, and Herbert Marcuse, "The Individual in the Great Society," in *A Great Society*, ed. Bertram Gross, pp. 58–90 (New York: Basic Books, 1968) ("Ubiquitous organization [is] characteristic of, and indispensable for, the functioning of advanced industrial society"; p. 77). Libertarians condemn both Marxist-Leninist elitism and Social Democratic bureaucracy. As a left libertarian has expressed the final goal of liberation: "Socialism is not a backyard of leisure attached to the industrial prison. It is not transitors for the prisoners. It is the destruction of the industrial prison itself" ("Socialism or Barbarism" [London: Solidarity pamphlet, n.d.]).

47. Quoted in Paul Cardan, *Workers' Councils* (Philadelphia: Solidarity, 1974), p. 13 n.

48. Bellah, "Religion and Polity in America," p. 120; C. B. Macpherson, "Individualist Socialism? A Reply to Levine and MacIntyre," *Canadian Journal of Philosophy* 6 (June 1976): 195–200. The question "What is to be done?" is answered in somewhat riotous diversity in an anthology of contemporary anarchist writings edited by DeLeon and others: *Reinventing Anarchy: What Are the Anarchists Thinking These Days?* (London: Routledge and Kegan Paul, forthcoming 1978).

But doesn't all of this assume a technologically advanced society? Not necessarily. Self-management, even in an industrially "primitive" system, would make greater use of local initiative and experience, possibly resulting in maximum flexibility, experimentation, and overall efficiency. Workers might be more interested and therefore more motivated. This should stimulate higher productivity, along with fewer overpaid, unproductive, and interfering managers. While it may be true that state socialism could direct a poor country more rapidly toward a nuclear bomb, a mammoth military establishment, superhighways, and an elite with villas in the countryside, those are scarcely my fondest dreams.

GENERAL REFERENCE
BIBLIOGRAPHY

INTERGALACTIC ANARCHIST NEWS

While documentation for my thesis can be found in the footnotes, the purpose of this bibliography is to provide the most utilitarian general reference for writings by and about anarchists. The items were chosen on the basis of availability (usually in English) and importance. Naturally some works are readily available but of only minor significance, and others are important but are out of print and extremely rare. The publication dates cited are usually those of the most recent editions. In cases where little has been written, such as on Max Stirner and Benjamin Tucker, I have included all the items I found, for the sake of "completeness." For a topic like the Sacco and Vanzetti case, where there is a library of polemical literature, I have made a representative selection. I have ignored such minor anarchists as Francisco Ferrer, although there are comments on them in the general studies section. A few subjects, like workers' control, syndicalism, and novels by or about anarchists, are also under-represented because they were not directly related to my research or because they have not been central to American radicalism. Foreign language studies have been restricted primarily because American anarchists have seldom read them—indeed, most American anarchists seem ignorant of most works in their own language, although many of the major anarchist theorists of the last fifty years have written in English (Goodman, Read, Bookchin, Ward, and Wolff).

The categories are usually self-explanatory, but there are a few obscure listings. Writings by and about Tolstoi have been placed under his name in "Related Primary Sources." This is not because of my skepticism about his later-life qualifications as an anarchist but is required by the paucity of literature on Tolstoi the anarchist. For some literature on the Spanish Civil War, see George Orwell in "Related Primary Sources." Any references to "Horowitz" or "Krimerman and Perry," followed by pagination, signify reprints in their respective anthologies. For a full citation, see "General Anarchist Studies and Anthologies." There are also some allusions to Staughton Lynd, ed., *Nonviolence in America* (Indianapolis: Bobbs-Merrill, 1966).

Let me conclude on a note of despair. While this bibliography is the best single reference on anarchism, any listing on such a broadly (un)defined subject is necessarily incomplete.

Order of Bibliography

I. MANUSCRIPT COLLECTIONS

(Limited to those consulted for this study)

Baskette Collection, University of Illinois, Urbana, Illinois. Includes about a dozen letters and postcards from Tucker to Ewing C. Baskette during the 1930s, along with letters from Josiah Warren to Stephen Pearl Andrews.

Brown University Library, Providence, Rhode Island. Has a miscellaneous collection on Ezra Heywood, consisting of the complete volumes of the *Word*, letters about Heywood, some photographs, and his death mask.

Ishill Collection, Houghton Library, Harvard University, Cambridge, Massachusetts. Contains more than two hundred letters by Tucker and some items about him. The library also has letters by Voltairine de Cleyre, Dyer D. Lum, Jo Labadie, Henry Bool, Peter Kropotkin, and Elisèe Reclus.

Labadie Collection, University of Michigan Graduate Library, Ann Arbor, Michigan. The most complete single accumulation on American anarchism.

Library of the Workingmen's Institute, New Harmony, Indiana. Best collection on Josiah Warren.

New York Historical Society, New York City. Includes a small collection on Lysander Spooner.

New York Public Library. Manuscripts Division, New York City. Has some of the papers of Emma Goldman and Benjamin Tucker (whose private library is now in the Berg Collection). For further primary bibliography of Goldman, see Richard Drinnon's biography, *Rebel in Paradise* (Chicago: University of Chicago Press, 1961), pp. 315–16.

State Historical Society of Wisconsin, Madison, Wisconsin. The Andrews Collection has some of the papers of Stephen Pearl Andrews and Josiah Warren. For information on lesser manuscript sources on Andrews, consult Madeline Stern's *The Pantarch* (Austin: University of Texas Press, 1968), p. 180.

Suffolk County Historical Society, Riverhead, Long Island, New York. Materials on the City of Modern Times, Long Island.

II. BIBLIOGRAPHIES AND ENCYCLOPEDIAS

Bettini, Leonardo. *Bibliographica dell'anarchismo*. Italy, 1972 (publications in Italian, 1872–1971).

Egbert, Donald Drew, and Persons, Stow, eds. *Socialism and American Life*. Bibliography, vol. 2 (of 2), compiled by T. D. Seymour Bassett. Princeton: Princeton University Press, 1952.

Faure, Sébastian ed. *Encyclopédie anarchiste*. 4 vols. Paris: 'La Librairie Internationale,'' 193?–34.

Filler, Louis, ed. *A Dictionary of American Social Reform*. New York: Philosophical Library, 1963.

Goehlert, Robert. "Anarchism: A Bibliography of Articles, 1900–75." *Political Theory* 4 (February 1976): 113–28 (includes many articles from small journals like *Anarchy*, not indexed here).

Hacker, Andrew. "Anarchism." In *International Encyclopedia of the Social Sciences*, 1: 283–85. 16 vols. New York: Macmillan and Free Press, 1968.

Jaszi, Oscar. "Anarchism." In *The Encyclopedia of the Social Sciences*, edited by Edwin R. A. Seligman and Alvin Johnson, 2:46–53. 15 vols. New York: Macmillan, 1937–44.

Kropotkin, Peter. "Anarchism." In *Encyclopaedia Britannica*, 1: 914–19. 11th ed. 1910. A classic summary by the leading theoretician of Communist Anarchism.

Kunitz, Stanley, J., and Haycroft, Howard, eds. *American Authors 1600–1900*. New York: H. W. Wilson, 1938. The article on Tucker has more than a half-dozen errors.

Lasswell, Harold; Casey, Ralph D. and Smith, Bruce L. *Propaganda and Promotional Activities: An Annotated Bibliography*. Chicago: University of Chicago Press, 1969.

Lehning, Arthur. "Anarchism." In *The Dictionary of the History of Ideas*, edited by Philip Wiener, pp. 70–76. New York: Scribner's, 1973.

Nettlau, Max. *Bibliographie de L'anarchie*. New York: Burt Franklin Reprints, 1967 (1897).

Reese, Rena. *List of Books and Pamphlets in a Special Collection in the Library of the Work-ingmen's Institute, New Harmony, Ind.,* New Harmony, Ind., 1909.

Sibley, Mulford Q. "Anarchism." In *A Dictionary of the Social Sciences*, edited by Julius Gould and William L. Kolb, p. 25. Glencoe, Ill.: Free Press, 1964.

Stammhamer, Josef. *Bibliographie des Socialismus und Communismus.* 3 vols. Jena, 1893–1909. Includes an extensive bibliography on anarchism.

Woodcock, George. "Anarchism." In *Encyclopedia of Philosophy*, edited by Paul Edwards, 111–15. 8 vols. New York: Macmillan and Free Press, 1967.

Yarros, Victor S. "Individualist or Philosophical Anarchism." In *New Encyclopedia of Social Reform*, edited by William D. P. Bliss and Rudolf Binder, pp. 41–45. New York: Funk and Wagnalls, 1910. See also "Anarchist Communism," by Clarence Lee Swartz, pp. 45–50, and his comment on Tucker, p. 1240.

Zimand, Savel. *Modern Social Movements: Descriptive Summaries and Bibliographies.* New York: H. W. Wilson, 1921.

III. GENERAL ANARCHIST STUDIES AND ANTHOLOGIES

Albert, Michael. *What Is to Be Undone? A Modern Revolutionary Discussion of Classical Left Ideologies.* Boston: Porter Sargent, 1974.

"Anarchism: The Idea and the Deed." *Times Literary Supplement*, no. 3278 (24 December 1964); pp. 1153–54.

Anderson, Thornton. "The Anarchists." In *Russian Political Thought*, pp. 231–47. Ithaca: Cornell University Press, 1967).

Apter, David, and Joll, James, eds. *Anarchism Today*. London: Methuen, 1971.

Arvon, Henri. *L'Anarchisme*. Paris, 1951.

Avakumovic, I. "Books on Anarchism and Anarchists" (review article). *Russian Review* 33 (Janaury 1974) 86–88.

Avrich, Paul. *The Russian Anarchists*. Princeton, N.J.: Princeton University Press, 1967. Printed in journals were "Anarchism and Anti-Intellectualism in Russia." *Journal of the History of Ideas* 27 (1966): 381–90; "The Anarchists in the Russian Revolution," *Russian Review* 26 (October 1967): 341–50; and "Russian Anarchists and the Civil War," *Russian Review* 27 (July 1968): 296–306. See also his more recent work, *The Anarchists in the Russian Revolution*. Ithaca: Cornell University Press, 1973.

Baldelli, Giovanni. *Social Anarchism*. Chicago: Aldine-Atherton, 1971.

Barber, Benjamin. *Superman and Commonmen*. New York: Praeger, 1972.

Bartsch, Günter. *Anarchismus in Deutschland*. 3 vols. Hannover: Fackeltrager-Verlag, 1972–73.

Berman, Paul, ed. *Quotations of the Anarchists*. New York: Praeger, 1972.

Bland, Georges. *La Grande Armée du Draplau Noir*. Paris: Presses de la Cité, 1972.

Bookchin, Murray. *Post-Scarcity Anarchism*. Berkeley, Calif.: Ramparts Press, 1971. Probably the most systematic and intelligent of all anarchist theoreticians, past and present. But see the critical review by Todd Gitlin, *Nation* 214 (6 March 1972): 309–11.

Bose, A. *History of Anarchism*. Mystic, Conn.: Verry, Lawrence, 1967.

Boyd, J. "From Far Right to Far Left, and Farther, with Karl Hess." *New York Times Magazine,* 6 December 1970, pp. 48–49.

Buchanan, James. *The Limits of Liberty: Between Anarchy and Leviathan*. Chicago: University of Chicago Press, 1975.

Burrow, J. W. "Anarchists (Who Are with Us Again)." *Horizon* 11 (summer 1969): 32–43.

Carlson, Andrew. *Anarchism in Germany:* Vol. 1. *The Early Movement (1830-1889)*. Metuchen, N.J.: Scarecrow, 1972.

Carter, April. *The Political Theory of Anarchism*. New York: Harper, 1971.

Catlin, George. "Individualists and Anarchists." In *The Story of the Political Philosophers*, pp. 405–31. New York: McGraw-Hill, 1939.

Chomsky, Noam. "Notes on Anarchism." In *Reasons of State*, pp. 370–86. New York: Pantheon, 1973.

Christie, Stuart, and Meltzer, Albert. *Floodgates of Anarchy*. London: Kahn and Averill, 1969.

Coker, Francis. "Anarchism." In *Recent Political Thought*, pp. 192–228. New York: Appleton-Century, 1934.

Cole, G. D. H. *A History of Socialist Thought: Marxism and Anarchism, 1850-1890*. Vol. 2 (of 5). New York: Macmillan, 1934.

Comfort, Alex. "Latterday Anarchism." *Center Magazine* 6, no. 5 (1973): 4–8.

Congress, U.S. House of Representatives: Committee on Immigration and Naturalization: Sixty-sixth Congress, second session. Report no. 504. *Exclusion and Expulsion of Aliens, of Anarchists and Similar Classes*. Washington, D.C., 1920.

Congress, U.S. House of Representatives: Subcommittee of the Committee on Immigration and Naturalization: Sixty-sixth Congress, second session. *Communist and Anarchist Deportation Cases*. Washington, D.C., 1920.

Coy, Peter E. B. "Social Anarchism: An Atavistic Ideology of the Peasant." *Journal of Inter-American Studies* 14 (May 1972): 133–49.

Crawford, K. "Desperate Romantics." *Newsweek* 76 (14 September 1970): 46.

De Leon, Daniel. "Socialism versus Anarchism." New York: New York Labor News, 1970.

Doctor, Adi H. *Anarchist Thought in India*. Bombay: Asia Publishing House, 1964.

Douty, H. M. "The Word and the Deed—Anarchism Revisited." *Monthly Labor Review* 89 (January 1966): 15–18.

Duberman, Martin. "Anarchism, Left and Right." *Partisan Review* 33 (fall 1966): 610–15.

————. "The Relevance of Anarchy." In *The Uncompleted Past*, pp. 151–61. *New York: Random House, 1969*.

Duerr, Hans Peter. *Ni Dieu ni Mètrè. Anarchistische Bemerkungen zur Bewusstseins und Erkenntnistheorie*. Frankfurt am Main: Suhrkamp Verlag, 1974.

Dulles, John W. *Anarchists and Communists in Brazil, 1900-1935*. Austin: University of Texas Press, 1974.

Ehrlich, Howard; Ehrlich, Carol; DeLeon, David; and Morris, Glenda. *Re-Inventing Anarchy: What Are the Anarchists Thinking These Days*. London: Routledge and Kegan Paul, 1978 (forthcoming).

Eltzbacher, Paul. *Anarchism: Exponents of the Anarchist Philosophy*. Translated by Steven Byington, edited by James J. Martin, with an appended essay on Anarcho-Syndicalism by Rudolf Rocker. New York: Libertarian Book Club, 1960 (1st Amer. ed. 1906). Rocker's essay is reprinted from *European Ideologies*, ed. Feliks Gross, pp. 343–89. New York: Philosophical Library, 1948.

Forman, James. *Anarchism: Political Innocence or Social Violence?* New York: Laurel-Leaf, 1976.

Fowler, R. B. "Anarchist Tradition of Political Thought." *Western Political Quarterly* 25 (December 1972): 738–52.

Fried, Albert, and Sanders, Ronald, eds. *Socialist Thought: A Documentary History*. Garden City, N.Y.: Anchor, 1964.

Ghio, Paul. *L'anarchisme aux Etats-Unis*. Paris: A. Colin, 1903. A section, "L'anarchisme insurrectionnel aux Etats-Unis," was printed in the *Journal des Economistes*, ser. 5, 55 (September 1903): 335–59. The article is very condensed, emphasizing the cities of Paterson, New Jersey, and Chicago, and with little on Tucker.

Gray, Alexander. *The Socialist Tradition.* New York: Longmans, Green, 1947.

Green, Gil. *The New Radicalism: Anarchist or Marxist?* New York: International, 1971.

Guérin, Daniel. *Anarchism.* New York: Monthly Review Press, 1970.

_____, ed. *Ni dieu ni maître: Anthologie historique du mouvement anarchiste.* Paris: Edition de Delphes, 1965? This is the best anthology of classical anarchist writings.

Hall, Bowman Newton. "A History and Critique of American Individualist Anarchists' Economic Theories." Ph.D. diss., Duke University, 1971.

Hobsbawm, E. J. "Bolshevism and Anarchists," and "Reflections on Anarchism." In *Revolutionaries,* pp. 57–70, 82–91. New York: Pantheon, 1973.

Hoffman, Robert L. "Anti-Military Complex: Anarchist Response to Contemporary Militarism." *Journal of International Affairs* 26,1 (1972): 87–97.

_____, ed. *Anarchism.* Chicago: Atherton, 1970.

Horowitz, Irving Louis, ed. *The Anarchists.* New York: Dell, 1964. A rather undiscriminating grabbag of libertarian literature.

Hostetter, Richard. *The Italian Socialist Movement.* Vol. 1 (of 2). Princeton: Princeton University Press, 1958.

Individualist Anarchist Pamphlets: An Original Arno Press Compilation. New York: Arno Press, 1971.

Ishill, Joseph, ed. *Free Vistas.* Vol. 2 (of 2). Berkeley Heights, N.J.: Oriole Press, 1935–37.

Jacker, Corinne. *Black Flag of Anarchy: Antistatism in the United States.* New York: Scribner's, 1968.

Joll, James. *The Anarchists.* 1st American ed. Boston: Little, Brown, 1965.

Kedward, Roderick. *The Anarchists: The Men Who Shocked an Era.* London: Macdonald, 1971.

Krämer-Badoni, Rudolf. *Anarchismus.* Munich: Verlag Fritz Molden, 1970.

Krimerman, Leonard, and Perry, Lewis, eds. *Patterns of Anarchy: Collection of Writings on the Anarchist Tradition.* Garden City, N.Y.: Anchor, 1966.

Lang, Olga. *Pa Chin and His Writings.* Cambridge: Harvard University Press, 1967.

Longoni, J. C. *Four Patients of Dr. Deibler.* London: Lawrence and Wishart, 1970. Deibler was the public executioner of four anarchists.

Lunn, Eugene. *Prophet of Community: The Romantic Socialism of Gustav Landauer.* Berkeley, Calif.: University of California Press, 1973.

Lusk Committee (New York, Legislative Joint Committee Investigating Seditious Activities). *Revolutionary Radicalism.* 8 vols. New York: Da Capo, 1971 (1920).

Madison, Charles A. "Anarchism in America." *Journal of the History of Ideas* 6 (January 1945): 46–66. See also "The Anarchist Background." in his *Critics and Crusaders: A Century of American Protest,* pp. 157–74. 2d ed. rev. New York: Ungar, 1959.

Maitron, Jean. *Histoire du mouvement anarchiste en France (1880–1914).* Paris: Société Universitaire d'Editions et de Librairie, 1951. See "Anarchisme individualiste," pp. 483–91.

Manas, editors of *The Manas Reader.* New York: Grossman, 1971.

Mancini, Matthew Joseph. "The Covert Themes of American Anarchism, 1881–1908: Time Space and Consciousness as Anarchist Myth." Ph.D. diss., Emory University, 1974.

Manicas, Peter. *The Death of the State.* New York: Putnam, 1974.

Martin, James J. *Men against the State: The Expositors of Individualist Anarchism in America, 1827–1908.* Foreword by Harry Elmer Barnes. Colorado Springs: Myles, 1970 (1953).

Marx, Karl; Engels, Friedrich; and Lenin, V. I. *Anarchism and Anarcho-Syndicalism: Selections.* New York: International, 1972.

Maurer, Charles. *Call to Revolution: The Mystical Anarchism of Gustav Landauer.* Detroit: Wayne State University Press, 1971.

Miller, William D. *Dorothy Day and the Catholic Worker Movement.* New York: Liveright, 1972.

Newbrough, Michael. "Individualist Anarchism in American Political Thought." Ph.D. diss., University of California, Santa Barbara, 1975.

Nomad, Max. "Evolution of Anarchism and Syndicalism: A Critical View." In *European Ideologies*, edited by Feliks Gross, pp. 325–42. New York: Philosophical Library, 1948.

Novak, Derry. "Anarchism and Individual Terrorism." *Canadian Journal of Economics and Political Science* 20 (May 1954): 176–84.

———. "The Place of Anarchism in the History of Political Thought." *Review of Politics* 20 (July 1958): 307–20.

Nozick, Robert. *Anarchy, State and Utopia*. New York: Basic Books, 1974. Discussed in M. F. Plattner's "New Political Theory," *Public Interest*, no. 40 (summer 1975), pp. 119–28, and H. Steiner, "Anarchy, State and Utopia," *Mind* 86 (January 1977): 120–29.

Ostergaard, Geoffrey, and Currell, Melville. *The Gentle Anarchists: A Study of the Leaders of the Sarvodaya Movement for Non-Violent Revolution in India*. New York: Oxford University Press, 1971.

Parsons, Albert R. *Anarchism: Its Philosophy and Scientific Basis as Defined by Some of Its Apostles*. New York: Kraus Reprint, 1971 (Chicago, 1887).

Pennock, J. Roland and Chapman, John W., eds. *Anarchism*. New York: New York University, 1978.

Perlin, Terry. "Anarchist Communism in America, 1890–1914." Ph.D. diss., Brandeis University, 1970.

———, ed. *Contemporary Anarchism*. Rutgers, N.J.: Transaction Books, 1978.

Perry, Lewis. *Radical Abolitionism: Anarchy and the Government of God in Antislavery Thought*. Ithaca, New York: Cornell University Press, 1973. A partial summary is found in "Versions of Anarchism in the Antislavery Movement," *American Quarterly* 20 (winter 1968): 768–82.

Plekhanov, George. *Anarchism and Socialism*. Translated by Eleanor Marx Aveling. Chicago: Kerr, 1909. A Marxian critique of anarchism, centering on the views of Bakunin. Other studies in the same broad category are Marx's *Indifference in Political Matters*, Engel's *On Authority*, Lenin's *State and Revolution*, and Stalin's *Anarchism or Socialism*.

Powell, Wiliam. *The Anarchist Cookbook*. New York: Lyle Stuart, 1971.

Read, Herbert. *The Philosophy of Anarchism*. London: Freedom Press, 1941.

Reclus, Elisée. "An Anarchist on Anarchy," *Contemporary Review* 45 (May 1884): 627–41. Tucker reprinted this as a pamphlet; it is somewhat sentimental but is valuable for evoking anarchist emotion: "after so much hatred we long to love each other, and for this reason we are enemies of property [Tucker would disagree] and despisers of the law" (p. 641).

Reichert, William O. "Anarchism, Freedom and Power," *Ethics* 79 (January 1969): 139–49.

———. *Partisans of Freedom: A Study in American Anarchism*. Bowling Green, Ohio: Bowling Green University Popular Press, 1976.

———. "Toward a New Understanding of Anarchism." *Western Political Quarterly* 20 (December 1967): 856–65.

Resnick, P. "Political Theory of Extra-Parliamentarianism." *Canadian Journal of Political Science* 6 (March 1973): 65–88.

Richards, Vernon, comp. and ed. *Errico Malatesta: His Life and Ideas*. London: Freedom Press, 1965. See also P. Holgate's *Malatesta*, (London: Freedom Press, 1956).

Riley, Thomas. *Germany's Poet-Anarchist: John Henry Mackay*. New York: Revisionist, 1972.

Rist, Charles. "The Anarchist." In *History of Economic Doctrines from the Time of the Physiocrats to the Present Day*, by Charles Rist and Charles Gide, pp. 610–36. London: Harrap, 1915.

Ritter, Alan. "Anarchism and Liberal Theory in the Nineteenth Century," *Bucknell Review* 19 (fall 1971): 37–66.

Rocker, Rudolf. *Pioneers of American Freedom: Origin of Liberal and Radical Thought in America*. Translated by Arthur Briggs. Los Angeles: Rocker Publications Committee, 1949.

Rosenthal, D. "Anarchism, Past and Future." *Nation* 213 (1 November 1971): 439–40.

Rothbard, Murray, and Hess, Karl eds. *Libertarian Forum, 1969–1971*. New York: Arno, 1971.

Runkle, Gerald. *Anarchism: Old and New*. New York: Delacorte, 1972.

Russell, Bertrand. *Roads to Freedom: Socialism, Anarchism and Syndicalism*. London: Allen and Unwin, 1918.

Sampson, Ronald V. "Power, the Enshrined Heresy." *Nation* 212 (4 January 1971): 14–20.

Scalapino, Robert, and Yu, George. *The Chinese Anarchist Movement*. Berkeley, Calif.: Center for Chinese Studies, 1961.

Schaack, Michael J. *Anarchy and Anarchists*. Chicago: F. J. Schulte, 1889. An analysis from the point of view of a Chicago police captain.

Schiller, Marvin. "Anarchism and Autonomy." *Bucknell Review* 21; 2/3 (1973): 47–59.

Schirer, Heinz. "Anarchism—Past and Present" (review of six books). *Survey* (Great Britain) 18,3 (1972): 205–8.

Schuster, Eunice Minette. "Native American Anarchism: A Study of Left-Wing American Individualism," *Smith College Studies in History* 17 (October 1931–July 1932): 5–197. AMS Reprint, 1970.

Sergeant, Alain, and Harmel, Claude. *Histoire de l'Anarchie* Paris, 1949.

Shatz, Marshall, ed. *The Essential Works of Anarchism*. New York: Bantam, 1971.

Shaw, George Bernard. "The Impossibilities of Anarchism." Fabian Tract no. 45. London: Fabian Society, 1893. Excerpted in Krimerman and Perry, pp. 500–514. Shaw divides anarchism into two schools, represented by Kropotkin and Tucker, and criticizes both. For a short description of Shaw's early politics, see Geoffrey Ostergaard, "G. B. S.—Anarchist." *New Statesman* 46 (21 November 1953): 628. Consult also the two volumes by his official biographer, Archibald Henderson.

Silverman, Henry, ed. *American Radical Thought: The Libertarian Tradition*. Lexington, Mass.: Heath, 1970.

Simon, S. Fanny. "Anarchism and Anarcho-Syndicalism in South America." *Hispanic-American Historical Review* 26 (February 1946): 38–59.

Sprading, Charles T., ed. *Liberty and the Great Libertarians*. Los Angeles, 1913.

Stafford, David. *From Anarchism to Reformism: A Study of the Political Activities of Paul Brousse within the First International and the French Socialist Movement, 1870–1890*. Toronto: University of Toronto Press, 1971.

Straus, Reed. "The Anarchist Argument: An Analysis of Three Justifications of Anarchism." Ph. D. diss., Columbia University, 1973.

Suskind, Richard. *By Bullet, Bomb and Dagger: The Story of Anarchism*. New York: Macmillan, 1971.

Taft, Philip. "Anarchism." In *Movements for Economic Reform*, pp. 98–120. New York: Holt, Rinehart, 1950.

Tassi, A. "Anarchism, Autonomy, and the Concept of the Common Good." *International Philosophical Quarterly* 17 (September 1977): 273–83.

Taylor, Michael. *Anarchy and Cooperation*. New York: John Wiley, 1976.

Tuchman, Barbara. "The Anarchists." *Atlantic Monthly* 211 (May 1963): 91–110. A fuller treatment can be found in her book *The Proud Tower* (New York: Macmillan, 1966), pp. 63–113. Her comments are "full of sensational nonsense" and have "a wealth of melodramatic detail" (Nicolas Walter, with whom I agree, "Anarchist Anthologies," *Anarchy* [London], no. 70 [December 1966], p. 380).

Tucker, William R. *The Anarcho-Fascism of Robert Brasillach*. Berkeley: University of California Press, 1975.

Tullock, Gordon, ed. *Explorations in the Theory of Anarchy*. Blacksburg, Va.: Center for the Study of Public Choice, 1972. Tullock later edited *Further Explorations in the Theory of Anarchy* (same publisher, 1974).

Veysey, Laurence. *The Communal Experience: Anarchist and Mystical Counter-Cultures in America*. New York: Harper and Row, 1973.

Vizetelly, Ernest. *Anarchists, Their Faith and Their Record: Including Sidelights on the Royal and Other Personages Who Have Been Assassinated*. New York: John Lane, 1911 (Kraus, 1972). Primarily interesting for its stereotypes.

Voline (V. M. Eichenbaum). *The Unknown Revolution*. (1 vol. in 2 sections). New York: Free Life Editions, 1975. Written during 1939–45, this is a Russian anarchist's account of the Bolshevik revolution.

Walter, Nicolas. "Anarchism." *Listener* (London) 79 (1968): 232–34.

Ward, Colin. *Anarchy in Action*. New York: Harper and Row, 1974.

Weisbord, Albert. "American Liberal-Anarchism," and "American Revolutionary Industrial Unionism." In *The Conquest of Power* pp. 1:225–36, 312–33. 2 vols. New York: Covici, Friede, 1937.

Weiss, Thomas G. "The Tradition of Philosophical Anarchism and Future Directions in World Policy." *Journal of Peace Research* (Norway) 12, 1 (1975): 1–17.

Widmer, K. "Anarchism in Revival." *Nation* 21 (16 November 1970): 501–3.

Wolff, Robert Paul. *In Defense of Anarchism*. New York: Harper, 1970. See also Jeffrey Reiman's response, *In Defense of Political Philosophy* (New York: Harper and Row, 1972). Wolff's ideas were vigorously debated in many articles, of which the following are only a selection. David Sobers, "Wolff's Logical Anarchism," *Ethics* 82 (January 1972): 173–76; Donald Stewart, "A Pseudo-Anarchist Belatedly Replies to R. P. Wolff," *Journal of Critical Analysis* 4 (July 1972): 51–61; Harry G. Frankfurt, "The Anarchism of Robert Paul Wolff," *Political Theory* 1 (November 1973): 405–14; Michael Pritchard, "Wolff's Anarchism," *Journal of Value Inquiry* 7 (winter 1973): 296–302 (preceded by M. B. E. Smith's "Wolff's Argument for Anarchism," pp. 290–295, and both followed by Wolff's reply, on pp. 303–6); and Rex Martin, "Wolff's Defense of Philosophical Anarchism," *Philosophical Quarterly* 24 (April 1974): 140–49.

Woodcock, George. *Anarchism*. Cleveland: Meridian Books, 1962.

――――. "Anarchism: The Rejection of Politics." In *Power and Civilization*, ed. D. Cooperman and E. V. Walter, pp. 491–98. New York: Crowell, 1962 (a revised selection from Woodstock's *Anarchy or Chaos* [London: Freedom Press, 1944]).

――――. "Anarchism Revisited." *Commentary* 46 (August 1968): 54–60.

――――., ed. *The Anarchist Reader*. Atlantic Highlands, N.J.: Humanities Press, 1977.

Wreszin, Michael. "Albert Jay Nock and the Anarchist Elitist Tradition in America." *American Quarterly* 21 (summer 1969): 165–89. His argument is elaborated in *The Superfluous Anarchist: Albert Jay Nock* (Providence: Brown University, 1972). While claiming that there is an "anarchist elitist tradition," Wreszin fails in his article to quote from such major anarchist theoreticians as Godwin, Proudhon, Bakunin, or Goodman. Besides this deficiency of documentation, he does not properly emphasize that anarchism is "antidemocratic" mainly in its rejection of the "sovereignty of the people" (i.e., the majority or the most powerful minority) for the "sovereignty of the individual." In this sense, it could more justifiably be called radically democratic.

Yarmolinsky, A. *Road to Revolution: A Century of Russian Radicalism*. London: Cassell, 1957.

Yaroslavsky, E. *History of Anarchism in Russia*. New York: International, 1937. Supports the Communist thesis that anarchism cannot overthrow capitalism and build socialism.

Zenker, Ernest V. *Anarchism: A Criticism and History of the Anarchist Theory*. New York: G. P. Putnam's, 1897.

Zuccoli, Ettore. *L'Anarchia*. Turin: Fratelli Bocca Editori, 1906.

IV. THE ANARCHIST HERITAGE

A. THEORISTS AND ACTIVISTS

1. *Stephen Pearl Andrews*

a. *Primary (all by Andrews)*

"Cost, the Scientific Limit of Price." *Merchant's Magazine* 24 (March 1851): 332–39.

"Great American Crisis." *Continental Monthly* 4 (December 1863): 658–70; 5 (1884): 87–99; 300–317.

Love, Marriage and Divorce, and the Sovereignty of the Individual: A Discussion by Henry James, Horace Greeley and Stephen Pearl Andrews. Boston: B. R. Tucker, 1889 (1853). The 1889 edition contains further comments by Andrews and James.

Science of Society. No. 1, "The True Constitution of Government in the Sovereignty of the Individual as the Final Development of Protestantism, Democracy and Socialism." No. 2, "Cost the Limit of Price—A Scientific Measure of Honesty in Trade as One of the Fundamental Principles in the Solution of the Social Problem." New York: Kraus Reprint, 1971 (1852, 1854).

b. *Secondary*

Adams, Grace, and Hutter, Edward. "The Intellectuals Look at Marriage." In *The Mad Forties*. New York: Harper, 1942.

"Andrews, Stephen Pearl." *New Encyclopedia of Social Reform*, edited by William D. P. Bliss, p. 51–52. New York: Funk and Wagnalls, 1910.

Baldwin, Roger. "Stephen Pearl Andrews." *Encyclopedia of the Social Sciences*, edited by Edwin R. A. Seligman and Alvin Johnson, 1:59. New York: Macmillan, 1937.

Bernard, Luther and Bernard, Jessie. *The Origins of American Sociology*. New York: Crowell, 1943. Refers to Modern Times, Andrews, and Warren (pp. 161–76, 313–86).

Dorfman, Joseph. "The Philosophical Anarchists: Josiah Warren, Stephen Pearl Andrews." In *The Economic Mind in America*, 2:671–78. New York: Viking, 1946. Also, "Philosophical Anarchism," ibid., 3:35–42.

Hall, B. "The Economic Theory of Stephen Pearl Andrews: Neglected Utopian Writer." *South African Journal of Economics*, March 1975, pp. 45–55.

Sachs, Emanie L. *"The Terrible Siren": Victoria C. Woodhull, 1838-1927*. New York: Harper's 1928. This is still the best biography, being certainly of higher quality than two later works that are more "colorful" and "spicy" than thoughtful: *Mrs. Satan*, by Johanna Johnston (New York: Putnam's, 1967) and *Vicky*, by M. M. Marberry (New York: Funk and Wagnalls, 1967).

Shively, Charles. "Option for Freedom in Texas, 1840-1844." *Journal of Negro History* 50 (April 1965): 77–96.

Stern, Madeleine B. *The Pantarch: A Biography of Stephen Pearl Andrews*. Austin: University of Texas Press, 1968.

Trowbridge, John T. "A Reminiscence of the Pantarch." *Independent* 55 (26 February 1903): 497–501.

Wish, Harvey, "Stephen Pearl Andrews, American Pioneer Sociologist." *Social Forces* 19 (May 1941): 477–82.

(In addition to this, see especially the section on Josiah Warren)

2. Michael Bakunin

a. Primary

Bakunin, Michael. "Bakunin and Nechayev: An Unpublished Letter." Edited by M. Confino. *Encounter* 39 (July 1972): 81–91, 39 (August): 85–93.

————. *Bakunin on Anarchy*. Edited by Sam Dolgoff. New York: Knopf, 1972.

————. *Bakunin's Writings*. Edited by Guy Alfred. New York: Kraus Reprint, 1971 (1947).

————. *God and the State*. Preface by Carol Cafiero and Elisée Reclus. New York: Mother Earth Publishing Association, 1916? Translated and first published by B. R. Tucker, but reprinted without acknowledgment or permission. Also in Dover paperback (New York, 1970).

————. *Oeuvres*. 5th ed. Paris: Stock, 1907–13.

————. *The Political Philosophy of Bakunin: Scientific Anarchism*. Compiled and edited by G. P. Maximoff; preface by Bert Hoselitz; introduction by Rudolf Rocker; biographical sketch of Bakunin by Max Nettlau. Glencoe, Ill.: Free Press, 1953.

Kennard, Martin P. "Russian Anarchist Visits Boston" (date: 1861; text of an account written some twenty years after). Edited by Oscar Handlin, *New England Quarterly* 15 (March 1942): 104–9.

Thorp, Annie Longfellow. "Laughing Allegra Meets an Ogre" (sketch by Longfellow's daughter of Bakunin's visit to Boston). Edited by David Hecht. *New England Quarterly* 19 (June 1946): 243.

b. Secondary

Avrich, Paul. "Legacy of Bakunin." *Russian Review* 29 (April 1970): 129–42.

Berlin, Isaiah. *Karl Marx*. 2d ed. London: Oxford University Press, 1948.

Bloom, Solomon F. "The 'Withering Away' of the State." *Journal of the History of Ideas* 7 (January 1946): 113–21. Marx and Engles on the future of the state.

Carr, Edward Hallett. *Michael Bakunin*. London: Macmillan, 1937. Earlier studies were "Bakunin; or, the Slippery Path," in *Romantic Exiles* (New York: Frederick A. Stokes, 1933), and "Bakunin's Escape from Siberia," *Slavonic Review* 15 (January 1937): 377–88.

Cole, G. D. H. "Bakunin." In *A History of Socialist Thought: Marxism and Anarchism, 1850–1890*, 2:213–36. New York: Macmillan, 1964.

Halbrook, Stephen. *The Marx-Bakunin Controversy*. Ph.D. diss, Florida State University, 1972.

Hodges, Donald Clark. "Bakunin's Controversy with Marx: An Analysis of the Tensions within Modern Socialism." *American Journal of Economics* 19 (April 1960): 259–74.

Kaltenbrunner, Gerd-Klaus. "Das Lustprinzip Revolution: Michael Bakunin und der Anarchismum." *Wort und Wahrheit* 25 (1970): 248–65.

Lavrin, Janko. "Bakunin the Slav and the Rebel." *Russian Review* 25 (April 1966): 135–49.

Masters, Anthony. *Bakunin: The Father of Anarchism*. New York: Saturday Review Press, 1975.

"Michael Bakunin," *Canadian-American Slavic Studies* 10 (winter 1976).

Nettlau, Max. *Michael Bakunin*. 3 vols. in one. Milan: Feltrinelli, 1971.

Nomad, Max. "Michael Bakunin, 'Apostle of Pan-Destruction.'" In *Apostles of Revolution*, pp. 151–213. Rev. ed., New York: Collier's, 1961.

Prawdin, Michael. *The Unmentionable Nechaev*. London: Allen and Unwin, 1961.

Pryziur, Eugene. *The Doctrine of Anarchism of Michael A. Bakunin*. Chicago: Regnery, 1968 (1955).

Rezneck, Samuel. "Political and Social Theory of Michael Bakunin." *American Political Science Review* 21 (May 1927): 270–96.

Russell, Bertrand. "Bakunin and Anarchism." In *Proposed Roads to Freedom: Socialism, Anarchism and Syndicalism*, pp. 32–55. London: Allen and Unwin, 1918.

Venturi, Franco. "Bakunin," and "Bakunin and Lavrov." In *Roots of Revolution: A History of the Populist and Socialist Movements in Nineteenth Century Russia*, translated by Francis Haskelll; introduction by Isaiah Berlin, pp. 36–63, 429–69. London: Weidenfeld and Nicolson, 1960.

Voegelin, Eric. "Bakunin: The Anarchist." In *From Enlightenment to Revolution*, pp. 217–39. Durham, N.C.: Duke University Press, 1975.

————. "Bakunin's Confession." *Journal of Politics* 8 (February 1946). 24–43.

Wilson, Edmund. "Historical Actors: Bakunin." In *To the Finland Station*, pp. 260–87. New York: Harcourt, Brace, 1940.

————. "Marx, Engels and Bakunin." In *Readings for Opinion*, edited by Earle Davis and William Hummel, pp. 382–86. Englewood Cliffs, N.J.: Prentice-Hall, 1960.

Woodcock, George. "Bakunin: The Destructive Urge." *History Today* 11 (July 1961): 469–78.

3. Adin Ballou

a. Primary

Ballou, Adin. "Adin Ballou Charts a Course for Nonresistants" (a selection from his writings). In *Instead of Violence: Writings by the Great Advocates of Peace and Nonviolence throughout History*, edited by Arthur and Lila Weinberg, pp. 325–77. New York: Grossman, 1963.

————. "Adin Ballou Explains the Hopedale Community." In *The Era of Reform, 1830–1860*, edited by Henry Steele Commager, pp. 46–48. Princeton, N.J.: Van Nostrand, 1960.

————. *Autobiography of Adin Ballou, 1803–1890*. Edited by William S. Haywood, New York: Da Capo. 1969 (1896).

————. "Christian Doctrine of Non-Resistance" (correspondence with Tolstoi). Edited by Lewis Wilson, *Arena* 3 (December 1890): 1–12.

————. *Christian Non-Resistance*. New York: Da Capo. 1969 (1910 edition). Excerpt, "Christian Non-Resistance" (1846), in *The Faith of Our Fathers: An Anthology Expressing the Aspirations of the American Common Man, 1790–1860*, edited by Irving Mark and Eugene Schwab, pp. 242–43. New York: Knopf, 1952.

"Non-Resistance" (a review of *Christian Non-Resistance*, by Ballou). *Christian Examiner* 44 (January 1848): 86–113. The disowning of a Christian radical by respectable Christianity.

Tolstoi, Leo. "Letter from Tolstoy" (about Ballou). Edited by F. I. Carpenter. *New England Quarterly* 4 (October 1931): 777–82. Also relevant is Tolstoi's "Message to the American People," *North American Review* 172 (April 1901): 503. This has been reprinted in *Tolstoy's Writings on Civil Disobedience and Non-Violence* (New York: Bergman Publishers, 1967), p. 5.

b. Secondary

"Ballou, Adin." In *New Encyclopedia of Social Reform*, edited by William D. P. Bliss, p. 88. New York: Funk and Wagnalls, 1910 (article on Hopedale, p. 578).

Calverton, Victor F. "Hopedale: An Adventure in Religious Cooperation," In *Where Angles Dared to Tread*, pp. 225–35. Indianapolis: Bobbs-Merrill, 1941.

Cary, George L. "Adin Ballou and the Hopedale Community." *New World* 7 (December 1898): 670–83.

Eliot, Samuel A., ed. "Adin Ballou, 1803–1890." In *Heralds of a Liberal Faith*, 2:297–300. 4 vols. Boston: American Unitarian Association, 1910–52.

Holloway, Mark. "Excitements and Institutions." In *Heavens on Earth*, pp. 116–32. New York: Dover Press, 1966.

Noyes, John Humphrey. "Hopedale." In *History of American Socialisms*, pp. 119–32. New York: Hillary House, 1961.

Padelford, Philip S. "Adin Ballou and the Hopedale Community." Ph.D. diss., Yale, 1942.

Perry, Lewis. "Adin Ballou's Hopedale Community and the Theology of Antislavery." *Church History* 39 (September 1970): 372–89.

Reichert, William. "The Philosophical Anarchism of Adin Ballou." *Huntington Library Quarterly* 27 (August 1964): 357–74.

Rollins, Richard M. "Adin Ballou and the Perfectionist's Dilemma." *Journal of Church and State* 17 (autumn 1975): 459–76.

Thomas, John L. "Antislavery and Utopia." In *The Antislavery Vanguard*, edited by Martin Duberman, pp. 240–69. Princeton: Princeton University Press, 1965.

Tyler, Alice Felt. "The Hopedale Community." In *Freedom's Ferment: Phases of American Social History to 1860*, pp. 116–71. Minneapolis: University of Minnesota Press, 1944.

Wilson, Lewis G. "Hopedale and Its Founder." *New England Magazine*, n.s. 4 (April 1891): 197–212. Includes twelve photos and drawings.

4. Alexander Berkman

Berkman, Alexander. *A.B.C. of Anarchism*. 3d ed. London: Freedom Press, 1964. This contains parts 2 and 3 of *Now and After: The A.B.C. of Communist Anarchism* (New York: Vanguard, Jewish Anarchist, 1929). An excerpt from the 1929 edition is in Krimerman and Perry, pp. 336–45. See also *What Is Communist Anarchism?* (New York: Dover, 1972), taken from this larger work.

_____., ed. *Blast* (San Francisco). Vols. 1–2, 1916–17. New York: Greenwood Reprint, 1970.

_____. *The Bolshevik Myth (Diary 1920-1922)*. New York: Boni and Liveright, 1925. Also printed as *The Kronstadt Rebellion* (Berlin: for Der Syndikalist, 1922). Excerpts: Horowitz, p. 495–506; "Kronstadt Rebellion," in *The Verdict of Three Decades*, edited by Julien Steinberg, pp. 84–112 (New York: Duel, Sloan and Pearce, 1950).

_____. *Nowhere at Home: Letters from Exile of Emma Goldman and Alexander Berkman*. Edited by Richard and Anna Maria Drinnon. New York: Schocken, 1974.

_____. *Prison Memoirs of an Anarchist*. Introduction by Paul Goodman. New York: Schocken, 1970 (1912). Another edition by Frontier Press had an introduction by Kenneth Rexroth.

Obituaries. *Nation* 143 (11 July 1936): 31; *News Week*, 8 (11 July 1936): 23; *Time* 28 (13 July 1936): 12.

Portrait and article. *World's Work* 45 (April 1923): 601.

Ward, John William. "Violence, Anarchy, and Alexander Berkman." *New York Review of Books* 15 (5 November 1970): 25–30.

5. Dorothy Day

(See the major studies on the Catholic Worker Movement for pre-1970 commentaries.)

Betten, Neil. "The Great Depression and the Activities of the Catholic Worker Movement," *Labor History* 12 (spring 1971): 243–58.

The Catholic Worker, 1933–present. The Greenwood reprint edition has an introduction by Dwight Macdonald, also published as "Revisiting Dorothy Day." *New York Review of Books* 16 (28 January 1971): 12 ff.

Colaianni, James. *The Catholic Left*. Philadelphia: Chilton, 1968.

Coles, Robert, and Erikson, Jon. *A Spectacle unto the World: The Catholic Worker Movement*. New York: Viking, 1973.

Cort, J. C. "Dorothy Day at 75." *Commonweal* 97 (23 February 1973): 475–76; discussion, 98 (13 April 1973): 135–37.

"Curtis to Publish Old-Line Catholic Radical." *Publisher's Weekly* 202 (17 July 1972): 99.

Day, Dorothy. "House on Mott Street" (1938 reprint). *Commonweal* 98 (10 August 1973): 163–64.

_____. Interview with Colman McCarthy. *New Republic* 168 (24 February 1973): 303.

_____. *The Long Loneliness*. New York: Harper and Row, 1952. One of several autobiographical works.

_____. "Reminiscence at 75." *Commonweal* 98 (19 August 1973): 424–25.

Deedy, J. "Honoring the Deserving." *Commonweal* 97 (27 October 1972): 74.

"Dorothy Day." *Commonweal* 96 (31 March 1972): 76.

"Dorothy Day and the Catholic Worker Movement" (symposium, with editorial comment). *America* 127 (11 November 1972): 380–99.

Gray, Francine du Plessix. *Divine Disobedience: Profiles in Catholic Radicalism*. New York: Knopf, 1970.

Grumbach, D. "Father Church and the Motherhood of God." *Commonweal* 93 (11 December 1970): 268–69.

Hennacy, Ammon. *Autobiography of a Catholic Anarchist*. New York: Catholic Worker Books, 1954. A selection from the book *Two Agitators: Peter Maurin–Ammon Hennacy* is in Staughton Lynd's *Nonviolence in America*, pp. 191–215. Hennacy's philosophy is partially expressed in "The Only Good State...." *Liberation* 1 (May 1956): 11.

Lobue, W. "Public Theology and the Catholic Worker." *Cross Currents* 26 (fall 1976): 270–85.

McCarthy, A. "Confronting Dorothy Day." *Commonweal* 104 (13 May 1977): 297.

Mayer, Milton. "Dollar for Dorothy." *Progressive* 41 (November 1977): 40–41.

Miller, William D. "The Church and Dorothy Day." *Critic* 35 (fall 1976): 62–70.

_____. *A Harsh and Dreadful Love: Dorothy Day and the Catholic Worker Movement*. New York: Liveright, 1973. Some reviews: R. Leucke, *Christian Century* 90 (29 August 1973): 834–35; George Woodcock, *Nation* 216 (19 March 1973): 373–74.

Mounier, Emmanuel. *A Personalist Manifesto*. New York: Longmans, 1938.

Novitsky, A. "Peter Maurin's Green Revolution: The Radical Implications of Reactionary Social Catholicism." *Review of Politics* 37 (January 1975): 83–103.

Vishnewski, S. "Dorothy Day: A Sign of Contradiction." *Catholic World* 209 (August 1969): 203–6.

Woodward, K. L. "Dorothy's Way." *Newsweek* 88 (27 December 1976): 61.

6. *William Godwin*

a. *Primary*

Godwin, William. "An Account of the Seminary...at Epsom in Surrey." In *Four Early Pamphlets, 1783-1784*. Facsimile reproductions; introduction by Burton Pollin. Gainesville, Fla: Scholars' Facsimiles and Reprints, 1966.

_____. *Caleb Williams: or, Things as They Are*. Introduction by Walter Allen, ed. Herbert Van Thal. London: Cassell, 1966.

_____. *The Enquirer: Reflections on Education, Manners and Literature*. Dublin: J. Moore, 1797.

_____. *An Enquiry concerning Political Justice and Its Influence on Morals and Happiness*. Photographic facsimile of the 3d edition, correlated and edited, with variant readings of the 1st and 2d editions, with a critical introduction and notes by F. E. L. Priestly. Toronto: University of Toronto Press, 1946.

_____. *Thoughts on Man: His Nature, Productions and Discoveries*. London: E. Wilson, 1831.

Shelley, Percy Bysshe. *Prometheus Unbound: A Variorum Edition*. Edited by Lawrence John Zillman. Seattle: University of Washington Press, 1959. Read also his *Masque of Anarchy*.

b. Secondary

Beauchamp, Tom, and Witkouski, Ken. "A Critique of Pure Anarchism." *Canadian Journal of Philosophy* 2 (June 1973): 533–39.

Clark, John P. *The Philosophical Anarchism of William Godwin*. Princeton: Princeton University Press, 1977.

Crampton, David. "Shelley's Politcal Optimism." Ph.D. diss., University of Wisconsin, 1973.

Fleisher, David. *William Godwin: A Study in Liberalism*. London: Allen and Unwin, 1951.

Garrett, Roland W. "Anarchism or Political Democracy: The Case of William Godwin," *Social Theory and Practice* 1 (spring 1971): 111–20.

Kramnick, I. "On Anarchism and the Real World." *American Political Science Review* 66 (March 1972): 114–28; replies by T. Hone, T. M. Perlin, and others, ibid. 66 (December 1972): 1316–17; 67:193–94, 576–77; 69:162–70.

McCracken, D. "Godwin's Literary Theory: The Alliance between Fiction and Political Philosophy." *Philological Quarterly* 49 (January 1970): 113–33.

Munro, David Hector. *Godwin's Moral Philosophy: An Interpretation of William Godwin*. London: Oxford University Press, 1953.

Paul, Charles Kegan. *William Godwin: His Friends and Contemporaries*. 2 vols. London: Kings, 1876.

Pollin, Burton R. *Education and Enlightenment in the Works of William Godwin*. New York: Las Americas Publishing Company, 1962.

————. *Godwin Criticism: A Synoptic Bibliography*. Toronto: University of Toronto Press, 1967. The standard bibliographic reference on Godwin.

Preu, James. *The Dean and the Anarchist*. Tallahassee: Florida State University Press, 1959.

Ritter, Alan. "Godwin, Proudhon and the Anarchist Justification of Punishment." *Political Theory* 3 (February 1975): 69–87 (see also related correspondence).

Rodway, A. E., ed. *Godwin and the Age of Transition*. London: Harrap, 1952.

Rogers, A. K. "Godwin and Political Justice." *International Journal of Ethics* 22 (October 1911): 50–68.

Rosen, F. "Principle of Population as Political Theory: Godwin's *Of Population* and the Malthusian Controversy." *Journal of the History of Ideas* 31 (January 1970): 33–48.

Sedelow, Walter A., Jr. "New Interest in Godwin" (review essay), *American Journal of Economics* 29 (January 1970): 108–12.

Thomas, James Andrew. "The Philosophical Anarchism of William Godwin." Ph.D. diss., University of Southern California, 1964.

Todd, Francis M. *Politics and the Poet: A Study of Wordsworth*. London: Methuen, 1957.

Woodcock, George. *William Godwin: A Biographical Study*. Foreword by Herbert Read. London: Porcupine Press, 1946.

7. Emma Goldman

a. Primary (all by Goldman)

Anarchism and Other Essays. New York: Dover, 1970 (1911). Excerpts in Lynd, pp. 119–34, and Horowitz, pp. 266–83.

"Assassination of McKinley." *American Mercury* 24 (September 1931): 53–67.

"Free Speech and Unpopular Ideas" (a speech given at the 1917 Berkman-Goldman draft conspiracy trial). In *The Agitator in American Society*, edited by Charles W. Lomas, pp. 102–12. Englewood Cliffs, N.J.: Prentice-Hall, 1968.

"Johann Most." *American Mercury* 8 (June 1926): 158–66.
"Letters from Prison." In *"Little Review" Anthology*, edited by Margaret Anderson, pp. 62–63. New York: Hermitage House, 1953.
Living My Life. 2 vols. New York: Dover, 1970 (1934).
Mother Earth Bulletin (editor of; New York, 1906–18). New York: Greenwood Reprint, 1970.
My Disillusionment in Russia. New York: Apollo, 1970. (1923).
My Further Disillusionment in Russia. Garden City, N.Y.: Doubleday, 1924. The second volume of *My Disillusionment in Russia*, with the "further" added by the error of the publisher. Excerpt in Krimerman and Perry, pp. 98–115.
Nowhere at Home: Letters from Exile of Emma Goldman and Alexander Berkman. Edited by Richard and Anna Maria Drinnon. New York: Schocken, 1974.
Red Emma Speaks. Edited by Alix Shulman, New York: Random House, 1972.
"There Is No Communism in Russia." *American Mercury* 34 (April 1955): 393–401.
"The Traffic in Women and Other Essays in Feminism." Washington, N.J.: Times Change Press. All the essays in this superbly printed pamphlet are also included within *Anarchism and Other Essays*.
"Voyage of the Buford." *American Mercury* 23 (July 1931): 276–86.
"Was My Life Worth Living?" *Harper's* 170 (December 1934): 52–58.
"Woman without a Country." In *Free Vistas*, edited by Joseph Ishill, 1:121–35. 2 vols. (Berkeley Heights, N.J.: Oriole Press, 1933).

b. Secondary

"Berkman and Goldman." *Outlook* 123 (24, December 1919): 529–30.
Dell, Floyd, *Women as World Builders*. Chicago: Forbers, 1913.
Drinnon, Richard. *Rebel in Paradise: A Biography of Emma Goldman*. Chicago: University of Chicago Press, 1961.
"Emma Goldman." *Ramparts* 10 (February 1972): 10–12.
Goldberg, Harold J. "Goldman and Berkman View the Bolshevik Regime." *Slavonic and East European Review* 53 (April 1975): 272–76.
"Goldman, Emma." In *New Encyclopedia of Social Reform*, edited by Wiliam D. P. Bliss, p. 555. New York: Funk and Wagnalls, 1910.
Goldsmith, Margaret. *Seven Women against the World*. London: Methuen, 1935.
Hapgood, Hutchins. "Emma Goldman's Anarchism." *Bookman* 32 (February 1911): 639–40.
Harris, Frank. "Emma Goldman, the Famous Anarchist." In *Contemporary Portraits*, pp. 223–51. New York: Kennerly, 1915.
Kern, Robert. "Anarchist Principles and Spanish Reality: Emma Goldman as a Participant in the Civil War, 1936–39," *Journal of Contemporary History* 11 (July 1976); 237–59.
Lynn, Kenneth. "Living My Life." In *Views of America*, pp. 149–56. Westport, Conn.: Greenwood Press, 1973.
Madison, Charles A. "Emma Goldman: Anarchist Rebel." In *Critics and Crusaders*, pp. 214–37. 2d ed. rev. New York: Ungar, 1959.
Pachter, Henry. "Private Lives of Rebels." *Harper's* 251 (August 1975): 83–84.
Rich, Andrea, and Smith, Arthur. *Rhetoric of Revolution*. Durham, N.C.: Moore, 1972.
Shulman, Alix. *To the Barricades*. New York: Crowell, 1971.
"Tragedy of the Political Exiles." *Nation* 139 (10 October 1934): 401–2.

8. Peter Kropotkin

a. Primary (all by Kropotkin)

"Brain Work and Manual Work." *Nineteenth Century* 27 (March 1890): 456–75.

"Cause of So-Called Industrial Idleness." *Craftsman* 13 (March 1908): 669–74.
Conquest of Bread. New York: Blom, 1968.
The Essential Kropotkin. Edited by E. Capouya and K. Tompkins. New York: Liveright, 1975.
"Ethical Need of the Present Day." *Nineteenth Century* 56 (August 1904): 207–26.
Ethics. New York: Blom, 1968.
Fields, Factories and Workshops. New, rev. and enl. 2d ed. New York: Blom, 1968.
Kropotkin's Revolutionary Pamphlets. Edited by Roger N. Baldwin. New York: Blom, 1968.
Memoirs of a Revolutionist. 2 vols. Introduction by Paul Goodman. New York: Horizons Press, 1968. Goodman's introduction is reprinted as "Kropotkin at This Moment," in *Dissent* (November–December 1968): 519–22. The *Memoirs* were first published in vols. 82–84 (1898–99) of the *Atlantic Monthly*. There has also been an edition from Dover Press (1970).
"Morality of Nature." *Nineteenth Century* 57 (March 1905): 407–26.
Mutual Aid, a Factor in Evolution. Foreword by Ashley Montagu, and "The Struggle for Existence," by Thomas H. Huxley. Boston: Extending Horizons Books, 1955.
"Russia's Point of View on the War." *Review of Reviews* 51 (February 1915): 230–31.
Selected Readings on Anarchism and Revolution. Edited by Martin Miller. Cambridge, Mass.: MIT Press, 1970.
"An Unpublished Essay on Leo Tolstoy." Edited by D. Novak. *Canadian Slavonic Papers*, 3 (1958): 7–26.
"What the Attitude of a Radical Should Be toward the War." *Current History Magazine, New York Times* 5 (October 1916): 109–11.

b. Secondary

Avrich, Paul. *The Anarchists in the Russian Revolution*. Ithaca: Cornell University Press, 1973.
Bogardus, Emory S. "Kropotkin and Co-operative Social Thought." In *Development of Social Thought*, pp. 381–91. 4th ed. New York: Longmans, Green, 1960.
Cole, G. D. H. "Anarchists and Anarchist-Communists—Kropotkin." In *A History of Socialist Thought: Marxism and Anarchism, 1850–1890*, 2:315–60. New York: St. Martin's Press, 1965.
D'Agostino, Anthony W. "Marxism and the Russian Anarchists." Ph.D. diss., University of California, Los Angeles, 1971.
Hulse, James W. *Revolutionists in London: A Study of Five Unorthodox Socialists*. New York: Oxford University Press, 1970.
Punzo, V. C. "The Modern State and the Search for Community: The Anarchist Critique of Peter Kropotkin." *International Philosophical Quarterly* 16 (March 1976): 3–32.
Reyler, Andre. "Peter Kropotkin and His Vision of Anarchist Aesthetics." *Diogenes* 78 (summer 1972): 52–63.
Rogers, James A. "Prince Peter Kropotkin, Scientist and Anarchist: A Biographical Study of Science and Politics in Russian History." Ph.D. diss., Harvard University, 1957.
Shub, David. "Kropotkin and Lenin." *Russian Review* 12 (October 1953): 227–34.
Woodcock, George, and Avakumović, Ivan. *The Anarchist Prince: A Biographical Study of Peter Kropotkin*. London and New York: T. V. Boardman, 1950 (also in Kraus Reprints).

9. Johann Most

Goldman, Emma. "Johann Most." *American Mercury* 8 (June 1926): 158–66.

Lore, Ludwig. "Most, Johann." In *Encyclopedia of the Social Sciences*, edited by Edwin R. A. Seligman and Alvin Johnson, p. 53. New York: Macmillan, 1937.

Most, John. "The Beast of Property." In *The Agitator in American Society*, edited by Charles W. Lomas, pp. 30–41. Englewood Cliffs, N.J.: Prentice-Hall, 1968. Examples of Most's pamphlets are *Down with the Anarchists!* (New York, 1901) and *The God Pest* (New York: n.d.).

Nomad, Max. "Johann Most, Terrorist of the World." In *Apostles of Revolution*, pp. 257–99. New York: Collier, 1961.

Obituary. *Reader* 7 (May 1906): 664–65. A hostile summary.

Rocker, Rudolf. *Johann Most, das Leben eines Rebellen.* Glashütten im Taunus: Detlov Auvermann, 1973 (1924).

10. Pierre Joseph Proudhon

a. Primary

Engels, Friedrich. "How Proudhon Solves the Housing Question." In *The Housing Question*, pp. 19–42. New York: International Publishers, 1935. A more complete collection of Marxist criticism is available as *Selected Writings of Marx, Engels, Lenin on Anarchism and Anarcho-Syndicalism*. New York: International, 1972.

Marx, Karl. *The Poverty of Philosophy*. New York: International, 1963.

Proudhon, Pierre Joseph. *Carnets*. 3 vols. Paris: Rivière, 1960–68.

———. *Correspondance de P.-J. Proudhon*. 14 vols. Paris: Librairie Internationale, 1875.

———. *General Idea of the Revolution in the Nineteenth Century*. Translated by John Beverly Robinson. New York: Haskell House, 1970 (1923).

———, *Oeuvres completes de P.-J. Proudhon*. Edited by D. Bouglé and H. Moysset. 19 vols. Paris: M. Rivière, 1923–59.

———. *Selected Writings of P. J. Proudhon*. Edited by Stewart Edwards. New York: Doubleday, 1969.

———. *System of Economical Contradictions; or, The Philosophy of Misery*. Translated by B. R. Tucker. Boston: Tucker, 1888.

———. *What Is Property? An Inquiry into the Principle of Right and of Government*. Translated by B. R. Tucker. New York: Humboldt, 189? A 1968 edition was also printed by Fertig Publishers, New York.

b. Secondary, Books

De Lubac, Henri. *The Un-Marxian Socialist: A Study of Proudhon*. New York: Sheed and Ward, 1948.

Dolleans, Edouard. *Proudhon*. Paris, 1948.

Gurvitch, Georges. *Proudhon: Sa vie, son oeuvre, avec un exposé de sa philosophie*. Paris: Presses Universitaires de France, 1965.

Guy-Grand, Georges. *La pensée de Proudhon*. Paris: Bordas, 1947.

Hall, Margaret. *The Sociology of Pierre Joseph Proudhon*. New York: Philosophical Library, 1971.

Hoffman, Robert. *Revolutionary Justice: The Social and Political Theory of P.-J. Proudhon*. Urbana: University of Illionois Press, 1972.

Jackson, John Hampden. *Marx, Proudhon and European Socialism*. New York: Macmillan, 1958?

Lu, Shi Yung. *The Political Theories of P. J. Proudhon*. New York: M. R. Gray, 1922.

Ritter, Alan. *The Political Thought of Pierre-Joseph Proudhon*. Princeton: Princeton University Press, 1969.

Woodcock, George. *Pierre-Joseph Proudhon: A Biography*. New York: Schocken, 1972 (1956).

c. Secondary, Articles

Barth, Hans. "The Idea of Sanction: Jeremy Bentham and Pierre-Joseph Proudhon." In *The Idea of Order*, pp. 144–59. Dordrecht, Holland: Reidel Publishing Company, 1960.

Bowle, John. "Proudhon's Attack on the State." In *Politics and Opinions in the Nineteenth Century*, pp. 152–67. New York: Oxford University Press, 1954.

Carr, Edward Hallett. "Proudhon: Robinson Crusoe of Socialism." In *Studies in Revolution*, pp. 38–55. London: Macmillan, 1954.

Cole, G. D. H. "Proudhon." In *A History of Socialist Thought: The Forerunners, 1789–1850*, pp. 201–18. New York: Macmillan, 1964.

Dillard, Dudley. "Keynes and Proudhon." *Journal of Economic History* 2 (May 1942): 63–76.

Douglas, Dorothy. "P. J. Proudhon: A Prophet of 1848." *American Journal of Sociology*, 34 (March 1929): 781–803; ibid. 35 (July 1929): 35–59.

Downs, Robert B. "Attack on the State." In *Molders of the Modern Mind*, pp. 241–44. New York: Barnes and Noble, 1961.

Faguet, Emile. "Proudhon." In *Politicians and Moralists of the Nineteenth Century*, pp. 111–64. London: E. Benn, 1928.

George, William H. "Proudhon and Economic Federalism." *Journal of Political Economy* 30 (August 1922): 531–42.

Harbold, William H. "Justice in the Thought of Pierre-Joseph Proudhon." *Western Political Quarterly* 22 (December 1969): 723–41.

————. "Progressive Humanity: The Philosophy of P. J. Proudhon." *Review of Politics* 31 (January 1969): 28–47.

Hoffman, R. "Marx and Proudhon: A Reappraisal of Their Relationship." *Historian* 29 (May 1967): 409–30.

King, Preston. "Federalism: Pierre-Joseph Proudhon." In *Fear of Power: An Analysis of Anti-Statism in Three French Writers*, pp. 43–67. London: Frank Cass, 1967.

Lewis, Wyndam. "'The Woman,' Proudhon's Only Revolutionary Discovery," and "Proudhon and Rousseau." In *The Art of Being Ruled*, p. 196–98; 330–75. London: Chatto and Windus, 1949.

Noland, Aaron. "Pierre-Joseph Proudhon: Socialist as Social Scientist." *American Journal of Economics* 26 (July 1967): 313–23.

————. "Proudhon and Rousseau." *Journal of the History of Ideas* 28 (January 1967): 35–54.

————. "Proudhon's Sociology of War." *American Journal of Economics* 29 (July 1970): 289–304.

Ritter, Alan. "Proudhon and the Problem of Community." *Review of Politics* 29 (October 1967): 457–77.

Schapiro, Jacob S. "Pierre Joseph Proudhon: Harbinger of Fascism." *American Historical Review* 50 (July 1945): 714–37. For a thorough criticism of this controversial article, see Nicola Chiaromonte, "P. J. Proudhon, an Uncomfortable Thinker," *Politics* 3 (January 1946): 27–29.

Soltau, Roger. "A Socialist Individualist: Proudhon." In *French Political Thought in the Nineteenth Century*, pp. 268–91. New Haven: Yale University Press, 1931.

Tsanoff, Radoslav. "French Positivism in Morals." In *Moral Ideas of Our Civilization*, pp. 472–85. New York: Dutton, 1942.

Watkins, Frederick M. "Proudhon and the Theory of Modern Liberalism." *Canadian Journal of Economics and Political Science* 3 (August 1947): 429–35.

Woodcock, George. "Solitary Revolutionary." *Encounter* 33 (September 1969): 45–55.

11. Lysander Spooner

a. Primary (all, except for the first item, by Spooner)

(Death of Spooner, editor's comment on) *New England Magazine* 4 (June–July 1887):83.

Letter to Grover Cleveland on His False Inaugural Address: The Unsurpations and Crimes of Lawmakers and the Consequent Poverty, Ignorance, and Servitude of the People. Boston: B. R. Tucker, 1886. Serialized in *Liberty*, vols. 3 and 4.

Letter to Thomas F. Bayard Challenging His Right and That of All the Other So-Called Senators and Representatives in Congress.... Reprinted in *Rampart Journal of Individualist Thought* 1 (spring 1965): 16–24.

"Limitations Imposed on the Majority." In *Voices in Dissent: An Anthology of Individualist Thought in America.* New York: Citadel Press, 1964. Originally from Spooner's *Trial by Jury*.

Natural Law; or, The Science of Justice. A Treatise on Natural Law, Natural Justice, Natural Liberty and Natural Society—Showing That All Legislation Whatever Is an Absurdity, a Usurpation, and a Crime. Part 1 (remaining portions never completed). Boston: B. R. Tucker, 1882.

No Treason. No. I, "The Suppression of the Rebellion Finally Disposes of the Pretense That the United States Government Rests on Consent." No. II, "The Constitution of No Authority." Boston: Lysander Spooner, n.d. No. VI reprinted, with introduction by James J. Martin, in *Rampart Journal of Individualist Thought* 1 (fall 1965): 38–90. Excerpt in Krimerman and Perry, pp. 242–50. His *Collected Works* were also published by M & S Press (Weston, Mass., 1971), along with an anthology from Arno Press, entitled *Let's Abolish Government* (1972).

b. Secondary

Alexander, A. John. "The Ideas of Lysander Spooner." *New England Quarterly* 23 (June 1950): 200–217.

Wise, David. "Father of the 3¢ Stamp." *Coronet* 42 (August 1957): 131. For another popularized view, see Ernest A. Kehr, Henry Goodkind, and Elliot Perry, "Look before You Lick," *Readers' Digest* 50 (June 1947): 125–27.

Yarros, Victor S. "Palladium of Liberty: Trial by Jury." *Arena* (April 1895): 209–17.

12. Max Stirner (Johann Kaspar Schmidt)

Adler, Max. "Stirner, Max." In *Encyclopedia of the Social Sciences*, edited by E. R. A. Seligman, 14: 393–94. New York: Macmillan, 1930.

Arvon Henri. *Aux sources de L'existentialisme: Max Stirner.* Paris: Presses Universitaries de France, 1954.

Basch, Victor. *L'individualisme anarchiste, Max Stirner.* Paris: F. Alcan, 1904.

Carlson, Andrew. "Anarchism in Germany; The Early Movement." Ph.D. diss., Michigan State University, 1970.

Carroll, John. *Break-out from the Crystal Palace: The Anarcho-Psychological Critique: Stirner, Nietzsche, Dostoevsky.* Boston: Routledge and Kegan Paul, 1974.

De Casseres, Benjamin. "Max Stirner: War-Lord of the Ego." In *Forty Immortals*, pp. 272–82. New York: J. Lawrien, 1926.

Eltzbacher, Paul. "Max Stirner." In *Anarchism*, translated by Steven Byington, edited by James J. Martin, pp. 61–76. New York: Libertarian Book Club, 1960.

Emge, Carol August. *Max Stirner.* Mainz: Verlag der Akademie der Literatur; in Kommission bei F. Steiner, Wiesbaden, 1964.

Fleischmann, E. "The Role of the Individual in Pre-Revolutionary Society: Stirner, Marx and Hegel." In *Hegel's Political Philosophy*, edited by Z. A. Pelcynski, pp. 220–29. Cambridge; Cambridge University Press, 1971.

Helms, Hans. *Die Ideologie der anoymen Gesellschaft*. Koeln: Verlag du Mont Schamberg, 1966.

Hook, Sidney. "Marx against der Einzige." In *From Hegel to Marx*. Ann Arbor: University of Michigan Press, 1962. Excerpt in Krimerman and Perry, pp. 537–42. For Marx's opinion of Stirner's "ego," see part 2 of the *German Ideology*, by Marx and Engels.

Huneker, James. "Max Stirner." In *Egoists: A Book of Supermen*, pp. 350–72. New York: Scribner's, 1921.

Kuczynski, Jurgen. "Stirner, Max." In *International Encyclopedia of the Social Sciences*, edited by David Sills, 15:271–73. New York: Crowell, 1968.

Lachmann, Benedict. *Protagoras, Nietzsche, Stirner*. Berlin: L. Simion, 1914.

Mackay, John Henry. *Max Stirner, sein Leben und sein Werke*. 2d ed. rev. Tretow, 1910.

Masaryk, Thomas G. "Individualism." In *Ideals of Humanity*, translated by Marie J. Kohn-Holocek; revised by H. E. Kennedy, pp. 35–51. London: Allen and Unwin, 1938.

"Max Stirner, the Predecessor of Nietsche." *Monist* 21 (July 1911): 84–88.

"Max Stirner's Anarchist Gospel." *Current Literature* 42 (May 1907): 535–38.

Paterson, R. W. K. *The Nihilistic Egoist: Max Stirner*. London: University of Hull Press, 1971.

Read, Herbert. "Max Stirner." In *The Tenth Muse*, pp. 74–82. New York: Horizon Press, 1957.

Ruest, Anselm. *Max Stirner*. Berlin: H. Seemann, 1906.

Schultheiss, Hermann. *Stirner*. Ratibor: Gedruckt bei F. Lindner, 1906.

Stepelvitch, Lawrence. "Revival of Max Stirner." *Journal of the History of Ideas* 35 (April–June 1974): 323–28.

Stirner, Max. *The Ego and His Own*. Translated by Steven Byington. New York: Libertarian Book Club, 1963 (1st American ed. 1906). Excerpts in Krimerman and Perry, pp. 165–84, 260–69; and Horowitz, pp. 292–311. The work was also available in Kraus Reprint (1971) and an abridged version by John Carroll, *Max Stirner: The Ego and His Own* (New York: Harper, 1971).

————. "The False Principle of Our Education; or, Humanism and Realism." Translated by Robert Beebe; edited and with an introduction by James J. Martin. Colorado Springs: Ralph Myles, 1967.

————. *Geschichte der Reaction*. 2 vols. New York: Burt Franklin, 1967 (1852).

Thomas, Paul. "Karl Marx and Max Stirner." *Political Theory* 3 (May 1975): 159–79.

Woodcock, George. "Stirner, Max." In *The Encyclopedia of Philosophy*, edited by Paul Edwards, 8:17–18. New York: Macmillan, 1967.

Zuccoli, Ettore. *I Gruppi Anarchici degli Stati Uniti e L'Operá di Max Stirner*. Modena, 1901.

13. Benjamin R. Tucker

a. Primary

"Benjamin R. Tucker—in Appreciation" (comments by George Bernard Shaw, H. L. Mencken and others). In *Free Vistas*, edited by Joseph Ishill, pp. 261–308. Berkeley Heights, N.J.; Oriole Press, 1937.

Byington, Steven T. "Benjamin Ricketson Tucker." *Man!* 7 (August 1939): 517–18.

Cleyre, Voltarine de. *The Selected Works of Voltarine de Cleyre*. Edited by Alexander Berkman. New York: Mother Earth Publishing Association, 1914.

Eltzbacher, Paul. "Benjamin R. Tucker." In *Anarchism*, translated by Steven Byington, edited by James J. Martin. New York: Libertarian Book Club, 1960 (1st American ed., 1906).

Ghio, Paul. "Les anarchistes intellectuels (Benjamin R. Tucker)." In *L'anarchisme aux Etats-*

Unis, pp. 79–132. Paris: A. Colin, 1903. See also his "Un anarchiste americain,"*Journal des Economistes*, ser. 5, 55 (July–September 1903): 335–50 (the authenticity of some of Ghio's research can be questioned).

"Henry George, Traitor" (reference to Tucker article). *New York Times*, 25 October 1897, p. 3.

Ishill, Joseph, ed. *Benjamin R. Tucker: A Bibliography*. Berkeley Heights, N.J.: Oriole Press, 1936.

Kelly, Florence Finch. *Flowing Stream*. New York: E. P. Dutton, 1939.

Nettlau, Max. *Der Vorfrühling der Anarchie, Ihre historische Entwicklung vor den Anfangen bis zum jahre 1864*. Berlin, 1925. Considers the influence of Warren, Tucker, and Individualist Anarchism in Europe, pp. 125–32.

Osgood, Herbert L. "Scientific Anarchism." *Political Science Quarterly* 4 (March 1889): 1–36. Also included in *Socialism and Anarchism*, published by Ginn and Company (Boston), 1889.

Raffalovich, Sophie. "Les anarchistes de Boston." *Journal des Economistes*, ser. 4, 4 (March 1888): 375–88. Vilfredo Pareto read this article and was prompted to write six long letters especially for Tucker's paper, *Liberty*. Note 4 (1 January 1887):4; 6 (29 September 1888): 6–7; 6 (10 November 1888):5; 6 (5 January 1889):7–8; 6 (5 October 1889):6–7; 7 (15 November 1890):2; 7 (2 January 1891):3; 8 (20 August 1892):2.

Schumm, George. "Benj. R. Tucker—A Brief Sketch of His Life and Work." *Freethinkers' Magazine* 11 (July 1893): 436–40.

Seymour, Henry. "The Genesis of Anarchism in England (A Few Recollections on My Early Life in the Movement)." In *Free Vistas*, edited by Joseph Ishill, pp. 119–29. Berkeley Heights, N.J.: Oriole Press, 1937.

Shaw, George Bernard. "The Impossibilities of Anarchism." Fabian Tract no. 45. London: Fabian Society, 1893.

"Socialists as Incendiaries: Boston *Liberty's* Charges." *New York Times*, 1 April 1886, p. 2.

Traubel, Horace, ed. *With Walt Whitman in Camden*. 5 vols. New York, etc., 1914–64?

Tucker, Benjamin R. "Attitude of Anarchism toward Industrial Combinations." In *Chicago Conference on Trusts...1899*. Chicago: Civic Federation of Chicago, 1900, pp. 253–61.

———. "Beast of Communism." In *Violence and the Labor Movement*, by Robert Hunter, pp. 70–74. New York: Macmillan, 1914.

———. *Individual Liberty*. Edited and with introduction by Clarence Lee Swartz. New York: Haskell House, 1969 (1926). Primarily a condensation of Tucker's 1893 *Instead of a Book*, but with some selection from his post-1893 writings.

———. *Instead of a Book, by a Man Too Busy to Write One; A Fragmentary Exposition of Philosophical Anarchism*. New York: Haskell House, 1969 (1893). A collection of articles from *Liberty*. Selections appear in Staughton Lynd (pp. 111–18), Krimerman and Perry (pp. 251–59), and Horowitz (pp. 169–82).

———, ed. *Liberty; Not the Daughter but the Mother of Order*. Boston and New York, vol. 17, nos. 1–403; 1881–April 1908; biweekly or irregular. New York: Greenwood Reprint, 1970 (with an introduction by Herbert Gutman). Further reference to his publishing career can be found in my dissertation, "The American as Anarchist" (University of Iowa, 1972).

———. "May Not Pride Be Carried Too Far?" (letter to the editor). *Spectator* 114 (30 January 1915): 152–53. For Max Eastman's interpretation of this letter, see *Masses* 9 (June 1917): 28–29; ibid., 9 (September):9.

———. "Mr. Benjamin R. Tucker's Story." In *The Terrible Siren: Victoria Woodhull, 1838–1927*, by Emanie Louise Sachs, pp. 236–66. New York: Harper's, 1928.

———. "Quaker Anarchists" (letter to the editor). *Outlook* 49 (17 February 1894): 334 (with a reply by the editor).

———. "State Socialism and Anarchism: How Far They Agree, and Wherein They Differ" (first published in 1888), Krimerman and Perry, pp. 61–69.

———. "Walt Whitman and Comstock." New York *Herald*, Paris edition, 23 November 1930; reprinted in *Free Vistas*, edited by Joseph Ishill 2:109–15. Berkeley Heights, N.J.: Oriole Press, 1937.

———. "Why I Am an Anarchist." *Twentieth Century Magazine* 4 (29 May 1890): 5–6.

Williams, Michael. "Views and Reviews." *Commonweal* 30 (7 July 1939): 275.

Yarros, Victor S. "Anarchism: What It Is, and What It Is Not." *Arena* 7 (April 1893): 595–601.

———. "Individualist or Philosophical Anarchism." In *New Encyclopedia of Social Reform*, edited by William D. P. Bliss and Rudolph Binder, pp. 41–45. New York: Funk and Wagnalls, 1910.

———. "Philosophical Anarchism: Its Rise, Decline and Eclipse." *American Journal of Sociology* 41 (January 1936): 470–83. This should be used with great care, since many of his data are inaccurate, and his interpretations may be consciously or unconsciously motivated by a rancor toward Tucker, of whom he was once an intimate friend.

———. "Philosophical Anarchism, 1880–1910." *Journal of Social Philosophy* 6 (April 1941): 254–62.

b. Secondary

Coker, Francis. *Recent Political Thought*. New York: Appleton-Century, 1934, pp. 198–200.

DeLeon, David. "The American as Anarchist: A Socio-Historical Interpretation." Ph.D. diss., University of Iowa, 1972. Primarily, in this version, a study of Tucker.

Destler, Chester MacArthur, ed. Comment on "Shall the Red and the Black Unite?" In *American Radicalism, 1865–1901: Essays and Documents*. New London, Conn., 1946. First printed in the *Pacific Historial Review* 14 (December 1945): 434–51.

Ebner, David. "Benjamin R. Tucker: The Ideology of an Individualist Anarchist in America." Ph.D. diss., New York University, 1968.

"Gentle Anarchist of Ste. Devote." *Bulletin: Old Dartmouth Historical Society* (New Bedford, Mass.), winter 1961.

Ingils, Agnes, comp. "Benjamin R. Tucker: Data." Unpublished compilation in the Labadie Collection, University of Michigan. The final copy was corrected by Pearl Johnson, B. R. T.'s companion.

Johnston, Dale Allen. "The American Anarchist: An Analysis of the Individualist Anarchism of Benjamin R. Tucker." Ph.D. diss., University of New Mexico, 1973.

Levitas, Irving. "The Unterrified Jeffersonian: Benjamin R. Tucker." Ph.D. diss., New York University, 1974.

Madison, Charles A. "Benjamin R. Tucker: Individualist and Anarchist." *New England Quarterly* 16 (September 1943): 444–67. Also printed in his *Critics and Crusaders* (New York: Ungar, 1959).

Mann, Arthur. *Yankee Reformers in the Urban Age*. Cambridge: Belknap Press of Harvard, 1954. Many of his facts are taken from a flawed article by Victor S. Yarros in the *American Journal of Sociology*. Mann also failed to use the main monographs by Schuster and Martin.

Martin, James J. *Men against the State: The Expositors of Individualist Anarchism in America, 1827–1908*. Colorado Springs: Myles, 1970 (1953). See especially "Benjamin R. Tucker and the Age of *Liberty*, I" and "Benjamin R. Tucker and the Age of *Liberty*, II," pp. 202–73. The entire study is also available in its Michigan Ph.D. form through University Microfilms, Ann Arbor, Michigan.

———. "Tucker, Benjamin R." In *Dictionary of American Biography*, edited by Allen Johnson, Dumas Malone, and others, vol. 22, suppl. 2, pp. 669-71. 22 vols., plus supplements, New York: Scribner's 1928–1958.

"Playboy after Hours" (includes some trivial comments on native American anarchists). *Playboy* 15 (April 1968): 23.

Riley, Thomas A. "Anti-Statism in German Literature, as Exemplified by the Work of John Henry Mackay." *PMLA* 62 (September 1947): 828–43.

_____. "John Henry Mackay, Germany's Anarchist Poet." Ph.D. diss., Harvard University, 1946.

_____. "New England Anarchism in Germany." *New England Quarterly* 18 (March 1945): 25–38.

Rocker, Rudolf. *Pioneers of American Freedom: Origin of Liberal and Radical Thought in America*. Translated by Arthur Briggs. Los Angeles: Rocker Publications Committee, 1949.

Zuccoli, Ettore. "La Critica Individualistica: B. R. Tucker." In *L'Anarchia*, pp. 229–55. Torino: Fratelli Bocca Editori, 1906.

14. *Josiah Warren*

a. Primary

Bailie, William. *Josiah Warren: The First American Anarchist*. New York: Kraus Reprint, 1971 (1906).

Conway, Moncure D. *Autobiography*. 2 vols. Boston and New York, 1905, 1:264–68.

_____. "Modern Times, New York." *Fortnightly Review* 1 (July 1865): 421–34.

"Death of Josiah Warren." *Index* 5 (23 April 1874): 197.

Ellis, John B. "Modern Times." In *Free Love and Its Votaries; or American Socialism Unmasked*, pp. 381–402. New York: United States Publishing Company, 1870.

Greeley, Horace. *Hints toward Reforms, in Lectures, Addresses and Other Writings*. New York: Harper's, 1850.

_____. *Recollections of a Busy Life*. New York: Ford, 1868.

Holmes, George F. "The Theory of Political Individualism." *De Bow's Review* 22 (February 1857): 133–49.

"Josiah Warren." *Index* 5 (23 April 1874): 198–99.

Kent, Austin. " 'Labor Cost' the 'Limit of Price.' " *Index* 6 (24 June 1875): 297. Reply by E. D. Linton, ibid., p. 345.

Nichols, Thomas Low. *Forty Years of American Life, 1821-1961*. New York: Stackpole Sons, 1937 (1864). Comments on Modern Times, Warren, and Andrews, pp. 238–41.

Noyes, John Humphrey. "Connecting Links." In *History of American Socialisms*, pp. 93–101. New York: Hillary House, 1961.

Owen, Robert Dale. *Threading My Way: Twenty-Five Years of Autobiography*. London, 1874.

Pare, William. "Equitable Villages in America." *Journal of the Statistical Society of London* 19 (June 1856): 127–43.

"Trialville and Modern Times." *Chambers' Edinburgh Journal* 18 (18 December 1852): 395–97.

Warren, Josiah. "The Cost Principle." *Index* 4 (11 December 1873): 504–5.

_____. *Equitable Commerce: A New Development of Principles for the Harmonious Adjustment and Regulation of the Pecuniary, Intellectual and Moral Intercourse of Mankind, Proposed as Elements of a New Society*. New Harmony, Ind., 1846 (reprint by Burt Franklin, New York, 1965). Excerpts, "The Pattern of Life in an Individualist Anarchist Community," and "Equitable Education" in Krimerman and Perry, pp. 312–23, 445–48.

_____. "Josiah Warren's Last Letter." *Index* 5 (30 April 1874): 207–8.

_____. "Labor the Only Ground of Price." *Index* 5 (28 May 1874): 260–61.

_____. "Letter from Josiah Warren." In *A Documentary History of American Industrial Society*, edited by John R. Commons and others, 10:133–37. 10 vols. Cleveland: Arthur H. Clarke, 1910.

_____. *True Civilization: An Immediate Necessity and the Last Ground of Hope for Mankind*. New York: Burt Franklin, 1967 (1863). A selection from, and comment on this work is found in *Passport to Utopia*, edited by Arthur and Lila Weinberg, pp. 60–67 (Chicago: Quadrangle, 1968). An excerpt from a different book, *True Civilization: A Subject of Vital and Serious Interest to All People; but Most Immediately to Men and Women of Labor and Sorrow,* in Horowitz, pp. 321–30.

b. Secondary

Adams, Grace, and Hutter, Edward. "Promoting Utopia and a New Messiah," and "The Sovereigns Seek Harmony at Modern Times." In *The Mad Forties*, pp. 271–94. New York: Harper, 1942.

Arieli, Yehoshua. "Individualism Turns Anarchism—Josiah Warren." In *Individualism and Nationalism in American Ideology*, pp. 289–96. Cambridge: Harvard University Press, 1964.

Barclay, Harold. "Josiah Warren: The Incomplete Anarchist." *Anarchy* 8 (March 1968): 90–96.

Bernard, Luther, and Bernard, Jessie. "The Direct Influence of Comte: The Modern Times Experiment"; "The Warren-Andrews Phase of Social Science: Antecedents and Point of View"; "The Warren-Andrews Phase of Social Science: Content and Criticism." In *The Origins of American Sociology*, pp. 161–76, 313–38. New York: Crowell, 1943.

Calverton, V. F. "Modern Times: Anarchism in Practice." In *Where Angels Dared to Tread*, pp. 288–310. Indianapolis: Bobbs-Merrill, 1941.

Clement, Edward H. "Warren of the West." *New England Magazine*, n.s. 35 (October 1906): 185–89.

Douglas, Dorothy. "Warren, Josiah." In *Encyclopedia of the Social Sciences*, edited by E. R. A. Seligman and Alvin Johnson, 15: 365–66. New York: Macmillan, 1937.

Dorfman, Joseph. "The Philosophical Anarchists: Josiah Warren, Stephen Pearl Andrews." In *The Economic Mind in America* 2:671–78. New York: Viking, 1946. See also "Philosophical Anarchism," ibid. 3:35–42.

Dubin, Barbara. "A Critical Review of the Social and Educational Theories of Josiah Warren and His Individualist School of Anarchism." Ph.D. diss., University of Illinois at Urbana-Champaign, 1973.

Fellman, Michael. "The Substance and Boundaries of Utopian Communitarianism: Albert Brisbane and Josiah Warren." In *The Unbounded Frame: Freedom and Community in Nineteenth Century American Utopianism, pp. 3–19.* Westport, Conn.: Greenwood Press, 1973.

Hall, Bowman N. "The Economic Ideas of Josiah Warren, First American Anarchist." *History of Political Economy* 6:1 (1974): 95–108.

Hawkins, Richard Laurin. "Josiah Warren," and "The Village of Modern Times." In *Positivism in the United States, 1853–1861*, pp. 11–24. Cambridge: Harvard, 1938. Includes illustrations of Warren and Modern Times.

Lockwood, George B., and Prosser, Charles. *The New Harmony Movement*. New York: Appleton, 1907. Contains comments on Warren, an illustration of him and some of his labor notes, and a chapter about him by William Bailie, pp. 294–306.

Martin, James J. "American Prophets. I: Josiah Warren." *Liberation* 2 (December 1957): 10–14.

Rexroth, Kenneth. "Josiah Warren." In *Communalism*, pp. 235–40. New York: Seabury, 1974.

Richard, Jerry. "The Whole Man Minding the Store." *Nation* 219 (28 December 1974): 695–98.

Schneider, Robert E. *Positivism in the United States: The Apostleship of Henry Edger*. Rosario, Argentina, 1946. Has a facsimile of New York *World* article on the Modern Times community.

Seligman, Edwin R. A. "Economists," In *Cambridge History of American Literature*, 3:437. 4 vols. New York: Putnam's, 1921.

Stern, Madeleine B. "Stephen Pearl Andrews and Modern Times, Long Island." *Journal of Long Island History*, vol. 4 no. 4 (summer 1964). J. W. Gaskins made a favorable comment on another anarchist colony in "The Anarchists at Home, Washington," *Independent* 68 (28 April 1910): 914–22 (includes several photographs). For a closer study of this colony, see Stewart Holbrook's "Anarchists at Home," *American Scholar* 15 (October 1946): 425–38. Non-American examples of communities are given in Charles Gide's *Communist and Cooperative Colonies* (New York: Crowell, 1928), pp. 155–69, and W. H. G. Armytage, in *Heavens Below*, p. 305–15, 342–58 (Toronto: University of Toronto, 1961).

"Warren, Josiah." in *New Encyclopedia of Social Reform*, edited by William D. P. Bliss, p. 1275. New York: Funk and Wagnalls, 1910.

15. Two Recent Anarchists

(See also anthologies, especially *Reinventing Anarchy*.)

Paul Goodman was undoubtedly the most famous and prolific anarchist of our time; his writings are approached, in quantity at least, only by the late poet and critic Herbert Read. Almost all of Goodman's many books are still in print, and his essays and articles are usually readily available. Therefore, I will list only a few of his works. For the writings of Read, Alex Comfort, Tony Gibson, Colin Ward, and others, one might write Freedom Press in London. Note also the listings for Murray Bookchin (Anarcho-Communist) and Murray Rothbard (essentially Anarcho-Capitalist).

By Goodman: "Black Flag of Anarchism," *New York Times Magazine* 14 July 1968, pp. 10–11+; *Communitas: Means of Livelihood and Ways of Life*, 2d ed. rev., 1960; *Compulsory Mis-education* (1966); *Growing Up Absurd: Problems of Youth in the Organized System* (1960); "Getting into Power; The Ambiguities of Pacifist Politics," *Liberation* 7 (October 1962): 4–8 (in Horowitz, pp. 545–51); *Like a Conquered Province: The Moral Ambiguity of America* (1967); "Notes on Decentralization," in *The Radical Papers*, edited by Irving Howe (1966); *Utopian Essays and Practical Proposals* (1962)—and many other works.

About Goodman: William Hamilton, "Exile from Paradise: A Garland for Paul Goodman," *Christian Century* 84 (16 August 1967): 1046–48; Michael Harrington, "On Paul Goodman," *Atlantic* 216 (August 1965): 88–91; Nat Hentoff, "Village Anarchist," *Reporter* 29 (18 July 1963): 54–55; George Steiner, "On Paul Goodman," *Commentary* 36 (August 1963); 158–63; Colin Ward, "Communitas Revisited," *Liberation* 7 (June 1962): 11–16. For an anarchist's criticism of Goodman's anarchism, see George Molnar, "Meliorism," *Anarchy* 8 (March 1968): 76–83; reply by Ross Poole, ibid., pp. 83–87.

The reader is particularly directed to works on Goodman's influence in libertarian educational theory: Paul Beebee, "Toward an Anarchistic Conceptual Framework of Alternative Learning Experiences" (Ph.D. diss., University of Virginia, 1975); John Anthony Bucci, "Philosophical Anarchism and Education" (Ph.D. diss., Boston University School of Education, 1974); M. Green, "Paul Goodman and Anarchist Education," in *Social Forces and Schooling*, edited by N. K. Shimarhara and Adam Scrupski, pp. 313–16 (New York: McKay, 1975); Joyce Hamby, "The Gentle Anarchist: The Political and Social Thought of Paul Goodman" (Ph.D. diss., University of Missouri-Columbia, 1974); Lawrence Rogers, "Anarchism and Libertarian Education" (Ph.D. diss., University of Nebraska, 1975); William Vaughn, "Toward an Anarchist Theory of Education: A Systematic Examination of the Educational Thought of Paul Goodman" (Ph.D. diss., University of Kentucky, 1970); Stephen Weiner, "Educational Decisions in an Organized Anarchy" (Ph.D. diss., Stanford, 1973).

By Read: "Anarchism and Modern Society," in *The Anarchists*, edited by Irving Horowitz

(1964), pp. 344–54; *Anarchy and Order*; "Art and the Revolutionary Attitude," *Southern Review* 1 (1935): 239–52; "Intellectuals in Exile," *New Statesman* 17 (18 February 1939): 244–45; "Lost Leader; or, the Psychopathology of Reaction in the Arts," *Sewanee Reveiw* 63 (fall 1955): 51–66; *The Philosophy of Anarchism: Poetry and Anarchism* (1941); *The Politics of the Unpolitical* (1946); "The State and the Individual," *New Statesman* 21 (24 May 1941): 532; *To Hell with Culture* (1963).

About Read: Dennis Joseph Enright, "There Was a Time: Herbert Read's Autobiographies," in *Conspirators and Poets*, pp. 102–5 (London: Chatto and Windus, 1966); Bernard Bergonzi, "Retrospect I: Autobiography," in *Heroes Twilight*, pp. 46–70 (New York: Coward-McCann, 1965); C. H. Grattan, "Gentlemen, I Give You Herbert Read," *Harper's* 194 (June 1947): 535–42; R. McLaughlin, "English Poet-Critic-Philosopher," *Saturday Review* 30 (28 June 1948): 17; J. Simon, "Notes of a Noble Anarchist," *Saturday Review* 46 (17 August 1963): 18; Stephen Spender, "Dialogue with a Recognizer," in *The Struggle of the Modern*, pp. 177–85 (Berkeley: University of California, 1963).

B. SOME EVENTS IN AMERICA

1. Haymarket "Riot"

a. Primary

Accused and the Accusers: The Famous Speeches of the Eight Chicago Anarchists in Court. New York: Arno, 1969 (1886).

Altgeld, John (governor of Illinois). "Reasons for Pardoning Fielden, Neebe, and Schwab" (1896). Printed in *The Mind and Spirit of John Peter Altgeld*, edited by Henry M. Christman, pp. 63–104. Urbana, Ill.: University of Illinois, 1960.

Brown, John, Jr. "John Brown and the Haymarket Martyrs." Edited by Louis Ruchames. *Massachusetts Review* 5 (1964): 765–69.

Chicago Tribune. "The Anarchist Can Be Legally Punished," In *A Century of Tribune Editorials, 1857–1947*, pp. 61–63. Chicago: Chicago Tribune, 1947.

Drescher, Nuala McGann, ed. " 'To Play the Hypocrite': Terence V. Powderly on the Anarchists." *Labor History* 13 (winter 1972): 60–62.

Forner, Philip, ed. *Autobiographies of the Haymarket Martyrs.* New York: Humanities Press, 1969.

Gary, Joseph (presiding judge at the trial). "The Chicago Anarchists of 1886: The Crime, the Trial, and the Punishment." *Century Magazine* 23 (1892–93): 803–37.

Godkin, E. L. "The Execution of the Chicago Anarchists." *Nation* 45 (1887): 366.

Kebadian, John, ed. *The Haymarket Affair and the Trial of the Chicago Anarchists, 1886: Original Manuscripts, Letters, Articles and Printed Materials.* New York: Kraus Reprint, 1970 (1886).

Kogan, Bernard, ed. *The Chicago Haymarket Riot: Anarchy on Trial.* Boston, D. C. Heath, 1959.

Lum, Dyer D. *A Concise History of the Great Trial of the Chicago Anarchists in 1886.* New York: Arno, 1969 (1886).

Three of those captured
at Haymarket Square,
May 4, 1886.

SPECIMEN RIOTERS—I. From Photographs taken by the Police Department.

McLean, George N. *The Rise and Fall of Anarchy in America*. New York: Haskell, 1972 (1888).

Parsons, Albert R. ed. *The Alarm: An Ararchistic Monthly* (Chicago, 1884–89). New York: Greenwood Reprint, 1970.

———. *Anarchism: Its Philosophy and Specific Basis as Defined by Some of Its Apostles*. New York: Kraus Reprint, 1971 (1887).

———. "The Board of Trade: Legalized Theft." In *The Agitator in American Society*, edited by Charles Lomas, pp. 41–45. Englewood Cliffs, N.J.: Prentice-Hall, 1968.

Parsons, Lucy, ed. *Famous Speeches of the Eight Chicago Anarchists*. New York: Arno, 1969 (1910).

———. *Life of Albert R. Parsons*. Chicago: Lucy Parsons, 1889.

Powderly, Terence V. "To Play the Hyprocrite: Terence V. Powderly on the Anarchists." Edited by N. M. Drescher, *Labor History*, 13 (winter 1972): 60–62.

Schaack, Michael J. (Chicago police captain). *Anarchy and the Anarchists*. Chicago: F. J. Schulte, 1889.

Schwab, Michael, and Spies, August. "Speeches in Court, 1896." A selection in *Nonviolence in America*, edited by Staughton Lynd, pp. 109–11. Indianapolis: Bobbs-Merrill, 1966.

b. Secondary

Adamic, Louis. *Dynamite: The Story of Class Violence in America*. Rev. ed. New York: Chelsea House, 1970 (1931; rev. ed. 1934).

Bernard, Harry. *"Eagle Forgotten": The Life of John Peter Altgeld*. Indianapolis: Bobbs-Merrill, 1938.

Calmer, Alan. *Labor Agitator: The Story of Albert R. Parsons*. New York: International, 1937.

Carter, Everett. "The Haymarket Affair in Literature." *American Quarterly* 2:3 (1950): 270 ff.

Commons, John R., and others. "The Chicago Catastrophe." In *A History of Labor in the United States*, 2:386-94. 4 vols. New York: Macmillan, 1918.

David, Henry. *The History of the Haymarket Affair: A Study in the American Social-Revolutionary and Labor Movements*. 2d ed. New York: Russell and Russell, 1958.

Fraser, Russell. "John Peter Altgeld: Governor for the People." In *American Radicals*, edited by Harvey Goldberg, pp. 127–44. New York: Monthly Review, 1957.

Ginger, Ray. *Altgeld's America: The Lincoln Ideal versus Changing Realities*. New York: Funk and Wagnalls, 1958.

Harris, Frank. *The Bomb: A Novel*. Introduction by John Dos Passos. Chicago: University of Chicago Press, 1963.

Hillquit, Morris. "The Chicago Drama." In *History of Socialism in America*, pp. 221–29. New York: Funk and Wagnalls, 1910.

Hunter, Robert. *Violence and the Labor Movement*. New York: Arno, 1970 (1914).

Johnson, Michael R. "Albert R. Parsons: An American Architect of Syndicalism." *Midwest Quarterly* 9 (January 1968): 195–206.

Kirk, Clara, and Kirk, Rudolf. "William Dean Howells, George William Curtis, and the 'Haymarket Affair.' " *American Literature* 40 (1969): 487–98.

Naden, Corinne. *Haymarket Affair, Chicago, 1886*. New York: Watts, 1968.

Synder, Wendy. *Haymarket*. Cambridge, Mass.: MIT Press, 1971.

Werstein, Irving. *Strangled Voices: The Story of the Haymarket Affair*. New York: Macmillan, 1970.

Wish, Harvey. "Governor Altgeld Pardons Anarchists." *Illinois State Historical Society Journal* 31 (December 1939): 424–48.

Yellen, Samuel. "American Propagandists of the Deed." In *American Labor Struggles*. New York: Harcourt, Brace, 1936; reprinted in Horowitz, pp. 418–39.

2. Homestead Strike

a. Primary

Black, Chauncey. "Lesson of Homestead: A Remedy for Labor Troubles." *Forum* 14 (September 1892): 14–25.

Brooks, G. "Typical American Employer: Mr. Andrew Carnegie." *Blackwood's* 152 (October 1892): 556–73.

Burgoyne, Arthur. *Homestead*. New York: Kelley, 1975 (1893).

Chamberlain, W. J. "Labor Troubles at Homestead." *Harper's Weekly* 36 (23 July 1892); 713–14 (including 13 drawings).

"Homestead Conflict" (collection of newspaper comments). *Public Opinion* 13 (16 July 1892): 345–48.

"Homestead Strike" (articles by William Oates, George Ticknor Curtis, and T. V. Powderly). *North American Review* 155 (September 1892): 355–75.

Ogden, R. "Pulpit on the Homestead Riots." *Nation* 55 (21 July 1892): 40.

b. Secondary

David, Henry. "Upheaval at Homestead." In *America in Crisis*, edited by Daniel Aaron, pp. 130–70. New York: Knopf, 1952.

Wolff, Leon. *Lockout: The Story of the Homestead Strike of 1892; A Study of Violence, Unionism and the Carnegie Steel Empire*. New York: Harper and Row, 1965.

(see related listings for Alexander Berkman)

3. McKinley Assassination

a. Primary

"Criminality of Anarchism." *Independent* 53 (19 September 1901): 2250.

"Czolgosz, Product of a Materialistic, Greed-Crazed World." *Arena* 27 (January 1902); 100–101.

Fallows, Samuel, ed. *The Life of William McKinely Our Martyred President. . .and a History of Anarchy, Its Purposes and Results*. Chicago: Regan Printing House, 1901.

Goldman, Emma. "Assassination of McKinley." *American Mercury* 24 (September 1931): 53–67.

Halstead, Murat. *The Illustrious Life of William McKinley Our Martyred President. . .[along with the story of] Anarchy, Its History, Influence and Dangers, with a Sketch of the Assassin*. Chicago, 1901.

Townsend, George Washington. *Our Martyred President. . .With a Full History of Anarchy and Its Infamous Deeds*. Philadelphia, 1901.

b. Secondary

Fine, Sidney. "Anarchism and the Assassination of McKinley." *American Historical Review* 60 (July 1955): 777–99.

Morgan, H. Wayne. *William McKinley and His America*. Syracuse, New York: Syracuse University Press, 1963.

4. Antianarchist Laws

"Anarchist Deportations." *New Republic* 21 (24 December 1919): 96–98.

"Anarchist Exclusion Law." *Outlook* 75 (21 November 1903): 678–79.

"Anarchy and Its Suppression." *Harper's Weekly* 45 (5 October 1901): 997.

"Bill against Anarchists." *Nation* 74 (20 February 1902): 145.

Burrows, Senator J. C. "The Need for National Legislation against Anarchy." *North American Review* 173 (November 1901): 727 ff.

Chafee, Zechariah, Jr. "Legislation against Anarchy." *New Republic* 19 (23 July 1919): 379–85.

"Control of Anarchists." *Nation* 82 (7 June 1906): 463–64.

"Deportations and the Law." *Nation* 110 (31 January 1920): 131.

"Deporting a Political Party." *New Republic* 21 (14 January 1920): 186.

Dowell, Eldridge. "The History of Criminal Syndicalism Legislation in the United States." *Johns Hopkins University Studies*, vol. 57, no. 1 (1939). From a 1936 dissertation at Johns Hopkins University: "A History of the Enactment of Criminal Syndicalism Legislation in the United States." An update appeared as "Criminal Syndicalism Legislation, 1935–1939," *Public Opinion Quarterly* 4 (June 1940): 299–304.

Duke of Arcos (Spanish envoy to the United States). "International Control of Anarchists." *North American Review* 173 (November 1901): 758–67.

"Exclusion and Expulsion of Anarchists from the United States." *Congressional Record* 56 (21 June 1918): 8777–90. "Includes a chronological list of plots, crimes, etc., involving the destruction of health, life or property in the United States."

Freund, Ernst. "Burning Heretics" (letter to the editor). *New Republic* 21 (28 January 1920): 266–67.

"Immigration and Anarchists." *Independent* 64 (12 March 1908): 554–55.

Koppes, C. R. "Kansas Trial of the IWW, 1917–1919," *Labor History* 16 (summer 1975): 338–58.

Pinkerton, Robert A. "Detective Surveillance of Anarchists." *North American Review* 173 (November 1901): 609–17.

Post, Louis F. *The Deportations Delirium of Nineteen-twenty*. Chicago, 1923.

Preston, William. *Aliens and Dissenters: Federal Suppression of Radicals, 1903–1933*. Cambridge: Harvard University Press, 1963.

Scott, S. C. T. "Congress and Anarchy: A Suggestion." *North American Review* 173 (October, 1901): 433–36.

Sims, R. C. "Idaho's Criminal Syndicalism Act: One State's Response to Radical Labor." *Labor History* 15 (fall 1974): 511–27.

Turner, John. "The Protest of an Anarchist." *Independent* 55 (December 1903): 3052–54.

United States. Congress. House of Representatives. Committees on Immigration and Naturalization. "Exclusion and Expulsion of Aliens of Anarchistic and Similar Classes." Washington: Government Printing Office, 1919. Consult also the 1920 congressional hearings on "Communist and Anarchist Deportation Cases" and "Exclusion and Explusion of Aliens of Anarchistic and Similar Classes."

Wallace, Lew. "Prevention of Presidental Assassinations." *North American Review* 173 (November 1901): 721–26.

Whitten, Woodrow. "Criminal Syndicalism and the Law in California, 1919–1927." Ph. D. diss., University of California-Berkeley, 1946.

――――. "The Trial of Charlotte Anita Whitney, 1920." *Pacific Historical Review* 15 (September 1946): 286–94.

5. Industrial Workers of the World

(see also Syndicalism and Workers' Control)

The reader should note that this is a minimal selection from the stupifyingly vast literature on the IWW.

Some of the primary sources of the early period of the IWW are still in print, such as Big Bill Haywood's *Autobiography* (New York: International, 1969), R. Chaplin's *Centralia* (Chicago:

Kerr, 1972), and such anthologies as Joyce Kornbluth's *Rebel Voices: An I.W.W. Anthology*
Ann Arbor: University of Michigan Press, 1964). Several of the older scholarly works have also
been reprinted, including John S. Gambs's *Decline of the I.W.W.* (New York: Russell, 1966
[1932]). Continuing research on the IWW can be found in both original essays and review articles in the excellent journal *Labor History*. See, for example, V. Jensen's "I. W. W." (*Labor
History* 11 [summer 1970]: 355–72), with a reply by M. Dubofsky.

Bercuson, D. J. "Western Labour Radicalism and the One Big Union: Myths and Realities."
  Journal of Canadian Studies 9 (May 1974): 3–11.
Brissenden, Paul. *The I.W.W.: A Study of American Syndicalism.* New York: Russell and
  Russell, 1957 (1919).
Brooks, John. *American Syndicalism.* New York: Arno, 1969 (1913).
Chaplin, Ralph. *Wobbly: The Rough-and-Tumble Story of an American Radical.* Chicago:
  University of Chicago Press, 1968.
Conlin, Joseph R. *Big Bill Haywood and the Radical Union Movement.* Syracuse, New York:
  Syracuse University Press, 1969.
_____. *Bread and Roses Too: Studies of the Wobblies.* Westport, Conn.: Greenwood Pub-
  lishers, 1969.
Dubofsky, Melvyn. *We Shall Be All: A History of Syndicalism in the United States.* Chicago:
  Quadrangle, 1969.
George, Harrison. *I.W.W. Trial.* New York: Arno, n.d.
Hill, Joe. *Letters of Joe Hill.* Edited by Philip Foner. New York: Quick Fox, 1965.
Preston, William, Jr. *Aliens and Dissenters: Federal Suppression of Radicals, 1903-1933.*
  Cambridge: Harvard University Press, 1963.
Renshaw, Patrick. *The Wobblies: The Story of Syndicalism in the United States.* Garden City,
  N.Y.: Doubleday, 1967.
Saposs, David J. *Left Wing Unionism.* New York: Russell, 1967 (1926).
Smith, Gibbs. *Joe Hill.* Salt Lake City: University of Utah Press, 1969.
Soltau, Roger. "The Syndicalist Challenge to the Sovereign State." In *French Political Thought
  in the Nineteen Century,* pp. 442–85. New Haven: Yale University Press, 1931.
Tyler, Robert L. *Rebels of the Woods: The I.W.W. in the Pacific Northwest.* Eugene: Univer-
  sity of Oregon Press, 1967.
Werstein, Irving. *Pie in the Sky.* New York: Delacorte, 1969.

6. Sacco and Vanzetti Trial

A five-volume edition of the trial transcript was published by H. H. Holt during 1928–29
(and is more recently available from Paul Appel of Mamaroneck, New York, 1969), and the letters of Sacco and Vanzetti were printed by Viking in 1928 (and reprinted by Octagon in 1971). I
have usually included only recent comments on this dramatic case of class justice.

Bagdikian, B. H. "New Light on Sacco and Vanzetti." *New Republic* 149 (13 July 1963):
  13–17.
Colp, R., Jr. "No Pardon of Sacco and Vanzetti." *Nation* 190 (21 May 1960): 454–55.
Deedy, J. "Sacco and Vanzetti: Still Nagging the American Conscience." *Commonweal* 90
  (25 July 1969): 466–68.
Dickinson, Alice. *The Sacco-Vanzetti Case, 1920-1927.* New York: Watts, 1972.
Di Giovanni, N. T. "Progress of Sacco and Vanzetti." *Nation* 188 (18 April 1959): 331–32.
Dos Passos, John. *Facing the Chair: The Story of the Americanization of Two Foreignborn
  Workingmen.* New York: Da Capo, 1970 (1927).
Eastman, Max. "Is This the Truth about Sacco and Vanzetti." *National Review* 11 (21 October
  1961): 261–64; reply by James Burnham, ibid. 11 (4 November 1961): 314.

Ehrmann, Herbert. *The Case That Will Not Die*. Boston: Little, Brown, 1969.

_____. *Untried Case: The Sacco-Vanzetti Case and the Morelli Gang*. New York: Vanguard, 1960.

Felix, David. *Protest: Sacco and Vanzetti and the Intellectuals*. Bloomington: Indiana University Press, 1965. Reviewed by A. M. Bickel, *New Republic* 154 (2 April 1966): 23–24 + ; discussion, ibid. 154 (24 June 1966): 36–37.

Frankfurter, Felix. *The Case of Sacco and Vanzetti: A Critical Analysis for Lawyers and Laymen*. New York: Universal, 1962.

Grossman, J. "Sacco-Vanzetti Case Reconsidered." *Commentary* 33 (January 1962): 31–44; discussion, ibid. 33 (May 1962):443; ibid. 33 (July 1962): 72–73; ibid. 33 (September 1962): 253–56.

Joughlin, Louis, and Morgan, Edmund. *The Legacy of Sacco and Vanzetti*. Chicago: Quadrangle, 1964.

Lyons, Eugene. *Life and Death of Sacco and Vanzetti*. New York: Da Capo, 1970 (1927).

Musmanno, Michael A. *After Twelve Years*. New York: Knopf, 1939.

Russell, Francis. *Tragedy in Dedham*. New York: McGraw-Hill, 1962. This was a major work of conservative revisionism. Its strong points and flaws were examined by Michael Musmanno in *New Republic* 148 (2 March 1963): 25–30, with a discussion in the issue of 23 March 1963 (pp. 37–38). Other reviews: *Christian Century* 79 (26 September 1963): 1168, and *New Yorker* 38 (8 December 1962): 235–36. Further articles by Russell: "Sacco Guilty; Vanzetti Innocent?" (with a rejoinder by M. A. Musmanno), *American Heritage* 14 (February 1963): 92–93; "How I Changed My Mind about the Sacco-Vanzetti Case," *Antioch Review* 25 (winter 1965–66): 592–607; "Sacco-Vanzetti: The End of the Chapter," *National Review* 22 (5 May 1970): 454–66.

Sinclair, Upton. *Boston: A Novel*. New York: Boni, 1928 (also in Scholarly Reprints).

Weeks, Robert, ed. *Commonwealth vs. Sacco and Vanzetti*. Englewood Cliffs, N.J.: Prentice-Hall, 1958.

NOTE: The governor of Massachusetts publicly affirmed the innocence of Sacco and Vanzetti in 1977.)

V. SYNDICALISM AND WORKERS' CONTROL
(see also Industrial Workers of the World)

"Ancestry of Guild Socialism." *Contemporary Review* 227 (September 1975): 133–36.

Arum, Peter Marshall. "Georges Dumoulin: Biography of a Revolutionary Syndicalist, 1887–1923." Ph.D. diss., University of Wisconsin, 1971.

Beetham, D. "From Socialism to Fascism: The Relation between Theory and Practice in the Work of Robert Michels." *Political Studies* 25 (March 1977): 3–24.

Bell, Daniel. "Work, Alienation and Social Control" (on guild socialism). *Dissent* 21 (spring 1971): 207–12.

Benello, C. George, and Roussopoulos, Dimitrios, eds. *The Case for Participatory Democracy*. New York: Grossman, 1971.

Bercuson, D. J. "Western Labor Radicalism and the One Big Union: Myths and Realities." *Journal of Canadian Studies* 9 (May 1974: 3–11.

Bertrand, Charles. "Italian Revolutionary Syndicalism and the Crisis of Intervention: August-December 1914." *Canadian Journal of History* 10 (December 1975): 349–67.

_____. "Revolutionary Syndicalism in Italy, 1912–1922." Ph.D. diss., University of Wisconsin, 1969.

Brown, Geoff. *The Industrial Syndicalist*. London: Spokesman, 1974.

Butler, James. "Fernand Pelloutier and the Emergence of the French Syndicalist Movement, 1880–1906." Ph.D. diss., Ohio State University, 1960.

Carby-Hall, J. *Worker Participation in Europe*. Totowa, N.J.: Rowman and Littlefield, 1977.

Carr, Edward Hallett. "Sorel: Philosopher of Syndicalism." In *Studies in Revolution*, pp. 152–65. London: Macmillan, 1950.

Clark, Marjorie. "French Syndicalism (1910–1927)." Ph.D. diss., University of California-Berkeley, 1928.

Clarke, Robert Hamilton. "The Politics of French Agricultural Syndicalism." Ph.D. diss., Princeton University, 1965.

Coates, Ken, and Topham, Anthony, eds. *Industrial Democracy in Great Britain*. London: MacGibbon and Kee, 1968.

DeLucia, Michael. "The Remaking of French Syndicalism, 1911–1918." Ph.D. diss., Brown University, 1965.

Douglas, Dorothy. "The Doctrines of Guillaume de Greef: Syndicalism and Social Reform in the Guise of a Classificatory Sociology." In *An Introduction to the History of Sociology*, edited by Harry Elmer Barnes, pp. 538–52. Chicago: University of Chicago Press, 1948.

———. "Guillaume de Greef: The Social Theory of an Early Syndicalist." Ph.D. diss., Columbia University, 1925.

Ellis, Jack. "French Socialist and Syndicalist Approaches to Peace, 1904–1914." Ph.D. diss., Tulane University, 1967.

Estey, James. "Revolutionary Syndicalism: An Exposition and a Criticism." Ph.D. diss., University of Wisconsin, 1911.

Fitzgerald, Edward. "Emile Pouget, the Anarchist Movement and the Origins of Revolutionary Trade-Unionism in France (1880–1901)." Ph.D. diss., Yale University, 1973.

Forst, R. D. "Origins and Early Development of the Union Marocaine in Travail." *International Journal of Middle East Studies* 7 (April 1976): 271–87.

Fox, R. W. "Two Views of French Radicalism." *Nation* 215 (25 September 1972); 247–48.

Fredericks, Shirley. "The Social and Political Thought of Federica Montseny, Spanish Anarchist, 1923–1937." Ph.D. diss., University of New Mexico, 1972.

George, William. "French Political Theory since 1848 with Special Reference to Syndicalism." Ph.D. diss., Harvard University, 1921.

Godfrey, Edwin. "The Non-Communist Left in Post War France." Ph.D. diss., Princeton University, 1952.

Gorz, André. *Strategy for Labor*. Boston: Beacon, 1967.

Grinevald, T. "The Christian Trade Union Movement." *International Labour Review* 72 (November 1955): 448–52.

Hansen, E. "Workers and Socialists: Relations between the Dutch Trade-Union Movement and Social Democracy, 1894–1914." *European Studies Review* 7 (April 1977): 199–226.

Hayward, J. E. S. "Solidarist Syndicalist: Durkheim and Duguit." *Sociological Review*, n.s., 8 (July-December 1960): 185–202.

Hess, Karl, and Morris, David. *Neighborhood Power: The New Localism*. Boston: Beacon, 1975.

Hodges, Donald. "The Rise and Fall of Militant Trade Unionism." *American Journal of Economics* 20 (October 1961): 483–96.

Hunnius, Gerry, and others, eds. *Workers' Control*. New York: Vintage, 1973.

Hunt, Persis. "Revolutionary Syndicalism and Feminism among Teachers in France, 1900–1921." Ph.D. diss., Tufts University, 1975.

Johnson, M. R. "Albert R. Parsons: An American Architect of Syndicalism." *Midwest Quarterly* 9 (January 1968): 195–206.

Laidler, Harry. "French Syndicalism." In *Social-Economic Movements*, pp. 277–315. New York: Crowell, 1944.

Levey, Jules. "The Sorelian Syndicalists." Ph.D. diss., Columbia University, 1967.

Levine, Louis. "The Labor Movement in France: A Study in Revolutionary Syndicalism. Ph.D. diss., Columbia, 1912.

McGrath, William. "The Theory of Value and Market in Syndicalism." Ph.D. diss., University of Southern California, 1970.

McMechan, William. "The Building Trades of France, 1907-1914: An Exploration of Revolutionary Syndicalism." Ph.D. diss., University of Wisconsin, 1975.

Mattick, Paul. "Workers' Control." In *The New Left*, edited by Priscilla Long, pp. 376-98. Boston: Porter Sargent, 1969.

Meisel, J. II. "Georges Sorel's Last Myth." *Journal of Politics* 12 (February 1950): 52-65

Melitz, T. "Trade Unions and Fabian Socialism." *Industrial and Labor Relations Review* 12 (July 1959): 554-67.

Nomad, Max. "Evolution of Anarchism and Syndicalism: A Critical View." In *European Ideologies*, edited by Feliks Gross, pp. 325-42. New York: Philosophical Library, 1948.

Papayanis, Nicholas. "Alphonse Merrheim and Revolutionary Syndicalism, 1871-1917." Ph.D. diss., University of Wisconsin, 1969.

————. "Alphonse Merrheim and the Strike of Hennebont." *International Review of Social History* 16,2 (1971): 159-83.

Pernicone, Nunzio. "The Italian Anarchist Movement: The Years of Crisis, Decline and Transformation (1879-1894)." Ph.D. diss., University of Rochester, 1971.

Roberts, David. "The Italian Syndicalists: From Marxism to Fascism." Ph.D. diss., University of California-Berkeley, 1972.

Root and Branch, eds. *The Rise of the Workers' Movements*. New York: Fawcett, 1975.

Sikes, Earl. "Anarchism and Syndicalism." In *Contemporary Economic Systems*, reve ed., pp. 116-41. New York: Holt, 1951.

Simon, S. F. "Anarchism and Anarcho-Syndicalism in South America." *Hispanic American Historical Review* 26 (February 1946): 38-59.

Spitzer, Alan B. "Anarchy and Culture: Fernand Pelloutier and the Dilemma of Revolutionary Syndicalism." *International Review of Social History* 8 (1963): 379-88.

Storchi, F. "Free Syndicalism and Marxist Syndicalism." In *Philosophy of Communism*, edited by Guiseppe Bettiol and others, pp. 151-59. Fordham University Press, 1952.

Sykes, Thomas. "The Practice of Revolutionary Syndicalism in Italy, 1905-1910." Ph.D. diss., Columbia University, 1974.

————. "Revolutionary Syndicalism in the Italian Labor Movement: The Agrarian Strikes of 1907-08 in the Province of Parma." *International Review of Social History* 21,2 (1976): 186-211.

Taft, Philip. "French Socialism and Syndicalism" and "Spanish Anarcho-Syndicalism." In *Movements for Economic Reform*, pp. 167-83, 568-79. New York: Rinehart, 1950.

Talmon, J. L. "The Legacy of Georges Sorel." *Encounter* 34 (February 1970): 47-60.

Vanek, Jan. *The Economics of Workers' Management*. London: Allen and Unwin, 1972.

Vanek, Jaroslav. *The General Theory of Labor-Managed Economics*. Ithaca: Cornell University Press, 1970.

————. *The Participatory Economy*. Ithaca: Cornell University Press, 1971.

————, ed. *Self-Management*. Baltimore: Penguin, 1975.

Westmeyer, Russell. "Anarchism," "Syndicalism in France," and "Syndicalism in the United States and Great Britain." In *Modern Economic and Social Systems*, pp. 293-307, 308-23, 324-44. New York: Farrar, 1940.

Wright, A. W. "Guild Socialism Revisited." *Journal of Contemporary History* 9 (January 1974): 165-80.

Wright, G. "Revolutionary Syndicalism Demythologized" (review article). *Social Research* 39 (spring 1972): 183-90.

VI. ANARCHISM AND ART

Aubery, Pierre. "The Anarchism of the Literati of the Symbolist Period." *French Review* 42 (October 1968): 39–47.

Avrich, Paul. "Conrad's Anarchist Professor: An Undiscovered Source." *Labor History* 18 (summer 1977): 397–402.

Baron, Lawrence. "The Eclectic Anarchism of Erich Muhsam." Ph.D. diss., University of Wisconsin, 1975.

Carr, Barbara. "Variations on the Anarchist: Politics Reflected in Fiction." Ph.D. diss., Indiana university, 1976.

Egbert, Donald Drew. *Social Radicalism and the Arts*. New York: Knopf, 1970.

———. *Socialism and American Art*. Princeton: Princeton University Press, 1967.

Fleishman, Avrom. "Conrad's Politics: Community and Anarchy in the Fiction of Joseph Conrad." Ph.D. diss., Johns Hopkins University, 1963.

Hogue, Herbert. "The Anarchic Mystique of Five American Fictions." Ph.D. diss., University of Washington, 1971.

Langbaum, Robert. "Thought on Our Times: Three Novels on Anarchism." *American Scholar*, spring 1973, pp. 227 ff.

Lynch, Honora. "Patterns of Anarchy and Order in the Works of John Rechy." Ph.D. diss., University of Houston, 1976.

McCracken, D. "Godwin's Literary Theory: The Alliance between Fiction and Political Philosophy." *Philological Quarterly* 49 (January 1970): 113–33.

Maloney, Philip. "Anarchism and Bolshevism in the Works of Boris Pilnyak." *Russian Review* 32 (January 1973): 43–53.

Martin, E. A. "Puritan's Satanic Flight: Don Marquis, Archy and Anarchy." *Sewanee Review* 83 (fall 1975): 623–42.

Mills, J. "Love and Anarchy in Sergeant Musgrave's Dance." *Drama Survey* 7 (winter 1968–69): 45–51.

Nash, C. "More Light on the Secret Agent." *Review of English Studies*, no. 20 (August 1969), pp. 322–27.

Ossar, M. "Anarchism and Socialism in Ernst Toller's *Masse-Mench*." *Germanic Review* 51 (May 1976): 192–208.

———. "Anarchism in the Drama of Ernst Toller." Ph.D. diss., University of Pennsylvania, 1973.

Reyler, Andre. "Peter Kropotkin and His Vision of Anarchist Aesthetics." *Diogenes* 78 (summer 1972): 52–63.

Sanders, D. "The Anarchism of John Dos Passos." *South Atlantic Quarterly* 60 (winter 1961): 44–55.

Sarracino, Carmine. "Henry Miller, Spiritual Anarchist." Ph.D. diss., University of Michigan, 1974.

Sherman, W. D. "J. P. Donleavy: Anarchic Man as Dying Dionysian." *Twentieth Century Literature* 13 (January 1968): 216–28.

Sherry, N. "Conrad's Ticket-of-Leave Apostle." *Modern Language Review* 64 (October 1969): 749–58.

———. "Greenwich Bomb Outrage and the Secret Agent." *Review of English Studies* 18 (November 1967): 412–28.

Steinke, Gerhardt. "The Anarchistic, Expressionistic and Dadaistic Phases in the Life and Work of Hugo Ball." Ph.D. diss., Stanford University, 1955.

Ward, John William. "Another Howells Anarchist Letter." *American Literature* 22 (January 1951): 489–90.

Williams, Michael. "Politics without Love: Anarchism in Turgenev, Dostoevsky, and James." Ph.D. diss., University of Michigan, 1974.

Woodcock, George. *The Writer and Politics*. London: Porcupine Press, 1948.
Youens, Anne. "Romance and Anarchy: The Epic Vision of Armand Gatti." Ph.D. diss., Carnegie-Mellon University, 1973.

(See also the listings for William Godwin, Paul Goodman, Herbert Read, and Leo Tolstoi, along with reference to general studies.)

VII. RELATED PRIMARY SOURCES

Bookchin, Murray. *The Limits of the City*. New York: Harper, 1974.
_____. *Our Synthetic Environment*. Rev. ed. New York: Harper, 1974.
Cleyre, Voltairine de. "Making of an Anarchist." *Independent* 55 (24 September 1903): 2276–80.
_____. *Selected Works*. Edited by A. Berkman and H. Havel. New York: Revisionist Press, 1972 (reprint actually published?) [1st. ed. 1914].
Cohn-Bendit, Daniel, and Cohn-Bendit, Gabriel. *Obsolete Communism: The Left-Wing Alternative*. London: Deutsch, 1968.
Commons, John R., and others, eds. *A Documentary History of Industrial Society*. 10 vols. Cleveland, 1910.
Drachkovitch, Milorad, ed. *The Revolutionary Internationals*. Palo Alto, Calif.: Stanford University Press, 1966.
Fried, Albert, and Saunders, Ronald, eds. *Socialist Thought*. Garden City, N.Y.: Doubleday-Anchor, 1964.
Greene, William B. *Socialistic, Communistic, Mutualistic, and Financial Fragments*. Westport, Conn.: Hyperion, 1975 (1875).
Haskell, Burnette G. "Shall the Red and the Black Unite? An American Revolutionary Document of 1883." In *American Radicalism*, ed. Chester McArthur Destler, pp. 78–104. New London, Conn.
Hedman, Carl G. "An Anarchist's Reply to Skinner on 'Weak Methods of Control.' " *Inquiry* 17 (spring 1974): 105–11.
Hess, Karl. *Dear America*. New York: Morrow, 1975.
Hospers, John. *Libertarianism: A Political Philosophy for Tomorrow*. Los Angeles: Nash Publishers, 1971.
Kurtz, Paul. "Conservative Anarchism: An Interview with Dwight Macdonald." *Humanist* 33 (January-February 1973): 13.
Labadie, Charles Joseph ("Jo"), and Ely, Richard T. "The Ely-Labadie Letters," edited by Sidney Fine. *Michigan History* 36 (March 1952): 1–32. See also Lawrence Conrad's article, "Jo Labadie—Poet," *Michigan History Magazine* 16 (spring 1932): 218–24 (portrait on p. 219), and Robert Zieger, ed. "A Letter from Jo Labadie to John R. Commons," *Labor History* 11 (summer 1970): 345–46.
La Boétie, Etienne de. *The Politics of Obedience*. New York: Free Life, 1975. Discussed by N. O. Keohane in "The Radical Humanism of Etienne de La Boétie," *Journal of the History of Ideas* 38 (January 1971): 119–30.
Mett, Ida. *The Kronstadt Uprising*. Montreal: Black Rose, 1971.
Morris, William. *News from Nowhere*. London: Routledge and Kegan Paul, 1970 (1891).
Nettlau, Max. *Anarchisten und Sozialrevolutionäre*. Glasshütten im Taunus: D. Auvermann, 1972.
_____. *Der Vorfrühling der Anarchie*. Glasshütten im Taunus: D. Auvermann, 1972.
_____. *Geschichte der Anarchie*. Glasshütten im Taunus: D. Auvermann, 1972.
New York (State) Legislature. Joint Committee Investigating Seditious Activities: *Revolutionary Radicalism*. Albany: J. B. Lyon, 1920.

Nock, Albert Jay. *Our Enemy, the State*. New York: Free Life, 1973.

Oppenheimer, Franz. *The State*. New York: Free Life, 1975.

Orwell, George. *Homage to Catalonia*. New York: Harcourt, Brace, 1952. A classic account, sympathetic to the anarchists, by a participant in the Spanish Civil War. Other significant studies are Gerald Brenan's *The Spanish Labyrinth* (Cambridge: Cambridge University Press, 1950); Vernon Richards, *The Lessons of the Spanish Revolution* (London: Freedom Press, 1953); Gabriel Jackson, "The Origins of Spanish Anarchism," *Southwestern Social Science Quarterly* 36 (September 1955): 135–57; Hugh Thomas, *The Spanish Civil War* (New York: Harper, 1961); Franz Borkenau, *The Spanish Cockpit* (Ann Arbor: University of Michigan Press, 1963); Gerald Meaker, "Spanish Anarcho-Syndicalism and the Russian Revolution, 1917–1922," Ph.D. diss., University of Southern California, 1967; Temma Kaplan, "Spanish Anarchism and Women's Liberation," *Journal of Contemporary History* 6,2 (1971): 101–10; T. Kaplan, "The Social Base of Nineteenth-Century Andalusian Anarchism in Jerez de la Frontera," *Journal of Interdisciplinary History* 6 (summer 1975): 45–70; Murray Bookchin, *The Spanish Anarchists: The Heroic Years, 1886–1936* (New York: Free Life, 1976); B. Chatwin, "Anarchists of Patagonia" (review article), *TLS*, no. 3903 (31 December 1976): 1635–36+ ; Sam Dolgoff, ed. *The Anarchist Collectives* (New York: Free Life, 1974); Abel Paz, *Durruti: The People Armed* (Montreal: Black Rose, 1976); and Temma Kaplan, *Anarchists of Andalusia, 1863–1903* (Princeton: Princeton University Press, 1977).

Rocker, Rudolf. *Aus den Memoiren deutscher Anarchisten*. Franfurt am Main: Suhrkamp, 1974.

Rothbard, Murray. *Conceived in Liberty*. 2 vols. New Rochelle, N.Y.: Arlington House, 1975 (Anarcho-Capitalist).

———. *For a New Liberty*. New York: Macmillan, 1973.

———. *Man, Economy and the State*. 2 vols. 2d ed. Menlo Park, Calif.: Institute for Humane Studies, 1970.

———. *Power and Market: Government and the Economy*. Menlo Park, Calif.: Institute for Humane Studies, 1970.

Serge, Victor. *Memoirs of a Revolutionary*. London: Oxford University Press, 1967.

Sirianni, Carmen. *Lenin, Leninism and Workers' Control*. Montreal: Black Rose, 1976.

Spring, Joel. *A Primer of Libertarian Education*. New York: Free Life, 1975.

Tannehill, Morris, and Tannehill, Linda. *The Market for Liberty*. New York: Arno Press, 1972.

Thoreau, Henry David. *Walden* and *Civil Disobedience*. Edited by Owen Thomas. New York: W. W. Norton, 1966.

Valuable interpretations of Thoreau as an anarchist are Joseph L. Blau, "Henry David Thoreau: Anarchist," in *Men and Movements in American Philosophy*, pp. 131–42 (New York: Prentice-Hall, 1953); George E. G. Catlin, "Individualists and Anarchists," in *Story of the Political Philosophers*, pp. 196–205 (New York: McGraw-Hill, 1960); Richard Drinnon, "Thoreau's Politics of the Upright Man," in *Thoreau in Our Time*, edited by J. H. Hicks, pp. 154–68; (Amherst: University of Massachusetts Press, 1966); and John Morris, "Thoreau, America's Gentle Anarchist," *Religious Humanism* 3 (spring 1969): 62–65. Staughton Lynd once provoked a spirited discussion of Thoreau's politics with his essay "Henry Thoreau: The Admirable Radical," *Liberation* 7 (February 1963): 21–26. The April 1963 issue of *Liberation* contains such replies as "Thoreau and the New Radicals: The Direct Actionists versus the Bird Watchers," and "Who Are the Anarchists?" A fair summary of Thoreau's probable place in anarchist theory was made by Clarence Lee Swartz: "Thoreau, while not properly labeled an anarchist, was certainly a free spirit" (introduction to B. R. Tucker's *Individual Liberty* [New York: Vanguard, 1926]).

Tolstoi, Leo. *Works*. 21 vols. Oxford: For the Tolstoy Society, Oxford University Press, 1928–37. See especially *The Kingdom of God Is within You*, *The Slavery of Our Time*, and *What I Believe*.

Some articles of particular interest to Americans are "Garrison and Non-Resistance," *Independent* 56 (21 April 1904): 881–83; "How Are the Working People to Free Themselves?" *Independent* 58 (15 June 1905): 1333–36; "The Law of Love and the Law of Force," *Fortnightly* 91 (March–April 1909): 460–85, 689–720; "Power and Slavery," *Independent* 58 (May 1905): 981–82; "A Message to the American People," *North American Review* 172 (April 1901): 503.

One of the best studies of Tolstoi is Ernest Simmon's *Leo Tolstoy* (New York: Vintage, 1960). For a Marxian critique of pacifist anarchism, read Lenin's *Tolstoy and His Time*. For an English, pragmatic critique, see Aylmer Maude, in *The Works of Tolstoy*, 2:221–24. Also helpful are "What Tolstoy Means to America," *Current Literature* 45 (October 1908): 402–4; E. Lampert, "On Tolstoi, Prophet and Teacher," *Slavonic Review* 25 (December 1966): 604–14, and Perry Gianakos, "Ernest Howard Crosby: A Forgotten Tolstoyan Anti-Militarist and Anti-Imperialist," *American Studies* 13 (spring 1972): 11–29.

Tuccille, Jerome. *It Usually Begins with Ayn Rand*. New York: Stein and Day, 1972.

———. *Radical Libertarianism*. Indianapolis: Bobbs-Merrill, 1970.

———. *Who's Afraid of 1984? The Case for Optimism*. New Rochelle, N.Y.: Arlington House, 1975.

Wilde, Oscar. *The Soul of Man under Socialism*. New York: Oriole Chapbooks, 1971 (1891).

Wollstein, Jarrett B. *Society without Coercion*. New York: Arno Press, 1972.

VIII. RELATED SECONDARY SOURCES

Abbott, Myron James. "Anarchy and Anarchism: Santayana on the Nature of Moral and Political Authority." Ph.D. diss., Vanderbilt University, 1974.

Ackelsberg, Martha. "The Possibility of Anarchism: The Theory and Practice of Non-Authoritarian Organization." Ph.D. diss., Princeton University, 1976.

Albertson, Ralph. *A Survey of Mutualistic Communistic Communities in America*. New York: AMS, 1973 (1936).

"Anarcho-Nihilism" (Latin American correspondence). *Economist* 237 (24 October 1970); 28, 31.

Arieli, Yehoshua. *Individualism and Nationalism in American Ideology*. Cambridge: Harvard University Press, 1964.

Avrich, Paul. *Kronstadt, 1921*. Princeton: Princeton University Press, 1970.

Berneri, Marie Louise. *Journey through Utopia*. London: Routledge and Kegan Paul, 1950.

Bestor, Arthur E., Jr. "The Evolution of the Socialist Vocabulary." *Journal of the History of Ideas* 9 (June 1948): 259–302.

Bondurant, Joan. *Conquest of Power*. Princeton: Princeton University Press, 1958.

Boyd, J. "From Far Right to Far Left, and Farther, with Karl Hess." *New York Times Magazine* 6 December 1970, pp. 48–49+ .

Brecher, Jeremy. *Strike!* San Francisco: Straight Arrow Books, 1972.

Buber, Martin. *Paths in Utopia*. London, 1949.

Bunzel, John. *Anti-Politics in America*. New York: Knopf, 1967.

Cantor, Milton. *The Divided Left: American Radicalism, 1900–1975*. New York: Hill and Wang, 1977.

Carr, Reginald. *Anarchism in France: The Case of Octave Mirbeau*. Montreal: McGill-Queen's University Press, 1977.

Carroll, R. and Collings, A. "Stuttgart Four" (on Baader-Meinhof). *Newsweek* 85 (16 June 1975): 34–35.

Clement, Travers, and Symes, Lillian. *Rebel America*. Introduction by Richard Drinnon. Boston: Beacon, 1972 (1934).

Cogswell, F. "Amateur Anarchist" (review article). *Canadian Literature*, no. 62 (autumn 1974), pp. 93–95.

Cohn, Norman. *The Pursuit of the Millennium*. London: Secker and Warburg, 1957.

Cole, G. D. H. *A History of Socialist Thought*. London, 1953–60.

Commons, John R., and others. *History of Labour in the United States*. 4 vols. New York: Macmillan, 1918–35. See "From Socialism to Anarchism and Syndicalism, 1876–1888," 2:269–300; bibliography on socialism and anarchism, 2:584–87.

Ellul, Jacques. *The Political Illusion*. New York: Knopf, 1967.

Fishman, William. *Jewish Radicals, from Czarist Stetl to London Ghetto*. New York: Pantheon, 1976.

———. "Rudolph Rocker: Anarchist Missionary (1873–1958)." *History Today* 16 (January 1966): 45–52.

Footman, David. "Nestor Makhno and the Russian Civil War." *History Today* 6 (December 1956): 811–20.

Freeman, David. "Anarchy Revisited: Two Schools of Thought." Ph.D. diss., Claremont Graduate School, 1976.

Friedman, Milton, and Schwartz, Ann Jacobson. *A Monetary History of the United States, 1867–1960*. Princeton: Princeton University Press, 1963.

Gellner, E. "Beyond Truth and Falsehood" (review article). *British Journal of Philosophy* 26 (December 1975): 331–42; reply by Paul Feyerabend, ibid., 27 (December 1976): 381–91.

Goldberg, Harold. "The Anarchists View the Bolshevik Regime, 1918–1922." Ph.D. diss., University of Wisconsin, 1973.

Gombin, Richard. *The Origins of Modern Leftism*. Baltimore: Pelican, 1975.

Gray, Alexander. *The Socialist Tradition*. London, 1946.

Hart, John Mason. *Anarchism and the Mexican Working Class, 1860–1931*. Austin: University of Texas, 1978.

Herreshoff, David. *American Disciples of Marx*. Detroit: Wayne State University Press, 1967.

Hinds, William Alfred. *American Communities*. New York: Corinth, 1961 (1878).

Hobsbawm, Eric. *Primitive Rebels*. New York: W. W. Norton, 1965.

———. *Revolutionaries: Contemporary Essays*. New York: Pantheon, 1973.

Hodden, H. J. "The Political Ideas of Thorstein Veblen" [evaluated in terms of philosophical anarchism]. *Canadian Journal of Economics* 22 (August 1956): 347–57.

Horowitz, Irving Louis. *Radicalism and the Revolt against Reason*. Carbondale: Southern Illinois University Press, 1961.

Iviansky, Z. "Individual Terror: Concept and Typology," *Journal of Contemporary History* 12 (January 1977): 43–63.

Jaher, Frederic Cople. *Doubters and Dissenters*. Glencoe, Ill.: Free Press, 1964.

Jarrell, Willoughby Given. "Some Anarchistic Implications of the Political Writings of Thomas Paine." Ph.D. diss., Emory University, 1974.

Johns, Patricke. "The Anarchist Movement in the Nineteenth Century." Ph.D. diss., University of Wisconsin, 1946.

Joll, James. *The Second International*. London, 1955.

———. "Singing, Dancing and Dynamite" (review article). *Times Literary Supplement*, no. 3887 (10 September 1976), pp. 1092–93.

Landauer, C. "From Anarchism to Reformism: A Study of the Political Activities of Paul Brousse, 1870–1890" (review article). *Journal of Modern History* 44 (March 1972): 124–25.

Large, S. S. "Romance of Revolution in Japanese Anarchism and Communism during the Taisho Period." *Modern Asian Studies* 11 (July 1977): 441–67.

Laquer, Walter. "Visionaries." *Atlas* 9 (January 1965): 49–51.

Levin, B. "Breaking the Shame Barrier." *Horizon* 19 (March 1977): 88–89.

LeWarne, Charles Pierce. *Utopias on Puget Sound, 1885–1915*. Seattle: University of Washington Press, 1975 (especially the chapter "Home").

Lichtheim, George. *The Origins of Socialism*. New York: Praeger, 1969.

Mailer, Philip. *Portugal: The Impossible Revolution*. New York: Free Life, 1976.
Miller, B. J. "Anarchism and French Catholicism in *Esprit.*" *Journal of the History of Ideas* 37 (January 1976): 163–74.
Munch, P. A. "Anarchy and Anomie in an Atomized Community." *Man* 9 (June 1974): 243–61.
Newton, Lisa Perkins. "Dimensions of a Right Revolution." *Journal of Value Inquiry* 7 (spring 1973): 17–28.
Nomad, Max. *Apostles of Revolution*. Rev. and enl. ed. New York: Crowell, Collier and Macmillan, 1961.
_____. *Dreamers, Dynamiteurs and Demagogues*. New York: Waldon Press, 1964.
_____. *Political Heretics*. Ann Arbor: University of Michigan Press, 1963.
_____. *Rebels and Renegades*. New York: Macmillan, 1956.
Nordhoff, Charles. *The Communistic Societies of the United States*. New York: Schocken, 1966 (1875).
Osgood, Herbert. "Socialism and Anarchism." Ph.D. diss., Columbia University, 1889.
Palij, M. *The Anarchism of Nestor Makhno, 1918-1921: An Aspect of the Ukrainian Revolution*. Seattle: University of Washington Press, 1976. Derived from his 1971 dissertation at the University of Kansas: "The Peasant Partisan Movement of the Anarchist Nestor Makhno, 1918–1921."
Passmore, J. "Second Thoughts on a Paradise Lost." *Encounter* 43 (August 1974): 46–48.
Perlin, Terry. "Anarchism and Idealism: Voltairine de Cleyre (1886-1912)." *Labor History* 14 (fall 1973): 506–20.
_____. "Anarchism in New Jersey: The Ferrer Colony at Stelton." *New Jersey History* 89 (1971): 133–48.
Rapaport, E. "Anarchism and Authority in Marx's Socialist Politics." *European Journal of Sociology* 17,2 (1976): 333–43.
Reszler, A. "Essay on Political Myths: Anarchist Myths of Revolt." Translated by P. Rowland. *Diogenes*, no. 94 (summer 1976), pp. 34–52.
Schumacher, E. F. *Small Is Beautiful*. New York: Harper, 1973.
Shuford, Robert Weir. "Anarchism and Social Action in America: A Case Study of an Alternative Health Care Facility." Ph.D. diss., Northwestern University, 1974.
Stauber, Leland. "The Implications of Market Socialism in the United States." *Polity* 8 (fall 1975): 38–62.
Stevenson, Billie Jeanne Hackley. "The Ideology of American Anarchism, 1880-1910." Ph.D. diss., University of Iowa, 1972.
Stoehr, Taylor. " 'Eloquence Needs No Constable': Alcott, Emerson and Thoreau on the State." *Canadian Journal of American Studies* 5 (fall 1974): 81–100.
Svoboda, G. J. "Anarchism in Bohemia: The Prague Anti-Habsburg Revolutionary Society, 1868-1872." *East European Quarterly* 11 (fall 1977): 267–91.
Vallance, Margaret. "Rudolph Rocker—A Biographical Sketch." *Journal of Contemporary History* 8 (July 1973): 75–95.
White, J. D. "Despotism and Anarchy: The Sociological Thought of L. I. Mechnikov." *Slavonic and East European Review* 54 (July 1976): 395–411.
Wittke, Carl. *The Utopian Communist: A Biography of Wilhelm Weitling*. Baton Rouge: Louisiana State University Press, 1950.
Yoast, Richard Alan. "The Development of Argentine Anarchism: A Socio-Ideological Analysis." Ph.D. diss. University of Wisconsin, 1975.
Zablocki, Benjamin. *The Joyful Community*. Baltimore: Penguin, 1971.

INDEX

Aaron, Daniel, 137
Abbot, Francis Ellingwood, 74
Abolitionism, 4, 43, 44, 55, 70, 127; and anarchism, 164 n. 20, 176 n. 54; and Lysander Spooner, 76
Adams, John, 53
Adams, Sam, 109, 127
Adorno, T. W., 161 n. 25
Alcott, Bronson, 22
Alger, Horatio, 32, 57–58, 141, 171 n. 19
Alinsky, Saul, 193 n. 27
Altgeld, John, 89
Anarchism. *See* Anarcho-Capitalism; Anarcho-Communism; Anarcho-Individualism; Libertarianism, left; Libertarianism, right
Anarcho-Capitalism, 5, 9, 117, 123, 126, 127, 128, 130–31, 147; directory of, 188 n. 10; and pacifism, 190 n. 10. *See also* Tucker, Benjamin R.
Anarcho-Communism, 5, 9, 31, 85, 92, 94, 117, 122, 123, 181 n. 21. *See also* Berkman, Alexander; Goldman, Emma; Goodman, Paul; Kropotkin, Peter
Anarcho-Individualism, 82–83, 122, 123, 127, 181 n. 22; continuity of, 189 n. 5
Andrews, Stephen Pearl, 72, 73, 76; on organization, 78–79, 81, 177 n. 61; at Radical Club, 175 n. 41
Aquinas, Saint Thomas, 29
Arnold, Thurman, 59

Articles of Confederation, 53, 127
Augustine, Saint, 26

Babbitt, Irving, 112
Bakunin, Michael, 12, 73; cited by New England Libertarian Alliance, 189 n. 4; cited by Sacco and Vanzetti, 176 n. 47; publication of *God and the State* by, 74; quoted, 156; rooted in village life, 94
Baldwin, James, 8
Baldwin, Roger, 96, 182 n. 27
Ballou, Adin, 86, 87
Bell, Daniel, 166 n. 23, 193 n. 27
Bellamy, Edward, 89, 90–93, 105, 180 n. 15; criticism of, by individualists, 181 n. 26
Bellow, Saul, 34, 100
Bentham, Jeremy, 169 n. 2, 172 n. 11
Berger, Victor, 183 n. 2
Berkeley, University of California at, 114
Berkman, Alexander, 82, 94, 96, 98, 99, 131, 190 n. 10
Bicentennial, 185 n. 13, 186 n. 21
Black Panthers, 23, 113, 120
Black struggles, 4, 8, 9, 21, 23, 35, 42, 43, 44, 129; American Revolution and, 52; civil rights movement and, 59, 68; and historical identity, 161 n. 22; ideological spectrum of, 113; individualist anarchism on, 79; and liberalism, 55,

237

The Johns Hopkins University Press
This book was composed in Compugraphic Garamond text and display type by Britton
Composition Company from a design by Susan Bishop. It was printed and bound by The
Maple Press Company.